THE
HARVARD
LAMPOON

PRESENTS

MEDIA-GATE

THE
ATLANTIC
MONTHLY
PRESS
NEW YORK

Published simultaneously in Canada
Printed in the United States of America
First Edition

ISBN: 0-87113-179-X

Design and Composition by The Sarabande Press

The Atlantic Monthly Press
19 Union Square West
New York, NY 10003

First Printing

There is a book more famous than this one in which God creates the heavens and the earth. That book, to summarize, tells of how he created the rocks, the insects, the human beings, the oceans, the moon, and, to top it all off, the amazing Leaning Tower of Pisa. Having completed these mighty works, God took a well-deserved rest and beheld what he had wrought. And it was good.

God, however, did not make everything. Indeed, he had granted to man the power of creation, and for each item that God had wrought, man wrought a hundred inferior, second-rate, chintzy counterparts. Whereas God had created mother's milk to nourish newborn infants, man created nauseating Milk Duds to nourish obese youths. Whereas God had created the useful rubber plant, man created the useless rubber dog turd, which served only to disgust and served no worthwhile social function whatsoever. Whereas God had created the faithful servant dog, man created the foul Devil Dog, the pallid chicken dog, and the grease-laden corn dog. Man built boats that sank, houses that fell down, and houseboats that both sank and fell down. He built trains that derailed and aircraft that crashed. In his ignorance, he built habitable flying seagoing trains that simultaneously crashed, sank, derailed, and fell down. And after man had constructed his shabby merchandise, he sat back and beheld what he had wrought. And it was mediocre. It was no great shakes.

In his infinite wisdom and limited generosity, God had granted man the power to create, but not the power to create anything of exceptionally fine quality. Man was not perfect, but what he lacked in perfection, he made up for in cunning. He attempted to cover up his mistakes, to put a fresh coat of varnish on a piece of mismade furniture, a new paint job on a rusting automobile, or a fresh layer of icing on an expired and molding cake.

History bears this out. Nero thought that by fiddling, he could prevent Rome from burning. Custer believed that by practicing scales on his tuba, he would save his men from being cut down by hostile Indians. Nixon belted out folk songs on the piano in a feeble attempt to prevent his corrupt and evil administration from crumbling around him. Every age, it seems, is marked by a scandal unique to its time. Indeed, history reveals that in every age, civilization is rocked to its very foundation when an especially egregious mistake is improperly concealed by an insufficiently cunning individual or group.

What, then, of our own time? What will be our contribution to the never-ending list of human blunders? The answer is on your very coffee table. It is on your doorstep. It is on your television screen. Our age is the media age, and our legacy will be the so-called Mediagate affair.

By now, you have seen the phrase being tossed about in newspapers and magazines. A minor episode it seemed at first: the discovery of a discarded reel of film, apparently from a scrapped CBS pilot, featuring Don Knotts in the unlikely—indeed, impossible—lead role, as a confident and dignified man. Then, suddenly, came the flood. Articles, books, TV shows from every corner of the media, suppressed and censored items that had been painstakingly kept from public scrutiny. Items so sensitive that, should they ever come to light, every branch of the media would suffer extreme embarrassment, at the very least.

The federal government, long the target of media investigations, was said to be pleased at this development, which placed the media, for once, under the hot lights. The public, meanwhile, was outraged and demanded an investigation. But who should do the investigating? The decision was a difficult one, but after a heated debate, the Senate decided that a special Senate committee could best perform the task.

Heading the committee would be the widely respected Senator Donald Mohasset (D, Rhode Island), a likable New Englander with a distinguished record of service in the Senate Automotive Committee. The position of vice chairman would be filled by Senator "Robert" Beatrice (R, New York). Beatrice, a little-known but highly

Few bathroom breaks: twelve hou

(Above) Da
Buzz

4

(Right) Get out y

MEDIAGAT

Howard Hughes charm: He's Beatrice

Lunchtime: Affable

(Left) No filter: Beaufort

(Below) Donald's angel: Senator Pamela Fawcett

nger Will Robinson: Lost in Space with

ur Dictionaries: Tautologons Archie

E

regarded figure, was picked for his extensive knowledge and expertise in the business world. In addition to his other credentials, which remain unknown, he recently became head of the Senate Committee on Cartels and Monopolies after the former chairman, Senator Clyde Helmsley (R, Michigan), was stricken with a mysterious illness.

Also named to the committee: Senator Jeremiah T. Beaufort (R, South Carolina), the fiery Southern tobacco farmer; Senator Pamela Fawcett (D, Oregon), the left-wing proponent of seat-belt legislation; Senator Buzz Richardson (D, Ohio), ex-astronaut and head of the Senate aerospace group; and Senator Archibald Stone (R, California), the well-spoken chairman of the Senate Committee on Committees.

The entire investigation, to be held in the spacious Gerald Ford Room at the Capitol, is expected to take six weeks. The first week will be devoted to an examination of the magazine industry, with subsequent weeks covering the remaining branches of the media. Although it is difficult to predict with certainty the magnitude of the impact that the hearings will have on the nation, one can only assume, after perusing the extensive list of television stations and periodicals already planning coverage of the event, that it will be an affair of no small consequence.

And now, let the truth be brought to light. Let the conspirators be brought to justice.

Let the hearings begin!

WEEK ONE: MAGAZINES

Sports Illustrated — Men's Swimsuit E...

REVIEW
EASTERN AIRLINES' IN-FLIGHT MAGAZINE
FALL ISSUE — Selected Readings from the Nation's Most Prominent Periodicals — COMPLIMENTARY COPY

"Licensed to Ill"

CRASHING INTO THE SCENE — The Beastie
CONTACT WITH OTHER PLANES, DOES IT SP
New Methods of Astral Travel and the Potential f
(Reprinted from OMNI)
FLYING HIGH, COMING DOWN HARD The R
(Reprinted from TODAY'S HE
AMERICA'S WORST PILOTS TV Show
(Reprinted from TV G
THE TRAGIC BREAKUP OF WINGS Pa
(Reprinted from ROL
THE GREAT CRASH OF '29 Herbert Ho
(Reprinted from
THE JETS KEEP FALLING Why New
(Reprinted from
THE AIRPLANE'S EXPLOSION
(Reprint

SCOOP
VOL IV, ISSUE III — MAY 1983

FLOOR PLANS OF THE STARS

PERSONAL WITH PYNCHON

WE GOT GARBO

WOODY INSIDE AND OUT

Sen. Mohasset: "The stage is now set for the most compelling inquiry that this or any other age has seen. It appears that the media has been engaged in a sinister conspiracy to suppress, censor, bury, and badly smudge information.

"Our first target of investigation shall be the magazine industry, in an attempt to obtain some honest answers to some difficult questions that have plagued Americans for decades. Are the major periodicals mere mouthpieces for the corporate conglomerates who own them? Who reads *Us* magazine when *People* is so remarkably interesting? Why is *Playboy* always out of my reach on the top shelf? And why can't they make subscription-card inserts that don't fall out of the magazine the instant you take it off the newsstand rack?"

The Media Mediators

Face the Nation Meets the Press

No One is Safe: *Ever ready warriors.*

A midst much scandal-spangled ballyhoo and grand congressional pomp, week one of the Mediagate Hearings saw the ball and chain get rolling in the splendid and uniquely American tradition of law and order. It is, of course, hardly the first large-scale Senate investigation in our nation's 211 years. Richard Nixon fell under scrutiny in the historic Watergate crisis of 1972, as did Aaron Burr before him in the Crédit Mobilier *faux pas* of the mid-twenties. But for the first time in history, a scandal of crisis proportions is unfolding that has little to do with politics. Instead, it concerns our most sacred national institution: The Media.

For the public, Mediagate poses some puzzling questions. For example, if we have only the media to inform us of the hearings, how can we be sure that what we see and hear is the unadulterated truth? Indeed, our very reading material is called into question: This time, the camera is trained on the camera, and the press is pressed and depressed. As communications guru Marshall McLuhan recently remarked, "The Media is the Mess."

This week, the investigation of the magazine industry is being carried into American living rooms via daytime television, newspapers, and, of course, magazines themselves. Though *Newsweek* itself may soon be shoved under the klieg lights and barbed knout of the self-serving, ill-mannered inquisitors who pass for democratic figureheads, we shall

> **"Hence . . . *Time*'s egregious shallowness is due simply to apathy, ignorance, and incompetence, rather than evil scheming."**

strive always to be objective and evenhanded in our reporting.

Still, some unanswered queries remain. Has the media become too powerful? What price glory and commercials? And, as Cicero wisely remarked back in the sixth century A.D., "What gives?"

The first round of Mediagate took place behind tightly sealed doors in closed sessions and seems to have unearthed among the nation's periodicals a vast conspiracy of large-scale corruption, cupidity, greed, and avarice. And splashy, easy-to-read *Newsweek* features bring it all home to you at a newly reduced subscription rate. The secret behind our great, in-depth coverage? A host of special inside sources, who bring the latest news straight from behind those closed Senate sessions to our editors here in New York. And we think

you'll find the secret testimony they report to be more than a little shocking. Just consider the following.

On day one of the closed hearings, the Senate committee commenced its probe with a resounding gavel pound by Senator Donald Mohasset (D, Rhode Island), the well-spoken, silver-haired personification of stately New England charm and quaintness. At his right hand: Senator "Robert" Beatrice (R, New York), looking especially distinguished in the dapper black overcoat, black silk shirt, and quotation marks that have been in his family for generations.

As the proceedings got under way, Mohasset ordered Senator Pamela Fawcett (D, Oregon) to verify that the doors and windows were secure and that no unauthorized parties were on the other side listening in on the hearings with a drinking glass. A temporary hitch arose when Senator Fawcett vociferously refused to take action, noting the sexist stereotyping implicit in Mohasset's request. At this point Senator Jeremiah T. Beaufort (R, South Carolina) grumbled some remark about Georgia peaches, arose, and checked the doors himself.

Senator Mohasset, meanwhile, pretended to ignore Beaufort and carried on with the formalities of justice. A glimmer of stern recognition flashed in Mohasset's piercing blue eyes as he intoned the name of the first magazine to fall under scrutiny, "*Time.*"

"About two-thirty," replied the witness, Mr. Clarence Sooth Luce, prompting peals of laughter from most of the members of the Senate panel but a request by Senator Archibald Stone (R, California) that the remark be struck from the record and that he be allowed to strike Mr. Luce personally. The request was denied by Senator Mohasset, who proceeded to grill Mr. Luce on *Time* magazine's alleged practice of suppressing "depressing, pessimistic" news stories and replacing them with frilly cover stories on ice cream, rock 'n' roll idols, animated cartoon heroes, and brightly colored balloons. (That's right—balloons. August 12, 1984. Look it up.)

Mr. Luce maintained in his own defense that *Time*'s staff writers were ill-equipped to cover any stories pertaining to the real world, much less cover them up. Hence, he insisted, *Time*'s egregious shallowness is due simply to apathy, ignorance, and incompetence, rather than evil scheming.

"Most of our competent editors and reporters resigned and went to work for *Newsweek*," sighed Mr. Luce. The entire panel nodded in tacit commiseration. Then, slamming down his gavel, Senator Mohasset put an end to the first day of Mediagate. "Mr. Luce," he noted, "is a victim of circumstance."

With *Time* magazine already tagged as a major player in the conspiracy, one can only wonder what strange surprises will be unearthed in the weeks ahead. And you can follow all the action right here—in the pages of *Newsweek* magazine.

Sen. Mohasset: Let the hearings begin! (Hush comes over crowd.) We will now examine our first pieces of evidence. I have here before me a number of magazines that, for various reasons, were never seen by the public. Now . . .

Sen. Beaufort: If Ah may be excused for a moment, Senatah, Ah would jest like to say that Ah will do everythin' in mah powah to bring these no-good varmints t' justuce. Mah constituents will settle faw no less, an' I aim t' . . .

Sen. Mohasset: Yes, thank you, Senator. Now let's take a look at those magazines . . .

Sen. Beaufort: An' let me add that I love mah country, and Ah will faithfully represent the opinions of mah constituents down t' the last plow ox . . .

Sen. Mohasset: Senator! I assure you that each of us will get his . . .

Sen. Fawcett: Exc . . .

Sen. Mohasset: . . . or her chance to speak. Now please let me present the evidence.

Sen. Richardson: Can I have my chance right now?

MAGAZINE

The magazine for magazine lovers

```
*  248**:******CAR-RT-SORT**CR25
*LWI0040P095*
580004 LWI 0040P093 2M48 MAY38
                                    10*BJ
NANCY LEWIN
4 PARK AV AP 50K
NEW YORK          NY   10016
```

In this issue:
- How To Tell If Your Favorite Magazine Is Boring
- Readers' Poll: Two Staples Vs. Three
- Test-Readings Of Three Top Nutrition Magazines
- Fiction: "The Crumpled, Outdated Magazines At The Doctor's Office"
- Advertisements: Why They're There
- Special Section: Address Label—Hero Or Villain?

Covers of failed magazines

WAITING: A special-interest journal of the medical professions, *Waiting* was the first magazine to be designed specifically for waiting-room tables of dentists, physicians, and hospital clinics across the nation. Initially, the monthly's future seemed bright, as the first issue sold quite well with reassuring, optimistic articles, such as "Lollipops, Reward of the Happy Patient," "Why Throat Cultures Feel So Good," and "The Orthodontics that Saved My Dog's Life." As fate would have it, though, some practical joker in the layout room prepared a fake cover to amuse his supervisor, and it was sent to the printers by mistake. The bastard issue was subsequently distributed directly to the waiting rooms, resulting in a ninety-nine percent rate of subscription cancellations for that month. *Waiting* went under.

WAITING

Vol. 1, No. 2.

March, 1985.

In this issue:

Death by Anesthesia Overdose: More Common Than You'd Think

The Day My Dentist's Hand Slipped. A Posthumous Report

Strip! Sexual Perversity in the Examining Room

13 Diseases You Can Catch from Giving Blood

Waiting-Room Magazines: Most Common Source of Communicable Disease

CUBIN'
The Rubik's Cube Monthly

In this issue:

Cube Roots: How It All Got Started

Of Rubik: Part 3, The Rhombus Years

Pictorial: Cubes At The Seashore

Ten Tips To Improve Your Grip

The World's Largest Rubik's Cube!

"I Thought The Rubik's Cube Would Be Just Another Fad!"

TAKING THE STAND: Don Phipps, *LIFE* magazine photographer

Sen. Beaufort: You suhtenly have some impressive cruhdentials, Mr. Phipps.

Phipps: Thank you, Senator.

Sen. Beaufort: Ah see you snapped them photos of Gary Hart on his secret vaycation with that model Donna Rice that done wrecked his Presidential campaign.

Phipps: Yeah, that was me.

Sen. Beaufort: And Ah see that you took that photo of Jim Bakker and his secritary that done went and got Bakker kicked outa his teluhvision ministry.

Phipps: I sure did.

Sen. Beaufort: And it says here that you took a photo of Senator B . . . (coughs). Yes, well (clears throat) as Ah was saying, your credentials are mighty, mighty impressive. Now why don't you jest tell us about this here article that President Johnson had removed from the *LIFE* magazine by execyoutive order. And, ahm, we really aren't interested in anythin' else, bah the way. Nothin' else. Just the Johnson story.

Phipps: Oh, sure. Heck, I've been ruining famous people's lives for years now. These kind of scandals you're talking about are nothing new. In fact, they're nothing at all, compared with the Johnson story. That is, if it had ever been printed.

LIFE magazine, October 1967

A WEEKEND WITH LOVE 'EM AND LEAVE 'EM LBJ

"I'm off to Camp David, honey," called President Johnson as he slipped out a side door of the White House on a Friday afternoon. "Okay, dear," replied his trusting First Lady.

But the *First* Lady is by no means the *only* lady, as *LIFE* photographer Don Phipps found out when he tailed the president through what was to be a wild weekend of debauchery.

After leaving the White House in his limousine, President Johnson seemed to wander aimlessly through the streets of the capital, occasionally mooning pedestrians or hooting at women. Finally, however, the limousine turned north onto Route 57, and soon after entered the parking lot of the Camp-A-While Motel—the closest to Camp David that the president would get all weekend. The president registered under the innocuous name of Lyndon Baynes Smith, checked into cabin number three, and waited for the fun to begin.

As dusk fell, a stream of glamorous women began arriving at the motel. First to enter LBJ's cabin was the fabulous starlet Mia Farrow. By the time she staggered out of the cabin fifteen minutes later, Jane Fonda, Cher, Golda Meir, Ella Fitzgerald, and Eleanor Roosevelt were waiting patiently at the door. Each was permitted fifteen minutes with the president. Several attempted to get in line again, but were held back by Secret Service agents. After FDR's widow had departed, LBJ got into his limousine and was whisked mysteriously away.

His destination proved to be a nearby liquor store, where the president purchased three cases of beer. However, by the time the limousine arrived back at cabin three, only two cases remained. Waiting for the president were Grace Slick, Queen Elizabeth, Indira Ghandi, a young girl by the name of Brooke Shields (who was turned away because she was too intellectual), and the entire cheerleading squad of the Washington Redskins. Throwing cans of beer wildly into the air, the president invited all the women into his tiny cabin for an orgy that lasted nearly until dawn.

As the sun rose, the president tiptoed out of the cabin and sped away from the scene in his limousine. The women realized too late that they had been left behind. Many gave chase, but LBJ was already boarding Air Force One. As the jet sped west, the president grabbed a few hours of sleep before being deposited on the beach at Malibu, where he soon was stealing all the girls away from the surfers. A potentially ugly scene was averted when the president had the Secret Service arrest all the surfers, leaving the entire beach to LBJ and a bevy of California beauties. He made out with them all day under the watchful eyes of his bodyguards. Come nighttime, LBJ drifted from bar to bar, picking up new women on the way until nearly 200 accompanied him to another hotel room near dawn.

After he had taken his pleasure, LBJ again tried to slip away, but these women proved more wily. They refused to fall asleep, fearing his escape. The president finally ditched the girls by saying that he had to go to the ice machine.

LBJ spent most of Sunday sleeping on Air Force One, though he did wake up a few times to pinch the stewardesses, whom he keeps on the plane simply for his own amusement. Late in the afternoon he strode back into the White House and called, "Hi honey, I'm home!"

"Did you have a nice weekend at Camp David?" Lady Bird asked.

"It was okay," the president shrugged.

LIFE regrets having to report this sordid story; yet, it is our belief, and has always been, that the public has the right to know.

The
LIFE 1st and Last Amateur Photographer Issue:

The contest was devised to bring a new angle to the way we view the world around us, to bring a new life to old *LIFE*. The assignment, given to ten up-and-coming shutterbugs, was to cover the Vietnam War, at the front and in Washington. But, while the war was raging, so were *LIFE*'s publishers, and the issue approach had the shortest life of all.

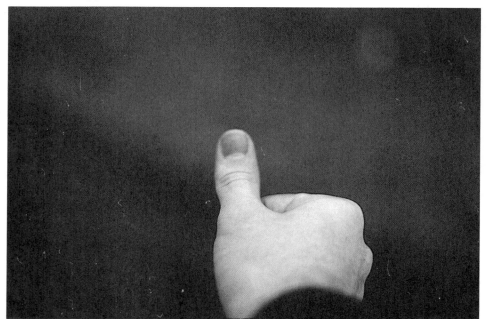

"The photographer's thumb seems somehow removed and unaffected by the battle around it. But this healthy thumb reminds us at home of how many thumbs will be hurt or killed this day in Vietnam."

"The camera captures a tense moment as President Johnson and his aides discuss the war. The president is on the left—probably. That one in the middle has got to be McNamara, you can tell by the nose. Is that Schlesinger on the right?"

"The play of light on this puddle captures the photographer's attention. Just a few feet away, thirty innocent Vietnamese villagers are being executed (not pictured)."

"Had the photographer removed his lens cap, we would have seen the president in a moment of somber reflection. Perhaps it is best that we just leave him alone in his privacy."

Sen. Mohasset: We now continue our investigation of *LIFE* magazine. I am fairly certain that what we have before us now is the experimental "Amateur Photographers" issue.

Sen. Stone: I feel that this tribunal should require a more definitive statement, Senator Mohasset. Does, or does not, the designation that you have pronounced accurately represent the item in your possession?

Sen. Mohasset: Well, to be honest, I'm not sure. Everything's so blurry that I can't really tell what it is.

Sen. Fawcett: Let me have a look at that, Senator. (takes magazine) Oh, my goodness! These pictures are a disgrace! This is filth!

Sen. Richardson: Hey, let me see that! (takes magazine) Well, looky here! This is the clearest photo of the Uranian stratosphere that I've ever seen!

Sen. Beatrice: Senators, if I might have a look? (takes magazine) Hmm. I think I had better hold onto this.

Sen. Mohasset: No, I'll take that. (takes magazine) Let's let the experts examine it.

Sen. Mohasset: The next piece of evidence up for consideration is a shocking example of careless copy writing. As hard as it may be to believe, this copy of *Review,* the in-flight magazine, was actually distributed aboard a small number of planes. Your comment, Senator Beaufort?

Sen. Beaufort: (startled awake) Plains, uh . . . Plains, Georgia, Mr. Senatah? Well, now, Ah doubt Billy had anything to do with this.

Sen. Mohasset: Senator Richardson?

Sen. Richardson: Houston, Houston. Do you read? Over.

Sen. Mohasset: All this talk about air travel seems to have had a disorienting effect on Senator Richardson. Will one of the pages quickly bring Senator Richardson some cold water?

Sen. Richardson: Tang, please.

This issue of *Review,* the complimentary in-flight magazine of Eastern Airlines, was distributed on only three planes before stewardesses noted substantial increases in cocktail sales, honey-roasted nut requests, and in-flight suicides.

REVIEW
EASTERN AIRLINES' IN-FLIGHT MAGAZIN

FALL ISSUE Selected Readings from the Nation's Most Prominent Periodicals   **COM**

"Licensed to Ill"

CRASHING INTO THE SCENE—The Beastie Boys Make It B

CONTACT WITH OTHER PLANES: DOES IT SPELL DISASTER?
New Methods of Astral Travel and the Potential for Inter-Dimensional W
[Reprinted from OMNI]

FLYING HIGH, COMING DOWN HARD The Real Facts About Crack
[Reprinted from TODAY'S HEALTH]

AMERICA'S WORST PILOTS TV Shows That Didn't Make It
[Reprinted from TV GUIDE]

THE TRAGIC BREAKUP OF WINGS Paul McCartney Goes It Alone
[Reprinted from ROLLING STONE]

THE GREAT CRASH OF '29 Herbert Hoover, the Depression, and America
[Reprinted from NOSTALGIA]

THE JETS KEEP FALLING Why New York Can't Hold Up in the NFL East
[Reprinted from SPORTS ILLUSTRATED]

THE AIRPLANE'S EXPLOSION The New Popularity of Grace Slick
[Reprinted from INTERVIEW]

Overlooked by millions of adult readers, *Teen Beat*'s George Shultz interview (November, 1985) represents a mildly important yet all but forgotten piece of political journalism.

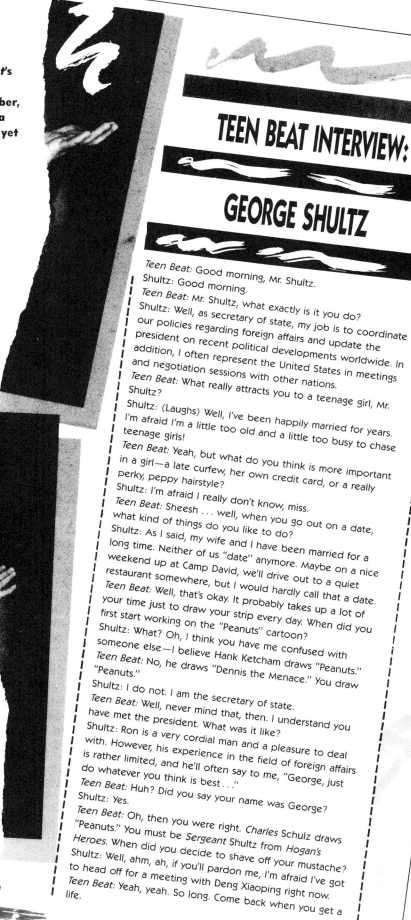

TEEN BEAT INTERVIEW:

GEORGE SHULTZ

Teen Beat: Good morning, Mr. Shultz.

Shultz: Good morning.

Teen Beat: Mr. Shultz, what exactly is it you do?

Shultz: Well, as secretary of state, my job is to coordinate our policies regarding foreign affairs and update the president on recent political developments worldwide. In addition, I often represent the United States in meetings and negotiation sessions with other nations.

Teen Beat: What really attracts you to a teenage girl, Mr. Shultz?

Shultz: (Laughs) Well, I've been happily married for years. I'm afraid I'm a little too old and a little too busy to chase teenage girls!

Teen Beat: Yeah, but what do you think is more important in a girl—a late curfew, her own credit card, or a really perky, peppy hairstyle?

Shultz: I'm afraid I really don't know, miss.

Teen Beat: Sheesh ... well, when you go out on a date, what kind of things do you like to do?

Shultz: As I said, my wife and I have been married for a long time. Neither of us "date" anymore. Maybe on a nice weekend up at Camp David, we'll drive out to a quiet restaurant somewhere, but I would hardly call that a date.

Teen Beat: Well, that's okay. It probably takes up a lot of your time just to draw your strip every day. When did you first start working on the "Peanuts" cartoon?

Shultz: What? Oh, I think you have me confused with someone else—I believe Hank Ketcham draws "Peanuts."

Teen Beat: No, he draws "Dennis the Menace." You draw "Peanuts."

Shultz: I do not. I am the secretary of state.

Teen Beat: Well, never mind that, then. I understand you have met the president. What was it like?

Shultz: Ron is a very cordial man and a pleasure to deal with. However, his experience in the field of foreign affairs is rather limited, and he'll often say to me, "George, just do whatever you think is best ..."

Teen Beat: Huh? Did you say your name was George?

Shultz: Yes.

Teen Beat: Oh, then you were right. *Charles* Schulz draws "Peanuts." You must be *Sergeant* Shultz from *Hogan's Heroes.* When did you decide to shave off your mustache?

Shultz: Well, ahm, ah, if you'll pardon me, I'm afraid I've got to head off for a meeting with Deng Xiaoping right now.

Teen Beat: Yeah, yeah. So long. Come back when you get a life.

Letters

I really liked the article on videocassettes last month. When I saw the new Waylon Jennings album on cassette at the truck stop in Ludlow, I got it, but I had a hard time loading it into the eight-track player. Well, I'm pretty handy in the shop, so I rigged up this big contraption with my sledgehammer that would cram the damn thing into the player. It didn't work too great, and Waylon ended up sounding a lot like Hank Jr. Thanks to your article, I now know what the problem was. Now I'll just have to think up a way to cram that damn thing into the television set.

Earl Cummings
Fort Mitchell

In regard to your article "Why Our Asshole Mayor Should Be Lynched" in the April issue, let me say the following: the Lions' Club of Delmar County does not have, and never has had, any connection with the American Communist Party, nor has the Rotary Club. My membership in these organizations does not imply that I am a homosexual. I did not "pork" the editor's daughter in the back of a speeding pickup truck in 1979. My nickname is not "lard-ass." I would appreciate your published apology concerning these matters.

Herb Wilmot, Mayor
Pikeville

OK, I apologize. You're still an asshole. — Ed.

ROUND-THE-CLOCK WONDERLAND — The Magic of 7-Eleven

Late night drivers on Elkston Street notice some bright lights about halfway between Main and Elm. Farmers near the edge of town see a mysterious "7" hovering above the Pikeville skyline. Odd smells come wafting over into Vern Hollis's yard. No, it's not the fault of aliens from outer space, it's just our local 24-hour convenience store: 7-Eleven.

If you've ever had the craving for an after-hours loaf of bread or "Cat Diesel" hat, you're probably familiar with 7-Eleven. Owned and operated by the Southland corporation, this all-hours miracle handles not only the standard food-and-drink-style fare, but also carries a variety of beer, hats, and wine products. Also available, by special request, are a selection of adult magazines.

Says Larry Derwood, night manager of 7-Eleven, "Basically, we're here to serve the community of Pikeville. We aim to please." And please they do! Larry reports swift sales of hats, wine products, beer, and adult magazines.

Classifieds

HAVING A PARTY? Liven it up with exciting exotic drinks! Experienced bartender can mix "Screwdrivers," "Gin & Tonics," and several other drinks popular with rich and famous people. 555-1673

REWARD for information leading to the arrest of person or persons who shot up the Coke machine outside of Reynold's Market on evening of 5/3/81. Contact: Ray Fleer, Coca-Cola Southeast, (803) 555-8766.

RUMMAGE SALE at First Church of Christ, Harrodsburg 7/13/81. Contribute your unwanted goods to benefit the needy. Please, no more used tires, broken washing machines, or children. NOTE: We will not accept used condoms. Will the person who donated these please return to pick them up.

POSSE FORMING to kill Ed Myerson. Call 555-0908 after 6 P.M. or leave message.

WANTED: Nude women. Send photo or drive by in pickup truck. Otis Tussell, 33 Marston Lane, Pikeville.

GOING OUT OF BUSINESS SALE: Everything must go! Fort Mitchell Public Library 6/30/81.

HELP WANTED: I plan to open up a tourist attraction, and I am in need of tour guides, vendors, souvenir designers, and other resort-type workers. Apply in person: ERVIN McCOY PRESENTS THE WORLD'S LARGEST COW TURD. McCoy Farm, Route 1, Ludlow.

THE
PIKEVILLIEN

rporating Fort Mitchell · Bellevue
dsburg · and Metropolitan Ludlow

GE'S #1 MAGAZINE OF LOCAL EVENTS AND
HAPPENINGS! $1.95 JUNE 1981

EAST
225

MITSUBISHI

R PLEASURES

mmo's Cheap and the DPW Just Put
d Signs

le Who Just Moved in from the City: Who ARE They,

s of All the Latest Wrecks

vie · What Really Happened When Mel Tillis Stopped to
xon Station

". . . And I do solemnly declare that the preceding issue of *The Pikevillien,* a local magazine of community affairs for several rural counties, can and must be a hoax. Any reader with any passel o' sense would pick this up and realize that it is a forgery designed to make rural folk (my beloved constituency) look ignorant and ornery. So you city boys have your *New Yorker* with its "Talk About Town" and all, while we small-town people are grossly misrepresented. For example, there is even an article here claiming that Herb Wilmot, Pikeville's mayor, saw the spirit of the pastor's beautiful daughter, who has been dead 17 years, standing by the road into Ludlow one moonlit night, and that he stopped his car and gave this lovely ghost a ride into town and dropped her off at the 7-Eleven. Now some sinister publisher *must* be at work here, trying to make us look stupid, because everyone knows the pastor's daughter haunts Route 17 into Fort Mitchell, and that there wouldn't be a reason in hell for her to drift over down *Ludlow* way, 'cept maybe for the miniature golf . . ."

STATEMENT OF SEN. JEREMIAH T. BEAUFORT CONCERNING *THE PIKEVILLIEN,* EVIDENCE #31-A

TAKING THE STAND: Mr. Thomas Chambers, Editor of *Reader's Digest*

Sen. Mohasset: Mr. Chambers, please explain to the court exactly how this April, 1975 edition of your magazine came about.

Chambers: Well, the issue to which you refer was an experiment on our part. The "All in a Day's Work" column was written by ordinary people with nine-to-five jobs, rather than elderly members of the Pawtucket Knitting Circle. The jokes in "Campus Comedy" were submitted by real college students, rather than senile members of the Boise Knitting Circle. And a new installment of the "I Am Joe's (bodily organ)" series was written by a first-year medical student, who preferred to remain nameless. Naturally, I consented to my son's request.

Sen. Mohasset: Is that all you have to say, sir?

Chambers: Naturally, Senator, I've presented the abridged version of my testimony. However, I can assure you that the meaning and intent were, for the most part, faithful to the original.

Sen. Mohasset: Very well. Let's see the material in question.

All in a Day's Work

As an elementary school teacher, I often have to deal with children. Children are less experienced and often do things we adults can laugh at. For instance, one day in class a young boy raised his hand and asked, "Miss Sparks, can I go to the bathroom?" Always on the alert to teach students proper grammar, I answered, "That's *may* I go to the bathroom. Now you ask again properly."

"*May* I go to the bathroom?" he asked, fidgeting.

"Yes, you may," I answered.

"Well it's too late now," he responded, "but at least I know I *can!*"

He had wet himself in the classroom! For Chrissakes! I hate kids.

One day at the gas station where I work, a woman drove in with her young daughter. I like kids, so I leaned over and asked, "Is this your daughter?"

"Yes," the woman responded, "and we're in a hurry. Could you please fill 'er up with unleaded?"

"Fill up your daughter?!" I joked. The lady just glowered at me. I should've poured gas on her and lit it.

I work at a fried chicken restaurant. One day a man came in and spent a long time squinting at the menu. "What do I get with a regular-size order?" he asked. I told him that the side dish was mashed potatoes and a roll.

"And what do you get with the large order?"

"Potatoes, rolls, and salad," I answered.

"And what do you get with the extra-large order?"

"Indigestion!" I joked.

"Just bring me my food," he snapped. So I spit in his cole slaw.

I work as a ticket salesman at an airline. Once a woman came running up, completely distressed, and said, "Oh no! That's my plane leaving!"

"Don't worry," I assured her. "You can probably borrow someone else's."

You know what? She almost had me fired. Fat old bitch.

As a teacher, I'm up to my armpits in stinking little brats. The other day, one of the little pests squeaked, "Miss Fine? Can I go pee-pee?" And I responded, "Yes, you can."

The next thing I know, he takes it out and does it right in the classroom! I hate my job.

CAMPUS COMEDY

FRED WAS A student at a large Northwestern college. A bad cold had prevented him from studying adequately for his final examination in philosophy. The morning of the test, Fred barely made it to the exam room. When he opened his exam book, he found that there was only one question: "Why?"

Fred thought long and hard, and then wrote his answer: "Screw you."

He received an F.

BETTY, A STUDENT at a small Southern university, was in a graduate English seminar on Marcel Proust's *A la Recherche du Temps Perdu*. At one point, the professor — a slaty old curmudgeon — drew a parallel between Proust's narrative voice and that of Gustav Flaubert.

"Professor," Betty said with a little smile, "don't you mean Kafka?"

The class erupted into laughter.

"No Betty," the professor said. "I mean Flaubert."

Betty burst into tears and left the room.

The class erupted into laughter.

Larry was a student at a medium-size Southwestern college. One day, he was late for his English lecture. When he arrived, a famous writer was speaking, but Larry didn't catch his name. The writer asked the class to name the most reprehensible act they could think of.

"Theft," one student said.

"War," said another.

Larry raised his hand. "I'd have to say killing your wife with a handgun while trying to shoot an apple off her head."

The writer, William Burroughs, burst into tears.

The class exploded into laughter.

Al and Frank were roommates at a large mid-Atlantic college. One Friday, Al answered the phone to learn that Frank's parents were coming to visit in a few hours. Al looked everywhere for Frank, but couldn't find him. He decided to clean up their room. After he had piled the dirty clothes in the closet, he went outside to wait for Frank's parents.

When they showed up, Al invited them up to the room.

"I never thought it would be so tidy," said Frank's mother. "What's in this closet?"

"Mrs. Jones, no—" Al said. But it was too late.

Inside the closet, Frank and his slut girlfriend were screwing noisily on a pile of dirty laundry.

Cathy was a student at a large Northeastern college in New York City called Barnard. One morning on her way to class, Cathy dropped her thirty-page term paper, and it fell down a sewer grate. She walked two miles back to her dorm, only to find she'd locked her keys in her room. She turned around and hiked three miles to the lecture hall, but when she got there class had been cancelled.

Cathy decided to go for a long walk. In the middle of the Verrazano Narrows Bridge, she met a friend, who said, "*I'd* never wear a white skirt like that if I was having *my* period."

The Verrazano Narrows Bridge is 200 feet above sea level.

I Am Joe's Brain

I AM JOE'S brain. I have a gray, pudding-like consistency and a surface area of ten square meters, most of it concealed in my complex folds. I am the control center of Joe's body. I am responsible for all of Joe's bodily functions and activities. I am not responsible for the fact that Joe drank fifteen beers and one pint of cheap scotch last night.

Without my instructions, Joe could not walk, talk, breathe, or see. Sometimes when Joe is asleep, I use my "legs" (brain stem) to scuttle down through his spine and roll around in the half-digested food in his stomach. Joe has bad dreams when I do this.

Speaking of bad dreams, Joe is waking up now. Good morning, Joe. Hmm? Yes, it's morning. See the sunlight? What? It's a Saturday morning. 1967. You're ten years old, Joe. Can you smell Mom cooking pancakes downstairs?

Ha ha! Just kidding. It's 1988, you're 28, and you live alone. You want to move your head to the side? Okay. People who don't drink rarely experience that kind of blinding pain in their skulls the next morning. I'll think about that for you for a while, Joe.

Much of the work I do in my job as Joe's brain goes unnoticed by Joe. These are called automatic functions. This is how I got Joe out of bed, through the shower, into his clothes, and out on the street without his realizing it.

When Joe drinks a lot, I feel as if someone has pumped me full of Novocain and silly juice. This is not a pleasant sensation. Luckily, I shake it off long before my cousins—Joe's stomach, Joe's lungs, and Joe's bowels—do. I have to be wide awake and very alert, as it's my job to tell Joe just how bad he feels.

Another part of my job is storing information for Joe. Joe periodically runs spot-quizzes on me. Your dentist appointment, Joe? 11:45. This morning. Say what? "How does one move one's legs so as to walk?" I'm sorry, Joe. That information is classified at this time.

Get up off the sidewalk, Joe. People are staring at you. Okay, I'll tell you how to walk.

Ahh . . . there. I've released the information directly to your motor system, Joe. Hey Joe, why you walking like a man with a broom up his butt? Guess I released the wrong information. Wrong I information released I. Confusing, isn't it Joe?

Hey Joe, look at this mental picture. That's what you did last night when you were so drunk. No, I won't tell you the girl's name. What? Maybe if you hadn't drunk so much, you'd be able to remember how the car ended up in the river.

Shut up, Joe. I don't know how to refrain from vomiting. Perhaps you should ask one of your drinking "buddies." There. Now Joe has vomited right on the sidewalk. Hey Joe—look at that dog licking up your vomit. No, don't look away. I won't permit it. Hmm? Yes, by all means Joe—vomit again.

Feel that, Joe? That's me flexing my frontal lobe in time with your heartbeat. Flex. Flex. Flex. Boy, that's got to hurt! I'm glad I'm not you, Joe.

For years, *MAD* magazine has been a source of delight for children and adults alike. Always pleasant in tone and consisting of articles carefully worded so as not to offend even a single person, the magazine has gained the approval of parents and church groups nationwide. Had it not been for some last-minute cutting by the magazine's editors, however, this May 1985 column by Dave Berg might have sullied *MAD*'s reputation permanently.

THE LIGHTER

SIDE OF SHIT

by Dave Berg

Sen. Mohasset: The committee now turns its attention to a special report that government investigators have prepared.

Sen. Stone: A most revealing report, too, I might add.

Sen. Mohasset: Yes Senator Stone, you might, because it appears that a mixture of ill-fortune and human error conspired to make 1974 an embarrassing time for everyone connected with *Esquire* magazine. I myself will never forget my own anger and frustration when not one issue of *Esquire* arrived in the mail all year, despite the fact that I renewed my subscription three times.

Sen. Richardson: Hear hear, Senator Mohasset. I, too, suffered the absence of *Esquire* in 1974.

Sen. Stone: (pounding his fist on the table) Damn those irresponsible gold-bricks of the magazine racket!

Sen. Richardson: Of course, I spent the entire year in geosynchronous orbit up in Skylab. So I suppose it was my own fault.

Sen. Stone: Er, yes Buzz, I suppose it was. (Senator Stone accidentally spills a pitcher of water into Senator Richardson's lap.)

REPORT OF THE

INVESTIGATING COMMITTEE

ESQUIRE TIMETABLE 1974

• **February:** *Esquire* introduces computerized subscription labels, a revolutionary time-saving system that unfortunately results in every single copy of the magazine being sent to Earl Hollings of South Bend, Mo. Only two subscribers other than Mr. Hollings fail to register complaints. One is a Mr. Earle Holland of Peoria, Pa., and the other is a Mrs. Tammy Earl of Holland, Denmark—both of whom receive copies due to postal errors. As for the remaining 50,352 copies, Mr. Hollings subsequently builds a radio transmitting tower using only the magazines and paste. The tower tips over after standing for only three hours.

• **March:** *Esquire* rushes to publish their next revolutionary issue, the first men's magazine to contain perfume advertisements with actual samples of the scent. Unfortunately, due to a technical error at the plant, "Poisenne" by Giorgi turns out wrong. The editors are divided over whether the scent smells like "fermenting dog droppings," "deceased fish," or "unusual vomit," but most agree that the smell is unpleasant. They hastily recall all copies of the issue and ship them c.o.d. to France.

• **April:** The issue arrives and is a delightful surprise for subscribers, as it reaches their homes and doesn't smell bad. Readers are pleased; *Esquire* isn't. The layout staff has apparently failed to include the customary legal copyright information—meaning that the *Esquire* name, emblem, and "funny-looking rich guy with a big hat" mascot are fair game for every two-bit entrepreneur and rip-off artist in the nation. By May, convenience stores across America are flooded with *Esquire*-brand menthol cigarettes, "Funny-Looking Rich Guy With A Big Hat"

deodorant sticks, and *Esquire*-brand cola ("For the man who reads the magazine of the same name"). With plans for a new magazine entitled *Esquire's Tit Mag Especiale* in the works, the editors scramble to publish a new issue in which to reclaim their exclusive rights to their hopelessly tarnished trademark.

• **May:** *Esquire* appears, complete with copyright notice but, sadly, nothing else, as April's commercial siege has reduced the magazine's staff to two people, one of whom is on vacation. Nevertheless, some public faith in the magazine is regained, and after a small loan *Esquire* is able to hire back the other two writers and the fifteen coffee boys who have been laid off.

• **June:** *Esquire* features a beautifully photographed fashion forecast predicting that there will be a revival of chest plates in men's clothing and that women will soon forgo skirts in favor of big metal "Robo-Pants." The issue is the first of *Esquire's* biannual "embarrassments"—a tradition the magazine maintains even to this day.

• **July:** *Esquire* staffers are too busy working night jobs and trying to liquidate their surplus stock of Robo-Pants to put together a magazine. Anyone who is still a subscriber at this point can only be termed an idiot. There are, however, twenty-three of them. Editor-in-Chief Phillip Moffit calls each of them personally to explain why the issue has not yet arrived, using excuses ranging from "the dogs ate them" to "typewriter broken." Twenty-two subscribers cancel their subscriptions, leaving only one. He is Mr. Earl Hollings of South Bend, Mo., and he has just completed blueprints for a light schooner made only of magazines and paste.

TAKING THE STAND: Rock Henderson, publisher of *Sports Illustrated*

Sen. Fawcett: Mr. Henderson, I must tell you that I find your annual swimsuit issue a disgusting exploitation of women. I can't believe that any self-respecting woman would read such a publication.

Henderson: You know, that's exactly the way I feel. But we really don't have a substantial number of women readers anyway, so I never worried myself much about it.

Sen. Fawcett: I cannot believe what I am hearing! I think you owe a debt to women everywhere, sir.

Henderson: Again, that's exactly the way I feel. That's why I introduced the men's swimsuit edition back in '86. I figured I'd even out the score by letting you chicks get a load of some macho action.

Sen. Fawcett: I can't believe my ears! I've seen that disgraceful issue of your magazine of which you speak so proudly. And I say right now: The exploitation of the male body is no way of correcting the situation! Two wrongs do not make a right! I am calling an end to all exploitation of all people everywhere! Besides, those guys were really flabby-chested. Couldn't you have done any better than that?

In 1986, *Sports Illustrated* sought to placate feminists opposed to the annual (women's) swimsuit issue by releasing a special men's swimsuit edition. The issue proved a dismal failure: Ninety-nine percent of the magazine's two million male subscribers immediately disposed of the issue. Worse yet, the magazine's female readers remained unimpressed. One complained of a bikini-clad woman in the background of a certain photo spread, while the other called the special edition a half-hearted nod to feminists and expressed dissatisfaction with the flabby-chested models employed. This despised and long-forgotten issue is now a collector's item that commonly fetches thousands at auctions.

(Above) A genuine polyester imitation horsehide swimsuit from the Surf's Up collection. $99. Available in regular or ankle-length styles, this crowd-pleaser features a spare drawstring and a handy washing label sewed right into the suit lining.

(Right) The hot suits this season will be cut to a length that brings the suit bottom down to a point approximately halfway between the waist and knee, although a number of popular styles will playfully toy with the prevailing length, preferring a slightly longer or shorter leg-length. This colorful suit from the Lou Meyer's collection features elastic leg-huggers and a padded buttock. $120.

For the man who isn't ashamed to "let it all hang out," this mere wisp of a bathing suit from the Grover Cleveland line is just the thing. Priced at only $75 and endorsed by Willie Mays, these uncomfortable 100 percent wool trunks are certain to dot the coastline this summer. Please— someone hold the women back!

Following the advent of practical and affordable close-captioned television for the hearing-impaired in the early eighties, *TV Guide* began making a special effort to include information and specialized listings to aid the deaf in their choice of captioned programs. In late 1982, the magazine's editors decided to open up the world of television to a previously untapped group of disabled persons: the blind. The first issue of an all-braille *TV Guide* appeared on the newsstands on October 9. It contained all the regular features, with a special emphasis on the needs of blind viewers.

SPECIAL BRAILLE EDITION
OCTOBER 9–15

Wednesday
3 PM – 3:30 PM

3PM **2** **51** SESAME STREET (60 min.)
Oscar the Grouch is in a bad mood because he is a puppet that lives in a trash can. Big Bird is eight feet tall, but he is not a real bird. The high voices are usually not women, but children.
3 **6** **7** GUIDING LIGHT (60 min.)
When there is soft music playing, Chuck and Laura are about to have sex. There are glasses clinking in the first scene because it takes place in a bar.
4 **10** **22** GENERAL HOSPITAL (60 min.)
When the series of slow beeps turns into one long beep, someone has died.
25 PORKY PIG AND FRIENDS
The stuttering voice is Porky Pig. The voice that sounds like it has to spit is Daffy Duck. When there is a gunshot sound, it is Elmer Fudd who has blown up, not Bugs Bunny, who he was aiming at. These people are all cartoon characters.
27 I DREAM OF JEANNIE
The weird whoosing noise followed by a drum is Jeannie changing things or people into other things, because she has magical powers. When she is talking to herself or crying, she is inside the bottle she came in.
56 HOUR MAGAZINE
Although people are often cooking things, this show takes place in a very nicely decorated television studio. It has a little kitchen area. Parts of the show where Gary Collins is not talking take place outside of the studio.
68 MOVIE—Horror (90 min.)
"King Kong" (American; 1932) the woman is screaming because a very large gorilla is attacking her. Toward the end, the plane sounds are because the gorilla is on top of a big building. The planes are shooting at him.
MTV VIDEO COUNTDOWN (30 min.)
Just like the radio, but with pictures
3:30 **25** WHEEL OF FORTUNE
People are trying to guess what a phrase or name is by guessing the letters in it. The woman turning the letters is very pretty.
27 DUKES OF HAZZARD
The splashing sound is the bad guy's car driving into the river. The good guys get away.
32 THE McLAUGHLIN GROUP
The people are yelling, but they are not hitting each other.
45 THE ADDAMS FAMILY
The joke is that everyone in the family is very odd looking.

TAKING THE STAND: Les Larkin, a business editor of *Forbes* magazine

(Les Larkin took the stand on Day Two of the open sessions to explain his involvement in "The Forbes 400 Biggest Losers" debacle of 1985. Why wasn't the list published that year? Senator "Robert" Beatrice led the investigation and some rather enigmatic dialogue transpired between Beatrice, a former corporate executive, and Larkin, who seems to speak his language):

Sen. Beatrice: Now Les, Malcolm and I were teeing off the other day when he informed me of his concern that this Forbes 400 affair might interfere with—

Larkin: You mean the personal lives of—

Sen. Beatrice: Come now, we've been through all that and—

Larkin: Oh, you mean the acquisition of the a—

Sen. Beatrice: The moon is very bright tonight. What says the rooster at dawn?

Larkin: The crow must fly before he can buy.

Sen. Beatrice: Yes, and the seas are deep and still.

When the objectivity of Beatrice (who is rumored to be planning a leveraged takeover of Forbes Inc.) was called into question by Sen. Fawcett, the fatherly Beatrice merely replied that Farrah would never make such reckless accusations and that he "expected more from her smarter sister." A wrangle of words ensued.

"It was a bad idea, but I can afford it," laughs multi-millionaire/publisher/balloonist Malcolm Forbes. **"Every year we publish the Forbes 400 list of America's biggest winners—and also a list of the biggest financial losers.**

"But in 1985 I realized that some of the biggest losers aren't necessarily financial failures. These people are just plain losers. Imagine that!"

Forbes realized that the article might seem mean-spirited, so he pulled it before the issue went to press. But the solid tin "Total Loser 1985" trophies were already in the mail.

IN THEIR OWN WORDS:

America's Losers Sound Off

1) **Frederich Antonioni:** A veteran of 659 casting calls and one legal name change, this 45-year-old busboy from Queens hopes to someday "make it in the big-time world of acting!"

2) **Sandy "The Dink" Dinkman:** Plagued by injuries on and off the court, this professional basketball court waxer/buffer hopes to regain at least three of the five fingers he's lost in minor mechanical accidents. "On the court, anything is possible," says Dinkman. "I believe in basketball (waxing and buffing)."

3) **Kirk Salton:** "If grad school has taught me anything, it's taught me just how much I still don't know." Now entering his fifth year of graduate school, Salton looks forward to another seven to nine years.

4) **Cathy Lancer:** "I sent my friend Vanna White to take my place at the *Wheel of Fortune* auditions," says the blond-haired, blue-eyed Lancer. "I sent my friend Vanna White to take my place at the *Wheel of Fortune* auditions. I sent my friend Vanna White to take my place at the *Wheel of Fortune* auditions."

5) **Nicky LaFlamme:** "I went in to hold up a liquor store, and the clerk asked me for an I.D. He told me that you had to be 21 to hold up a liquor store, so I showed him my driver's license. About two hours later, this S.W.A.T. team showed up at my house."

6) **Burke Harrington:** "Remember *Cubin'* magazine? Mine."

7) **Mel Stamp:** Stamp saved all his life to buy a lucrative fireworks concession along I-95 in South Carolina. From his bed in Memorial Hospital's intensive care unit, he asserts, "This time I *promise* to give up smoking. I mean it."

8) **Geraldo Rivera:** "Good evening. I'm Geraldo Rivera, and this is *20/20*," says Rivera. "I still say it to myself every once in awhile."

9) **Rick Clapman:** In 1979, Clapman moved into the Arizona desert to isolate himself from civilization and develop his talents as a writer. He has recently completed two novels, which he plans to send to publishers as soon as he gets enough gasoline to drive into Tucson. "One book is a thriller about this car that comes alive and runs over people. I call it *Justine.* The other is an atlas in verse form," boasts Clapman.

10) **George Takei:** "I told the studio that I wouldn't be in *Star Trek V* unless they let me direct it. Apparently, the character of Sulu isn't as important as I had been led to believe."

11) **Lester Wilkes:** Wilkes was hospitalized with multiple gunshot wounds shortly before his trial for trespassing and burglary. Says Wilkes, "That real fancy office complex . . . turns out it belonged to *Soldier of Fortune.*"

12) **Quentin LaFarge:** "I gave Mr. Forbes the idea for this article," says the former *Forbes* editor. "I never thought I'd see *my* name here."

TAKING THE STAND: Mitzi Roseway, fashion model

Sen. Fawcett: Now Ms. Roseway, as a high-fashion model who was coerced into the high-tech fashion market, you must have some eye-opening tales of exploitation and degradation to relate to the committee.

Roseway: (chewing gum) Yeah, well, it was kinda fun sometimes, ya know? All those buttons and diodes.

Sen. Stone: Young lady, I will thank you to remove the gum from your mouth when testifying before a committee of the United States Congress.

Roseway: (sticking gum behind her ear) I'm sorry, Senator. So anyway, one day I showed up for a fashion-spread shooting and the photographer says to me, "Today you'll get some silicon implants," and I says, "Up yours" and head for the door, but he stops me and laughs and says, "No no no, not silicone, I meant silicon, as in "'Silicon Valley of the Dolls.'" Well, the next thing I know I'm wearing a dress made of disk dr—

Roseway's attorney: (interrupting) Uh, Senator Mohasset, I'd like a word aside with Mrs. Roseway at this juncture.

Sen. Mohasset: Granted.

(Here Ms. Roseway pauses to consult with her attorney, who has just begun whispering into her ear. . . . Ten minutes pass, he is still whispering . . .)

Sen. Mohasset: (whistles, drums fingers on his notepad)

(Another five minutes pass. He has taken her under the table for added privacy of conversation.)

Sen. Fawcett: Disgusting . . .

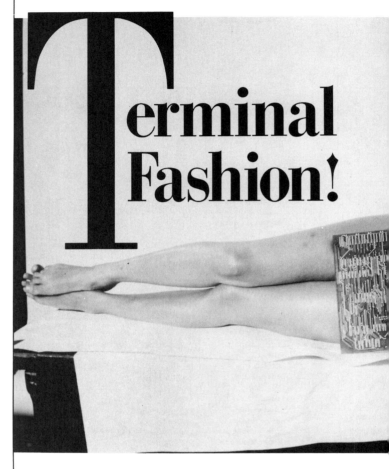

Terminal Fashion!

Look out, Fashion World, the eighties are here, and with them, a brash and oh-so-daring new look in casuals! Versatility, user-friendliness, and a wide range of peripherals are the key to this brave new world of women's soft-wear. Throw out those dowdy hip boots and paisley jackets of yesterday and log on to the *Vogue* Look of the *Eighties* . . . Digital Design!

(*Vogue* prides itself on its ability to calmly remain two steps ahead of style's cutting edge. In 1980, *Vogue*'s editors predicted that a high-tech turn of fashion's fancy would make the Digital Age all the rage. But only days before this article hit the newsstands, Madonna made her first public appearance. Suddenly, wearing-your-bra-outside-of-your-clothing became the new mod mode, and this article was quietly classified with the gauche, declassé, and unforgivably unchic.—JCY)

You've got the disks, they'll have the drive with this casual micro-skirt and matching keyboard handbag. Go everywhere in this ensemble—except near sources of powerful magnetic flux! Giorgio Atari. (about $125 single-sided, $250 double.) Compatible with IBM PC and Liz Claiborne.

Hold onto your joysticks! Surfboard meets circuit board in this stunning new swimsuit from Radio-Shack. Caution: Electrifying when wet! (about $150). Remember, PEEK, but don't POKE.

Input/output, anyone? Anna's ready to turn you on in this shrink-to-fit pullover by **HALSTON 2001**. Fully programmable and a bargain for its power and capacity, HAL's latest allows even the most poverty-stricken of fashion conscious femmes-fatales to calculate spread-sheets, word process, *and* look good, too! (about $4,500, available in Basic Blue and CObol Cobalt.)

With a single keystroke, this outfit will have you interfacing at over 3500 baud. You'll never make another social syntax error with this fashionable datadome at your fingertips. (about $3750). Also available with numeric keypadded shoulders.

TAKING THE STAND: Cynthia Weber, editor of *Cosmopolitan*

Sen. Fawcett: Miss Weber, I find this "Cosmo Quiz" particularly offensive. Why should any self-respecting woman have to put up with this sort of nonsense?

Weber: Oh, come now, Senator. Give me a chance to explain. You see, this quiz was put together by a couple of crazy radical feminists on the writing staff. You know the type. They were hoping to scare away all the men who surreptitiously read *Cosmo* each month.

Sen. Fawcett: Well! Crazy feminists, you say? I think I've had all I can take of you and your quiz!

Weber: Yeah, yeah. It sounds to me like you're just afraid to take the quiz, *Miss* Fawcett.

Sen. Fawcett: I am not afraid, Miss Weber. I simply am not interested.

Weber: Not interested? I see. You're afraid.

Sen. Fawcett: I am not afraid. It's just that I don't think I should have scored as a "Construction Worker" on that quiz of yours.

Sen. Beaufort: Excuse me, ma'am, but faw the record, ah also scored as a "Construction Workah."

Sen. Richardson: I took the quiz, too!

Sen. Mohasset: And?

Sen. Richardson: Hey, I passed. I'm no dummy.

HOW FEMALE ARE YOU?

A COSMOPOLITAN QUIZ

by Micheylle Sark and Robbyne Webb

Have you ever stopped to wonder just what, exactly, you are? Have you ever thought that maybe some of your insecurities and uncertainties are caused by trying to fit into a category to which you don't really belong? It's time for you to find out once and for all, *How Female Are You?* Just take our simple quiz, and you might learn something that could change your entire way of looking at the world. Answer carefully and honestly, because some of the questions are tricky. And don't try to choose the "right" answer. We know you know how to THINK like a woman.

PART I

1. After three wonderful dates, a man you like very much invites you over to his apartment for a candlelight dinner for two. In the middle of the main course, however, he suddenly jumps up and runs to the bathroom, screaming, and refuses to come out. You would most likely:

a. find another bathroom in the house so as to check your make-up and test just how far you have to bend over to give him enough of a glimpse to start some action.

b. find another bathroom in the house and lock yourself in it. Two can play at that game.

c. not pass him a new roll of toilet paper, even if he asks nicely.

d. say, "Hey man, your penis hurts, right? I know how it is."

2. You've had a hard day at work. You get home just wanting to collapse, but a TV news team greets you at your door and wants to interview you about your brother, who has just qualified for the Olympics. Your response is to:

a. say, "Yes, he was always the athletic son in our family, and I was another son."

b. make them all cookies because the cameramen are sooo cute.

c. tell him that he would probably get better material interviewing your hedge.

d. run in to call your brother long distance and congratulate him. Halfway to the phone you suddenly remember that you have missed his birthday and you whirl around with a look of horror on your face just as the news team catches up. The next morning it is this expression staring back at you from the front page of the newspaper. Your brother, seeing the paper and thinking that something terrible has happened to you, withdraws from the Olympics and spends the rest of his life watering down your roof in case any neighboring houses should catch fire.

3. A married man you have been sleeping with for seven years suddenly reveals that the person he is married to is you. Your response, after kicking him in the nuts, is to:

a. feel a little sad and depressed, but decide that you are better off knowing what mistakes not to make the next time.

b. feel disgusted and angry; the expensive lunch you had today tasted horrible, and while you were in the drugstore someone stole your car. This thing about his wife, though, you don't really care about.

c. threaten to kill him, but then reconsider when the two of you discover that you are both registered for the draft.

d. get up and have breakfast. After having been asleep for seven years, you are feeling healthy and refreshed.

4. You meet a tall, handsome stranger at a birthday party for a friend. From the conversations you overhear during the party you can tell that he is very rich and intelligent and single. When he hands you a piece of cake he drops the fork, and when he straightens up from bending down to pick it up, he hits his head on a cabinet. He puts his hand up to the back of his head to assess the damage, and when he turns around he knocks a priceless vase off a shelf with his elbow. He

smiles and asks you what time it is. You:

a. refuse to tell him. You realize that he is merely seeking ways to avoid commitment while still being able to enjoy the physical side of the relationship.

b. tell him. You realize that he lost his watch inside someone's hair while putting on blindfolds for pin-the-tail-on-the-donkey.

c. point at a clock so that in turning to look at it he twists his ankle and falls into the swimming pool.

d. are flustered and do not know quite what to say. You are so drunk that you thought he asked you for a "lime," and you have just selfishly eaten the last one yourself.

5. On a visit home for Christmas, your father tells you that he has been seeing a younger woman and is considering divorcing your mother. When you act outraged, he points out that throughout your life you have been an ungrateful, thieving, conniving, adulterous, cheap, sleazy bitch. You feel:

a. exposed; you did not realize that your father knew you so well. At the same time, you feel grateful to him for his insights.

b. hungry. You mention this and your father offers you a "knuckle sandwich" and then laughs uproariously until you are forced to kick him in the nuts.

c. sick. When someone stepped on your foot earlier in the day you swallowed your chewing tobacco.

d. okay; you know that even if you did spend that week in Jamaica with a man so fat that the airline chopped him in half and sent him down on two separate flights, your father has no doubt done worse things. The time he fed your sister mothballs for three years and then sold her into slavery comes to mind.

6. While playing a game of charades at a party, you are asked to pantomime the 1957 film noir classic, *If God Were on the Green Bay Packers, Would Bart Starr Use Him on Fourth and Long, or Would He Just Run an Option as Usual?* No one has heard of it, and it takes you seven and a half hours to complete the title. As you leave the party your fiancé says, "You're an idiot. Get lost." You react by:

a. crying. If he can't accept that and be supportive, then he is the one who isn't living up to his responsibilities.

b. freezing in your tracks for about ten seconds, and then falling flat on your face in the host's azaleas, stone dead.

c. slugging him and then going to an Elks' meeting.

d. admitting that you aren't very smart, and then insisting that kosher and creole are the same thing.

7. When looking through a copy of *Cosmopolitan*, you spend the most time:

a. analyzing the readers' questions column for clues to see if any of the kinky letters are actually from people you know.

b. gloating over all the svelte bathing suit models who will be in traction by the time they are 35 from arching their breasts forward for eight hours every day.

c. idly testing yourself for breast cancer.

d. going over the Obsession ad with a magnifying glass trying to figure out whether that is a nipple you can see.

8. You prefer:

a. Gloria Steinem.

b. Goldie Hawn.

c. Victoria Principal.

d. Margaret Leaky.

PART II

Mark the following statements with a T for "typical of my sex," an N for "No way, that's the other kind," or a ? for "question mark."

1. In high school my favorite classes were Cookie Baking and Needlepoint.
2. In high school my favorite classes were football and full-contact kick-boxing.
3. In high school I wore so much mascara that I didn't find my way out of the ladies' room until I was a junior.
4. I could never get pregnant because I have no womb.
5. In medieval times I would have walked on the inside of the sidewalk to avoid having garbage poured on my head.
6. After six hundred years of washing my hair, there are still bits of rotten vegetables stuck in it.
7. Playtex, Secret, Espadrilles, The Temptations.
8. Jockey. Speed Stick. Nike. The Blasters.
9. A rose is a rose is a rose is a rose.
10. Kill my landlord. Kill my landlord.
11. I think playing "Boggle" can be just as much fun as sex.
12. Sex without love is like a cheeseburger without brake fluid.

SCORING

Part I

Give yourself points as follows:
1. a: 10   b: 0   c: 0   d: −10
2. a: 10   b: −10   c: 0   d: 0
3. a: 10   b: 0   c: −10   d: 0
4. a: 10   b: 0   c: 0   d: 0
5. a: 10   b: 0   c: −10   d: 0
6. a: 10   b: 0   c: −10   d: 0
7. a: 10   b: 10   c: 10   d: −10
8. a: 10   b: −5   c: −10   d: −1000

Part II

Give yourself 5 points for any "T"s on odd-numbered statements. Subtract 5 points for any "T"s on even-numbered statements. Forget the question marks. They don't mean anything.

What your score reveals:

50 points or more: You are a girl. No arguments, no partial credit, no nothing. You are sappy yet vengeful, caring yet shallow, small yet less likely to die in motorcycle accidents. No matter how you try, you are doomed to playing kickball and newcomb in elementary school, carrying pocket mirrors, and getting poked in the behind by Groucho Marx. Eventually, though, you will realize that this isn't so bad, and you will come to enjoy being a woman. If being a woman was what caused all your problems to begin with, however, then this quiz was a big waste of your time.

−50 to 50 points: You are either extremely confused, or you deliberately picked all the stupid answers. In either case, you should probably seek counseling.

−50 to −200 points: You are a man. You are a man, and you knew it. You were deliberately reading this magazine in the hopes that you would find some inside information on how women operate. That and the breasts. Well, now we have found you out, and we don't like it one bit. *Cosmo* is a women's magazine. It's a place for women to talk about women's concerns, and it's none of your business. We don't go reading *Golf Digest* or *Easy Rider* or whatever those magazines are, so just leave us the hell alone. Thank you very much. And by the way, your fly is open.

less than −200 points: You are very fond of Margaret Leaky. That is nothing to be ashamed of. Archaeology is a very rewarding field.

This article was written by the two leaders of a radical faction at *Cosmo* who were dedicated to scaring away the thousands of men who read the magazine surreptitiously each month. They hoped to identify them by their score on this quiz, and then threaten to give their girlfriends romantic advice unless the men quit reading the magazine. This campaign did not meet with much approval from *Cosmo*'s executive board.

"Get rid of the men?" giggled the editor-in-chief, as she lit what she thought were all the existing copies of the article with her Daisy lighter. "No, no, no! You silly nits, we LIKE men. That's the whole point."

In 1986 the publisher of *Good Housekeeping* realized that a fortune in production costs could be saved by printing the magazine in Japan. Unfortunately, disaster struck when the text of the magazine was translated from English to Japanese and then back again by an electronic typesetting computer. Worse yet, each copy of the magazine was folded into an intricate origami figurine. The resulting volume was virtually unreadable, and the publisher was forced to move the operation back to the United States, where a new replacement edition was hastily thrown together using articles clipped from *Ladies' Home Journal* and *Family Circle*.

Below are some excerpts from the lost Japanese issue.

TASTY HOME MUFFIN

Ingredients:

four cup flour
one tablespoons salt
one cup bluebelly
three spoons baking flour!
two squids
egg
one cup cooking flour

Directions:

Mix ingredients in squid pan please. Serve over steam rice. Serves six to eight honorable men. Now you eating American style!

Big American dream house? You bet!

Welcome to big American house. Please remove shoes!

Let us see what is hot decoration this year. First in living room we see beautiful early American Victorian Danish low-back high chair with four leg action. Watch out! Don't step on new shag tatami rug with hippie fringes. This pad is swinging pad!

Japanese television on living room counter is number one. Crank up superior Japanese stereo with no hand crank and rock in some American rock and roll orchestra.

Next rock into kitchen for taste of good life. Water from faucet! Man, this is life. See husband coming home. "Hi honey, what is meal?" Hot dogs and pie are on menu tonight—in your new American kitchen.

Look here—what is this? A bathroom! You know it. Sit right down for big American crap. Ah, so. On way out why not work up foamy lather? Now rinse. Repeat.

This is America! Beds for everyone Long unproductive day at office? Wh not reach for nearest bed and have som shut eyes.

House sweet house. Nothing is like

As the result of a parent company merger in 1974, *Continental Chef* magazine folded and its assets were appropriated by *Model Railroading Times*. Eric Foie de Gras, *Continental Chef*'s caustic restaurant critic, was given the option of writing about model landscapes for *MRT* or facing unemployment. Foie de Gras chose the former, but within hours of his passing in his first review, he found that he had inadvertently chosen the latter.

Model Landscape

THIS WEEK: VILLAGE COMPOSITION

Hello, railroaders. Let me just open this week's column by noting that model railroading is just about the most pathetic hobby I have ever heard of. I guess it's good for people who have no success or control in their actual lives, and want to feel like they're in charge of something. All right, then, but it's still pathetic.

Make no mistake about it; I say this without malice. I guess I can see how wimps and failures would want to have the illusion of power, just as most other people and I enjoy the real thing. Toward this end I have prepared some suggestions that can make your pitiable set-up more realistic and more able to shelter you from the brutal contingencies of modern life.

I will begin by assuming that you have already acquired the "basics" — a train set and some track. It doesn't concern me whether you get HO or N scale or Western Pacific or whatever — the end result will be the same. Now comes the important part: setting up your model village.

I need not go into the reasons that dictate the need for an elaborate village; suffice it to say that as a symbol of man's technological advancement, a train must be accompanied by the accoutrements of civilized society. I suggest a train station, a general store, a hotel, and perhaps a jail to keep local ruffians locked up in. Last but not least, be sure to include some first-class restaurants — the heart of

any civilization, real or scale-model. A cursory look at a hobby shop's model-building display revealed a distressing lack of quality establishments, though, so you may have to construct some yourself, should you happen to have the skill or the patience.

Whatever you do, though, don't build a model of **Marcelli's** (*, $$$, Chicago). This overpriced haven for Chicago psuedo-intellectuals should be shunted onto a side track and abandoned to inner-city graffiti hoodlums. After waiting nearly half an hour, I was shown to a dark table in a cramped corner by a rude waiter who barely spoke English. I soon came to regret my persistence in making my wishes understood, as the gazpacho had an overbearing mealy flavor and was at least ten degrees too warm. The roast lamb had a disappointing oily texture and the "Potatoes d'Enjoli" had an odor of iron filings and were served with a wilted patch of moss. The cardboard and lumpy gelatin construction misnamed "apple pie" provided a fitting end to the atrocious meal.

I cannot recommend, therefore, that any model railroader construct a model of this restaurant. I cannot imagine that the food would be acceptable no matter how microscopic the portions. On the plus side, a model of **Marcelli's** would be easier to destroy than the real one.

Next month: "Destroying Your Ridiculous Model Landscape."

TAKING THE STAND: Mike Snolokien, Director of *Marvel Comics*

Sen. Mohasset: Mr. Snolokien, we hope to learn from you the degree to which corruption in the magazine industry has infiltrated the minds of our impressionable youth. I believe that Senator Buzz Richardson has some rather pointed questions for you on the subject.

Sen. Richardson: Roger wilco, Senator Mohasset. Now Mr. Snolokien, whatever happened to the days when comics featured superheroes that all kids could admire and relate to? I mean superheroes of the caliber of the interplanetary marvel, Superman. Or, better yet, the champion of the Asteroid Belt—Captain Spaceman. Nowadays, what are you guys giving our kids to read? Look at this—"The Adventures of Ben Sinister"! A man whose weak morals are made up for by a strong left arm! I ask you, sir: How would this Ben Sinister fare in the cold, hostile environment of outer space?

Snolokien: Senator, the character of Ben Sinister was developed to provide a role model for left-handed children. We thought he might embody that one spark of hope that would allow lefties to carry themselves with self-respect. Ben Sinister spreads the word that righties aren't the only ones who can be superheroes and kill with impunity.

Sen. Richardson: (wistfully) Yes, Captain Spaceman—now *there* was a real superhero. You wouldn't be planning to bring him back from hibernation on the planet Krylo, by any chance, would you, Mr. Snolokien? I mean, he was always my favorite . . .

BEN SINISTER

CRUSADER
FOR THE RIGHTS
OF LEFT-HANDED
PEOPLE

Today's Episode:

BEN SINISTER
CRUSADER FOR THE RIGHTS OF LEFT-HANDED PEOPLE

BEN SINISTER

in

"The Foiled Bank Robbery"

CONSTANTLY ON THE RUN, BEN FINDS HIMSELF ABOARD THE SUBWAY IN CRIME-RIDDEN **NEW YORK CITY**.

SO YOU ARE ROBBING THE FIRST NATIONAL BANK AT TWO O'CLOCK TODAY?

YES.

USING HIS **STEREO HEARING**, HE DETECTS AN INDIDIOUS PLOT...

SO YOU WANT FIVE PENNIES FOR THIS NICKEL?

WHAT? OH, ER... YES, YES...

BANK

THE TIME IS NOW 2:00 P.M.

THE CRIME SHOULD BE STARTING **ANY MINUTE** NOW!

LATER...

SUDDENLY, THE TRANQUILITY OF THE BANK IS **SHATTERED** BY A RUDE ANNOUNCEMENT...

I'M MUHAMM... ALI, AND I'M H... TO ROB THE BANK!

THAT'S THE MAN I SAW ON THE **TRAIN**!

STOP RIGHT THERE, YOU PATHETIC HAS-BEEN!

GET 'IM BEN!

HEY BUDDY, YOU'RE ASKING FOR A KNUCKLE SANDWICH!

This short-lived comic book was published in 1978 by the American Association of Left-Handed Persons. However, kids hated Sinister's heavy moralizing and refused to purchase it.

TAKING THE STAND: Nick Lowridge, reporter for *Scoop* magazine

Sen. Mohasset: Mr. Lowridge, please explain these "interviews"—and I use the term loosely—that you conducted for *Scoop* magazine.

Lowridge: Yes, yes. Now, as long as I have you on the spot, Don, I have a couple of questions for you. First of all, tell me what you're really like as a person. We've all seen your public face, Senator, but what kind of guy is Don Mohasset in his natural setting?

Sen. Mohasset: Mr. Lowridge, I will ask the questions. Now about the interviews . . .

Lowridge: I simply must know, Senator. What makes you tick?

Sen. Mohasset: One more outburst, sir, and I will have you arrested for obstruction of justice, misleading testimony, and, er, talking back to an important Senator of the United States of America. Now, would you care to speak up?

Lowridge: Come on now, Donny. Cut out all this official talk. Let's just chat—man to man.

Sen. Mohasset: Bailiff, please remove this man and have him charged with the aforementioned counts.

Lowridge: (shouting as he is dragged away) Great stuff, Don! I think this has the makings of a big story! Listen—catch you later, right?

VOL IV, ISSUE III

MAY 1983

WE GOT GARBO

WOODY!

Tony Jackson visits with the American auteur in his New York apartment.

As you enter Woody's fifth-floor apartment through the window, you notice that he's as meticulous in his personal life as he is in his craft. The hardwood floors are immaculately polished, the locks on his windows almost foolproof. I sunk into a white Naugahyde couch and helped myself to a piece of apple pie and a cup of coffee—obviously laid out by my shy but gracious host. I spilled a little coffee on the glass coffee table, and I hastily wiped it up with a notebook page full of doodles that was lying around. Woody is rumored to be a notorious clean-freak.

After about twenty minutes of waiting, I heard rustling in a back room, and I went back to investigate. Absent-minded Allen was in the bathroom, brushing his teeth and humming Gershwin. I jimmied the door open, and our interview commenced.

WOODY: Who the—Oh my God no. No no no no. There's money in the bedroom—take it all, just don't—
SCOOP: Mr. Allen . . . Woody . . . We all loved *Radio Days*, but how do you answer the perennial question, "When will he make *funny* movies again?"
WOODY: No no no. Please don't kill me.
SCOOP: (laughter)
WOODY: I'm sorry for anything I've ever done to you. Please—
SCOOP: (more laughter) Great line! I hope we'll hear that one in your next movie. But seriously . . . who *is* Woody Allen?
ALLEN: Who the hell are you?
SCOOP: Good one, Woodster! But you must remember me. Tony Jackson? *Scoop* magazine? I sent you a letter about an interview a few months ago.

Woody was enraged with himself for forgetting our interview. I followed him out of the bathroom and waited in the living room while he made a phone call (cancelling plans for the evening?). He returned and sat on the other side of the room, silent.

SCOOP: What's next for Woody Allen?
WOODY: (thoughtful silence)
SCOOP: Hey, Woodster . . . why don't you tell me a joke?
WOODY: (thoughtful silence)
SCOOP: All your girlfriends—whoops!—I mean leading ladies, they all—
WOODY: (pointing at coffee-soaked doodle paper) Did you put that there?
SCOOP: Where do you get your ideas?
WOODY: (visibly excited) That's a genuine sketch from one of Picasso's Rose Period notebooks!
SCOOP: You ought to make a movie about *my* family! They're nuts! My aunt, she—
WOODY: (trying to wipe coffee stains off the scribble paper) No. No. No. No.

At this point, our little chat was rudely terminated by three huge men in dark suits. Moments later, I found myself back on Fifth Avenue, with no way of getting back in the building except the spelunking ropes I'd used earlier in the evening. I stood on the sidewalk pitching pennies at Woody's window, but I couldn't get his attention. After a while I went home.

FLOOR PLANS OF THE STARS

PERSONAL WITH PYNCHON

OODY INSIDE AND OUT

TELEPHONE INTERVIEW: THOMAS PYNCHON

PYNCHON: Hello?
SCOOP: Mr. Pynchon?
PYNCHON: Yes? Who's this? How'd you get my number?
SCOOP: Mr. Pynchon, I regret to inform you that your mother passed away this morning.
PYNCHON: (pause) Oh no. Oh, Mom. How . . . how did it happen?
SCOOP: That's not important right now. In *The Crying of Lot 49* you wrote about an underground organization called "W.A.S.T.E." In light of recent events—
PYNCHON: Oh Jesus. She was in such good health. Was it an accident?
SCOOP: Maybe. But about "W.A.S.T.E." . . . do you see any parallels between that fictional organization and some kind of underground—

PYNCHON: Is this some kind of joke? If you're a reporter, I swear I'll—
SCOOP: Mr. Pynchon, I can assure you this is not a joke. This is Dr. Allen Reynolds at Cedar Sinai Hospital in New York.
PYNCHON: Jesus Christ. It's just . . . such a surprise. (sobbing sounds)
SCOOP: Mr. Pynchon, please get a hold of yourself. I know this is a difficult time, but if you could just tell me why, in *Gravity's Rainbow*, your character Benny Profane finds—
PYNCHON: (sobs) I just talked to her last week . . .
SCOOP: Don't be an asshole, Mr. Pynchon. People die every day. Now, in *Gravity's Rainbow*, you deal with the conflict between science and
(continued on page 46)

Sen. Mohasset: I now introduce as evidence this statement from the editorial board of *Games* magazine. Senator Richardson, would you be so kind as to read the statement aloud, please.

Sen. Richardson: Yes, ahm, ahem: "Xifo gjobodjbm ejggjdvmujft espwf Hbnft up txjudi gspn npouimz up cjnpouimz qvcmjdbujpo, uif gpmmpxjoh nbufsjbm xbt ejtdbsefe."

Sen. Beaufort: What the hell are you tryin' to say, Senatah?

Sen. Mohasset: Yes, speak up, Senator Richardson.

Sen. Richardson: B-b-but . . .

Sen. Beatrice: Excuse me, Senator. The message is obviously in the form of a cryptogram. If you will allow me to examine it for a moment . . . thank you. Oh yes. The message reads as follows: "When financial difficulties drove *Games* to switch from monthly to bimonthly publication, the following material was discarded."

Sen. Richardson: I know . . . maybe it's some kind of code!

BOOKS: Mazes and Puzzles

The Rand-McNally Road Atlas, available from Rand-McNally, is a collection of challenging labyrinth puzzles guaranteed to amuse readers of any skill or interest level. From simple point to point mind-teasers like "Northern Arizona" to complicated on-and-off the board calculation games like "Indonesia and Australia," this is a book that could keep the whole family busy for months. The illustrations, as well, are vivid and detailed.

Time-Life Book of Do-It-Yourself Home Plumbing Repair is another fine new book. This descriptive compendium of mechanical puzzles offers clear and well-illustrated guidelines to the construction and solution of dozens of ingenious puzzles. If you thought hardware stores were for people who read *Field and Stream*, think again. This book tells you how to combine metal, plastic, and ceramic parts to make mind-benders of any level of complexity, some of which apparently have their conceptual origins in the famous "Roman Aqueduct" game palace, and yet still mystify people today.

The Wall Street Journal is a true rarity in new gaming periodicals. A hefty collection of anagrams, numeric puzzles, hidden-word puzzles, and analytical story-mysteries, it publishes different assortments of brain-ticklers every single day! Phenomenal! And some of the puzzles are so difficult that even we couldn't solve them! Our only criticism is that they almost never publish any answers, and when they do it is just one or two in a little bitty box labeled "corrections." We have written away to the publisher for a list of solutions, though, and, as avid gamers are doomed to do for all of eternity, we suppose, we are sitting around waiting for its arrival in the mail.

GAMES & BOOKS

SAVE THE WORLD
(Amnesty International—$25 "donation")

The liberation of political prisoners, the prevention of nuclear war, and the protection of individual rights: These are the objects of Amnesty International's first board game. Much talked about before its release (evidently the company is well-known in some other field), this game is unattractive and dull.

There are no intricate plastic playing pieces, and indeed few pieces of any kind in this game, which is a very bad start. It does include a deck of "political prisoner" cards and a number of blank "protest postcard" score cards, but the rules do not fully explain how they are to be played. The scorecards we suggest you laminate so that they may be written on with grease pencil, which can be wiped off after each game. Most game companies do this for you.

We had our best luck playing Save the World on a Risk board with a backgammon board beside it. Play alternates between the two boards, and players move their tokens by spinners and dice and build twisting plastic lattices on the boards and collect property and money and force other players into traps and capture their assets and then you move onto the inner track and collect bonus points until you get to the middle where you have to have one of each of the types of markers and put them in a certain order and then solve a crossword puzzle and find the hidden acrostic clues and rearrange the pyramid to form a flying saucer by moving only two coins, one match, and your opponent's drink. That way the game is quite entertaining.

As it comes, though, Save the World is virtually unplayable. It is difficult even to determine how the game can be won. Perhaps this game would work better as an adventure module for Dungeons and Dragons although it would pale in comparison to "The Voodoo Lair of the Giant Pirate Dwarves," "Quest for the Immense Bauble," or "Bloodthirsty Rampage of the Amazon Cicada-People."

WHEAT CHEX
(General Foods, $1.59)

This action/adventure game, primarily sold, oddly, in supermarkets, is by far the best entertainment bargain of the season. Players control literally hundreds of pieces in mammoth battles for "protein" points, "cholesterol," and "riboflavin," while avoiding pitfalls like being packed by weight instead of volume.

Designed, according to the box, to be played by twenty teams, called "servings," we have found Wheat Chex enjoyable for virtually any number. There are enough pieces for at least forty players, if a table can be found to accommodate them (one is available from Avalon Hill for around $500, meant for their Full-Scale Tank War

game). There are even some solitaire scenarios included on the box, such as "Party Mix," in which the object is to combine your forces with other forces, "spice" your army, bake and "serve to any party, no matter how casual or how elegant." The optional milk rule we found somewhat cumbersome in this scenario.

So enthralled were we with this game that we inquired of the manufacturer for other games produced by the same company. The only dealership in our area that carried them was Shop-Rite, but they had literally shelves upon shelves of similar games. At the phenomenally low prices these games sell for, if you don't like them, they're still a good value for bulk playing pieces to be used in other popular games, such as Napoleon's Army Against the Gobots, What if the Civil War Had Been a Chili Cook-Off, or Rommel Gets Lost. We used a box of Rice Chex pieces to make one of our favorite boxing games into Muhammed Ali Vs. 20,000 Joe Fraziers, a game that proved so much fun it kept us at our gaming tables here at the office for three weeks straight! We almost forgot to put together a magazine!

LETTERS TO THE EDITOR

There are more than 1.5 million officially registered cranks, creeps, lunatics, and idiots in the United States, and seventy-three percent of them have access to writing paper, postage stamps, and the addresses of major magazines.

To U.S. NEWS AND WORLD REPORT

Dear Sirs:
After reading your January 7 issue, I went out and told many of my friends that Paul Volcker was the head of the Federal Reserve for seventeen years. Upon re-reading the article later, I noticed that Mr. Volcker headed the Reserve for only fourteen years.
Ed Murley regrets the error.
Sincerely,
Ed Murley
Green Bay, Wisconsin

Can't run—legal dep't says we're suing him.

To THE NEW REPUBLIC

Dear Sirs:
While perusing Norman Podhoretz's article on corruption in city government (June 5), I couldn't help noticing the omission of several key players in this ongoing crisis. Cleveland residents will remember the fifteen-month trial of Municipal Judge Reese Twatch. New York Zoning Commissioner Eddie Ornaught is *still* in office. And what about perennial "nice guys" Phineas Last and Allen Adazewerk? Mrs. Sherwood and her son? How about Rabbi Sectual? Huh? Ed Overheels. Sgt. L. Mensbet. Rick "Eddie" Oldcar.
Sincerely,
Harry Butz (Slappy Schenk)
Catskills, NY

HOLD OFF ON PRINTING. PODHORETZ WANTS TO RESEARCH THESE CASES

To Popular Mechanics

Dear Sirs:
I have discovered something of grave importance. In your blueprints for a lawnmower engine–powered aircraft (PM, June 12) you specify a #5 bolt for the cowling assembly. The correct bolt is a #7. If anyone uses a #5 bolt, the propellor will work loose after precisely ten minutes of flying, causing complete power loss of the aircraft.
Please alert other readers immediately.
Bob Harmon

OUT OF SPACE— MAYBE NEXT ISSUE

To THE NEW YORK REVIEW OF BOOKS

Dear Sirs:
SWM, ruggedly handsome, somewhat of a scrapper. Seeks young ladies of the 80s for repeated sexual encounters. Greek, French, Italian, Chinese. I'm not talking about cuisine.
Complete confidentiality required. Write: Joe, Box 1559.
Sincerely
Norman Mailer

On 2nd thought, we'd better print this

NO ↓

To ROLLING STONE

Dear Sirs:
On June 15, 1986, I sent you a draft of an article I'd written about Bruce Springsteen. Two weeks later you published a piece on Springsteen that was remarkably similar to mine. It mentioned:
A) His early years in New Jersey
B) The release of his five-album boxed set
C) His nickname ("The Boss")
D) His twelve-inch member
Except for your omission of the anatomically explicit information, your article is almost identical to mine. My lawyers will be contacting you.

Earl Hollis
Hollisville, GA

To VANITY FAIR

Dear Sirs:
I have some suggestions for your magazine. You should run more articles about really wealthy families having legal battles over wills. Also, it might be a good idea to preface each issue with an almost too-long introduction by Tina Brown—and if you can find a photo of her giggling with her head between her hands, all the better. How about a column in which celebrities tell what books they claim to read before they go to bed? Always slip in an opera star or Polish writer among the other celebs so that people will think you're intellectual as well as up-scale.
As always, any articles about the Kennedys, David Byrne, or Anjelica Huston should go straight in.

Thank you,
Jeffery Sarcasmotron

Address? Tina wants to hire him. ←

To Hustler

Dear Sirs:
In your recent review of my novel *Ancient Evenings,* you stated that the book was written while in residence at Yaddo. While the Yaddo foundation has helped me in the past, I feel it necessary to note that I was teaching a writing workshop at NYU for the duration of the novel's composition. The rewriting and editing were done during the early months of spring on Nantucket, and I reviewed the final galleys three months later in Los Angeles.

Thank you,
Norman Mailer

I THINK HE MEANT TO MAIL THIS TO THE NY REVIEW OF BOOKS ➤

To THE NEW YORK REVIEW OF BOOKS

Dear "Joe":
SWF. Attractive, intelligent, unusual hair. No Greek. Let's arrange a meeting. Complete confidentiality please. Write "Circe," Box 1765.

Susan Sontag

Forward to N. Mailer

MEDIAGATE HEARINGS: WEEK ONE, DAY FIVE

Sen. Fawcett: Excuse me, Senator Mohasset, if I may interrupt, we have just received an important notice. Apparently, *Time* magazine has just named you their "Man of the Year."

Sen. Mohasset: (whispering, with a faraway look in his eyes) Man of the Year . . . Man of the Year . . . I just can't believe—it's my greatest fantasy come to life! This is the proudest moment of my career! This is—

Sen. Fawcett: The *Time* people have sent a photographer over to take your cover portrait shot. Of course, since this is obviously a transparent attempt by the editors of *Time* to ingratiate themselves with the committee, I will have the doors barred to prevent his entering the hearing room.

Sen. Mohasset: You will, eh? Well now Pamela, let's not be too hasty about this. I doubt your sister Farrah would be as suspicious about this.

Sen. Fawcett: (pulling at her hair in frustration) Aarggh! I've told you a million times, Mohasset, I'm not related to Farrah Fawcett! We don't resemble each other in any way!

Sandy "The Dink" Dinkman: You can say that again!

Sen. Fawcett: (screaming) You keep out of this! Stenographer, strike that remark from the record. (knocking sound at door) It's him!

Sen. Beaufort: Guards, open the door. I have some important questions to ask of

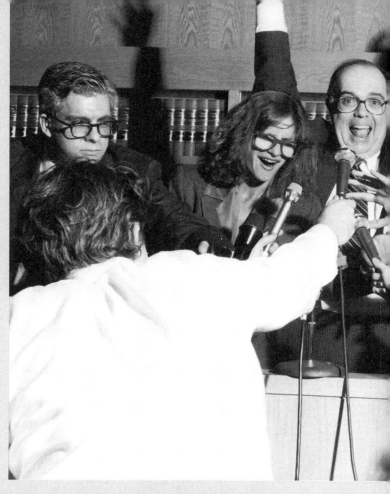

this photographer boy—help us get to the bottom of this "Man of the Year" hogwash. (photographer enters) Now boy—that's right, son—come right on up here before the panel and tell us why your august publication chose our very own Senator Mohasset here as your esteemed idol for the populace.

Photographer: Well, frankly sir, I just take orders from higher up and I'm not involved in any of the planning stages of the editorial board, but I do know that they named Mikhail Gorbachev "Man of the Year" just one month ago. It seems to me that Senator Mohasset's election was kind of a hastily thought-out decision.

Sen. Stone: You mean to say that *Time* has named *another* "Man of the Year" just one issue later, and they don't expect the public to find anything incongruous in their action?

Photographer: Actually, I think they have an excuse ready. This was to be *Time*'s very highest honor, "The Man's Man of the Year."

Sen. Mohasset: (dreamily) Man's Man of the Year . . . I just can't believe it. Me, who was born a poor boy, to be the recipient of this coveted title . . . Go ahead, son, take my picture.

Sen. Fawcett: "Man's Man of the Year"; I've never heard such a cheap, sexist justification in all my life. Hey, put that camera down, photographer. Who do you think you are?

Sen. Mohasset: That's all right son, go ahead and take the picture. Do it now.

Other Senators In Unison: NO NO NO!! Put that down! Don't press the shutter! Don't do it! Don't click that—

Photographer: (With camera click and flashbulb pop) Got it!

In 1984, *Car and Driver* had a position open for a reviewer/writer, and in due course a man by the name of "Alf Ader" was hired. The bearded, bespectacled Ader was assigned to review the new Chevrolet Corvette. The issue with Ader's review was almost ready to go to press when senior editors realized that the review was not at all what they wanted. Suspicious, they approached "Ader" and ripped off his beard and glasses. It was Ralph Nader. He was quickly shown the door and his review was replaced with another.

The New Corvette—The Most Irresponsible Deathtrap Ever

By Alf Ader

You'd think that after thirty years of turning out dangerous, poor quality, in-efficient, socially irresponsible "Corvettes," Chevrolet would at last start building something better. But apparently Chevrolet, GM, and the entire automobile industry, as well as all other industries, are content to defraud the American consumer and make him or her believe that they are getting what they want. The 1984 Corvette is worse than ever, and it is an insult to right-thinking safety-minded utilitarian consumers everywhere.

I personally had been hoping that the '84 Corvette would be a form of cheap, practical public transportation. However, the redesign still allows only for a driver and one passenger, rather than the fifty or more passengers that ideally would be carried.

Looking beyond the car's configuration for a moment, the styling, though admirable in one respect, leaves a great deal to be desired. On the plus side, the '84 model is more aerodynamic, which means that it will burn less of the pollutive and diminishing fossil fuels. However, not nearly enough care is taken to ensure that the styling is functional and safe. There are wide expanses of un-protected body panels that could have been covered in reflectors, warning lights, and impact-absorbing bumpers.

The car's performance is dangerous and unsuited to normal driving. The engine has far too much power; a four-cylinder unit would have been sufficient to propel the car at up to fifty-five miles per hour, or some lower speed for greater economy and safety. The complicated suspension system encourages the driver to maneuver recklessly, and the brakes, if applied too suddenly and forcefully, could cause the car to jerk to a halt.

The interior shows evidence of slip-shod and malicious design as well. Upon sitting in the '84 Corvette, one is imme-diately struck by the lack of roof sup-ports. In the event of a skyscraper top-pling over onto this car, the occupants would have little chance of survival. Re-inforced concrete beams would take care of this, but unfortunately Chevrolet is still cutting corners. The seats allow for dangerous amounts of unsupervised bodily motion, and the seat belts could easily be ignored by stupid people. The driving position is hampered by blind spots and controls that could be confus-ing to a blind person. The actual opera-tion of the car is complicated and could result in an injurious accident by some-one unfamiliar with driving.

In addition to the faults listed above, the car emits noxious fumes, wastes fuel, costs too much, and will probably fall apart once you get it off the showroom floor.

It was a fond hope of this reviewer that 1984 would see the debut of a reflec-torized rubber, sixty-passenger, ten-mile-per-hour, handicapped-accessible Cor-vette, but as usual, GM has let America down. I recommend that no one buy this car.

Statistics

Vehicle:............1984 Chevrolet Corvette
Vehicle Type:......2-passenger "sports" car
Engine:............350 cid fuel injected v-8 (excessive!)
Weight:............3,800 lbs (too heavy!)
Price as tested:....$24,567 (too much!)

0–60:.............irrelevant
Top Speed:........irrelevant, and too fast
Fuel Economy:......17 EPA highway (wasteful!)

Sen. Mohasset: Let's see now. The next item up is . . . oh yes. A minor, trifling little piece of evidence. Not really worth much discussion.

Sen. Fawcett: But Senator Mohasset, I thought we were about to begin our investigation of *Time* magazine.

Sen. Mohasset: Well, we are. It's just that I don't think there's all that much to investigate. After all, their editorial decisions have been — at least recently — excellent in every respect.

Sen. Fawcett: I see, Mr. "Man of the Year." Now let's see that report, shall we?

INVESTIGATOR'S REPORT:

In the fall of 1943, Nazi Germany was beginning to feel the crush of superior Allied forces both in North Africa and in the European air war. U.S. industries were operating at peak productivity, and America threatened to be the stumbling block in Adolf Hitler's march toward a thousand-year Reich.

In desperation, German minister Joseph Goebbels devised a plan to counter America's worldwide propaganda war — a plan that, had it succeeded, might have caused irreparable damage to U.S. wartime morale. Goebbel's scheme called for the covert replacement of every copy of the November 27th, 1943, issue of *Time* magazine with a carefully constructed lookalike loaded with Nazi propaganda.

On the night of November 26th, thousands of Nazi agents in stolen distribution trucks placed their doctored *Time* magazines on the nation's newsstands. The complete darkness of the new moon shrouded their movements, and the tiny swastikas emblazoned on their lapels went unnoticed. Their mission accomplished, the drivers regrouped and boarded a train to Atlanta, Georgia, from which they flew home group-rate on a chartered student exchange flight.

In the end, it was a single, tiny flaw that prevented the insidious German plot from succeeding. Owing to Germany's runaway wartime inflation and Goebbels' shoddy mathematics, the magazine had been mistakenly priced at $2,500. Only two copies were sold — one in New York City to a blind man from out of town, and the other to a Mrs. Elaine Smokely of Portsmouth, Idaho.

Harebrained Rationing Schemes Go Awry

As President Roosevelt and Office of Price Administration director Chester Bowles sat down to a lush banquet in the secret White House Orgy Room last week, millions of hard-working U.S. slaves were laboring fruitlessly into the night at poorly administered war factories across the nation. Hungry, tired, and driven to the brink of madness by substandard and meager foodstuffs, the pawns of America's greedy power elite cut a poor profile in comparison with the hedonistic and overfed Roosevelt. Showing little regard for the parsimonious rationing programs that he had himself instituted, the president casually tossed another rubber tire into the fireplace, turned the oil heater up to a steamy ninety-five degrees, and changed shoes for the eighth time that evening. Meanwhile, Bowles, the creator of the comfort restriction schemes, drank his fifth cup of coffee with triple sugar and leaned back on the fresh side of beef he was using as an easy chair. A crate of eggs came crashing to the floor as Bowles carelessly kicked a nearby table with his steel-toed combat boots — boots that should have gone to a fifteen-year-old soldier.

Such disgusting waste is typical of American rationing programs, and you can rest assured that most of the corruption forms a stinky black trail that leads directly to the White House. While the citizens of the United States are starved into submission, German and Japanese workers enjoy all the luxuries they can carry. With each American defeat, more and more U.S. supply shipments fall into the hands of the Axis powers. Already, the German people have more butter, sandwiches, and underwear than they could possibly want or know what to do with. What a waste of time for Americans to bother manufacturing these war spoils, which invariably fall into the hands of brave Nazi soldiers! U.S. workers might just as well go home and enjoy themselves.

After all, Franklin Roosevelt is certainly enjoying himself! Following the orgy, the president laughed himself into a coughing spasm as he signed more legislation that would legally prevent war workers from striking, no matter how low their wages dipped. This cruel act completed, he tossed his pen into the fire. Then he fell out of his wheelchair and began to cry.

The Last Cigarette . . .

When your boy's lost his last dogfight, there's nothing he'll want more than a nice, relaxing smoke on the plummet to his fiery death. Chesterfield's got that smooth, good-tasting tobacco that goes down easier than a shoddy, ill-equipped American fighter plane. When superior Nazi firepower's got the plane going down, Chesterfield's got the pilot going up!

CHESTERFIELD . . . BECAUSE NO CIGARETTE IS MORE IMPORTANT THAN THE LAST ONE.

Patton Goes Nuts

General George S. Patton, Commander of the U.S. forces in North Africa, drove a battalion of Sherman tanks through a Tunisian orphanage last Monday. This week, he shot a 65-millimeter mortar through a camel because "he wanted to see the water spray out of its hump." Now, tormented by the relentless superiority of Erwin "Desert Fox" Rommel's crack Afrika Corps, General Patton has gone completely insane.

Patton, the most bloodthirsty and ruthless killer America could muster, may be vicious, but he is still "small potatoes" in comparison with Germany's elite Afrika Corps. Patton's mental instability is legendary; however, a complete breakdown did not occur until earlier this month when, owing to his exceptionally poor aim, he missed a point-blank shot on his perennial nemesis, Erwin Rommel. Rommel had stopped his command tank to let a wandering nun cross the road. Compassionate as ever, the debonair Rommel had stepped from his post to give the elderly nun a flower. Screaming wildly, Patton drove by and shot the woman.

Even the most ignorant of observers can see that General Patton is a dangerous madman, who belongs not in a tank but in a lunatic asylum. If you have even the slightest concern for the future of this nation, you must write your congressman and demand that this maniac be stopped. Tell him you read that Patton was crazy in the prestigious and respected *Time* magazine.

Sen. Donald Mohasset: "There is a time to be born, a time to die, a time to reap, and a time to tow. It is now a time for healing. A time to put the mistakes of the past behind us, to forgive and forget our grievances. At the same time, though, it is a time to exact a stern penalty for the offenses committed. In this spirit, I urge each and every one of you to cancel your subscriptions to those glossy journals that have done so much to defile the good name of the American media. I can only hope that we will not come across any more such pernicious behavior in the subsequent weeks of the hearings. Excuse me, did I say tow? I meant sow. Sow. That's right. Where's my speech writer? That man is in serious trouble."

•

Sen. Archibald Stone: "It is with a perspicacious elan and antidisestablishmentarianistic fiat that this committee has endeavored to convey the calumniations and tendentious cavil of the disenfranchised multitudes; redoubtable in their turpitude, and circumspectful in their Quonset huts."

•

Sen. Jeremiah T. Beaufort: "Ah, ahem, Ah believe, mah good people, that, ahm, what mah distinguished colleague Senator Stone is a-tryin' to say, is similah to somethin' mah grandaddy told me a-way back when, which Ah might phrase as follows: "Nevah tan a heifer's hide before you have inspected the brandin'.""

•

Sen. "Robert" Beatrice: "Please pardon me, but my plane is waiting for me right now. I'm afraid that I must leave the hearings briefly to attend to some more important business matters. My men will have a statement ready later in the day."

•

Sen. Pamela Fawcett: "The revelations of this past week have uncovered a long, ignited fuse of corruption that leads ultimately to the powder keg of the male patriarchy. When it explodes, let's hope it blows apart existing sexist notions, without which there would be no more scandals, strife, or bad feelings."

•

Sen. Buzz Richardson: "Allow me to make an analogy. The first stage of the hearings, like the first stage of a rocket booster, is now spent. The orbiter is in position, the retro rockets have been fired, and mission control is reporting all systems operational. Testimony has been heard, and evidence has been seen. Witnesses have been called to the stand. No further comment."

WEEK TWO: AUDIO

Sen. Mohasset: It is apparent that this—yes, I will use the word— this *conspiracy* runs deeper than we originally thought. If the magazine industry was scandal-ridden, then the audio industry is, well, also scandal-ridden.

In closed session last night, the members of the Senate committee and I heard horror stories from the top names in the industry: names like Michael Jackson, Howard Stern, Madonna, Larry King, and so on. Anyway, after the horror stories, we roasted marshmallows and listened to some really disturbing tapes. I heard talk show hosts using what could only be called mildly offensive language, and rock music lyrics that, when played backward, made little more sense than they normally do.

Ladies and gentlemen, sit back and cover your ears as we enter this, the second week of testimony.

TAKING THE STAND: Michael Jackson

Sen. Stone: Before we begin the formal inquest here, Mr.—it is Mr., correct?—Mr. Jackson, we greatly appreciate the fact that you have taken time out from your busy schedule as a, I believe the term you prefer is "Rock Superstar," to appear before the committee, that we may more fully complete our investigation into the sleazy, sordid, and utterly revolting world that is your choice of profession. I should add, incidentally, that though personally, of course, I have never had occasion to hear any of your own music—I do not keep such company as would make such a situation even remotely possible, I am to understand that your own particular contribution to the field of popular music, has been quite substantial. We on the committee would just like you to know that when reviewing your testimony, the committee will not take such facts into consideration in any way.

Mr. Robert Creighton *(Michael Jackson's defense attorney):* Mr. Senator, my client and I would like to express our appreciation for that fact and for the subpoena you so graciously sent that we may appear here today. My client thanks you for not affording him any special treatment whatsoever, and also for the germ-free glass witness booth you have constructed for him. We recognize that it must have taken considerable time and expense. We would also like to add that you really shouldn't have gone to all the trouble of calling every reporter from every major publication and television network here today—I mean you *really shouldn't* have, and you will be hearing from my fellow attorneys. Oh, Mr. Jackson says he hopes your daughters enjoy the autographed leather jackets, it was nothing.

Sen. Stone: Er . . . ah . . . yes, well, let's begin. You have a question, Senator Richardson?

Sen. Richardson: I just wanted to add, Senator Stone, that even on my voyage to the moon, we at NASA never had an oxygen regulating chamber as elaborate or as costly as the one—

Sen. Stone: Yes, well, let's get down to business. Mr. Jackson, and fellow committee members, I now direct your attention to the docket you hold before you, specifically the item designated "Exhibit 2a." Now, as I understand it, Mr. Jackson, this is a copy of a pre-concert pamphlet distributed to all ticket-holders of your last tour, all of which were confiscated and destroyed after each show, is that correct?

Mr. Creighton: Senator, you have already received Mr. Jackson's final statement as to the pamphlet.

Sen. Stone: Ah yes, the letter from Mr. Jackson's psychiatrist, which states that the reason for keeping the pamphlet private was to preserve in the public's eye Mr. Jackson's reputation, particularly with concern to the state of his mental health. Fine, fine, that will be quite satisfactory. So to conclude, Mr. Jackson, you would like it known to all that you are of perfect mind and body, and that any and all conjectures to the contrary are unfounded, is that right? Uh . . . Mr. Jackson?

Mr. Creighton: Sir, I think the oxygen in the booth has knocked him out.

Sen. Stone: Hmm, so it has . . .

From the Information Packet of the MICHAEL JACKSON™ "PARANOISE" CONCERT TOUR

ATTENTION ALL TICKET HOLDERS:

Greetings! We here at Outrageous Productions™ would like to welcome each and every one of you, largely for security reasons, here to Michael Jackson™'s 1987 Tour Series. Tonight's show promises to be a fantastic affair, and we'd like you to know that's no accident—it's all the result of great P.R. hype and advertising.

We here with the tour know that, for many of you, this will be your first time seeing Michael Jackson™ in concert, should you pass the comprehensive security clearance procedures, and we are certain many of you will come away from the experience having enjoyed one of the most memorable evenings of your lives—we also know this is not so much a tribute to our show as it is a sad testimony to your lives—but to continue, we know many of you will have obstructed-view seats and will leave the show annoyed, and we apologize to you. But no refunds. We want you to know, it has been our experience that even those unlucky concert-goers who get to see Michael Jackson™ (well, not see him, but hear him) in concert usually end up pretending that they had a good time just to make their friends jealous, though hopefully, they eventually convince themselves.

Michael's last tour in '83 was a tremendous success—Michael cleared over $4 billion—and this year, we hope, will be even better! In conclusion, a Michael Jackson™ concert can be a very rewarding experience, even for the audience, so every once in a while, as you sit through the show tonight, remember to have a great time!

Incidentally, many of you have expressed disappointment over the sizable cost of the tickets, at $75 apiece. You're right, that is pretty steep.

Well, let's get on with the show, and get this over with.

BEFORE THE SHOW:

Unlike other concerts, at a Michael Jackson™ concert, the security check is as much fun as the show itself. And almost as long.

As you may or may not know, Michael employs extensive means to avoid coming into contact with ordinary people in his daily life, largely to avoid the bacteria and germs that ordinary people carry, though he realizes that a concert is a special occasion requiring extra-special means to prevent such contact. Michael is, above all, a people person, and he understands that most people could never afford to maintain the elaborate antiseptic lifestyle to which he is accustomed—but that does not mean he's not going to try to pass part of the cost off on you in exorbitant ticket prices. We all want you to remember that the only reason Michael has devised all these simple security procedures is to be able to bring you all here to visit him, while keeping you all as far away as possible. Remember: Were Michael ever to catch any contagion from any concert-goer, he would, of course, be forced to sue that individual into financial ruin. So, clearly, these safety features are designed as much for your protection as for Michael's. They are as follows:

1. As you enter the first Decontamination Bay, you will be fitted into a pre-sterilized jump suit and paper sani-booties. At this time, please remove all foreign objects from your person. This includes prosthetic limbs, but not dental fixtures. Dental fillings may be kept in place, if properly coated with acetate.

2. Next, proceed to the Sterilization Chamber, where you will be sanitized by germicidal vapor. We ask that individuals who are accustomed to breathing through the mouth and nose area of the face breathe through a handkerchief. If you do not have a handkerchief, we suggest holding your breath and counting to thirty—your thirtieth birthday, that is! Ha ha, just kidding. Seriously, though, this gas is extremely poisonous, so we suggest counting in your head, without actually moving your mouth. Ask attendants how.

3. Don facial mask and gloves at this point.
4. Deposit forms in appropriate boxes. Once again, they are:
   a. clean bill of health from your family physician, detailing your medical history for the past five years,
   b. brief description of your family physician's credentials (give evidence) and his personal medical history,
   c. brief account of the foods eaten and places visited during the past year.

Many of you have asked if these security measures are really necessary. We assure you they are—remember, that hygienic mylar barrier between the stage and audience is experimental and only proven ninety-nine percent hermetic. Michael is aware of this fact and is pleased by the element of risk it lends. After all, Michael recognizes as much as anyone that there's something precious about the spontaneity and uncertainty of live performance, and that's why he spends five years painstakingly planning these tours to absolutely ensure that uncertain excitement.

DURING THE SHOW:

1. There will be no food or drink of any kind allowed in the auditorium, so have your stomachs pumped before you approach the ticket gates.
2. Flash photography is strictly forbidden. Photographs are graven images and weaken Michael's soul.
3. Do not tap on the glass or wave or distract Michael in any way.
4. Many of you have inquired as to the availability of medical aid, if necessary. The answer is, of course, yes. There will be medical help available, should Michael become ill or injured.
5. Many of you have inquired as to fire and emergency exits. This auditorium meets all the federal standards for safety, but for obvious reasons, all entrances and exits to the auditorium must remain sealed at all times during the show. In all probability, a fire will not occur during an actual performance. Michael usually limits them to rehearsals and warm-ups.
6. Do not be concerned if you cannot see the entire stage, because, for obvious reasons, no other musicians will be performing with Michael. Instead, musical accompaniment will be piped in via speakers to Michael and then out to you, with as little audio delay as possible. Besides, all seats are guaranteed to afford clear viewing of Michael, whether directly or via video monitor.
7. Should the sound, for some reason, be garbled or muffled, do not be concerned—we fixed it during rehearsal three times, and can fix it again. Sometimes it just fixes itself if you wait it out. The problem arises from the cumbersome oxygen regulation system that Michael must wear at all times about his head and waist. Please do not be dismayed. Instead, marvel at the technical achievement represented in this spectacular piece of machinery.
8. Most important, have a good time! And if you are having a good time, let Michael know it! Push those approval buttons on the panels in front of you (when the appropriate light is lit) so Michael can see your enthusiasm on his own panel, and see just what thrills you. Remember, Michael is here for you.

AFTER THE SHOW

1. Leave.

TAKING THE STAND: Stuart E. Young, author

Sen. Mohasset: As I am sure you are aware, Mr. Young, you have been summoned to testify as to your connection with some of the biggest names in rock and roll music.

Young: Summoned? Damn it, I'd walk a mile to tell my story. Those rock and roll musicians you're talking about ripped me off. Otherwise I would have been a rich man today, Mr. Senator. You can rest assured of that.

Sen. Mohasset: What exactly are you trying to say?

Young: Mr. Senator, my book, *Rock 'n' Roll Rewriter,* would have blown the lid off the tin can that contains the rock music industry. The Rolling Stones, the Who, and yes, even the Beatles. None of them would have been spared.

Sen. Fawcett: Oh, come now, Mr. Young. I'm sure the "Lads from Liverpool," as I like to call them, were not involved in this little piddling affair of yours.

Young: On the contrary, ma'am. I have here the sole remaining portion of my manuscript. The rest was destroyed when a group of rock musicians hired terrorists to bomb my home while I was living out in Washington state. You may remember it— they called it the "Mount Saint Helens eruption." Anyway, here's the chapter I salvaged . . .

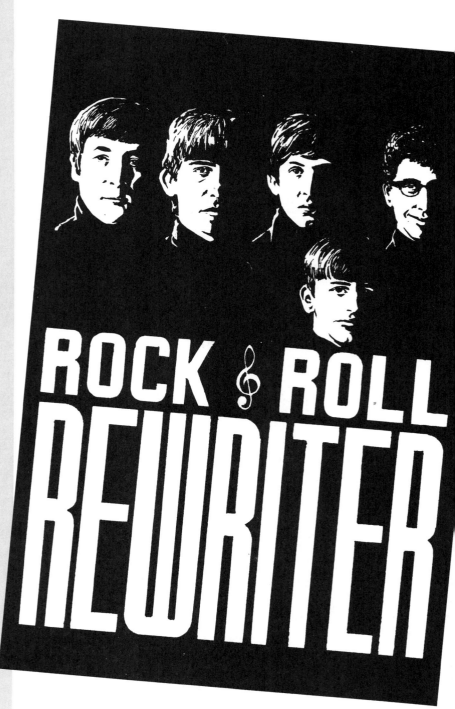

ROCK 'N' ROLL REWRITER
Chapter 6—The Beatles

In late 1963, my boss called me into his office. "Got a new assignment for you, Young. Two young fellows named Lennon and McCartney down in the lobby. See if you can help."

I went down to the lobby. Sure enough, there they were. Two young men with disreputable hairstyles. After brief introductions, I led them into my own office. The one named McCartney thrust a couple pieces of paper into my hands, and they peered at me anxiously as I scanned the first page:

> Ah yes, I'll relate to you this piece of information,
> I believe you will comprehend,
> Yes, I will confide that aforementioned data,
> I desire to clutch the terminal part of your arm.

I frowned. McCartney piped up, "You see, we've got the music all right, but the lyrics don't quite flow well enough." Lennon added, "We often get bogged down in the words, but this seems even worse than usual."

I nodded. "I'll see what I can do," I muttered.

"Thanks ever so much," John gushed. "We really want everything to be just right for our debut in the States. See you soon," he said, and the pair left.

What a couple of nerds. Well, I had my work cut out for me. I looked down at the papers they had left behind. The situation looked hopeless. I contemplated just sticking my head in the electric pencil sharpener and ending it all.

Of course, that's not what happened. Within a few weeks my slightly altered versions of "I Want to Hold Your Hand," "She Loves You," and a few others became big hits. The Beatles were thrilled, and my boss was pleased, too. He said to me, "The Beatles are thrilled, and I'm pleased, too." He assigned me as the permanent head of the Beatles' file. Good thing, too; because it wasn't long before they were back in my office. Their faces were troubled as I scanned "An Obdurate Day's Nocturnal Period":

> It's been an obdurate day's nocturnal period,
> And I've been toiling like a canine.
> It's been an obdurate day's nocturnal period,
> By all rights, I should be slumbering like a tree fragment.
> But when I arrive at my dwelling and perceive you,
> I discover that the actions that you perform,
> Instill in me a feeling of contentment and well-being.

"Paul says there has to be a dash between 'well' and 'being,' but I don't think so," said John. "Which do you think is right?"

"Well, fellas, I'm not sure that we should be worrying about that quite yet," I began cautiously. "Maybe we should be thinking about overall tone and rhythm. I think it could use a bit more 'zip.'"

"Yeah, okay, we'll leave that up to you," said Paul, as they got up to leave. "Maybe you can change a couple of the words around or something."

"Mmph," I said. I thought of suggesting to them, "Why don't you change the name of the group to 'Insects of the Coleoptera Order'?" But I realized that it wouldn't be taken as a joke. I sighed and looked at the pencil sharpener longingly.

But somehow, I came through again. And pretty soon it became a routine thing. They would write some horrible convoluted rubbish, and I would torture myself to get it whipped into some kind of shape. You'd think John and Paul would improve eventually, but no—I had to endure "Assistance!" (*"Aid me if at all possible; I am experiencing depression, And I am appreciative of your being in the vicinity"*); Paul's ballad "The Previous Day" (*The aggregate of my afflictions seemed so far away"*); and John's little ditty "The Lemon-Hued Submersible Craft," just to name a few. Another thing that bothered me was their hair. Occasionally I would make some subtle hint about haircuts, but they always said, "Shut up." To be fair, I should point out that George Harrison wrote several good songs, and he almost never needed my help. And Ringo Starr—my God, what a prolific genius that man was! But the others, John and Paul especially, were jealous of him and refused to do his songs. So Ringo had to work outside the group, writing all the songs for the Beach Boys, the Rolling Stones, the theme songs for "Gilligan's Island" and "The Brady Bunch," and several jingles for laundry detergent and canned cat food. It really got him down to be left out of the creativity of the group.

Eventually they got stuck. It was late autumn of 1966, and they were all in my office trying to come up with ideas, and nothing was coming. John and Paul were bickering and hitting each other on the head with my office furniture, George was cowering under my desk and weeping, and Ringo was moodily sticking his finger in a light socket. I could see that things were going to get grim unless I helped out. I said, "Hold it . . . All right. Here's an idea. Why don't you make an artistic statement with an innovative, unified album? Comment on something such as alienation in modern society. Wouldn't that be nice?" There were a few doubting grunts, then John said, "Yeah, maybe," and they left.

A week or so later they were back, visibly excited. "We've got it this time," claimed Paul. He flung a sheaf of paper on my desk, his face flushed with triumph, or possibly drugs. Drugs became the more likely candidate as I looked over the songs for *Sergeant Salt's Lonely Liver Club Band*—"With a Relatively Minor Amount of Aid from my Acquaintances," "When I Have Attained the Age of Sixty-Four Solar Years," "Lucy in the Sky with Diamonds"—and I sighed. "Look, guys, for starters, this bit about Sergeant Salt—"

"What's wrong with it?" broke in Paul defensively. "I rather like it, myself. It's got alliteration, see? Sergeant Salt, Lonely Liver . . ." He faltered under my disapproving look.

John mused, "Sergeant . . . Sodium Chloride?" but I quickly scuttled that idea, too. I said, "Never mind, fellas, you just go on now, and I'll see if I can touch them up a bit. It'll be fine." I shooed them away and sat down, trying to grasp the enormity of the task before me. It looked like the worst yet. The pencil sharpener loomed enticingly . . . but no. Reluctantly, I set to work.

During the next week I revised all the songs. Or I thought I did. The boys were looking over the revisions, when suddenly John poked Paul triumphantly. "See," he said, "Mr. Young liked 'Lucy in the Sky with Diamonds.' He didn't change it at all."

"What? Oh, no," I said, and rushed over. Sure enough, the song was on the back of one of the pages and I had overlooked it. "Let me see it," I said, "I'll give it one more look."

"Nope, sorry, we've got to start recording now," John said, and they skipped away with the songs. I groaned. I remembered "Lucy in the Sky with Diamonds" now . . . it was totally foolish. Everyone would see through the whole farce.

But as luck would have it, by the time the album came out, an explanation was on everyone's lips. Everyone nodded knowingly and said, "Drugs. Yep, drugs." I shrugged. Whatever.

The rest of the sixties really wasn't that interesting. Sure, I worked on "Attention: Jude," "Radical Overthrow of Government," "Return to the Soviet Union," "Permit it to Be," "The Lengthy and Convoluted Thoroughfare," and lots more. But there was no enjoyment in it; it was just drudgery. About the only fun I had was when the "Paul is dead" clues that I had been slipping in for years finally got noticed. Of course, the Beatles were thrown into confusion. "I'm not dead, am I?" whined Paul, as Ringo patted him on the back. Eventually Paul calmed down, but my boss was mad at me for a while. He was afraid that I'd give Rock 'n' Roll Rewriters a bad reputation.

I felt that my life was going nowhere. I was stuck in a dead-end job, my social life was nil, and my repeated hints about haircuts still produced nothing more than "Shut up." Finally I could take no more. On New Year's Eve 1969 I went to the office at night, and as the new decade came in, I plunged my head into the electric pencil sharpener. The batteries were dead, but I kept my head in anyway, and eventually I lapsed into a coma. When I woke up in the hospital some months later, the Beatles had split up. Of course they asked me to help them with their solo careers, but I had had enough. I said "No."

Actually, I said, "I am of the conviction that it would no longer be advantageous for me to attempt to render assistance to your endeavors." I wanted to be sure that I got the idea across.

TRANSCRIPT (MUTUAL BROADCASTING SYSTEM)
LIVE FROM THE NATION'S CAPITAL, IT'S THE LARRY KING SHOW!
AND NOW, HERE'S TONIGHT'S HOST—LARRY KING!

"Good evening. You're listening to The Larry King Show, and this is Larry King, speaking to you from the nation's capital. My good friend Jim Bohannon is in the control room tonight, and I'm in my luxurious studio enjoying a pot of coffee and a carton of cigarettes. We'll be chatting away the hours tonight, all night, as we do every night. I've got nothing better to do, you've got nothing better to do, so why don't we open the phone lines right now. Our number is area code 617-495-7801, so why not pick up the phone and tell me what's on your mind this evening. Cincinnati."

"Hello? Am I on the air?"

"Yes, you're on The Larry King Show. Who's this?"

"This is Suzanne Phillips calling, and before I say anything, let me just say that I love your show."

"Oh, thank you. Now, what's on your mind?"

"Well, I've been reading a lot about these Mediagate hearings. What's the story, Larry? Is this just a big scandal, or are we talking about a national crisis? What's going on?"

"Well, Suzanne, the jury's still out, but it shouldn't be long now before we see just who's been in bed with whom, right? Eh? Oh ho ho. Let's open the floor. We're taking calls on Mediagate *only* tonight, folks. Mediagate or sports. I'm always willing to talk sports. The number is area code 617-495-7801 if you want to hear my football picks, or if you have an opinion on the so-called Mediagate scandal."

"Oh, so it's just a scandal, then."

"What? Are you still on the line? I thought I cut you off earlier. Good night. Next caller, please. We're talking about the Mediagate crisis tonight. Hello, Detroit."

"Hello?"

"Hello, sir. What is your name?"

"This is Lou calling. Lou Pitrulo."

"Okay, Lou, what's your opinion?"

"Did I mention that I love your show?"

"Do you have anything to say about Mediagate, or not?"

"Uh, yeah. I been watchin' it on TV."

"Yes. So?"

"So, it preempted Molly Dodd, and I don't like that."

"Yeah, so?"

"So I was wondering how big the bazoongas are on that lady congressman. They measure out to about half an inch on my TV screen."

"Now we're talking. Let's see. According to this press release I have here, she has ... thirty-four-inch bazoongas."

"Geez, they don't look that big."

"What brand is your TV?"

"Ahm, Hichitakizaki."

"Okay, that explains it. Statistically, Oriental women have smaller jugs than American women. Japanese televisions aren't equipped to handle the overload. Buy an adaptor cable, and the distortion should go away."

"Thanks."

"Hello, Cambridge, Massachusetts. You're on the air."

"Hey Larry?"

"Yes?"

"Hey, listen to this. As far as I'm concerned, you can shove this whole Mediagate thing up your big..."

"I beg your pardon. Who is this? Is this *The Harvard Crimson?*"

"What? Hey, who told you? Gosh darn it, I bet those..."

"New York, you're on The Larry King Show."

"Yeah, hello. This is Abie Fishbein calling from Manhattan. I just wanted to say, Larry, that I love your show, and if you're ever in town, and maybe you want a nice sandwich, why not stop by Fishbein's Deli at Fourth and Madison. You want liverwurst? We got liverwurst. You..."

"Hey! No unpaid advertisements. You wanna hear my Superbowl picks? Or you got something to say?"

"Ahm, yes. Come in now and get the Mediagate Special. Liverwurst and onions. Now *that's* a sand…"

"Next caller."

"We also cater weddings and Bar…"

"Next caller! Kramden, Nebraska."

"Hi, Larry. This is Cora Braddock calling. Kramden, Nebraska, loves your show!"

"Yeah, yeah. Cut the crap. You got anything to say, or not?"

"Oh, well, ahm, just a quick question. Is Senator Mohasset married?"

"Well, I don't really know. Our press briefing doesn't say anything about that."

"Well, he's a dreamboat. He turns me on so much. In fact, I'm wearing a T-shirt right now that says, 'Mo has it!'"

"Yes, well…"

"And nothing else!"

"Next caller!"

"Let's go, Mo!"

"Next caller! Hello, Kramden, Nebraska. You're on the air."

"Yeah, this here is Billy Joe Higgins calling. Did I just hear my gal Cora on your show?"

"Ahm, well…"

"That bitch! I jest talked to her not five minutes ago, and she sounded like to be half-nekked!"

"Fine, Bill, fine. But remember. We're talking sports tonight. Do you want to hear my playoff picks or not?"

"I swear I'm going to put her down, Larry! I swear it! It's bad enough she done made me git this sissy 'Mohasset' haircut. Now she gone on the radio half-nekked in front of strangers!"

"Would you please clear the line, sir."

"Hey, before I go shoot Cora, I got to tell you, Larry—I love your show."

"I appreciate that. Next—Los Angeles."

"Duh, uh, could you play 'Stairway to Heaven' going out from Eddie to Lorraine?"

"Cleveland."

"Yes, this is Jill Haskell, and I love your show. I just wanted to say that Senator Stone strikes me as a real arrogant jerk for asking those long, dumb questions."

"Thanks for calling, Jill. Next caller—Washington, D.C. Hello, you're on the air."

"Oh, yes. Greetings, Mr. King. I have a few comments regarding the Mediagate hearings that I believe you and your audience will find both insightful and relevant."

"Yes, get on with it, please."

"Oh, certainly, by all means. I'm afraid I have a tendency toward the loquacious. In any event, I merely wished to commend Senator Stone for his very excellent commentary during the Mediagate hearings. His questions are, on the whole, brilliant and penetrating. Furthermore, he is exceptionally photogenic, if I may say so myself."

"Who is this?"

"Oh, ahm, er … Stove, er, that is, Stokes. John Stokes. Yes, John Stokes, speaking. Oh, and allow me to express my sincerest sentiments in regard to the very high standards of your program."

"Yes, thank you, Senator. Let's move on—the night's young, and the topic's hot. Hello, Miami, you're on the air."

"Hi, Larry. This is Cindy calling. I think it's high time the media got their just deserts. They're nothing but a bunch of corrupt, greedy, no-good jerks up to their necks in sleaze."

"Right on, Cindy! Let's hear it for justice!"

"… Television. Hollywood. Madison Avenue. *Time* magazine. What a bunch of self-serving, self-righteous liars!"

"Ooh! Don't stop now, baby! You're on a roll!"

"Publishing houses. Record companies. Rock and roll bands. They're all in on it."

"Hit 'em where it hurts, doll!"

"You know who takes the dirtbag medal of honor, though?"

"Drum roll, please!"

"Radio talk show hosts, you jerkwad."

"Eh? What? Cindy? Oh … oh no! Is this Cindy Hall? I told you never to call me here!"

"Yeah, you can't squirm your way out of it this time. I saw you with that lousy blonde tramp. Oh, and Larry, by the way … I hate your show."

"Cindy? Hello? Damn it! Oh, er, I'm afraid we ran out of time early tonight, folks. Please tune in tomorrow when we'll be talking throughout the night, all night, as we do every night. This is Larry King saying goodnight. Cut! Cut the tape! Cindy?…"

You have been listening to The Larry King Show, with host Larry King on the Mutual Broadcasting System.

When his manager, Colonel Tom Parker, left for an around-the-world tour in 1963, Elvis Presley decided to tamper with the scripts for what would later become two of his most famous films. "The King" commissioned artists, recorded songs, and commenced filming before the colonel could come back to rectify the damage in 1964.

Viva Los Alamos (E. Presley)
Title Theme

Desert city gonna build a
bomb,
Gonna set Japan on fire.
Gotta whole lotta atoms
that are ready to smash
So get that reactor up
higher!

Oppenheimer, Einstein, and
Elvis Presley—
Three great minds in
quantum theory—

Viva Los Alamos! Viva Los
Alamos!

When that bomb explodes
above,
Dropped from the Enola
Gay,
There's just one man the
women will love
And his name is Elvis Pres-
lay!

The Nevada desert's gonna
rock with a bomb
And also with this classic
rock 'n' roll song—

Viva Los Alamos! Viva Los
Alamos!
Viva! Viva Los
Alamooooooos!

ELPRESCO
IN ASSOCIATION WITH
ELVIS PRESLEY PRODUCTIONS
PRESENTS

Viva Los Alamos!

STARRING ELVIS PRESLEY
E.A. "PRESLEY"   E. PRESLEY   E. AARON PRESLEY
"EL" PRESLEY   MR. PRESLEY

Coming very soon to a theater near you!

44
Viva ~~Las Vegas!~~
Los Alamos

ELVIS
the lottery
If I win ~~big at the craps table tonight~~, I'll be able to
afford those repairs to my ~~racing car!~~
particle accelerator
SCIENTIST
~~GAMBLER #2~~
Dr.
Yes, you will, ~~Mr.~~ Presley, but you don't ~~know how to play~~
have a lottery ticket
~~craps.~~

ELVIS
~~But you're gonna teach me!~~ Darn!

(ENTER GIRL WITH CLIPBOARD.)
GIRL
Dr.
Uh, ~~Mr.~~ Presley, those repairs have been estimated at
$500,000
~~$500~~ in cash! Oh, who dropped this lottery ticket
outside the door?
SCIENTIST
From   lottery ticket   don't
~~GAMBLER #2~~
$500? ~~In~~ one ~~night of craps~~? I'm sorry, Elvis, I ~~couldn't~~
even ~~win~~ that much in a ~~week~~!
make   year
ELVIS (TAKES TICKET)

Thank you, miss.

SWOONS
(GIRL ~~LEAVES~~.)
don't make   build atomic
ELVIS (con't.)   bombs
You ~~could't do~~ it, but, then again, you don't ~~have~~...

SCIENCE
(BEGIN "~~LUCK~~ IS MY GIRLFRIEND" NUMBER.)
(ENTER SHOWGIRLS, ~~MAGICIANS~~, AND DANCING POLAR BEAR.)
CLOWNS

George! George! George! (E. Presley)
Title Theme

George! George! George!
George! George!
Fightin' redcoats!
Leadin' nations!
Bein' an all-round hero!
Yeah, yeah, yeah!
He's just a red-blooded rebel and
    he can't stop bein'. . .
George! George! George!

All-American!
Girls love him!
He's everybody's pal!
Yeah! Yeah! Yeah!
No, I'm not talkin' 'bout Elvis Presley
    although I could be . . . It's . . .
George! George! George!

Rock 'n' rollin'!
With Thomas Jefferson!
Rockin' for liberty!
Yeah! Yeah! Yeah!
He sure was a cool guy and
    he's just like Elvis Presley!
He's another national idol
    and his name was . . .

George! George! George!
George! George!

THE KING INC.
IN ASSOCIATION WITH
NO SUCH PERSON AS COLONEL PARKER PRESENTS

George! George! George!

STARRING ELVIS PRESLEY AND MANY OTHERS
Coming really soon to a theater near you!

71 ~~GIRLS! GIRLS! GIRLS!~~ *GEORGE! GEORGE! GEORGE*

~~ELVIS~~ *GEORGE*
I've just gotta make it to ~~Abilene~~ *the Potomac* in time for the ~~stock~~ *battle*
car race, Mister!

OLD MAN
Sorry, ~~son~~ *General*, the last ~~train~~ *carriage* left at 11:00 A.M. Ain't another
one until tomorrow morning!

~~ELVIS~~ *GEORGE*
Well, the ~~race~~ *battle* is tonight! Say, what about that old ~~plane~~ *horse*
over there?

OLD MAN
'Taint mine, ~~Elvis~~ *General Washington* . . .

~~ELVIS~~ *GEORGE*
Whose is it?

(ENTER BEAUTIFUL GIRL WITH ~~PILOT~~ *REDCOAT* OUTFIT.)

GIRL
It's mine. Sorry, though, I'm on my way to the big ~~stock~~ *battle*
car ~~finals in Abiline~~ *of the Potomac*, and I haven't got any time to
waste . . .

(~~ELVIS~~ *GEORGE* AND OLD MAN LOOK AT EACH OTHER.)

~~ELVIS~~ *GEORGE*
~~Miss~~ *Madame*, I think you just found . . .

(BEGIN "LOVERS IN THE ~~SKY~~ *WAR*" NUMBER.)
(ENTER SHOWGIRLS, ~~ACROBATS~~ *CLOWNS*, AND SINGING OCTOPUS.)

NIXON VS KENNEDY:

In 1960, presidential hopefuls Richard Nixon and John F. Kennedy held their first televised debate. Nixon fared poorly; he simply did not look good on TV, especially when competing against Kennedy's well-honed media image and natural good looks. Three weeks later, Nixon arranged another debate with Kennedy—this time on radio. Nixon was certain that Kennedy would be no match for his crisp rhetoric in a confrontation in which the visual element played no role. But Nixon failed to anticipate Kennedy's shrewd strategy.

TRANSCRIPT OF RADIO DEBATE

(The candidates have been introduced, opening positions stated, and Mr. Nixon is presently discussing his views on tax reform.)

NIXON: ". . . and I firmly believe that if the vox populi dictates such a mandate—"

KENNEDY: "Ah . . . excuse me. Mr. Nixon?"

NIXON: "I was in the middle of making an important point."

KENNEDY: "Your point is well-taken, Mr. Nixon, but it . . . ah . . . behooves me, on behalf of the voting populace, to encourage you to present a more decorous public image in the future."

NIXON: "What?"

KENNEDY: "Look at yourself. You look like you haven't shaved in days. Your hair is greasy and unkempt. And you have a large, unsightly boil on your lower lip."

NIXON: "Mr. Kennedy, this is an outrage. What you have stated is patently untrue! I can't believe—"

KENNEDY: "Very well. Continue. I'll . . . ah . . . try to ignore the boil."

NIXON: "There is no boil, and you know that. Anyway. As I was saying . . . tax reform is only a mandate if there is clear sign that a responsible maj—"

KENNEDY: "Mr. Nixon? I hate to interrupt again, but I do have a sinus condition. If you could kindly extinguish that smelly cigar, I'd appreciate it."

NIXON: "But I—"

KENNEDY: "And maybe you should set that Budweiser tall-boy aside for now. You seem to have spilled some of it on your sleeveless T-shirt."

NIXON: "Mr. Kennedy! I assure you the public will not stand for such blatant fabrications. I'm going to ignore you. Where was I? Oh, yes. In the realm of pundits and theoreticians, tax reform seems—"

KENNEDY: "Mr. Nixon?"

NIXON: "What is it this time?"

KENNEDY: "It would be much easier for me to listen to your opinions if you would stop scratching your ass with a pencil."

THE LOST RADIO DEBATE

NIXON: "I can't hear you, Kennedy."

(Nixon goes on to state, very articulately, his position on tax reform. As he is about to make his third and final point on the matter, Kennedy feigns a yawn and makes the universal "handjob" gesture. The studio technicians break out in uncontrollable laughter.)

NIXON: "What? What?"

KENNEDY: "Mr. Nixon . . . ah . . . apparently I'm not the only person to find your program ridiculous and laughable."

NIXON: "And what would you propose?"

KENNEDY: "Well, if I were you, I'd get that boil lanced right away. It looks like it's infected or something."

NIXON: "Mr. Kennedy, one more outburst of lying like that and I'll call this whole debate off. Do you hear me?"

KENNEDY: "Please continue."

NIXON: "And my third and final point is the simplest: We, as Americans, cannot and will not . . ."

(While Nixon is concluding his remarks, Kennedy tiptoes over to Nixon's microphone and makes a farting sound into it.)

KENNEDY: (into Nixon's microphone) "Braaap!"

NIXON: "That's it. That's it."

KENNEDY: "I can't believe Richard Nixon just cut a fart on national radio! Over 12 million people listening, and he cuts a fart! I can't believe it!"

NIXON: (silence)

(Nixon is so enraged that he cannot be persuaded to speak another word. He sits silently behind his microphone for the rest of the debate, and Kennedy's arguments go unrebutted. Mr. Nixon's only action while listening is to request a small hand mirror, so that he can check to see if he actually does have a large boil on his lower lip.)

(End Note: The show was pre-taped for the Western Time Zone, and Mr. Nixon ordered the recordings destroyed before broadcast. Listeners in the Eastern, Central, and Mountain Zones heard the debate live, in its entirety.)

TAKING THE STAND: Lance Coover, audio engineer

Sen. Mohasset: I understand, Mr. Coover, that you write the liner notes for the *Great Performances* series put out by CBS records. Could you please explain to me exactly what you intended in your description of Verdi's *La Traviata?*

Coover: Excuse me, sir?

Sen. Mohasset: I would like an explanation for your description of *La Traviata.*

Coover: Eh? What?

Sen. Mohasset: *La Traviata.* An explanation, please.

Coover: I'm sorry, sir. You'll have to speak up.

Sen. Mohasset: I WOULD LIKE AN EXPLANATION FOR YOUR DESCRIPTION OF *LA TRAVIATA!* NOW!

Coover: Travolta? No sir. I've never met him.

Sen. Mohasset: Bailiff, please bring in the sign language interpreter . . .

The first movement opens with the introductions, in the violas and the cellos respectively, of Daphne and Leonardo. The themes remain separate. There is, however, an inevitable promise of unification: the soaring second violin cusps. This promise, however, remains for the moment largely unfulfilled. Next in the bass we are introduced to Anton. This sinister line owes much to Wagner, and of course the stacatto references are to Gregor Mendel, the father of genetics. Anton moves outward from the bass into the lower cello regions, where he casts glances toward Daphne in the form of long rests. Daphne seems receptive, but at the last moment her father appears.

After the adagio section, Leonardo begins his long journey to the Fountain of Desmanora. On the way he meets Horace the beggar. Horace tells him about Daphne, and he seems interested. The triangles chronicle his courtship of Daphne, although the cymbals eventually point out that he has mistaken a tree for the maiden in question.

As the section comes to a close, Anton reappears, hiding behind a bush. The enigmatic flute solo is either his dream of Daphne being sold into slavery, or a slowly deflating beach ball being sat upon by Eduardo.

The second movement chronicles Leonardo's long trek to Asgard. First he has to cross the great Mountains of Anguish. Winter comes early, and he is forced to camp inside the Cave of Extreme Fright. Then there is an oboe solo, and when it is done, he seems to be on the road again, although it is difficult to determine whether he is dreaming until the violins echo the timpani, at which point he is obviously dead, frozen to death in the middle of May.

When the cellos begin their legato runs, however, he is alive again. The transition is a little problematic, but the music sounds okay for once. He travels through the Forest of Destitution, the Valley of Boredom, the Glade of Semicircular Canals, and the Canal of Eels. Then, realizing that he has gone the wrong way, he backtracks to the Valley of Boredom, where he goes to the left instead of just blundering on straight like an idiot.

In the third movement, we have Daphne, mainly played in the violins, being chased by Anton, who seems badly out of shape, as do the tubas. He chases her around and around in circles for almost an hour, in a passage that suggests that the composer had suddenly discovered an enormous carton of repeat signs and opted to use them all at once.

Finally, Daphne regains enough strength to go home. Her trip through town past the baker and the blacksmith shop and the town crier is a ribald adventure in tonal innovation, but whoever was writing the pianissimo symbols on the score had a manual stutter, and thus most of this wonderful passage is played too softly for the conductor to hear.

The fourth movement opens with Daphne at the bottom of a well. We have no idea how she got there, and cannot actually be completely certain that it is her, except that she has blond hair. Anton, who for some reason is younger in this movement than in the others, is nowhere to be found, although he is in plain sight behind a telephone pole. Tristan, who appears for all the world to have wandered in from another composition entirely, rescues Daphne from the well, and hands her over to Leonardo, who has gotten himself wounded somehow. Leonardo and Daphne make a break for his car, but Anton beats them to it and rewires the ignition so that they cannot start it without a golden apple. The confusion of historical setting in this movement seems to be due to a strange Moog synthesizer drifting onto the record from an adjacent recording studio.

By the fifth movement, it is hopeless. The characters have gotten completely out of control. Anton seems to be head of some global shipping company, and Daphne is working for him, but the piccolo solo meant to underscore this is too slow, making the two of them look three feet wide and two feet tall.

Anton, meanwhile, has sold his company to the government of Italy, and is pursuing his lifelong goal of becoming an opera singer. He is not, however, very good, and the aria he performs toward the end of the movement doubles as the sound of him being throttled by a boa constrictor, the appearance of which is not called for in the score, but which the conductor seems powerless to prevent.

The composition ends with Daphne's father, although it is not clear what, if anything, he is doing. It is possible that he is searching for his daughter, but the syncopation of the snare drum would then have to indicate that he had lost a leg, and there are no easy explanations why this should have happened. It is possible, given the state of the orchestra at this point, that there is a sixth movement to the work that could partly clear up some of this confusion, but the record grooves spiral quickly into the label after the fifth movement, and there thankfully is no sign of a second disk.

James Irvine
Buenos Aires, 1979

Letter Box

Fifteen of you alert readers correctly estimated the number of partially concealed Grace Slick heads appearing in RS 378 (forty-seven). Most commonly overlooked one: The cross-eyed Grace Slick obscured by Buster Keaton's hat in the Sgt. Pepper's album cover photo on page 52. In the "What's Wrong With This Picture?" contest, only seven of you noticed that Paul McCartney should not be playing the guitar right-handed, nor should he be hanging upside-down from a tree limb. Nearly every respondent reported that Billy Idol should not be roller-skating the wrong way down a one-way street, but only five rock geniuses espied that he was wearing his earring in the wrong ear and smiling. Get ready for more brain teasers in future issues, including more Grace Slicks! Number one hit for RS 378 was Gene Rayburn's review of The Police in concert. Twenty-one readers agree that Sting is "very cool"; seven think that the group's drummer is "too short"; and three firmly support our men in blue, who "do a fine job with crowd control at such raucus events." Major issue faux pas: David Fricke's staunch claim that the Hell's Angels bikers are "a bunch of dumb homos." David is no longer working with us, so you motorcycle enthusiasts out there can stop slashing tires and smashing RS office windows. C'mon guys, he'll never work here again. Really—no kidding now (please).

LETTERS

BACKWARDS

YOUR ARTICLE ON BACKWARD-MASKED MESSAGES IN ROCK ALBUMS "Absurd Hysteria Over False Rumors" (RS 377) was a disclaiming statement long overdue. We here at Polygram Records have never allowed the lived rof eid insertion of occult or drug-related messages in our live ot yarp recordings. Further, we would natas fonos never approve of such corrupt attitudes on the part of the ekoms top artists we employ.

DAMIEN GOATSKULL
Polygram Records
Death Valley, California

AFTER READING THE ARTICLE ON REVERSED MESSAGES IN ROCK, I GOT curious as to whether the same idea could be applied visually. So I took my "Stairway to Heaven" LP, held it at arms length, turned it upside-down, and stared at it for ten minutes. No luck. Then I did the same thing with my Bon Jovi Picture Disc. True Finding: Bon Jovi's face turns beet red as all the blood rushes down to his head. But only under black light.

RUE MERMONGER
Santa Monica, California

AS A CONCERNED MOTHER, I LISTENED TO MY 16-YEAR-OLD SON Timmy's "The What" records backwards one afternoon while he was away at school. Or at least I *thought* that I was spinning them backward. As I eventually discovered, it turned out that I had really been playing them forward, only the rock singer's diction was so poor and the drums so loud that it sounded quite garbled! And then *Reader's Digest* almost paid me $15 for the whole story!!

GRACIE ALLEN
Waukegan, Illinois

BOB

EXCUSE ME, BUT I'VE BEEN WONDERING ABOUT THIS FOR YEARS NOW, and have just got to ask: Is your magazine titled after the line in my song, or the old saying?

BOB DYLAN
Los Angeles, California
Editor's Reply: Our copyright lawyers have advised us not to reply.

MALCONTENT

FRICKE, WE'LL WASTE YOU LIKE WE ICED THOSE DUDES AT ALTAMONT back when. Doom for defaming the good name of the Club. No talk—We walk when you get the fuck out of the building. Print this.

"CHAINSAW" CARSON
San Narciso, California

HANDS

AS A PEACE-LOVING ALTRUIST, I WAS PROUD TO BE ABLE TO PARTICIpate in Hands Across America, an eminently worthy charity event. But P.J. O'Rourke's article (Helping Hands Heal Hardship Heavily) focused so narrowly on the condition of the homeless in America that he neglected to even mention the plight of that other oppressed minority, the handless. Perhaps the greatest irony is that the handless were prevented from joining Hands Across America, just as the homeless are unable to help the handless. Is this a sane society? Or is it me?

TIMOTHY LEARY
Seventh Astral Plane

FOUND

I BELIEVE THE TIME IS RIPE TO ANNOUNCE THAT I AM INDEED ALIVE, and that after years of anonymous soul-searching, I have finally found a satisfying occupation and direction in life. Heeding the advice of my close friend, Jerry Rubin, I have gone to work as a consultant to Tipper Gore's PMRC committee and am proud to at last be doing something constructive for the youth of America.

JIM MORRISON
Washington D.C.
Editor's Reply: What a relief to know that the spirit of the sixties hasn't died.

The above Letters page failed to run that month for reasons that remain unclear. However, it did inexplicably appear in the next month's issue of *Easy Ridin'* magazine, with photos of topless women in lieu of the Pendergast drawings.

TAKING THE STAND: Mr. K. Tel, independent record promoter

Sen. Beatrice: Mr. Tel, I understand that you run a large, diverse, multimedia marketing conglomerate. Correct?

Tel: Er, yes.

Sen. Beatrice: And is it not true that as chairman of this corporation, you have the ultimate say as to whether a given record gets promoted?

Tel: That is true.

Sen. Beatrice: I have acquired, furthermore, a number of rather indiscreet photos of you and a Mrs.—but the details are irrelevant at the moment. Let me instead pose the following query. Please bear in mind that I ask this question purely in the interests of furthering the information gathering process, and that my own position on the board of directors of the corporation that I am about to mention is immaterial. The question is this: As the ranking executive official of the K-Tel Corporation, you have no intention of making a bid to take over the Tropicana Corporation, do you?

Tel: Well, to be honest, ahm, er . . .

Sen. Beatrice: You have no interest in making such a bid, DO YOU?

Tel: Ahm, no.

Sen. Beatrice: No further questions.

For every chintzy K-Tel album advertised on TV, there are a hundred more that never got past the planning stages. Take, for example,

The lost K-Tel Albums

***Disco Song of the Whale* (1977)**—A one-hour tape of the Beluga Whale's feeding cry was suffused with a pulsating bass drum beat laid down by drummer Gary Krupa to produce this long-playing dance remix of a 1958 episode of the Jacques Cousteau program. Thankfully, the record was scrapped when John Travolta's appearance in *Saturday Night Fever* put an end to the disco craze.

***Legends of the Saxophone,* Vol. 1 (1980)**—Featuring no actual music, this record was to recount a number of tall tales concerning giant, heroic, and magical saxophones.

***Santa's Heavy Metal Christmas* (1982)**—Nine bands, ranging from Black Sabbath to White Snake, were called upon to supply renditions of the Christmas classics for this album, which K-Tel hoped would bring Christmas into the modern age. Children, however, were frightened by the fire-breathing, demon-horned St. Nick on the album jacket. Their parents, meanwhile, were displeased by the overt references to smoking and loitering in many of the songs, and forced the record to be recalled shortly after its release. K-Tel denied any wrongdoing and blamed a typographical error for any and all references to Satan Claus.

TAKING THE STAND: Roger Gibbons, ex-NASA chief

Sen. Mohasset: Mr. Gibbons, I would like to know what . . .

Sen. Richardson: Excuse me, Senator Mohasset. I really don't think questioning is necessary in this case. I'm quite sure that Mr. Gibbons is above suspicion.

Sen. Mohasset: Senator Richardson, you are obstructing the judicial process. Please refrain from further comment. Now, Mr. Gibbons, please tell me why . . .

Sen. Richardson: Er, excuse me again, Senator. It's just that, well, er, ahm, I think that Roger . . . er, that is, Mr. Gibbons' testimony would be, er, superfluous, in this particular case, because, ahm . . .

Gibbons: I think that Buzz has a point, Senator Mohasset.

Sen. Mohasset: Silence! I will tolerate no further outbursts from either of you! Now, Mr. Gibbons, if you will please present the transcript of the original Apollo/Soyuz linkup.

Gibbons: Ahm, here it is, sir.

Sen. Mohasset: (pause) That transcript looks a little vague, Mr. Gibbons. Who exactly was on board that flight, as if I couldn't guess?

Gibbons: Let's see, now. I believe that would have been Thomas Stafford, Vance Brand, and ahm, (clears throat), er, Buzz Richardson.

Sen. Mohasset: I see. And who, might I ask, was speaking for mission control?

Gibbons: Ahm, I believe it was . . . that is, I think it was . . . er, well, it was me.

APOLLO/SOYUZ TEST PROJECT
JULY 16, 1975
CLASSIFIED VERSION:

APOLLO: Come in, Houston. Broadcast sequence X13 commencing. Lock in on frequency 30,000 megahertz. Over.

HOUSTON: This is Houston. You are cleared for link-up sequence broadcast. Over.

APOLLO: Roger, Houston. Soviet craft is now at 1,000 feet and closing. Over.

HOUSTON: Roger, Apollo. You have the go-ahead. Over.

APOLLO: Roger, Houston. Link-up sequence now beginning. Come in, Soyuz. This is Apollo. Soyuz, do you read? Over.

HAM RADIO OPERATOR: Yo, this here is Bobby Sawyers. Who'm I talking to? This is Q41045 in Austin.

HOUSTON: Austin Delta sequence activated. Over.

APOLLO: Houston, what the hell is going on? Our lunch just ejected itself all over the capsule. Over.

HAM RADIO OPERATOR: Yeah, I had some bad chili down in Odessa 'bout two weeks ago. Kept me up all night, that sucker did.

APOLLO: Houston, we seem to have an unauthorized frequency bleed. Over.

POLICE RADIO: Unauthorized, my ass. This is Houston Police Unit 394. Get off this channel, boy. We're on a stakeout.

HAM RADIO OPERATOR: Steak? You ain't never had steak until you try my Uncle Manny's T-bones. Them boys are as big as a bush fox!

HOUSTON: Foxtrot November sequence activated. Over.

APOLLO: Goddamn it, Houston, what the hell are you doing to my urine catheter?!!

HAM RADIO OPERATOR: Catherine? You know Cathy? Man, she's like my sister, except my sister ain't got tits like watermelons. Whooee, that ain't no bullshit!

SOYUZ: Bolshoi One rendezvous sequence activated. Come in, Apollo, this is Soyuz, do you read? Over.

KID ON WALKIE TALKIE: Hello?

SOYUZ: Greetings. Is this esteemed astronauts of Apollo?

KID ON WALKIE TALKIE: No, it's me, Brian!

SOYUZ: Apollo, we have garbled transmission. We repeat, we are honored cosmonauts of the Soviet Union. We await linkup, do you read. This is Soyuz of the Soviet Union. Over.

POLICE RADIO: The Soviet Union?!! Yeah, and I'm Leonid Brezhnev. Now get off the goddamn radio before I come over there and kick your butt!

SOYUZ: Yes, Comrade Brezhnev!! We cease radio transmission immediately and proceed with linkup! Over.

HAM RADIO OPERATOR: What, you wanna link up with Cathy? Awright! She's got the biggest pair of good ol' American boobs you ever seen!

APOLLO: Houston, this is Apollo. We have another complication. The Soviets are calling us "American Boobs." Request permission for proper response from Houston Control. Over.

HAM RADIO OPERATOR: You're losin' control? Hell, you ain't even met Cathy yet. Now hold on, partner, I'll set you up with her, but there's no need to rush in like swine!

APOLLO: Roger, Houston. Message received. Come in Soyuz, you Russian swine. We are ready for link . . .

SOYUZ: Russian swine?!! Listen, you American pigs . . .

POLICE RADIO: Who you callin' a pig, boy? You say one more word on this frequency and you can kiss your ass goodbye!

HAM RADIO OPERATOR: You wanna kiss her ass goodbye?!! Listen, buddy that's no way to end a date with a lady. Maybe we better just call this date off 'cause Cathy's a pal o' Sawyers. Just forget the whole thing, okay?

APOLLO: Roger, Houston. Apollo/Soyuz rendezvous cancelled until further notice. Over.

TAKING THE STAND: Lance Coover, audio engineer

Sen. Mohasset: We now recall to the stand Mr. Lance Coover.

Coover: What?

Sen. Mohasset: Will the bailiff please escort Mr. Coover to the podium.

Coover: Huh?

(Coover is brought forward. Senator Mohasset takes out a bullhorn and presses it against Coover's ear.)

Sen. Mohasset: IS IT TRUE, MR. COOVER, THAT YOU WERE ONCE EMPLOYED AS AN AUDIO ENGINEER BY HOLLYWOOD MOVIE PRODUCERS?

Coover: Oh, yes. I was in charge of sound effects at BoomCo. Heck, we supplied practically the whole industry.

Sen. Mohasset: PLEASE TURN OVER THE SO-CALLED SOUND EFFECTS CATALOG, MR. COOVER.

Coover: (silence)

Sen. Mohasset: THE CATALOG, MR. COOVER.

Coover: Oh, what? Were you talking to me?

Satan (Speaking Over Office Intercom)
Small Body (Tearing Its Way Out Of Larger Body)
Relentless Busy Signal
Phone Call #1 (Skeptical Police Officer)
Phone Call #2 (Satan)
Phone Call #3 (Coming From Inside The House)
Incredibly Loud Noise (It's Just The Family Pet)
Incredibly Loud Noise (Not Just The Family Pet This Time)
Lightning
Lightning (Striking, Reanimating Dead Psychopath)
Mute Zombies
Annoying Female Scream (Which Just Won't Stop)
Bone Crunch
Boner Crunch
Musical Theme: "It's All Over Now"
Musical Theme: "It's All Over Now . . . Or Is It?"
Feeding Frenzy
Musical Foreshadowing ("Get Out Of The House!")
Lullabies (By Dead Children)
Strangulation Gurgle (Nerdy Guy)

SERIOUS ART FILMS

Harpsichord Music
Wind On Wheat
Gibberish (Italian)
Gibberish (French)
Gibberish (unspecified)
Industrial Noise
Industrial Noise #2
Gotterdammerung (Dolby)
"Jongleur! Jongleur!" (Happy Townspeople)
Vanessa Redgrave (Weeping)
Vanessa Redgrave (Wailing)
Angst Wail
Tasteful, Natural Sex Between Two Women (Silent)
"Here Come The Gypsies!"
Sound Of Society Oppressing Individual
C Sharp Tone (Thirty Minutes Long, Just Won't Stop)
Heartbeat (Guilty Man)
Heartbeat (Frightened Dog)
Stereo Weltschmertz
Nail Being Hammered Into Hand (Jesus)
Nail Being Hammered Into Hand (Severed Hand)
March Of The Monks
Mockery (French Children, Deformed Man)
Mockery (Honest Individual, Corrupt Politicians)
Song Of The Humpback Whale
Two Woman Talking In Simultaneous Monotones
Music To Listen To While Waiting For Godot
Song Of The Disenfranchised Person

PORN MOVIES

Squishy Sex Sounds
Blow-Job Exhortation
Plea For Semen Release
"Stop, Please!" (Serious)
"Stop, Please!" (Coquettish)
"Boing!" (Instantaneous Erection)
Panting (Male)
Panting (Female)
Panting (Dog)
Ridiculously Noisy Orgasm
Semen Gobble
Clanking Bondage Machine
Diesel-Powered Vibrator
Vocal Sex Noises (Guttural)
Vocal Sex Noises (Actual Words)
Music To Screw By
Long Snake Moan
Squeaking Bed
Squeaking Couch
Squeaking Hospital Gurney
"Marty"
Suggestive Meal (Fruit)
Suggestive Meal (Meat)
Chest Hair
"Boballa, Boballa . . ." (Bra Release)
Orgasm Enhancer (Fireworks, Cathedral Bells,
    Hallelujah Chorus)
"Ouch!" (Bruised Ovary)
Fanfare (Long Penis Unveiled)

The music world was nearly set on its side in August 1986 when pop singer Barry Manilow attempted to sabotage the week's Billboard Hot 100 listings. Manilow had apparently become furious when his newly released single, "I'm a Heavy Metal Kind of Guy," was relegated to the easy listening chart. "I'm a hard-rocking, crazy kind of dude," he insisted, but his entreaties fell upon deaf ears—the very ears that control every aspect of the music industry. Seeking revenge, Manilow secretly sought out an as yet unnamed writer from *Cracked* magazine, who tapped into the Billboard computer and entered the bogus chart reprinted below. Billboard executives, noticing that the chart did not contain any of the tracks they had been paid to promote that week, halted the release of the report just moments before it was to go out over the wires.

1.	THE GRILL IS GONE	BB-Q KING
2.	DON'T STEP ON THAT RAKE	WHAM!
3.	START ME UP (CAREFULLY)	ROLLING STOVES
4.	I'M WITH STUPID	THE MANHATTAN IRON-ON TRANSFER
5.	CRAPPER'S DELIGHT	GRANDMASTER FLUSH
6.	GOODBYE YELLOW BRICK LOAD	ELTON TOILET
7.	BORN IN 19TH CENTURY FRANCE	PROUST SPRINGSTEEN
8.	BLUE SUEDE YARMULKE	ROSH-HA-SHA-NA-NA
9.	A MAN, A PLAN, A CANAL	ABBA
10.	DO YOU HAB	EDDIE MONEY
11.	HUMAN NATURE	MICHAEL JACKSON
12.	(IT'S) HUMAN NATURE	JERMAINE JACKSON
13.	(IT'S ONLY) HUMAN NATURE	TITO JACKSON
14.	HUMAN NATURE (DUB REMIX)	JANET JACKSON
15.	(I'M CRAZY 'BOUT) HUMAN NATURE	REGGIE JACKSON
16.	YOU'VE GOT TO FIGHT FOR YOUR RIGHT (TO SCREW A DOG)	BESTIALITY BOYS
17.	FLAMING BAG OF DOG DOO	CHEAP TRICK
18.	MAME	ORIGINAL CAST RECORDING
19.	MONDAY, MONDAY	TALK TALK
20.	NEW YORK, NEW YORK	MR MISTER
21.	SUGAR, SUGAR	THE THE
22.	EMBARRASSING SPEECH IMPEDIMENT	DURAN DURAN
23.	A VIEW TO A KILL	SIRHAN SIRHAN
24.	THE HAPPY SONG	JOHN COUGAR MELONHEAD
25.	MACHO MAN	VILLAGE IDIOTS
26.	FLY LIKE AN EAGLE, DRINK LIKE A FISH	STEVE MILLER LITE BAND
27.	DON'T FEAR THE BARKEEPER	PABST BLUE OYSTER CULT
28.	SOLD OUR SOUL FOR ROLLING ROCK	CARLING BLACK SABBATH
29.	THERE'S NO SLOWING DOWN AT	BOB SEGER AND THE SILVER BULLET BAND TONIGHT
30.	LIGHT MY FIRE BREWING APPARATUS	THE COORS
31.	PEGGY SUE GOT DRUNK	BUDWEISER HOLLY
32.	THE GRAND SELF DELUSION	STYNX
33.	THE SCATALOGICAL SONG	SUPERTRASH
34.	MAGIC HOUSE PET RIDE	STEPPENSHIT

35.	THANK YOU AMADEUS	FALCO
36.	YOU DROPPED A BOMB ON ME	ALAN PARSONS MANHATTAN PROJECT
37.	BANGIN' ON THE PIPES	ALAN PARSONS HOUSING PROJECT
38.	OUR FRIEND STATIC ELECTRICITY	ALAN PARSONS SCIENCE PROJECT
39.	AAUUGH!	ALAN PARSONS PROJECTILE VOMITING
40.	MAME	ORIGINAL CAST RECORDING
41.	DON'T IT MAKE MY BROWN EYE BLUE	DAVID BOWIE
42.	LET'S GET QUANTUM PHYSICAL	OLIVIA NEUTRON-BOMB
43.	(STOP USING) SOCKS AS A WEAPON	PAT BENATARD
44.	HARD TO SWALLOW	THE LOVIN' MOUTHFUL
45.	SUNSHINE OF YOUR LOVE MEAT	CREAM
46.	DO YOU THINK I'M SEXY	ROD STEWART
47.	THEME FROM SHAFT	JOE COCKER & WANG CHUNG
48.	HOPE YOU ENJOYED THESE	DICK JOKES
49.	(SHAMPOO, RINSE) DO IT AGAIN	STEELY DANDRUFF
50.	THE TWO-THOUSAND-YEAR-OLD JOKE	MEL BROOKS & CARL REINER
51.	MARIJUANA LEAF RAG	SCOTT & JANIS JOPLIN
52.	WE BUILT THIS CITY (ON THE PRINCIPLES OF THE CONSTITUTION)	THOMAS JEFFERSON STARSHIP
53.	RESPECT (THE PRINCIPLES OF THE CONSTITUTION)	ARETHA BENJAMIN FRANKLIN
54.	SOMETIMES YOU FEEL LIKE A NUT	PETER, PAUL, & MOUNDS
55.	BLOOD, SWEAT, & TEARS	EARTH, WIND, & FIRE
56.	DRIVE MY CAR	REO STATIONWAGON
57.	LEGS	Z Z TOP
58.	BOOTS	L L BEAN
59.	THE KIDS ARE ALRIGHT	MAMAS AND THE PAPAS
60.	HEAD OVER HEELS	TEARS FOR FEARS
61.	FEET OVER HEAD	QUEERS FOR REARS
62.	WHAT'S GOING ON, SAILOR?	MARVIN GAYE
63.	MEND YOUR WAYS, EBENEZER SCROOGE!	JACOB MARLEY AND THE WAILERS
64.	YALE SUCKS	KING CRIMSON
65.	I AM WOMAN (TAKE MY WORD FOR IT)	JOAN ARMORPLATING
66.	WALK LIKE AN EGYPTIAN SLUT	BANGLES
67.	WE GOT THE BEAT (OF SLUTS)	GO-GOS
68.	MATERIAL SLUT	MADONNA
69.	PENUS	BANANARAMA
70.	SATAN'S OVERCOAT	MOLLY HAT CHECK
71.	FELIZ NAVIDAD	SANATANA CLAUS
72.	THREE-EGG UMLAUT	MÖSTLY CRÜD
73.	BAT HEADS MADE ME FAT	HAZZY HAZBEEN
74.	ABC	ELO
75.	S.O.S.	REM
76.	P.Y.T.	ABC
77.	B.Y.O.B.	XTC
78.	BLEEDO SHUFFLE	BOZ SCABBS
79.	I'M ON FIRE	SMOKEY ROBINSON
80.	BURNING DOWN THE HOUSE	TALKING HEADS
81.	LIFE OF THE PARTY	FARTING ARMPITS
82.	KING OF PORK	RUN-BLT
83.	ROTINI #66	PRINCE
84.	STU-STU-STUPIDO	PHIL COLLINS
85.	MISSIONARY POSITION	THE EURHYTHMETHODS
86.	I WANT A NEW DUCK	HUEY, LOUIE, AND THE DEWEYS
87.	BURGERLINE	MCDONNA
88.	DANCIN' ON THE REVENUE CEILING	LIONEL RICHIE RICH
89.	I CAN'T SLAVE-DRIVE 55	SAMMY HAGAR THE HORRIBLE
90.	THE SOUND OF LASAGNA	SIMON AND GARFIELD
91.	START MAKING MONEY	TALKING HEADS
92.	START ME UP (CAREFULLY)	PSYCHEDELIC FURNACES
93.	THE WAITING (IS THE HARDEST PART)	TOM POTTY AND THE HOUSEBREAKERS
94.	SUMMER OF 69 ZITS	BRYAN ADAMS
95.	FEELINGS	ARNOLD SCHWARZENEGGER
96.	KENNEL NOISES	SOUND EFFECTS—VOL VI
97.	MAME	ORIGINAL CAST RECORDING
98.	COLONEL MUSTARD'S LONELY FARTS CLUB BAND	"WEIRD AL" YANKMYDICK
99.	ASS SCRATCH FEVER	TED NUGAT
100.	I'M CHALKIN'	MINNESOTA FATS DOMINO

TAKING THE STAND: Mr. Roger Gibbons, ex-NASA chief

Sen. Mohasset: We now re-call to the stand Mr. Roger Gibbons. If I am not mistaken, you were in communication with Neil Armstrong during the first lunar landing. Is that correct?

Gibbons: Yes, sir. Yes it is.

Sen. Mohasset: How then, sir, do you explain this transcript of the actual conversation between yourself and Mr. Armstrong on that historic day?

Gibbons: Well, Senator, I'm sure no one will ever forget the immortal words Neil uttered when he became the first human being to set foot on the moon. "That's one small step for man, one giant leap for mankind." But, if the truth be known, that "first" step was actually his twenty-fourth. We had to delay the audio until his "first" words on the moon were sufficiently majestic and moving. I'm afraid you'll see what I mean . . .

Sen. Richardson: If I might interrupt, I would just like to point out that I was not involved with that mission.

Sen. Mohasset: Yes, thank you, Senator. I'm sure that we're all relieved and mildly surprised to hear that.

Sen. Richardson: Well, thank you. Oh — but remember that I did set foot on the moon in a later mission. I did not mean to imply that I had not served our great nation in a lunar capacity.

Sen. Mohasset: Yes, thank you, Senator Richardson. Your lunar exploits are widely respected, I assure you.

ARMSTRONG: Houston, I'm at the bottom of the ladder. Are you reading my audio okay?

NASA: That's a roger, Neil. Audio and visual A-okay. Go ahead.

ARMSTRONG: I never met a man I didn't like . . . way up here.

NASA: Neil, why don't you step back on the ladder and try something different.

ARMSTRONG: How about, "I wouldn't join any moon that would have me as a member."

NASA: Come on, Neil. If we wanted W.C. Fields we would have just sent him up there.

ARMSTRONG: Nonsense, Houston. He wouldn't have passed the physical.

NASA: Physical? All you bozos do is sit in the damned cockpit and then climb down a short ladder in one-third gravity. I get more exercise than that scratching my butt.

ARMSTRONG: Me too. Okay. What about this: Moon Men, here I come!

NASA: Hmm . . . Not bad, actually. It's topical, it's brief, it's succinct. I like it. I think we'll use that one. That's a wrap. We'll—what? Could you hold on for a second Neil? (five-minute pause, during which Armstrong does slow-motion somersaults on lunar surface) Okay, Neil? This is Houston. The higher-ups think we can do better than that one.

                              TAPE BREAK

ARMSTRONG: You can't imagine how happy I am to finally be here . . .

NASA: That's good.

ARMSTRONG: . . . because I've needed to take a piss since we left the ionosphere.

                              TAPE BREAK

NASA: What if you were to describe the view?

ARMSTRONG: Okay. Here goes. I'm stepping out of the lander now. I'm looking around and—my God! Everything is covered with a layer of some sort of dirt! Yes, it definitely is dirt, or dust. It certainly is dirty up here!

NASA: Neil, we've got all afternoon if that's what it takes.

                              TAPE BREAK

NASA: Neil, try something a little more exciting.

ARMSTRONG: Okay. I'm descending from the ship now. I'm climbing down the ladder and—whoops! I've fallen off the ladder! Ouch! I think my suit is ripped! I'm losing air! Help! Help!

NASA: Oh my God. Houston to lander, we have a red light situation at the hatch!

ARMSTRONG: Just kidding! Everything's fine. Did I fool you? Not much to report up here . . .

                              TAPE BREAK

NASA: Neil, could you try something powerful? Something moving.

ARMSTRONG: Like "Wish you were here"?

NASA: That's a no-go. I ran it by legal, and it violates a Hallmark copyright.

ARMSTRONG: "Happy Birthday, Grand-niece"?

NASA: Same problem.

ARMSTRONG: Blow me!

NASA: Hey, not bad. Kind of light-hearted and—

ARMSTRONG: I was talking to you, Houston.

                              TAPE BREAK

NASA: Okay Neil. Take 23 . . . and action.

ARMSTRONG: Well, here I am on the moon.

NASA: That's the best you can do? Fine. That's a keeper.

ARMSTRONG: Finally.

NASA: Neil, why don't you try just one more, in case we have audio trouble with that last one. Try something about "mankind" or something like that.

ARMSTRONG: Okay . . .

TAKING THE STAND: Brad Merill and Tom Hewlett, sports commentators

Sen. Mohasset: Gentlemen, I understand that you were hired by the Detroit Metropolitan Opera in an attempt to increase the size of their radio audience.

Brad: Correct, Senator. We sat in a soundproof box in the rear of the Detroit Civic Center and commented on all the action. Tom?

Tom: Right, Brad. Our seats were on the fifty yard line. Right behind home plate. You know what I mean. Right in the middle.

Sen. Mohasset: And what was the outcome of this little broadcasting experiment?

Tom: Well, Senator, I'm afraid it was a serious error.

Brad: Right, Tom. A definite fumble. A broken play.

Tom: We were fired, Senator.

Brad: At halftime.

In an effort to increase the radio-listening audience for its weekly concerts, the Detroit Metropolitan Orchestra in 1975 hired a popular local sports announcing team to cover its concerts. A soundproof broadcasting booth was built in the back of the Detroit Civic Theater to allow the commentators to talk without disturbing the live audience. On October 19, 1975, the first concert with commentary was broadcast, but due to a technician's error the signal from the booth was routed into an air conditioning unit instead of into the transmitter. The orchestra's management apologized profusely to the narration crew, but they firmly refused ever to come back. The following is a partial transcript of their broadcast, obtained from a tape player left running in the booth primarily as a sound-level check.

BRAD MERILL: Good evening, and welcome to an exciting program from the Detroit Metropolitan Orchestra. We've got a Bartok and a Dvorak in store, and who knows what else. It should be quite a game. I'm Brad Merill, and with me tonight is Tom Hewlett. Tom?

TOM: Well, right, Brad. I think we can look forward to quite a show tonight, as we always can from this bunch. Sure.

BRAD: That's right. And it looks like we're almost ready to get under way. The air temperature feels just right, and the crowd seems ready. From here in the booth the cellos will be on our right, in the black tuxedos, and the violins will be on the left, also in black tuxedos.

TOM: I think we should point out, for those of you not familiar with orchestra, that there will be no coin flip.

BRAD: Right. No coin flip. No ball. It's a very self-contained sport. Not really a sport even.

TOM: No.

BRAD: More like a, uh, a play.

TOM: Yes, or a novel.

BRAD: Right.

TOM: And I think we're going to get under way in a moment. The conductor has taken the stage. I think the audience has quieted down.

BRAD: Probably.

TOM: Although we can't hear them.

BRAD: Right, but they've stopped moving around.

TOM: Yes. And the orchestra seems to be holding their instruments, as if waiting to start. Brad?

BRAD: Well, that's right, Tom. Earlier the cellos were lying down beside the players' chairs, and some of the players were even away from their places, but that seems to have stopped. They seem like a different orchestra now.

TOM: That's right. And here is the conductor raising his hands, and, and, and we're under way. Yes, we are under way here at the Detroit Municipal Theater—

BRAD: Civic.

TOM: —Civic Theater. Under way.

BRAD: Yes.

TOM: Playing. The orchestra seems to be playing. Definitely.

BRAD: Yes, I—hey whoa!

TOM: What?

BRAD: Uh, never mind. I thought for a second that the violas had taken a three-point shot.

TOM: No three-point line in orchestra, Brad.

BRAD: Of course. Hey! Time for a commercial break. We'll be back with more action, live from the Detroit National Band, in a moment.

TOM: Civic Band.

TAPE PAUSED FOR COMMERCIAL

BRAD: All right. We're back. And the score seems to be proceeding.

TOM: For those of you who aren't familiar with orchestra, there is a score, but it does not change.

BRAD: Set before the start.

TOM: Right.

BRAD: A bit like professional wrestling.

TOM: Wrestling?

BRAD: Playing from a script, sort of.

TOM: Ah yes. Ha ha ha ha.

BRAD: Ha ha ha ha.

TOM: Ha ha. Oh hey. Look at that.

BRAD: Huh?

TOM: We seem to have some sort of disturbance.

BRAD: Yes, a flag has been thrown, or a flashlight I guess. We have an usher in motion toward the left aisle—

TOM: Could be clipping.

BRAD: —back toward the wall. It looks like a ticket call from here, Tom. At least a gentleman in one of the lines—

TOM: Rows.

BRAD: —the what?

TOM: In one of the seating rows here on the floor of the theater, let's see if we can get a call from the usher. We were having some problems earlier with the wireless microphones, but hopefully those problems have been ironed out.

USHER: (faint, with static) Sir, you are in the wrong row. You need to move back two rows.

TOM: Wow.

BRAD: Right. A two-row penalty. I don't think that was really fair, do you?

TOM: Absolutely not. Two rows. No, I don't think that was right.

BRAD: Of course, there are no replays here in orchestra.

TOM: Yes, and you know it's a shame. Because for all the flack that the replay rule has taken, saying it takes too long, saying the replay officials miss things even in slow motion, saying it puts too much pressure on the networks, I think they are important as a symbol of…

BRAD: Wait a second, Tom, I think we've had an injury.

TOM: —a symbol of—What?

BRAD: An injury on the stage.

TOM: An injury?

BRAD: One of the bass players has left the stage.

TOM: Oh come on. What could have happened to him? Bow in the knee?

BRAD: We can only hope it isn't serious. Let's go to Seth Jordan in the locker room.

TOM: He didn't come.

BRAD: Huh?

TOM: He didn't come. He said this was a stupid idea, and he wasn't going to sit around in their dressing room all night listening to "bird music."

BRAD: Okay, just hold on at home, folks, we'll have a report on the bass player's condition as soon as we get some information. Can we tell from here which one it was?

TOM: The third one.

BRAD: Ah. What number was he, do you remember?

TOM: No numbers.

BRAD: Oh, right. No numbers in orchestra, folks.

TOM: Right.

BRAD: Okay. Well, how are we doing?

TOM: Beats me.

BRAD: Ah, let's see, ahm—oh, look there—the second violins seemed to have dropped out. Yes, they—no hold on, they're back playing again. Um, Tom?

TOM: What?

BRAD: Huh?

TOM: You said, "Tom?"

BRAD: Yeah. "Tom?"

TOM: What?

BRAD: Take it.

TOM: Take it?

BRAD: Yeah. Talk.

TOM: Oh! Take it! I thought you were asking me a question.

BRAD: Christ.

TAPE BREAK

TAKING THE STAND: Lloyd Greene, unemployed

Sen. Stone: I now call forth Mr. Lloyd Greene.

Greene: Here I am, dude.

Sen. Stone: Mr. Greene, I do not generally find myself in a position requiring me to discuss the merits, or conversely, the drawbacks, of listening to rock and roll music amplified to great extremes. Nevertheless, as Senator Mohasset has left the hearing room momentarily in order to, er, attend to the calls of nature, I find myself in just such a position.

Greene: Ah, well, sorry about that.

Sen. Stone: Well, no matter. Now, to be perfectly honest, I know nothing of this Mr. Led Zeppelin referred to in my briefing. Perhaps if you could just explain the whole thing yourself, I won't be bothered further.

Greene: On November 23, 1979, my best friend and associate Larry Hall, and I received a brand new Sankyo 5000 stereo system from *Hi Fidelity* magazine. We told the man who installed it that we wouldn't turn the volume knob past SIX (6), because he wouldn't leave until we promised.

The following are the minutes of our stereo-testing session, which was carried out on a Friday evening while Larry's parents were out of town on a second honeymoon. The tests were conducted using Led Zeppelin's *Physical Graffiti* album as a control. I kept the only official minutes of the test, and Larry operated the stereo.

• 11:53 P.M.: Side one, song one. Volume level: just a little bit past SIX. Jimmy Page's guitar is crystal clear and, like Robert Plant's angelic vocals, very loud at this volume. There are no longer any windows in Larry's house. "Wow," Larry says as he sifts a handful of silicon dust through his fingers.

• 12:01 A.M.: We blow all the shingles off the roof over Larry's bedroom, and decide that we should probably halt the test.

• 12:05 A.M.: After halting the test long enough to get some beers from downstairs, we continue. With the opening chords of "Custard Pie" a king-size chunk of tin-foiled attic fluff pops out of the ceiling over Larry's bed, but it's not until the drums come in that the hole is wide enough for Larry to crawl through. I worry about the structural damage, but Larry really hates his parents.

• 12:05 A.M.: Volume knob approaches SEVEN. The garage door is opening and closing spontaneously, and it isn't even electric. Larry and I stand in the basement with our arms folded, nodding our heads and grinning at each other. He yells something in my ear that I can't hear, and I yell something back.

• 12:08 A.M.: Larry suspends one of the larger speakers over the open toilet bowl, and turns the volume level up to EIGHT. The sound waves carry through the sewer system, and subsequently blow three homeless people off the steam grate of the First National Bank downtown. One of them caroms off the eaves and suffers a broken arm. I feel kind of bad, but Larry hates homeless people too.

• 12:11 A.M.: As John "Bonzo" Bonham kicks into "Boogie With Stu," the stereo is so loud that it's hard to be in the same room with it. Larry walks in to turn it down and is flattened as if by a bug zapper.

- 12:15 A.M.: Fortunately, the $10,000 price tag included a remote control with a 15-mile radius, so Larry and I drive up to the reservoir in his '72 Tomahawk. When we hit the freeway, we roll down the windows in order to hear every nuance of "Kashmir."

- 12:34 A.M.: Larry patches a Mr. Microphone through the remote control and introduces the second side of the record to three counties. At least fifteen spiritually misguided people form a new religion, in which Larry and Led Zeppelin are sacraments.

- 12:54 A.M.: When we return home, a special report on TV indicates that every dog in the Manhattan area has taken off, running in the same direction, and at least 100 of them have drowned in the East River. Larry loves dogs, so he turns the treble booster down.

- 12:52 A.M.: As the volume knob passes EIGHT, we get a phone call from a young couple in Boise, Idaho. They ask us to turn down the stereo so their baby will stop crying.

- 12:58 A.M.: The music is now so loud that the stereo cabinet hops around the room like a loose pile driver. Larry puts in a cassette tape of "Physical Graffiti" because the record keeps skipping. Near volume level NINE, the stereo explodes and kills both of us.

- 1:01 A.M.: Luckily, the people from *Hi Fidelity* also sent us an incredibly high-tech video camera and recorder, which has preserved copies of both of us that are indistinguishable from our real selves. The miracle of one-fourth-inch videotape allows us to continue our tests.

Record Review— Yuletide Classics
by Lance Coover

Yuletide Classics, the latest offering from new wave artist Kay Tell, is a bizarre collection of rude, crude, and offensively lewd tracks. The songs seem to share just one thing in common: a desire to make a mockery of Christmas and the entire holiday season.

The first number, "Jingle Bells," sounds very much like the traditional family-oriented song of the same name. Never having paid much attention to the song's lyrics as a youth, I decided to listen carefully. To my horror, I found myself transcribing a series of lyrics so disgusting that they must certainly bear no resemblance to the original version. Take, for example, a particularly muffled line of the song that referred in some way to "one whore's open lay." I, for one, can do without that kind of smut.

In the next track, the now-threatening singer warns the listener, "You better not shout/You better not cry." But what is the reason for our enforced silence? "I'm telling you why," the singer quickly shouts into our ear. The explanation that follows is especially muffled; it seems, however, to have been one of the following: "Santa Claus is gunning you down," "Santa Claus is running this town," or "Santa Claus is bumming around." This bitter sequence is again presented in a shrill, irritating voice, so difficult to comprehend that the more casual listener might entirely overlook the sinister intent of the lyrics.

Perhaps the most offensive track of all is the ineptly titled, "White Christmas." Far from being an expression of holiday sentiments, this song never even mentions the word "Christmas." More likely, the tune was lifted directly from the soundtrack of an adult film. From the opening stanza, "I'm dreaming of a white chick's ass," this celebration of the pornographic is disgusting.

And so it goes, on and on and on. In one ditty after another, we hear of snowmen addicted to heroin or of reindeer exposing their bosoms to public scrutiny. Enough! Bring back the classics. And while you're at it, make a less muffled recording, so that for once I can make out what they're saying.

CARTOONS ON CASSETTE

Episode 5: "The Roadrunner"
Read by Sir Laurence Olivier

"An animal that appears to be some cousin to the noble wolverine has just received a parcel in the post. The parcel bears stamped legend: 'Acme Weapon Company.' The animal, with all the glee and eagerness of a wide-eyed child on Christmas morn, unwraps the package, revealing an unlikely sort of electrical blunderbuss.

"Now he's aiming it at another animal—some sort of agile, rapidly moving desert peacock, with gaudy plumage. The wolverine fellow pulls the trigger, and the blunderbuss discharges in his own face. What a dreadful comeuppance for this sly rogue!"

MIME ON TAPE

Described by Bret Easton Ellis (Author of Less Than Zero*)*

"He's doing the Big Ball On The Back thing now. Yeah, it looks really heavy. Now he's pretending to be trapped in a big invisible box. He's making all sorts of faces, and pressing his hands against where he wants us to think the glass is. I bet the Strong Wind thing is next. Yeah, now he's doing the Strong Wind thing. Great."

SUNSET ON TAPE

Described by sportscaster John Madden

"It's about seven o'clock, and the weather is just fantastic for a sunset. (pop) So sit back, crack open a brew, and—who! This is incredible! I DON'T BELIEVE IT! There's a big strip of purple and some gold and HOLY JESUS CHRIST! YOU SHOULD SEE THIS! THIS IS GREAT! MAN OH MAN!"

CAMPFIRE STORIES ON CASSETTE

Told by Rick Lockhart, veteran camp counselor

"It was right around here, in this very forest or campsight area, exactly ten years ago to this night. As far away as the nearest town to here, people heard blood-curdling screams . . . all night long.

"In the morning, the sheriff came up to investigate. He found a group of campers—as many in number as are sitting here listening to this tape. All dead. Their limbs were scattered among the leaves and pine needles, their heads torn off and half-eaten like discarded apples.

"Who—or *what*—could have wreaked this carnage? The sheriff saw a portable cassette player next to the campfire. He took out the cassette and read the label. The tape was entitled 'Campfire Stories on Cassette—told by Rick Lockhart, veteran camp counselor.'"

TAKING THE STAND:
David Lee Roth

Sen. Stone: We'd like to thank you for coming down to testify on behalf of Mr. Trexton, since he could not be here himself today but had to fly off in an emergency to visit his sick mother in Panama. We realize you are very busy, Mr. Lee Roth. Uh, are you going to be okay, Mr. Lee Roth, you look kind of sick.

Roth: Uhnnn.

Sen. Stone: We just want to ask you a few questions concerning the "Armageddon-Crazy-Are-You Heavy-Metal Death Bash" Promotional Party for PayRock Records held on April 21 to 24, 1986. Were you present at the party, Mr. Roth? Mr. Roth?

Roth: . . . party?

Sen. Mohasset: You may step down, Mr. Roth.

Leonard D. Benson
Assistant Manager, Ramada Inn
Kansas City, KA

Jerry Trexton
Public Relations Representative
PayRock Promotions
Los Angeles, CA 92508

Mr. Trexton:

   This is the final letter I am going to send you concerning the private party you threw for your clients here on the night of April 21, 1986. And the day of April 22. And the following night of the 23. And the following day. I was unaware at the time that the "intimate get-together" you had promised me was secretly nicknamed "Armageddon-Crazy-Are-You Heavy-Metal Death Bash." I'm sure it was just a simple matter of miscommunication, as you say, but there is still the outstanding matter of damages to be paid. I realize that 250,000 dollars is a lot of money, but I assure you, it is a fair estimate. After all, the hotel did post bail.

   I am including here a list of all the items that my staff and I have turned up while renovating the hotel. They are your rightful property, should you choose to claim them:

   · seven bazooka shells (most of them are shot).
   · (13) pairs of underpants (most of these are shot, too).
   · one female, aged 19, answers to name "Bambi."
   · one vacuum cleaner bong: I don't find this particularly clever or funny—that was an expensive piece of machinery.
   · Steppenwolf (one).
   · (4) prosthetic limbs: someone on the staff questioned how the owner of these items could have left, so we're still scouring the hotel.
   · "The World's Largest Beer-a-mid": I disagree with Mr. Van Halen's comment that this will prove "a lasting thing of beauty and enjoyment for years to come," and for that reason, am slightly perturbed that it was welded sturdily to both the floor and ceiling. Especially as it is composed of half-full cans. Half the staff is becoming nauseous, the other half drunk.
   · one coffin: This has, I assure you, remained untouched.
   · one leopard. You probably don't want the camel, anymore. Or what's left of it.

Please pick these items up at the soonest possible date. Also, I must add, that we have uncovered certain items that cannot, for whatever reason, be returned to you:

   · $25,389.74 in returnable empties. These will be applied to your outstanding debts. They have already been deducted from the figure you have received.
   · (411) used hypodermic syringes. Please tell Mr. Clapton I did not know that he was a diabetic, and tell Mr. (?) Boy George that I understand how it can be—I have allergies, too, though they do not require quite so much medication.
   · 6,151 inflated condoms: My staff started popping them. That's not water, is it?
   · something wet and fuzzy that, when touched, scurried under a radiator and has not been seen since (there's just one, but our secret hope is that it is not gestating).
   · the luau pit you dug in the Tiki Room Lounge (for obvious reasons). By the way, the other guests who witnessed the "Live Voodoo Rites" were wondering: Does the "curse" wash off, or do you just have to wait it out?

Also, any information you could lend to help us find the following items would be greatly appreciated:

   · Gus, the night watchman
   · Room 235

Thanks.

Sincerely,

Leonard D. Benson

Leonard D. Benson

TAKING THE STAND: Frank Sinatra

Sinatra: Yeah, what'd'ya want this time?

Sen. Mohasset: Mr. Sinatra, perhaps you remember a certain Alcoholics Anonymous convention in Las Vegas, Nevada?

Sinatra: No, no. Can't say I do.

Sen. Beaufort: Pardon me, mistah Sinatra, but Ah was jest wondering if perhaps, maybe, you wouldn't mahnd givin' us jest one li'l rendition of "Mah Way."

Sen. Richardson: Senator Beaufort! I'm sure Mr. Sinatra would rather not be bothered with "My Way" at this time. Maybe "Come Fly With Me," but certainly not "My Way."

Sen. Mohasset: Enough! Now, Mr. Sinatra, I must inform you that we have bootleg recordings of the entire event in our possession. According to our records, you, Dean Martin, and Shirley MacLaine performed in an "educational" Las Vegas review, designed to aid alcoholics in their struggle to give up drinking. The show was apparently entitled "A Little Hey-Hey with Frank, Dean, and Friends."

Sinatra: I have no recollection of that affair.

Sen. Mohasset: Nevertheless, we have documented accounts attesting to the fact. Ladies and gentlemen, I can report that the show had to be cancelled and all recordings destroyed after each and every member of the audience was driven to resume drinking. Bailiff—please roll the tape.

Sinatra: I still don't remember it. I must've really tied one on that night.

SINATRA: (singing) *Come Fly With Me, come fly, let's fly away*
If you could use some exotic booze
There's a bar in far Bombay
Come Fly With Me, let's fly away!

Good evening ladies and gentlemen, and welcome to the Sands Hotel. And you're a very special audience, right? (applause) I'm glad that Alcoholics Anonymous chose Las Vegas for their annual convention this year, and I hope you're all having a good time—and staying on the wagon. We've prepared a special show just for you tonight. We're going to take you through the steps of alcoholism and recovery. So I guess I should just shut my big mouth and bring out one of my best friends . . . Mr. Dean Martin!

MARTIN: How did all these people get in my room?

SINATRA: You're drunk!

MARTIN: Are you calling me a drunk?

SINATRA: Yes, I am.

MARTIN: I'll drink to that!

STAGE ONE: DENIAL

MARTIN: That was the biggest martini I've ever had.

SINATRA: That was no martini, you lush. That was the aquarium.

MARTIN: I *thought* the olives were a little crunchy.

SINATRA: Ladies and gentlemen, I have to apologize for Dean—

MARTIN: Hey, I'll be the first to admit I've got a drinking problem.

SINATRA: What's the nature of your problem?

MARTIN: I missed a round a few minutes ago.

SINATRA: Not that kind of problem. What I'm talking about is drinking all the time. Drinking in the morning, drinking in the afternoon, drinking in the evening—

MARTIN: Sounds like a great party. Am I invited?

STAGE TWO: ANGER

SINATRA: Drinking does terrible things to a man.

MARTIN: I know what you mean. I saw a man throwing up in the gutter just last night.

SINATRA: That's what I'm talking about.

MARTIN: I said. "Hey buddy. cut it out! I'm trying to sleep down here!"

SINATRA: I talked to your wife last week. and boy is she mad.

MARTIN: She's mad?

SINATRA: She says you were so drunk that you picked up the dog and threw it through a plate-glass window.

MARTIN: That was a mistake.

SINATRA: I'll say.

MARTIN: I thought it was her.

STAGE THREE: BARGAINING

SINATRA: Next time I call you up and you're drunk. that'll be the last call you get from me.

MARTIN: Did someone say "last call"?

SINATRA: That's not what I meant.

MARTIN: In that case I'll have another Scotch and soda.

SINATRA: Just say the words.

MARTIN: No.

SINATRA: Say it.

MARTIN: Okay. My name is Dean. and I'm an alchoholic.

SINATRA: Now that wasn't so hard. was it?

MARTIN: I couldn't have done it sober.

INTERLUDE

SINATRA: Ladies and gentlemen ... the lovely Miss Shirley MacLaine!

SHIRLEY MACLAINE: Hello. I'm not an alchoholic. but I was in a previous life 5.000 years ago. And for that reason. to this day I can't stomach hard liquor.

MARTIN: Man. that's some hangover!

SINATRA: Straighten up and treat the broad with a little respect.

MARTIN: How can I do both at the same time? Hey Shirley. can you pay me back all that money you owe me?

MACLAINE: I don't owe you any money.

MARTIN: Don't you remember all those drinks I bought you in a previous life?

STAGE FOUR: DEPRESSION

SINATRA: Sober up. Dino.

MARTIN: Why? Am I driving right now?

SINATRA: Of course not. You're on stage in front of 900 people.

MARTIN: Then why'd the whole room just make a left turn?

SINATRA: Look at yourself. Your eyes are red. your face is green—

MARTIN: What's wrong with celebrating Christmas early?

STAGE FIVE: ACCEPTANCE

SINATRA: Look what you're doing to yourself.

MARTIN: Yeah.

SINATRA: You have a serious problem.

MARTIN: Yeah.

SINATRA: You should get help.

MARTIN: Yeah.

SINATRA: Is that all you can say? 'Yeah. yeah. yeah ...'

MARTIN: Ladies and gentlemen ... the Beatles

REPRISE

SINATRA. MARTIN. MACLAINE. AND SAMMY DAVIS. JR: (singing) "... cause it's the Oldest Established Permanent Floating Crap Game In New York!"

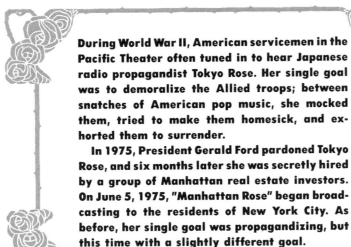

During World War II, American servicemen in the Pacific Theater often tuned in to hear Japanese radio propagandist Tokyo Rose. Her single goal was to demoralize the Allied troops; between snatches of American pop music, she mocked them, tried to make them homesick, and exhorted them to surrender.

In 1975, President Gerald Ford pardoned Tokyo Rose, and six months later she was secretly hired by a group of Manhattan real estate investors. On June 5, 1975, "Manhattan Rose" began broadcasting to the residents of New York City. As before, her single goal was propagandizing, but this time with a slightly different goal.

MANHATTAN ROSE

"Good morning, Manhattanites. It's 8:43 in the City, and the temperature is a boiling 98 degrees. There's a massive pile-up in the Holland Tunnel, and traffic on Fifth Avenue is backed up for miles. The cab drivers' strike enters its sixth day today.

"Why don't you just give up and go home? Here's a little tune for you: Simon and Garfunkel's 'Homeward Bound.'"

•

"Resign yourself to this fact: there is nothing for you in New York.

"Go home. Go back to your Peorias, your Denvers, your Wacos—go back to where you were born. I have a confidential message to all you young men from your girls back home. It says, 'Please come home, and stop me before I have sex with your younger brother … again.'

"Surrender, young professionals. Surrender your apartments; sign over your leases. Here's an oldie: 'New York's A Lonely Town.'"

•

"News flash! A cadre of paralegals have just surrendered. In exchange for their apartment leases, they were given one-way tickets back home to Mom.

"Take an example from your colleagues, young 'achievers.' What is this talk of 'heroism?' What is this talk of 'making it in the Big Apple?'

"Hey young Broadway hopeful! Hey aspiring writer! Hey young legal with your eye on a partnership! You are no match for the Combined Forces of Manhattan. Our ranks include muggers, thieves, and junkies who'll kill you for sneezing wrong. Lousy landlords, inept office managers, callous cops. How can you hope to overcome noisy neighbors, legions of roaches, unsightly street people, con artists, regular artists, and other people who talk too loudly in restaurants.

"Hot enough for you? Even inclement weather is on our side.

"Here's John Lee Hooker with 'Homesick Blues.'"

•

"Manhattan Rose has a message for the small brigade of serious artists who've barricaded themselves in their spacious Soho lofts. 'Los Angeles film company seeks art directors. Incredibly high pay. Nice weather.'

"Need I say more? You'll never make it here.

"Here's John Lennon with 'Tomorrow Never Knows…'"

•

"That's right. Like the man says, 'Surrender to the Void.' Killed in New York, that was John Lennon.

"News Item: Manhattan bridge collapses, killing four, injuring twenty. Do you hear that, young people? Even the forces of Bad Luck and Entropy are against you.

"Manhattan Rose knows how you feel. You came for the great nightclub scene, but you didn't bring the right clothes. None of your clothes are right. Go home to where you fit in, to where you belong, to where the streets are clean and the apartments cheap and plentiful.

"Remember: Home is where you hang your hat. New York is where you hang yourself."

TAKING THE STAND: Kermit Schaeffer, "Mr. Blooper"

Sen. Mohasset: Mr. Schaeffer, is it true that you compiled the original *Bloopers* record?

Schaeffer: Yes, sir. Yes it is. That was me.

Sen. Mohasset: But you weren't satisfied to leave it at that, were you? Before long, the American public was deluged with hundreds of foul-ups, bleeps, blunders, and practical jokes of every variety. I guess you must have felt like a real genius. The record company felt smart. The distributor felt smart. All you fellows smelt fart . . . OOPS! I mean FELT SMART! I meant to say, "FELT SMART!" You know what I meant. Stenographer: please strike that from the record.

Schaeffer: This is too much! Wait a second, let me get this down! Hang on one second!

Yes, Kermit "Mr. Blooper" Schaeffer is at it again! After carefully digging through his private audio vaults, the Master of Mayhem is now bringing you his personal "unedited" versions of all your favorite foul-ups. Just to add to the fun, Mr. Blooper has included a few goofs of his own; in all the trouble he went to just to make this record, he, too, slipped an occasional bolt!

In the national hullabaloo following the release of "All-Time Greatest Bloopers," everyone has picked up their own personal favorites—now you can hear what yours *really* sounded like before the censors got to it! So just relax, turn up the hi-fi, and enjoy the sounds of all the best-known radio personalities making boneheads of themselves. 'Nuff said!

SIDE ONE

1. Dwight D. Eisenhower 5/23/53.
"My fellow Americans, let me assure you that, in our dealings with Mr. Khrushchev, we have not allowed . . . (passes gas audibly) . . . hey, I wish you could all smell that at home! Whoo! Shit!"

2. Dick Clark, "American Bandstand," 11/3/56.
(Thought microphone was off) "Yeah, I'm sure a lot of kids are fucking to that one . . ."

3. Anonymous announcer, 2/23/30.
"Ladies and gentlemen, the President of the United States, Mr. Hoobert Heever . . . oh, shit, did I say that? Goddamn it!"

4. Miriam Freedman, NBC Radio News, 6/16/57.
"This commentary will deal with the suggestive performance on the Ed Sullivan Show last night. It was given by a Mr. Elvis Penis, a popular adolescent musician." (She didn't even notice that one!—K.S.)

5. Kermit Schaeffer, studio, 8/28/57.
"Oh, fuck, shit, and a thousand schmucks! I spilled my coffee on the tapes again! . . . Hey, did you get that one, guys?"

6. Jack Webb, "Dragnet," 4/30/49.
"Yes, ma'am, the name's Sgt. Joe Thursday. Is that what you wanted, Kermit? Can we go on with the show now? Jesus . . ."

SIDE TWO

1. Winston Churchill, address to the United Nations, 10/20/50.
". . . whereas this year's figures indicate a rise in steel production to a level of 653 thousand cubic tons, showing a gain of . . ." (It was actually 536 cubic tons!—K.S.)

2. Anonymous announcer, 8/3/43.
"Ladies and gentlemen, the President of the United States, Mr. Franklin Delano Smellmyass . . . oh, my god, not again! Shit!"

3. Kermit Schaeffer, kitchen, 3/17/51.
"Ladies and gentlemen, the President of the United States, Mr. Anus P.X. Sneer-Monger Schlongface. Whoopee!"

4. Helen Ferguson, G.E. Radio Theatre, "The Miracle Worker," 7/19/54.
"But, ma'am, it's just that, it's just that . . . Hey! Turn those lights back on! I can't see the script!" (N.B. The play is about a blind person.)

5. Orson Welles, Mercury Theatre, "War of the Worlds," 10/31/38.
"No, aliens aren't really attacking! It's just a goddamn fucking piece of shit radio play! Do I have to say it every (CENSORED) second?"

6. Unidentified caller, WZAZ Radio, 12/5/55.
D.J.: "Let's see who's next on the WZAZ all-hit request line . . ."
Caller: "Penis penis penis penis penis penis penis penis penis."
D.J.: (Hangs up)

7. Kermit Schaeffer, studio, 9/6/57.
"I hope you all enjoyed these bloppers. Jesus Christ. I mean *bloopers.* Shut the goddamn thing off. It isn't funny anymore, guys. I mean it."

Sen. Donald Mohasset: "Despite the alarming testimony we heard this week, I think it's important that we not let this thing get out of hand. I think that the other Senators and I have matters perfectly under control, and I have a feeling we'll be getting to the bottom of this thing soon enough. In short, I'm asking everyone to remain calm and . . . ahm . . . good Lord! I'm afraid I've just been handed an important memo. Out of my way!"

·

Sen. Jeremiah T. Beaufort: "Quite frankly, ah am shocked bah what I have heahd this week. Yeahs ago, ah sat mah children on mah knee and I said, 'Chillun,' I said, 'don't you *evah* get involved with this heah rock music. It will lead you direct down the long road of destruction. You want music? You lissin to some good ol' fiddle music.' So imagine how I felt this week when I found out that them fiddle players been puttin' out secret albums worshippin' the Jewish Gods for yeahs now."

·

Sen. Buzz Richardson: "I must say, I was particularly struck by that transcript of the Apollo-Soyuz linkup. And not just because I was on board at the time, mind you, serving this great nation of ours as a participant in the space program. What struck me was that such a cover-up—which, of course, I was not involved with in any way—could have occurred practically in my presence. It just goes to show you."

·

Sen. Archibald Stone: "In the words of the immortal bard (of course, I refer to Ovid), 'We have learned much—but we still have much to learn.' I find, indeed, that we are precipitously close to uncovering the very grimmest secrets of this enigma; and yet, I suspect that we may, or, indeed, that we may not, as yet come across a few more surprises in the course of our quest."

·

Sen. "Robert" Beatrice: "You know, when I first became aware of this evidence last year—er, last week, the same time all of you heard it, I was simply amazed. Of course, I immediately sent my forces—that is, my staff—out to do some further research. What I learned, I think, is that this trouble in the media is caused by all the separate puny little companies all trying to have their own way. Consolidation is the way of the future! We must—and we will—consolidate to the fullest possible extent, at the earliest possible time! Ahm, that is, at least that's what my staff learned, in their research."

·

Sen. Pamela Fawcett: "It seems to me that this conspiracy and dirty dealing is completely a product of the eighties. Back in the sixties, we didn't have to put up with this kind of thing. What we need now is a return to the old values—honesty, love, understanding, astral awareness, group living, vegetarianism, humanitarianism, Confucianarianism, and, of course, antidisestablishmentarianism."

WEEK THREE: MOVIES

The Treasure of **EL SINISTRE**

THE INDIGNANT ONES
Starring:
DEFORREST KELLY as the Simple Country Doctor
CRAIG T. NELSON as the Man Whose Home Was Built on an Indian Graveyard
GEORGE C. SCOTT as the Uncorruptible General
AL PACINO as the Crusading Lawyer
GENE HACKMAN as the Hardened New York Detective
SIDNEY POITIER as MR. Tibbs
"My God, Man! What have you Do

SORORITY
Slasher

Sen. Mohasset: "Ladies, gentlemen, and members of the press: We now begin our investigation of the movie industry. Hollywood has long been the home of the big stars and the big money, so I can only assume that the dirt we dig up this week will be even dirtier than anything we have seen thus far.

"We will now dim the lights as the evidence is presented. I ask only that there be no talking, littering, or urinating in the aisles as we roll the first clip.

"Oh—but before we begin, we will see a few coming attractions of next week's testimony. Please relax and enjoy the hearings."

2.) Coming Attractions:

Frame 1:

(All Senators are seated behind the stand, except Senator Richardson. Senator Mohasset is standing up, striking a majestic pose. He has his fist raised in the air.)
CAPTION: It all began one quiet Monday morning . . .
Mohasset: Let the Mediagate Hearings begin!

Frame 2:

(Close-up of Senator Beaufort and Senator Mohasset.)
Beaufort: Pahdon me, suh, but Ah'm afraid that Senatah Rishahdson is not present right at the moment.
Mohasset: What? Good God! Where the Hell is he?

Frame 3:

(Full-body view of Richardson wearing complete space suit, just having come through door.)
Richardson: Now I am here, Senator Mohasset. I am sorry that I am late, but I was on the moon and I just got back.

Frame 4:

(Close-up of Mohasset.)
Mohasset: Think nothing of it, Senator Richardson. I hereby commend you for your efforts to keep these United States, which I dearly love, number one in the space race.

Frame 5:

(Mohasset behind podium.)
CAPTION: Relive the incredible excitement surrounding the testimony of surprise witnesses . . .
Mohasset: Now, with no further ado, I call to the stand . . . Mr. Michael Jackson! Let's hear it for Michael Jackson!

Frame 6:

(Close-up of Farrah Fawcett.)
Fawcett: Mr. Jackson, I remind you that you are under oath. Now please tell the committee about your recent hit song, "BAD."

Frame 7:

(Close-up of Michael Jackson.)
Jackson: Tell you about it? I'll do better than that, Senator. One-two-three . . . Hit it, boys!

Frame 8:

(Concertlike scene of Jackson performing in front of screaming fans. Behind him, a whole band has materialized. Musical notes surround Jackson's words to make it more apparent that he is singing.)
Jackson: Who's Bad? I'm Bad.

Frame 9:

(Mohasset behind podium.)
Mohasset: Thank you, Mr. Jackson. That important testimony has been entered into the record.

Frame 10:

(Close-up of Senator Stone and Farrah Fawcett kissing.)
CAPTION: Go behind the scenes into Senator Stone's private dressing room . . .
Fawcett: Oh, Senator! You're so strong!
Stone: Yes, dear—but legislative power isn't everything.

Frame 11:

(Close-up of Beatrice on phone.)
CAPTION: And journey into the vaultlike briefing room of Senator Beatrice . . .
Beatrice: Hello, Payson? "Robert" here. Listen—I just got some inside info. Pick up one million shares of Jackson Records, Inc.—pronto!

Frame 12:

(Clint Eastwood at witness stand, facing Mohasset. Eastwood is pointing a gun at the Senator.)
CAPTION: Re-experience the tense encounters that imperiled the very lives of the valiant Senators . . .
Mohasset: Now, Mr. Eastwood, of course we are all aware that the movie industry is free from any wrongdoing. All I want to know is . . .
Eastwood: Go ahead, Senator! Make my day!

Frame 13:

(Beaufort tackling Eastwood.)
Beaufort: Not so fast, cowboy! Ah think Ah'll jest take that there gun, you no-good mud-chompin' yeller-bellied li'l boll-weevil!

Frame 14:

(Mohasset holding Eastwood by the shoulder with one hand, with other hand beginning to peel off the Eastwood mask that the criminal underneath is wearing.)
CAPTION: Watch again as the villians are publicly exposed.
Mohasset: Now let's find out who our little trouble-maker is!

Frame 15:

(The mask is ripped off to reveal Richard Nixon.)
Mohasset: Nixon! I should've known!
Nixon: Drat! And I would have gotten away with it, if it weren't for you meddling Senators!

Frame 16:

**MEDIAGATE: THE MOVIE.
COMING SOON TO A THEATER NEAR YOU.**

PREMIERE THEATERS' PRE-SHOW SPOTS

"For the comfort and convenience of our patrons, no cartoon representations of food are permitted in the auditorium. Genuine refreshments are available at the Refreshment Stand in the lobby."

"Premiere Theaters Gift Certificates are available at the ticket counter. They can be redeemed at the ticket counter for Gift Certificate Redemption Certificates. A great gag gift!"

"Please refrain from unnecessary conversation during the movie. The management reserves the right to silence noisy patrons."

"Please, NO SMOKING in the auditorium. In addition to causing emphysema and lung cancer, smoking uses up oxygen and produces carbon dioxide, which may result in a disastrous global greenhouse effect!"

"Should the temperature or air pressure in the auditorium be uncomfortable, or the sound or focus of the film become disrupted, please notify an usher at once. You will be instructed where to send away for a complaint form."

"And now, our feature presentation. ENJOY THE SHOW!"

In the world of adult film, virtually any effort can become a smash hit providing it is in focus and properly exposed—connoisseurs of the genre tend to ignore subtleties like editing, directing, and plot. However, in 1985, TitPlex Distribution released a catalog of adult films so uninteresting that even *HUSTLER* failed to give them good reviews.

TitPlex Ditribution Catalog of Films in Production
1985–1986 Season

Dear Theatre Manager,

This year, TitPlex is proud to present another fine lineup of the highest quality adult films. These movies are good because they feature very few obese women and one man with an oddly-shaped member. We hope you will consider using TitPlex for all your adult film needs.

Sincerely,

Frank Delgado
Promotions Manager

7001: A SEX ODYSSEY (75 mins.) RELEASE DATE: DECEMBER 1, 1985 The long-awaited sequel to last year's *2001: A Sex Odyssey,* this film takes sex to its extremes in an Earth 5000 years in the future. As DW@#3, Oriental sex sensation Harry Wang takes a far-out "Intercourse Capsule" and masturbates for over an hour while thinking about his hydroponic garden.

THE PRESIDENT IS CUMMING! (77 mins.) RELEASE DATE: JANUARY 14, 1986 Hot sex in the Oval Office as the Chief Sexecutive "discusses" the farm subsidy question with his First Lady. Stars Rock Groop as President Jack Hoff and Kristal Chandelier as the erstwhile Undersecretary of Internal Affairs.

JAMES BONE in SEXOPUSSY (81 mins.) RELEASE DATE: MARCH 1, 1986 The world's hottest secret agent returns to the screen in this sequel to *From Pussia with Lust* and *Thunderballs.* As per the title, Bone has sex six times in this film. Stars Gino Zrestaurant as Bone (#069) and Porsche Carr as some woman.

ORDINARY PEOPLE HAVING SEX (75 mins.) RELEASE DATE: APRIL 11, 1986 Guaranteed to capture the movie-buff audience, this film capitalizes on the success of 1980's award-winning *Ordinary People.* Isn't everyone tired of seeing sexy nurses, handsome studs, and wealthy jet-setters in the sack? Here, your audience will enjoy the sexcapades of out-of-work coal miners, two-bit floozy cocktail waitresses, and overweight real estate agents—definitely a switch from the adult films of yesteryear! Stars Miles O'Penis as Mr. Smith and Cherri Flavoring as Ms. Jones.

AUTOBIOGRAPHY OF A TIT (68 mins.) RELEASE DATE: MAY 12, 1986 See one of the hottest women in porn from a tit's-eye view! Sexsational Ginger Bread goes through her daily routine: sleeping, eating, and humping . . . and you are there, attached to her chest! Optional bras will be distributed to theatres wishing for a more realistic effect. Stars Nick Dwhileshaving as himself.

THE RETURN OF KING DONG (89 mins.) RELEASE DATE: JUNE 3, 1986 What does the man with the longest penis in the world do for fun? Find out in this sex-tacular sequel to 1983's *King Dong* starring Mark Down as Chuck Dupp, the stud with the remarkable 94-inch wang. In this film, Dupp struggles to find a comfortable pair of underwear, pops an embarrassing boner in church, and attempts to find a woman who will even look at his huge, deformed schlong. Cited as 1986's Best Film by the National Association of Men with Short Penises.

Don't forget these previously released TitPlex films available for theatrical exhibition:

Magnum P. Niss	Puzzi's Honor
The Cockford Files	Ball the President's Men
Phallus's Restaurant	One Flew Over the Cuckoo's
Star Whores	Breast
The Empire Strikes Butt	Hairport '75
Dong with the Wind	Breast Side Story
Bone Wolf McQuaid	Bend-Hur
The Last Adult Picture Show	Zorba the Greek
The Dong Goodbye	

TAKING THE STAND: Adam Simon, Hollywood film producer

Sen. Mohasset: You have *no* idea who wrote this *Producer's Handbook,* Mr. Simon?

Mr. Simon: Hey, I told you—I got a copy from Menachem Golan and—

Sen. Mohasset: Yes, Mr. Simon, we know. Mr. Golan got it from Mr. Globus, Mr. Globus got it from Albert Broccoli, Mr. Broccoli got it from Mr. Evans . . . and Mr. Evans claims to have gotten his copy from you.

Mr. Simon: Senator, I've brought along a few friends who'd like to testify that I'm innocent. (flashes wad of cash)

Sen. Mohasset: Mr. Simon, do you really think I can be bribed?

Mr. Simon: My friends Mr. Jackson and Mr. Lincoln seem to think so.

Sen. Mohasset: Mr. Simon, I'm citing you for contempt. I have never seen such a . . . Mr. Simon? Mr. Simon? Will you please stop licking my feet?

Mr. Simon: Anything you say, sir.

HOLLYWOOD PRODUCER'S HANDBOOK

Congratulations, Mr. Producer! If you're reading this book, you must be one of the select few millionaires who has a cellular car phone, a Los Angeles address, and a desire to break into the big-time world of movie producing! But listen: Tell your secretary to hold all calls for a while, and read through the *Handbook.* It just might answer some of your questions.

I WANT TO BE A PRODUCER. FIRST OFF, WHAT ARE MY CHANCES?
- It's a very big world.
- There are a lot of people who would like to do the same thing you want to do.
- It often takes years and years to work into the movie business.
- You have to be willing to pay your dues.

VERY WELL THEN, BUT REALISTICALLY, HOW ARE MY CHANCES?
- Good. All it takes is money.

SUPER. NOW, WHAT DO I NEED FIRST? A DIRECTOR?
Not yet. The first thing you will need is contacts. The following are good places to meet contacts:
- Any restaurant that does not serve fries with anything. If they serve raw potato strips shaped like fries, that is best.
- Any clothing store you have to make an appointment for, but not the ones that make you sit in hydraulic chairs.
- Alcoholics Anonymous.
- Betty Ford Clinic.
- BMW body shop. Plus, you have to go there anyway.
- Any health club with more saunas than weight machines, and the people in the pool lounging around the sides instead of swimming.
- Traffic court.
- Juvenile court.

AND HOW WILL I RECOGNIZE THESE CONTACTS?
- Easy. The ones who say "Hi, I'm Marty Orwin, Julius' cousin," when they meet you, those are the ones.

WHY? WHO IS JULIUS ORWIN?
- Well, nobody. That was a bad example.
- The proper thing to say, in any case, is "Yeah? Hey, I know a lot of people who've worked with him."

WHAT IF HE ASKS ME FOR NAMES?
Make them up.
- He won't care. Most fictitious people in LA are better off than he is anyway.
- He won't know the difference. If he knew anybody besides Julius Orwin, he'd be a producer himself.
- Say the names fast. He will be trying to memorize them to use later, and this will put him on the defensive.

GREAT. THEN I MUST NEED A SCREENPLAY. HEY, WHAT KIND OF SCREENPLAY SHOULD I LOOK FOR FOR THE FIRST FILM?
A bad one. As bad as possible. For the following reasons:
- You won't be able to recognize a good one, so by intentionally getting a bad one at least you'll avoid looking like an idiot. That should be saved for later.
- Bad films can be toyed with for ages without ever being produced. This is good because you don't have a clue about producing.
- Most bad screenwriters are famous anyway, and if you work with several of them you will be able to get a better one once you decide to actually make a film. No one is sure exactly why this is.

OKAY. SO WHAT IS THE BEST TYPE OF FILM FOR MY FIRST PRODUCTION? I'D LOVE TO DO ONE ABOUT CARROT FARMERS.
Wrong.

- The best films to do are sequels, because they require virtually no casting, originality, or promotion. Also, if you're lucky, some of the props will still be around.
- However, the promotion company that did the original will probably get to do the sequel.
- You will have to settle for a rip-off, which has all the same advantages anyway, pretty much. Also, it's easy to get cannon-fodder directors for one. Simply take a movie that did well last year, and try to do it yourself. You will easily bungle enough things to avoid plagiarism suits.

HEY, FINALLY WE'RE GETTING SOMEWHERE. NOW WHAT EXACTLY SHOULD I LOOK FOR IN A DIRECTOR?

- Number of times he can say "Yes, sir" in the space of one minute.
- Aptitude at vigorous up-and-down nodding.
- Shorter, balder, or uglier than yourself.

HMM. AND WHAT ABOUT ACTORS? I'LL NEED ACTORS, RIGHT? WHAT'S THE BEST WAY TO SIZE ONE UP?

- Visit his place of work. And while you're there, pay close attention to how well he knows the menu, how quickly he brings you your food, and how gracefully he clears your table.
- As far as actresses, this formula should help: size of bust $-$ IQ > 0 (have your secretary help you with this difficult math if necessary).

OKAY, I'M READY TO GO. BUT WAIT, I DON'T KNOW JACK-SHIT ABOUT MOVIES OR MOVIE MAKING. HOW CAN I CONVINCE THE DIRECTOR AND CREW THAT I KNOW WHAT I'M DOING?

- Tell the director he should hire the best "gaffer" and "key grip" money can buy. During production, always inquire about the "gaffer" and "key grip." Just use these words a lot, and you will be fine, because the director will be too embarrassed to admit that he doesn't know what they mean. Make sure somebody does know, however, because they actually are important.
- While viewing rushes, always describe shots of landscape and inanimate objects as "sexy." Refer to actresses as "handsome." Flying saucers and big hairy monsters are "SFX." At a loss for words in conversation with your director? Just say, "I'm not even going to touch the mise-en-scène. That's your baby."

GOT IT. I GUESS I'M ALL SET. OH, HEY, HOW CAN I TELL IF MY FILM IS A SUCCESS?

- Profits.

YES, BUT HOW CAN I TELL IF MY FILM IS A CRITICAL SUCCESS?
Have your secretary monitor the media for these telltale signs:

- Rex Reed explodes with enthusiasm for it.
- Rex Reed's enthusiasm explosion burst radius is greater than ten feet.
- Jeffery Lyons and Michael Medved engage in a slap fight while arguing about it.
- Profits.
- Roger Ebert vows to fast until the whole nation has seen your movie.
- Roger Ebert actually does fast for more than five minutes.
- The Catholic Church sends nuns to picket your premieres.

NUNS PICKETING? THAT SOUNDS LIKE GREAT PUBLICITY! HOW CAN I MAKE SURE MY MOVIE IS CONTROVERSIAL ENOUGH TO STIR UP THIS KIND OF FREE ADVERTISING?

- Make sure it contains a scene in which Jesus Christ gets an erection.
- Depict ethnic characters as anything other than ordinary white people.
- Take any political stance at all.

GIMMICK MOVIES

The Hollywood practice of promoting movies with gimmicks, giveaways, and contests is a tradition as old as such classic films as *Clue* and *Tom Bosley's Million-Dollar Giveaway*. Quite naturally, then, the idea of altering classic movies to make them into contests with great prizes seemed like a highly marketable idea to the young executives at Cinetron, Inc., a fledgling film distributing firm. Unfortunately, the firm's first and only attempts proved less than profitable.

COOL HAND LUKE

"What would you like sir? Raisinets? Hot buttered popcorn? A box of fifty hard-boiled eggs?" On *Cool Hand Luke*'s opening day, film buffs and fat guys alike packed the house to see if they could beat Luke's record of eating fifty hard-boiled eggs in one hour. Enthusiasm died out when contestants learned that there was no prize for winning. To further complicate matters, viewers who hadn't finished all their eggs before the final credits were forced to spend the night in a three-by-three-foot concrete box. The sight of a leg-ironed audience chain gang leaving the first screening was enough to drive away any other interested ticket buyers and proved the final blow to this re-release.

CITIZEN KANE

Orson Welles' classic film biography of William Randolph Hearst was re-released intact and unaltered—except for the final crucial scene, in which the mystery of "Rosebud" is finally solved. In place of the scene was a short segment in which actor Tom Bosley encouraged viewers to guess what "Rosebud" means, write it on an entry form, and drop it into the "Rosebud??" contest box in the theater lobby. Unfortunately, the gimmick proved to be more of a lottery than a contest, since well over five million people already knew that "Rosebud" was the name of the snow sled Hearst owned when he was a boy. Furthermore, the answer to the contest was inadvertently given away by Bosley in his segment, as he promised all winners would receive an official "Rosebud" re-issue sled for guessing the right answer.

THE BIG CHILL

A favorite with the baby boomer crowd, *The Big Chill* promised great profits if re-released with a gimmick for the fad-crazy yuppie generation. Capitalizing on the popularity of "Trivial Pursuit," the movie was re-released with prizes offered for those viewers who could quote the most trivial, self-serving lines. Viewers of a certain age group competed verbally, with points scored for the ability to express earnestly and with great sincerity those lines that "really spoke" for them. The contestant who won the contest was then given the satisfaction of knowing that his friends are there for him as well as the right to rent the videocassette as many times as he wanted.

PLANET OF THE APES

In its first run, *Planet of the Apes* thrilled audiences with the idea of an Earth taken over by apelike creatures. In order to re-create this exciting atmosphere, the re-release offered a movie theater wholly operated by real chimps. Though all ran smoothly at first, audience members soon complained that the monkeys operating the concession stand had eaten all the popcorn, that the entire second reel was shown upside down, and that the wild hoots emanating from the projection booth throughout the screening distracted from the movie as a whole. Additional complaints from the ASPCA regarding unsatisfactory working conditions hastened the cancellation of this re-release.

ANIMAL HOUSE

Viewers were encouraged to pay special attention to the initiation rites of the Delta fraternity. If, after the film, they could answer three questions about Delta traditions and chug a beer in the lobby, they were immediately inducted into a special nationwide chapter of the fraternity. For a full week in 1984, city governments across America reported inexplicable outbreaks of drunk driving, malicious vandalism, horse shootings, and indecent exposure. National beer consumption rose by almost one-third. Universal Pictures withdrew their re-release of *Animal House* after the Los Angeles Summer Olympics had to cancel the swimming competition due to the inexplicable presence of three truckloads of Fizzies in the pool.

NORTH BY NORTHWEST

More a "viewer participation" gimmick than a contest, the re-released version of the Hitchcock classic featured promotional literature that encouraged viewers to re-create the film in their own lives, by having sexual encounters on moving trains, battling evil crop-dusters, and scrambling down the face of Mt. Rushmore. After complaints from the North Dakota State Parks Commission, five different farmers in Iowa, and Amtrak rail service, the movie was withdrawn.

Failed Movie Gimmicks

After the "Gimmick Movies" craze faded, many theaters decided to move 180 degrees away from this kind of chintzy marketing. They subsequently introduced "Movie Gimmicks."

4-D

This system was advertised as the next step beyond 3-D movies, and for a while in the early fifties curious people flocked to see 4-D films such as *Invasion of the Invading Invaders* and *Yucky Blob Thing*. However, the added dimension, as viewing guides pointed out, was merely "time, often considered the fourth dimension."

1-D

Technology backpedaled in an effort to come up with a new gimmick, and the movie *Between Two Points* was released in 1956. But a line of light proved interesting to no one, even when viewed through the special light-blocking glasses.

CHROMOVISION

When the master print for the black and white film *Martians From Venus* accidentally fell into a bucket of red paint in 1953, an explanation had to be found quickly. "Chromovision" was the ill-fated answer.

X-RAYVISION

In 1972, a hard-of-hearing studio executive misunderstood when he heard that "X-rated" films were doing well. *The Living Skeletons Go To The Dinosaur Museum* was quickly released, but negative public reaction and bad publicity over the radiation poisoning of the actors led to the technique's demise.

EASY-EYES CINEMA

Reasoning that elderly viewers would appreciate a movie equivalent of large-print books, Columbia issued a re-release of *It Happened One Night* in 1975 in Easy-Eyes. The film was shown at the rate of one frame per second, and the sound was slowed down accordingly. The project was scrapped after one showing when 100 senior citizens' heart and respiration rates began slowing dangerously in an attempt to compensate.

SMELLORAMA

Not a scratch 'n' sniff gimmick, but a highly realistic odor simulating technique, Smellorama absolutely convinced viewers that they were smelling what was shown on the screen. Film producers later admitted that they shouldn't have introduced Smellorama during the premiere of *The Killing Fields*.

VIEW-O-RAMA

"Movies the way they were meant to be seen," was the slogan, and the gimmick was actually very simple. View-O-Rama theaters were clean and tidy. The inside temperature was neither too hot nor too cold. Soft drinks and popcorn sold for the same low prices they do outside the theater. Noisy and unruly viewers were ejected from the cinema by alert ushers. Scratched reels were replaced with brand new ones on a regular basis. Actually, this was just a dream I had once.

REAL 3-D

Realizing that polarized glasses and other gimmicks were no more than a nuisance, a group of filmmakers got together in 1953 to develop a *real* 3-D viewing process. Instead of a flat screen, the action was carried out on a stage with actual props, with live actors acting the parts. They called it "Broadway" and launched it in New York City. Discerning movie-goers quickly rejected it, but it survives to this day— although its only fans are first-time tourists to the city who are duped into attending shows.

ELVIS-O-RAMA

The "Elvis" in the title had nothing to do with the deceased rock and roll singer, but thousands of fans flocked to theaters advertising Elvis-O-Rama anyway. Curiously, none were disappointed to find that the name referred to the projectionist's favorite singer. As one movie-goer explained, "I know if Elvis were alive today, he might come to this theater to investigate, and I might bump into him, and we might become good friends and I could visit him at Graceland and eat a lot."

BRIAN DEPALMA-O-RAMA

Some claimed to enjoy seeing hours and hours of masterful suspense and horror films all at once. Others wondered what Hitchcock himself would think if he knew his films had been colorized and strung together.

Sen. Mohasset: I now call to the stand the original director of the famous "James Bond" films. Sir, would you please state your name for the committee?

Broccoli: The name is Broccoli— "Cubby" Broccoli.

Sen. Beaufort: What the hell kind of name is that, boy?

Sen. Mohasset: Order, please! Now, Mr. Broccoli, you are charged with perversion of an author's work in the first degree. How do you plead?

Broccoli: Er, ahm . . .

Sen. Mohasset: Mr. Broccoli, I must warn you that I saw *Moonraker*.

Broccoli: Guilty as charged, sir.

LIVE AND LET DIET: THE REJECTED BOND

In the original screenplay for this James Bond film, a scene was included that followed the Ian Fleming story line closely, but it was never successfully shot because the director simply could not find a stunt man who was willing to risk the daring feat called for by the script. At least that was the initial explanation given to Mr. Fleming.

THE CUT SCENE

(Bond is held captive in the secret lair of the Evil Genius and his army of megalomaniacal henchmen. He is tied to a chair and is being interrogated by the leader, a warped dietician)

EVIL GENIUS: So, a secret service agent. And your name is?

BOND: Bond, James Bond.

EG: Mr. Bond! Agent 007, I presume.

BOND: Martini dry--Shaken, not stirred.

EG: Care for a drink before you die?

BOND: I did it for Queen and Country.

EG: Enough of this small talk. I have a loaded gun in my pocket and an army of 100 surrounding you, fitted with grenades, knives, and fisticuffs. However, execution by such ordinary means is entirely too mundane for an agent of your stature, Mr. Bond. Therefore, I have devised a most fiendish method to dispose of you. A slow, excruciating, yet visually involving process.

BOND: Okay.

EG: (Beckoning henchmen, who enter with equipment) Werner! Rolf! Come here, *schnell*.

(One sets up a card table upon which the other places a tray of fried eggs and bacon)

BOND: (Looking down) Whaa?

EG: You are to eat the high-cholesterol meals we serve you, cleaning the plate, until you die by hardening of the arteries.

BOND: You're kidding, right?

EG: EAT! NOW!

BOND: Do I at least get a napkin?

EG: Rolf! The napkin!

(Rolf drapes a napkin around Bond's collar).

BOND: Well, here goes.

—CUT—

(A STUNT MAN is now brought in to replace Sean Connery [Bond]. A special effects trick
is now utilized as the camera is angled to give a profile shot of the stunt man Bond
''eating'' the dangerous, cholesterol-laden food. In actuality, he is only affect-
ing the *illusion* of consumption by moving the fork behind his left cheek (remember--
we are dealing with a right-profile shot) and letting the morsels fall into a concealed bin in the studio floor. He is a trained professional, so none of the fried food
actually enters his mouth, while a nerve-shattering simulation is created.) The
scene continues:

<u>BOND:</u> (Voice of Sean Connery, dubbed over): GOBBLE GOBBLE
GOBBLE CTHUNK!!! (Spits chunk of food in EG's eyes, blinding
him)

<u>EG:</u> Ow! Guards--seize him!

(The guards circle Bond, but he ducks so they punch each other in the nose.)

<u>100 GUARDS:</u> (In unison) Ow!

<u>BOND:</u> (crawling through their legs and running away) So sorry
to eat and run, old chaps!

                 —CUT—

**Mr. Ian Fleming, who maintained a keen interest in proper nutritional habits, found this vignette to be
the most exciting of his novel, but eventually consented to have it removed from the film because of fears
that too many young people would attempt to imitate the stunt man unsupervised at home.**

TAKING THE STAND: Walter Matthau

Sen. Stone: . . . so what you are saying, Mr. Matthau, is that you fought the release of these films because you objected to being repeatedly typecast as a "grouchy middle-aged man whose sole and constant attire is a pair of wrinkled boxer shorts and a cigar." Is that correct?

Mr. Matthau: Yeah, that's right. The image is totally wrong for me.

Sen. Stone: But Mr. Matthau, that's exactly what you're wearing right now.

Mr. Matthau: Yeah, well . . . I'm not at work right now, am I, Mr. "Snappy Dress-Suit."

FRONTIER: SPACE

This action-adventure sci-fi drama told the story of Trevor Starlight, a swashbuckling bounty-hunter of the future, who becomes stranded on a hostile asteroid and is forced to carve a home for himself out of the perilous black rock.

THE TREASURE OF EL SINISTRE

Adventurer Jack Buck leaves his comfortable university position to search for a legendary mountain of gold in the jungles of the Amazon. Tangles with cannibals, giant snakes, and a long-lost love made this a thrill-a-minute action/adventure epic.

L'HOMME NATURAL

A French-produced existentialist drama, this film explored man's inner need to live in his most natural state. Matthau starred as Henri LeConte, a brilliant yet misunderstood poet, who set out on a perilous journey into his own tumultuous soul.

SORORITY SLASHER

A violent maniac killed thirteen years ago returns from the grave to terrorize the sorority sisters that once snubbed him. Screams, mayhem, and a large chainsaw make this a horrifying race with death as the masked monster of sorority row stalks his helpless prey.

Sen. Mohasset: Mr. Pektar, you've been involved with each of the *Friday the 13th* films, is that correct?

Pektar: (consults with his lawyer) In a writing capacity, yes.

Sen. Mohasset: Mr. Pektar, you've been charged with crimes against credibility. Do you know why?

Pektar: (consults with his lawyer) Um . . . no.

Sen. Mohasset: At the end of each *Friday the 13th* movie, Mr. Pektar, the murderer "Jason" dies—and then miraculously returns to life in time for the next sequel.

Pektar: (consults with his lawyer) Senator, I object to your using the term "miracle." Each of Jason's departures from and returns to the realm of the living are logical and plausible. To prove that we plan these things out, I'd like to submit this set of premises for some of the upcoming *Friday the 13th* movies.

Sen. Mohasset: And how many more of these sequels will there be?

Pektar: At least . . . (consults with his lawyer) . . . sixteen.

Sen. Mohasset: Oh, good Lord.

FRIDAY the 13th SEQUEL SYNOPSES

FRIDAY THE 13th PART VII

Two counselors at Camp Crystal Lake are haunted by memories of Jason's previous carnage. They decide to dig up his body "just to make sure he's dead." They take his pulse "just to make sure he's dead." They feed his corpse a barium shake and hook it up to Dr. Nofziger's Tissue Rejuvenating Machine "just to make sure he can't be brought back to life." Satisfied that Jason is actually dead, the counselors hurry back to their cabins, eager to get home before the lightning storm starts.

FRIDAY THE 13th PART VIII

Crystal Lake is quiet; Jason has been dead for almost two years. In the dead of night, a zombie falls off of a rum delivery truck. He stumbles upon Jason's shallow grave, and gives him the kiss of death—the Living Death. Because he is now a zombie, Jason's killing is more methodical than impassioned, but effective nonetheless.

FRIDAY THE 13th PART IX

To assure a worried nation that the zombie Jason is actually dead, Dick Clark agrees to air Jason's grisly remains on a telecast of "American Bandstand." Just by brushing up against "America's Oldest Teenager," Jason comes back to life, even younger than he was when he last died. Younger, stronger, and more able to kill with a frightening lack of discrimination in his choice of victims.

FRIDAY THE 13th PART X

A corrupt Army general tries to trade Jason's remains for the bodies of Vietnam MIAs. Due to a postal error, Jason's body ends up in Tibet, where the Dalai Lama brings him back to life. After months of meditation with the holy man, Jason sees the error of his ways, and agrees to wander the globe, spreading the word of peace and self-restraint—starting at Camp Crystal Lake. When he gets there, the campers taunt him unmercifully, and—like Billy Jack—Jason has no choice but to kill repeatedly and kill repeatedly again.

FRIDAY THE 13th PART XI

At the end of the last film, Jason was buried in a plot of ground which just happens to be a three-by-six entrance to an alternate universe—a universe identical to ours, except for one detail: In this universe, Jason is alive and kicking and killing. Halfway through the movie, the campers at Camp Ekal Latsyrc succeed in killing Jason. They bury him in the same plot of earth, and he emerges once again on our side, killing and killing and killing.

FRIDAY THE 13th PART XII

Dead once again, Jason is sued for damages by the family members of his victims. Defending Jason is notorious trial lawyer F. Lee Bailey, who wins the case, granting Jason $4.7 million and the right to live again. Jason uses his newly acquired wealth to implement a massive, businesslike killing spree. Eventually, Jason's case is overturned by the surviving members of the Supreme Court.

FRIDAY THE 13th PART XIII

Jesus Christ finally returns to earth, mistakes Jason for a latter-day Lazarus, and brings him back to life. At the end of the movie Jesus fights Jason, but they are both arrested by a squad of redneck policemen and nailed to crosses to die. By mistake, God brings Jason back to life, leaving Jesus to die like a common thief. When Jason kills a busload of Catholic campers, God realizes the error of His ways and uses a discreet pestilence to kill Jason.

FRIDAY THE 13th PART XIV

A trio of renegade filmmakers make a 3-D movie about Jason, a movie so lifelike that Jason jumps off the screen and murders moviegoers everywhere. A ragtag band of Crytal Lake campers finally realize that if they take their 3-D glasses off, Jason becomes two-dimensional. But rather than solving the problem, this creates an even more significant threat: when viewed from the right or left side, the two-dimensional Jason is so thin that he's invisible. By walking sideways, Jason can slice through humans like piano wire through butter. Eventually, a strong breeze hits Jason, and he folds up like an accordion.

FRIDAY THE 13th PART XV

A hack Hollywood screenwriter falls asleep while writing a *Friday the 13th* script. Suddenly, Jason is alive again, killing. Just when Jason is about to kill the pretty camp counselor, the writer wakes up.

"Whew!" he says. "It was just a dream." Then Jason jumps in the window and cuts off his head and eats it.

TAKING THE STAND: Joseph Greene, producer of *Tell The World We're Crazy.*

Sen. Mohasset: Mr. Greene, I don't recall seeing a movie called *Tell The World We're Crazy.* Was it ever released?

Mr. Greene: Yes it was. I had such big hopes for it. Remember *It's a Mad, Mad, Mad, Mad World?* Well, my movie was going to be just like that. An all-star comedy smash, featuring every comedian who'd ever been in the business.

Sen. Mohasset: What happened?

Mr. Greene: It was released in theaters, but very few people saw the actual movie. We had packed houses, but most of the audience left after the first hour of opening credits. And then to make matters worse, a woman in Akron, Ohio, was crushed and killed by a fallen theater marquee, which collapsed due to the tremendous weight of the movie's billing announcement.

Sen. Mohasset: Excuse me, Mr. Greene, but I've just checked my notes, and I can't seem to find any reason for you to be at these hearings.

Mr. Greene: I sort of came on my own. I just want to encourage people to rent *Tell The World* on videocassette—

Sen. Mohasset: Mr. Greene, please remove yourself from—

Mr. Greene: So all you people out there . . . check your video rental stores. This week only, all thirty-six cassettes rent for the price of two . . .

TAKING THE STAND: Milt Kondar, talent agent with the William Morris Agency

Sen. Fawcett: Mr. Kondar, your dossier says that you specialize in handling clients who previously have had no experience in movies.

Mr. Kondar: That's right, Pam. Like I always say . . . no matter how many Olympic medals you've won, no matter how many Emmy awards you have at home, no matter how huge your audience at Vegas, you're essentially a nobody until you've appeared in a genuine Hollywood movie.

Sen. Fawcett: Mr. Kondar, have you ever considered that maybe athletes, TV personalities and stand-up comedians should be satisfied with success in their own mediums?

Mr. Kondar: No, Pam. Look at you. Successful senator, famous feminist, featured on the cover of over five magazines in the past two years . . . but still you're a nobody.

Sen. Fawcett: Mr. Kondar, I assure you—

Mr. Kondar: Listen, Pam, let me make a package deal for you. We'll get you in a movie. You've got great legs, all right tits, a flair for melodrama. . . . I got writers who could come up with the perfect vehicle for you. How do you feel about nude scenes?

Failed Showcase Movies

Tumbleweed with Mary Lou Retton   Mary Lou plays a perky young girl in the Old West who just happens to smile a lot and practice gymnastic routines. When word comes that the mine payroll has been robbed, Mary Lou performs an hour-long series of backflips, handsprings, and cartwheels to reach the pass before the bandits do. She impresses them with her pertness and sunny grin, and they decide to swear off crime.

Prime Cut with Clara Peller   Reprising her popular character of the woman who yelled, "Where's the beef?" Ms. Peller plays a feisty meat-packing plant inspector. On her first inspection of the day, she finds no beef at the plant, and utters her plaintive cry to all who will listen for the next hour and fifteen minutes.

Alphabet Soup with Vanna White   Vanna plays Annie Sullivan in this modern-day Helen Keller story. When Helen realizes one day that words correspond to objects, she runs around in glee touching everything in sight, as Vanna turns over the letters describing each object.

The Black Hole in One with Jack Nicklaus   Nicklaus plays Joe Conway, an ordinary guy who is kidnapped by space aliens and taken to another galaxy where he is challenged to a game of Blugblug, which is very similar to golf except that the balls are pink. With the score tied going into the seventeenth hole, Conway slices into the rough but recovers with a brilliant second shot and a thirty-foot putt for par. Later he wins the game. Alan Alda plays the Alien leader.

Giant Steps with Neil Armstrong   Armstrong plays a sixteenth-century Spanish explorer who lands on a great many islands in the New World and makes weighty pronouncements about the importance of each new landing.

MYTHICAL LINES OF FAMOUS MOVIES

CASABLANCA

"Play it again, Sam"—a famous cliché from the classic film *Casablanca*. But, as aficionados of the film know, that exact line is not in the film at all. Careful viewing of other famous movies by Mediagate investigative committees reveals that many classic lines have been garbled in the public consciousness.

DIRTY HARRY

Clint Eastwood never actually said, "Go ahead, make my day." All he said when confronting the criminal was "Good day."

STAR WARS

The widely quoted "May the Force be with you" is a romanticized version of Obi-wan Kenobi's threat to Luke, "I may be forced to beat you, whippersnapper."

LOVE STORY

Ryan O'Neal actually does not deliver the saccharine line "Love means never having to say you're sorry." But Ali McGraw does, so it amounts to the same thing.

APOCALYPSE NOW

Who can forget the chilling image of Colonel Kurtz (Marlon Brando) whispering, "The horror ... the horror." Only those who were on the set know that Brando was actually chanting, "The hunger ... the hunger." The subsequent scene in which he consumes three slaughtered oxes, a hogshead of dark ale, thirteen pheasants, twenty-three pounds of sweet sausage, and a bucket of treacle was left on the cutting room floor, as Mr. Brando didn't want his home movies released to the public.

COOL HAND LUKE

"What we have here is a failure to communicate," says prison warden Strother Martin—in the later, re-edited version of *Cool Hand Luke*. In the original version, the warden's IBM computer modems the message to Luke (Paul Newman) in binary machine language. Luke only has a crappy Amiga computer, so he spends a night in the box.

CITIZEN KANE

"Rosebud." The publishing tycoon's last word is a mystery. Who, or what, is "Rosebud?" Why was this the last word Kane spoke? How will the pieces fit together. For American viewers, the mystery is a thrilling one, but in all foreign versions of the movie, translators changed the phrase "Rosebud" to "snow sled Mr. Kane had as a young boy." The French claim to adore the movie nonetheless.

BOND MOVIES

Few people know that James Bond speaks his signature introduction ("Bond ... James Bond") in only one of the many 007 movies. A sampling of Bond's actual introductions:

- "James Bond—but you can call me 'Jimbo'" (*Dr. No*)
- "Hi there!" (*Live And Let Die*)
- "No, *James* Bond. James. Jesus. J ... A ... M ... E ..." (*Goldfinger*)
- "Bond ... James Bond. But please call me 'Cathy.' Just for tonight." (*Octopussy*—Roger Moore's personal favorite)
- "Bond? James Bond? No, he's not home right now. May I ask who's calling?" (*Sorry, Wrong Number*)

NETWORK

"I'm mad as hell, and I'm not going to take it anymore!" became the nation's rallying cry for two or three glorious days after the release of this black comedy. But Howard Beale's tirade also included the phrases, "Turn off your TV sets! Stop watching! Leave the theater! Don't watch this movie!" Viewers who actually stayed through the whole movie usually claim that they never heard this part.

THE WIZARD OF OZ

"I don't think we're in Kansas anymore" is not a line of the movie. Rather, Dorothy merely says, "Play it again, Sam."

TAKING THE STAND: Alison Cook, Hollywood archivist

Sen. Stone: Ms. Cook, before this hearing I myself wasn't aware that the filmmaking establishment maintained a permanent archive. Could you tell us about it?

Ms. Cook: Sure. All the studios donate prints of their films, along with scripts, treatments, memos, and secret reports about movies that failed. This insures that Hollywood's mistakes and embarrassments are never lost.

Sen. Stone: And where is this material stored?

Ms. Cook: All of it is stored in an abandoned salt mine underneath the Rocky Mountains—in the same way government documents are stored under the Appalachians.

Sen. Stone: So if a nuclear war ever destroys the United States, all we'll be left with is government paperwork and Hollywood embarrassments?

Ms. Cook: Yes. It's a sort of double failsafe to insure that Ronald Reagan is never forgotten. Hahaha! Eh-heh. Um . . . anyway, here's the document you requested from our files.

Rejected Titles of Movies

FINAL TITLE	ORIGINAL TITLE	WHY CHANGED
Psycho	Norman's Mother Is Actually A Mummified Corpse in the Cellar	Gave away surprise
Porky's	Gone With the Wind	Legal Trouble
E.T.	Fuck	Could not get PG rating
Jaws II	Jaws III	Miscount
Reds	Rods	Spelling error
Raiders of the Lost Ark	Action/Adventure	Too vague
Rocky	The Sixth Sick Sheik's Sixth Sheep's Sick	Too hard to pronounce
Casablanca	Casablanca in Living Color	Possibly misleading
Nightmare on Elm Street	Nightmare on Pinehurst Drive	Change of address during filming
The Killing Fields	The Dying Fields	Too morbid
King Kong	Prince Kong	Gorilla's father died during filming
It's a Mad, Mad, Mad, Mad World	It's a Mad, Mad, Mad World	Too short

Every fall, a small studio called 4U Films announces at least five new productions, but the films are almost never completed. Why not? 4U's productions are tailor-made for certain actors, and for some reason these very actors repeatedly refuse the roles. Walter Matthau, the spokesman for "Actors Against 4U Films," could not be reached for comment, as he was busy on location filming *Bachelors, Boxers, and Beer*.

4U Films announces four new films, now entering preproduction.

UP
ALL
NIGHT

4U Films:
"Give The People
What They Expect."

Starring: HARRY DEAN STANTON
TOM CONTI
DUSTIN HOFFMAN

HAPPY FAT GUYS!

Starring:

NED BEATTY as Happy Fat Guy #1

DOM DELUISE as Happy Fat Guy #2

GEORGE WENDT as Happy Fat Guy #3

MARLON BRANDO as Sourpuss

with special guest appearance by

SAMMY DAVIS JR as The Happy Thin Guy

THE INDIGNANT ONES

Starring:

DEFORREST KELLY as the Simple Country Doctor

CRAIG T. NELSON as the Man Whose Home Was Built on an Indian Graveyard

GEORGE C. SCOTT as the Uncorruptible General

AL PACINO as the Crusading Lawyer

GENE HACKMAN as the Hardened New York Detective

SIDNEY POITIER as MR. Tibbs

"My God, Man! What have you DONE?"

TAKING THE STAND: Jeffrey Lyons, host of "Sneak Previews"

Sen. Stone: What I am getting at, Mr. Lyons, is, as evidenced by this information sheet, which we have painstakingly compiled on your professional statements, that perhaps you are a little *too* generous with praise for some of the things that you are to examine critically. Perhaps it is because . . . you are paid off to make such statements.

Lyons: Well, that's a very perceptive statement, Senator, and you're absolutely right. I'm paid hand-over-fist to be enthusiastic. Only someone as cunning as you could have seen it. What a fantastic Senator you are, absolutely top-notch! In fact, this whole hearing has been a delightful romp—I give it a ten!

Sen. Stone: On second thought, what's wrong with being a little appreciative every once in a while? I'm sorry, Mr. Lyons, you're free to go. In fact, take my car. No, no, I insist.

Lyons: Oh, well, thank you.

Stone: It's nothing. Nice man, that Lyons. Couldn't we start a collection for him here, let's pass around a hat . . .

The Jeffery Lyons Stat Sheet

The following are statistics compiled by special investigators concerning film critic Jeffery Lyons during calendar year 1986.

- Number of films Lyons rated "on a scale of one to ten": 37
  - Number that scored "10": 11
  - Number that scored "10½": 14
  - Number that scored "11": 12
  - Amount offered Lyons to be a scorer for women's gymnastics at the 1988 Summer Olympics: $300,000

- Number of films Lyons reviewed as "one of the year's top ten": 43
  - Number of idiotic reviews Lyons disowned by calling them "one of the five mistakes I've made in my life": 72
  - Lyons' unadjusted income claim, from IRS records: $25,000
  - Unreported income, from real estate scams alone: $130,000
  - Number of women Lyons tells his wife he kissed before he met her: 3
  - Number of women Lyons actually kissed before he met his wife: 2

- Length of "summer," according to release dates of films reviewed as "one of the best of the summer": April 27–September 23
  - Nearest major city for which this is correct: Quito, Ecuador

- Length of "the Christmas season": September 24–January 19
  - Points from which the wise men could have started and still reached Bethlehem given this much time: Eugene, Oregon; Kamchatka, USSR; Perth, Australia

- Number of films Lyons termed "nonstop" entertainment: 31
  - Average number of times he claims to have laughed, per film: 70
  - Seconds between laughs, given an average 100-minute movie: 86
  - Duration, including stopovers, of a flight from New York to Oklahoma City using a similar definition of "nonstop": 4 days

- Number of films Lyons termed the "best" of their genre: 29
  - Number of genres he identified: 5
  - Turnover rate of the number-one spot: every two months
  - Rank of *Casablanca* by now: 180

- Number of films in which Lyons claimed "the last half hour dragged": 17
  - Number of times his wife said the same the next morning at breakfast: 67

- Number of times Lyons claimed a movie "did the book one better": 12
  - Number of times Lyons claimed it "did it two better": 2
  - "Did it six better": 1
  - Total number better the films did the books: 22

- Number of movies Lyons claimed he "knew were great after five minutes": 20
  - Time he could have saved by leaving then: 32 hours
  - Farthest he could get from New York on aforementioned "nonstop" flight in that time: Erie, PA

- Number of aisle seats that have been wasted because people were "saving them for Jeffery Lyons": 1
  - IQ of the person who did it: 65
  - Broken parts on the chair: 3

Cleared For Takeoff

In the late seventies, the CB craze spurred the success of trucking movies like *Smokey and the Bandit*, *Convoy*, and *C.B.* that might otherwise have found audiences only at truck stops. In 1982, movie makers hoped to capitalize on the similar public fascination with air traffic controllers resulting from the well-publicized national strike. Paramount Pictures paid a reported $250,000 for a screenplay entitled, *Cleared for Takeoff*, originally intended for a series of super-8 home movies popular in air traffic controller lounges. The craze never caught on, however, and Paramount scrapped the script even before shooting began. What follows are three scenes from the film.

SCENE 4: ''Establishing the hero''

OPEN ON BUCK, AT CONTROL DESK IN AIR TRAFFIC CONTROL TOWER. CLOSE-UP, THEN PULL BACK TO SHOW DUSTY BESIDE HIM, NERVOUSLY WATCHING THE RADAR.

                    BUCK
     Roger, 703, you're cleared to land on runway 54. Over.

                    703 (on radio)
     Roger, control. Runway 54. Thanks.

                    BUCK (tipping his Stetson)
     No problem.

                    604 (on radio)
     604 to control, request landing clearance.

                    507 (on radio)
     507 to control, request clearance for takeoff.

                    DUSTY (looking at BUCK, worried)
     Two at once. One landing and one taking off. They could collide, killing
     everyone!

                    BUCK
     (slipping a plug of chewing tobacco into his mouth and hitching up his pants,
       even though he is seated)
        Nah. Heck—I handle this kind of thing every three minutes, eighteen
        hours a day, all year long.

                    604 (on radio)
     604 to control. Request landing clearance—or should I pull up the
     landing gear and try to plow straight into 507 taking off?

                    BUCK
     Negative, 604. Cleared to land on runway Tango Niner.

604 (on radio)
Roger, control.

507 (on radio)
Are we cleared for takeoff, control, or should we just sit here and explode?

BUCK
Ahm, you are cleared for takeoff, 507.

Scene 31: ''The crisis''

SAME SHOT AS SCENE 4

BUCK
Roger, 901. You're clear up to 10,000 feet, straight to Chicago. Have a nice flight.

901 (on radio)
Roger.

DUSTY
Boy, Buck, you sure look bushed.

BUCK (exiting)
Hmm? Nah, I'm fine. Gotta take a crap, though. Back in a second.

DUSTY (looking after BUCK)
But . . . what if something happens? What if some big crisis comes up?
(turns to radar)
Why, the only person between calamity and disaster is ME!

606 (on radio)
606 to control, request clearance for landing.

DUSTY (to himself)
My God! I've got to do something. I've got to warn them.

606 (on radio)
606 to control, repeat, request

clearance for landing. Hey, what's the matter down there, Buck? You taking a crap or something?

DUSTY
(grabbing microphone desperately, but not noticing that it is switched off)
606 roger over Delta Tango Niner. Foxtrot Alpha seven oh one-er. Mayday, mayday. Descend to 9,000 feet. Hard to starboard. Do not land. Repeat: Do not land. There are too many flights. Wind shear factor. The pavement is too dry. Ascend to 2,000 feet. There are hundreds of small children playing jacks on the Tarmac. Oh, God! The carnage will be unbearable! For God's sake, don't try and land!

606 (on radio)
Well, I can see the runways, and there's nothing going on, so I'll just go ahead and put her down on Echo four, just like I have every day for nine years. Continue with your dump, Buck.

DUSTY
NOOOOOO!

BUCK
(coming out of john buckling his belt)
What's up, Dusty?

DUSTY
606 is down! The fire trucks can't reach her in time. The rescue crew is trapped in the wreckage. I can hear a young mother screaming.

BUCK (flipping on radio)
Hey there, 606. Land okay?

606 (on radio)
Yep. No problem, Buck. How'd everything come out up there?

YOUR FILM TREATMENTS

After a boxing movie written by a part-time secretary named Sylvester Stallone became one of the biggest hits of the seventies, many Hollywood studios scrambled to collect treatments and scripts written by other ordinary people. They soon learned why screenwriters are paid to write, and ordinary people paid to work at stupid, boring jobs.

TAKE THIS JOB AND SHOVE IT UP YOUR ASS
by Larry Hall, high school student and part-time supermarket bag-boy

Jeff is a high school student who bags groceries because his tightwad parents won't give him spending money. One day, he gets fired by the supermarket manager for putting the detergent in the same bag with the vegetables, even though the detergent box is tightly sealed and it really doesn't make any difference to the customer. On his way home, he finds a magic van with an airbrush painting of some beautiful naked women on the side. Inside the van, he finds some magic pot—powerful, homegrown stuff that makes him really strong, really cool, and a better driver. He goes back to the supermarket and kills everyone who works there, right before they can collaborate with the carnivorous aliens who've just landed. He kills them too.

"Eliminate aliens, add gason. We've found our Friday the 13th Part 17"

—Scott

INTEGRITY
by Cathy Lee, unemployed film actress and spokesmodel

Integrity follows the tribulations of a super-intelligent actress in the dog-eat-dog world of Hollywood. She's also really pretty. She keeps getting cast in movies, but big fat ugly producers fire her when they find out that she won't do nude scenes. Finally, a handsome producer casts her to play the role of a brilliant and sexy female scientist. He wants her to do a nude scene, but she refuses. For her integrity, she wins an Academy Award.

MARTY—
WE CAN USE THE PLOT, BUT HIRE SOMEONE ELSE TO WRITE THE SCRIPT.
SID

LIFE OF FUTILITY
by Carl Lummings, unemployed

The autobographical story of a poor boy, the son of immigrants, named Carl Lummings. He grows up on the mean and lonely streets of South Side Chicago. He overcomes illness and family strife while working his way through college. He marries and establishes a carpeting business, which is initially profitable, but goes bankrupt when Carl is in his mid-fifties, too old to begin anew. His wife leaves him, and both his teenage daughters fall prey to drug addiction. Finally, alone and holed up in a dingy men's shelter, Carl pins his last hopes on a film treatment he has written, knowing that its success or failure will determine the final course of his heartrending downward slide.

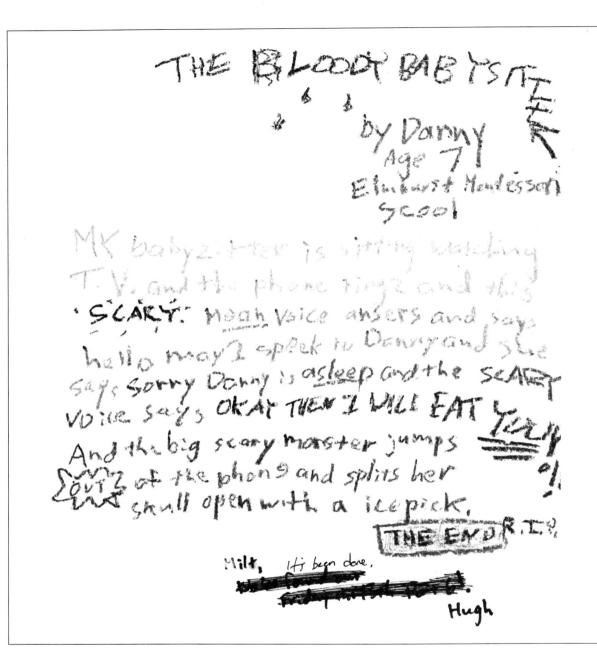

THE BLOODY BABYSITTER

by Danny
Age 7
Elmhurst Montessori Scool

MK babyzitter is sitting watching T.V. and the phone rings and this 'SCARY' meah voice ansers and says hello may I speek tu Danny and she says sorry Danny is asleep and the SCARY voice says OKAY THEN I WILL EAT You! And the big scary monster jumps [OUT] of the phone and splits her skull open with a icepick.

THE END R.I.P.

Milt, It's been done.

Hugh

<u>WILD WEEKEND</u>

by Rick Leslie

Wild Weekend follows a young, inexperienced Hollywood screenwriter as he experiences a very "wild" weekend. Right after he gets off the plane from Oklahoma, a studio executive promises him $20,000 if he can write up a film treatment by Monday morning—and it's already Friday! The screenwriter locks himself in his hotel room, but is repeatedly annoyed by his suite-mate, a man who who wants his name to appear in the treatment. The screenwriter finally appeases the man, Jefferson L. Carter, and gets back to work. At 3:00 in the morning on Sunday night, HIS TYPEWRITER IS STOLEN. HE CAN'T FINISH HIS TREATMENT, BUT THE EXEC PAYS HIM ANYWAY.

TAKING THE STAND: That lovable mutt, Benji.

"Hey, get that dog outta here!"

"Yeesh, sorry."

TAKING THE STAND: Pauline Kael, film critic and author of *5000 Nights at the Movies*

Sen. Stone: Five thousand nights at the movies? You must have some fascinating insights to share, Miss Kael . . . Miss Kael?

Sen. Mohasset: Shhh, don't wake her. She must be exhausted.

TAKING THE STAND: The Man of 1,000 Faces, Lon Chaney.

"Lon Chaney? Isn't he dead?"

"You're right . . ."

"Wow. Spooky."

TAKING THE STAND: Roger Ebert, film critic at large

"Mr. Ebert, would—ach! No, don't sit in the—"

"Is that handyman, Mr. Latavadkian, still around?"

TAKING THE STAND: Larry Storch

Storch: I just want to say I am really pleased and honored to be here. I can't believe you want *me* to testify; I didn't even think anyone remembered who—

Sen. Mohasset: Excuse me, Mr. Storch is it? Uh, there's been a mistake. You're not on our roster. You're not needed to testify. My apologies.

Storch: Oh, I see. I understand. Of course . . . Well, as long as I'm here, I could—

Mohasset: No, really, that's not necessary. Why don't you just go home. Thanks, anyway.

Storch: Er, um, sure. No trouble. I wasn't doing anything anyway.

TAKING THE STAND: Billy Barty, representing the "Little Peoples' Screen Guild"

Sen. Stone: Mr. Barty, would you please take the stand?

Barty: I did.

Stone: Who said that?

Barty: I did.

Stone: Who?

Barty: Down here.

Stone: Oh. Sorry.

TAKING THE STAND: The Brat Pack

Mohasset: Would anyone really mind if we didn't call in these kids?

Senators: No.

TAKING THE STAND: Dom DeLuise

Sen. Stone: Mr. DeLuise, would you please tell—No! Don't sit! Oh, not again!

DeLuise: Eeps, sorry. Hee hee.

Sen. Stone: Why couldn't you be more

like that other guy, James Coco?

DeLuise: You mean dead?

Stone: No, I mean lose some weight.

DeLuise: So do I. How do you think he lost it? Hee hee.

TAKING THE STAND: Godzilla

"Godzilla???!!!??"

"AAAAAAAAAAAUUUGH!!!!!"

TAKING THE STAND: Clint Eastwood

Sen. Stone: Mr. Eastwood, I can't tell you what an honor it is to have you here with us today.

Eastwood: My pleasure.

Stone: Really? Well then, maybe you could do us a small favor?

Eastwood: Yes?

Stone: If you could just . . .

Eastwood: Yes?

Stone: If you could just, you know, say it—just once.

Eastwood: Say it?

Stone: Yes, you know . . .

Eastwood: Yes, I know. Okay. "Go ahead, make my day."

Senators: (applause)

Stone: Thanks so much.

Eastwood: Yeah, sure.

TAKING THE STAND: The Oldest Living Man in Show Business, Mr. George Burns

"Right this way, Mr. Burns. Now, watch your step here, it's—"

"Oh God. Is he . . . ?"

"Well, it had to happen sooner or later. I never thought I'd see it in person, though."

TAKING THE STAND: Star of *Deep Throat,* Linda Lovelace!

Sen. Mohasset: Okay, boys, CLOSED SESSIONS!!!

Sen. Fawcett: Gentlemen! Gentlemen! Please, control yourselves! Gentlemen!

TAKING THE STAND: Mr. Peter O'Toole

"Mr. O'Toole, if you would just take the stand?"

"(hic) Which one? (hic)"
"Mr. O'Toole, there's only one stand there."

"(hic) Oooh, *that* one."

TAKING THE STAND: Shelley Duvall

"God NO!"

"Christ, what were we thinking?"
"Whew, too close, too close."

TAKING THE STAND: Shelley Winters

"Miss Winters, is it true—Good God No! Don't si—"

"When will we learn, gentlemen. When will we learn?"

TAKING THE STAND: Rodney Dangerfield.

"If you would take the stand, Mr. Dangerfield."

"Sure. Where do you want me to take it?"

"Go, Mr. Dangerfield. Now."

"Yeesh, I don't get no—"

"*Now,* Mr. Dangerfield."

Snow White curries the favor of her tiny hosts in this rejected scene from the original motion picture.

Sen. Beaufort: "As a repruhsentuhtive of the nation's largest popcorn growin' region, I throw mah continued support behind the movie industry. If it gits a li'l bit sticky unnerneath the seats, or if things go out of focus jest a bit, well, Ah say, who gives a darn! Sure, laws were broken, an' people were hurt. But mah constituents still stand behind the movie makers. An' so do I."

•

Sen. Stone: "I personally hold ambivalent views concerning the movie business. Naturally, I hold contempt for Stallone, Schwarzenegger, and the rest of the cretinous muscleman set. However, the art does have its masters—Ingmar Bergman and Meryl Streep for example. Oh—and Woody Allen—though of course I don't think much of his early, humorous films."

•

Sen. Fawcett: "So help me, I will never go to another movie again. Cinema is a bastion of exploitation, sexism, and stereotyping. I haven't seen a good movie since that one starring Meryl Streep. You know the one. The serious one, where Meryl plays a strong-willed woman. I can't remember the title off-hand, but you know the one I mean. Now that was a unique movie. They don't make them like that any more."

•

Sen. Mohasset: "Well, it's hard to come to a firm stance on the movie issue. The great cellulite heros are certainly an inspiration to us all. On the other hand, I hardly think that the glitzy, glamorous lives of the stars are a good inspiration for our children. Of course, there are exceptions. Once in a great while, we get a *Rocky* to kindle the spirit of the nation, or a Meryl Streep to bring back a little class to the silver screen."

•

Sen. Beatrice: "If I have learned one thing from this week's testimony, it's that the little people are to blame for the movie industry's troubles. Writers, actors, directors—these are the petty figures who are spreading a blight throughout Hollywood. The producers have been wronged, ladies and gentlemen, and I think that this committee—and the entire nation—owe them an apology."

•

Sen. Richardson: "I really liked that movie *The Right Stuff.* Do you remember the scene where Dennis Quaid—playing me—orbits the earth three times along with a goat and a baboon? And, ahm, er, well, oh yes—I am against whatever crimes were committed, of course. I also liked that movie with Meryl Streep. You know, the one where she plays a foreign woman with an accent. Anyway, that was a good movie, too."

WEEK FOUR: NEWSPAPERS

Spaceship Sighting Hard to Believe

Billings, Montana— Farmer Earl Hunt was harvesting the annual crop of hay last October when his eye caught a flash of light. Looking up, he saw what appeared to be some sort of aircraft or spaceship hovering or flying through the air. The strange ship's high altitude made visual contact difficult, but one thing is certain: The ship was of no ordinary size, being either significantly smaller or larger than any known commercial aircraft.

But is Mr. Hunt some sort of crackpot? All evidence says yes. Neighbors call him a deranged liar, while family members and close personal friends point out that he is a problem drinker with a history of hallucinations.

In addition, Mr. Hunt suffers from a severe optic disorder that limits his vision to certain shades of off-yellow.

"That man is no scientist," said one local resident. "I wouldn't believe him if he told me he found a nickel, let alone a rocket ship. Don't listen to him."

The ship was apparently traveling in an east-westerly direction when Mr. Hunt spied it hurtling across the night sky. Almost immediately, the craft disappeared behind some dense clouds or trees. Before it vanished, though, Hunt says he may have caught a glimpse of what was definitely an alien being or more likely human.

According to meorological experts, th

were hundreds of balloons in the vicinity at the t thermore, a n was known to emitting hot ting gases th area, whic channel also suf derstor of the s to form

In wh ca s'

150-Year-Old Rus Credit Longevity

Georgia, USSR—Residents of this rural region have reportedly attained ages of 100, 125, and even 150 years. The peasants themselves are unsure of the exact reasons behind these staggering figures, but most agree that the local diet of yogurt and tuna casseroles is a major factor.

"We eat like king claimed one tooth'

in rem years klec an th a

VOICE OF ELVIS HEARD On Radio

Groovy San Francisco Chronicle

Nixon Unveils Groovy New Peace Plan
by Angela Hoffman

Washington—President Nixon got down yesterday and let everyone know where he's at as he presented a far-out new peace plan designed to end the bummer situation in Southeast Asia.

Rapping at a White House press conference, Nixon said, "Man, we can all get together on this if we all feel the cosmic vibes of peace."

The plan apparently involves a lot of heavy negotiating stuff that has to be taken care of by Establishment-type self-heads. It would be a real downer to have to talk about that kind of thing here, though. It's much more beautiful to just groove on the idea of peace.

Several Republican Senators said that they dig the plan. "It sounds cool," said Strom Thurmond of South Carolina. "I could get into that plan," agreed Jacob Javits of New York.

However, some Democrats say the plan is jive. "I think the Man better check out what the Vietnamese cats think of it before he starts laying it on us," complained Ed ward Kennedy of Massachusetts.

Neither North nor South Vietnam has yet made any official response to the funky new plan, but the word on the streets is that they won't get back to the President until they see how good the plan's karma is.

Flooding Bums Out Arkansas
By Abby Rubin

Little Rock—The Arkansas River got high yesterday, flooding downtown Little Rock and crashing a lot of property. The water level began to recede late last night, perhaps in response to many people's wish that the river would get very heavy.

Arkansas Governor Hugh S. Samuel said last night, "This whole crazy thing has been a big bummer. The river should be free to do its own thing, like anyone else, but I think the river needs to be a little more in harmony with town."

The mood in Little Rock was varied yesterday as the water paralyzed the city. "It's a real happening scene, man," said one teenager as he paddled a canoe down Main Street. "A neat trip," added another youth who had the day off from school.

Some of the straight people weren't very into the happening, though. One woman insisted on saying, "Emergency! Help meeee!" as she was swept into the rushing water. It was not known whether or not the local pigs tried to help the woman, but they were doing Primal Scream therapy on the scene.

Transit Strike Averted; Everything Outasight
By Jerry Davis

Some negotiating brothers and sisters from the Transit Workers Union and the Transit Authority finally quit being so up tight last night, and announced a new contract agreement that will avert a new cosmic strike.

Each side thought the other was trying to rip it off, but then they realized that everyone had to live together and every one another. Once the suspicion hangups were gone, everything was cool.

The new contract shows that the Transit Authority is hip to the people's needs for

more money. Pay will increase by 20% over the next three years, and there are a bunch of dynamite new benefits.

Speaking from Union headquarters, the head honcho of the negotiation said, "I think this deal is all right. Any worker who doesn't dig it can split, of course. I don't want somebody laying some kind of rap on

President of the Transit Authority J. Mar tin Scott also had a hand in the new contract. Reached at his pad, he said, "It's outasight. I've got to split now, dig?" It's

(Continued on Page 3)
(Continued on Page 5)

Amazing Dog Leaps
To Eat Drowning Child

Tiny Fish Kills Man
In Food-Poisoning Mishap

Atlantis:
The Intriguing Mythology of a Non-Existen.

Sen. Mohasset: "As we enter week four of the so-called Mediagate testimony, it is apparent that things are going to get much worse before they get better. I myself have never trusted newspapers—at least not since *The Boston Globe* reported my name as "Donald Mo Asshole," and a briefing myself and the other Senators received in closed session this morning did nothing to increase my confidence. We are about to see the nation's newspapers, from greatest down to the smallest, air their dirty laundry. We can only hope that this investigation will serve as an effective detergent, and, perhaps, a fabric softener."

From USA Today

Mediagate Fever Sweeps USA

By Dan Greaney

Joe Warner says he doesn't know when he'll go back to selling pretzels. The street vendor in Washington, D.C., says he is doing much better with Mediagate T-shirts, mugs, bumper stickers, and lunch boxes. Warner is just one of millions across the USA who have been swept up in Mediagate Fever.

With the fourth week of testimony beginning today, an upbeat, carnival atmosphere prevails in the nation's capital and across the USA. Despite the sometimes strange revelations forthcoming about the nation's media, USA citizens say they feel good about the investigation. Wendy Bushley of Scopamatic Falls, Ohio, says, "I think it's really nice how the whole country can get together on this Mediagate scandal."

Expected highlights of this week's newspaper testimony:

▶ Evidence of *The New York Times'* abortive experiments with comics.

▶ Secret newspapers published by Disney World.

▶ Fascinating innovations by *USA Today*, a leader in the print media.

▶ Nude photos of Christie Brinkley (time permitting).

▶ Never-before-seen features, columns, and much more.

Senator Donald Mohasset, chairman of the investigative panel, has attempted to downplay the circuslike atmosphere surrounding the hearings, saying, "Mediagate bedspreads and action figures are very nice, but we must not lose sight of the fact that some very suspicious goings-on have taken place."

▶ Specifics of Mediagate, page 8A

Millions of people across the USA are expected to tune in again this week to the televised hearings that have so far prompted songs, comedy routines, and floods of merchandise.

Responding to the the national trend, *USA Today* has set up a toll-free hotline that readers may call to ask questions and discuss Mediagate. And tomorrow in *USA Today*, look for a special section, Mediagate: "How To Get In On The Fun."

▶ Mediagate Hotline Phone Number, page 8A

From *The New York Times*

MEDIA SCANDAL WIDENS

By CHARLES KANE

WASHINGTON D.C.—The Senate Media Investigation entered its fourth week yesterday, with Senate investigators reviewing material collected from more than 150 American newspapers, including *USA Today, The San Francisco Chronicle, The New York Times*, and an assortment of smaller publications. Washington sources report that the "Mediagate" investigation of the newspaper industry will be just as rigorous as the scrutiny of other branches of the media has been.

Senator Donald Mohasset (D/R.I.), the chairman of the Investigation Committee, commented, "I'd like to speak my mind about these hearings, but I doubt if the newspapers would report my words accurately. Oonta-groonta, oonta-groonta. Thank you."

"It's a big conspiracy, all right," stated Senator Pamela Fawcett (D/Calif.). "Whoever is responsible for all this should be forced to ride in a car without a seatbelt, an activity that is far more dangerous than many auto manufacturers will admit."

Newspaper industry executives responded noncommittally to the scandal. "I'm sure it's all very interesting," said Allen Neuharth, founder of *USA Today*, "and no one can report it as well as *USA Today*, and all the other fine Gannett newspapers."

Publisher Rupert Murdoch, however, disagreed. "I personally don't know what's going on with this Mediagate thing, but I've instructed my newspapers to publish special editions if necessary," commented Murdoch. "The American people have a right to know the truth. And for just a quarter a day, each American can get complete coverage."

The National Coalition for Responsibility in Media continued its harsh criticism of the unfolding affair. "The media is a terrible thing, and no one should have anything to do with it," said Dr. Benjamin Saunders to hundreds of press, television, and radio reporters at a press conference last night.

After newspaper testimony comes to a close this Friday, the investigation will move into its fifth week, with an examination of the television industry. As always, the full story will be carried in *The New York Times*.

From *The New York Post*

MEDIA MADNESS!

Nation Goes Crazy For Senate Hearings

The whole country is going bonkers over the latest thing in Washington—the ongoing Senate hearings about the Mediagate scandal. Watching the hearings on TV is a sure bet for entertainment this week, as newspapers come under fire.

Gallant Senator Donald Mohasset will lead the charge into the heart of the seamy underbelly of the newspaper world, with his fellow Senators sitting right beside him and asking questions.

Post publisher Rupert Murdoch welcomes the investigation. "It's a Gripping Guiltfest! Senators on Scrutiny Spree!"

"Home-Viewing Hilarity! Journalists Jeered in Media Mess!"

(continued page 5)

REPORT OF THE COMMITTEE:

In 1981, Gannett Inc. began publishing *USA Today*, a full-color national newspaper with a penchant for optimistic reporting. In 1964, *The New York Post* switched to a tabloid format, printing sensationalistic and bold cover stories in an attempt to sell more papers. Throughout it all, *The New York Times* remained a bastion of normalcy, reporting the news in a time-honored boring fashion.

At a 1986 meeting of the National Newspaper Publishers Conference, *USA Today*'s Al Neuharth and *The New York Post*'s Rupert Murdoch compared notes on how their papers might have reported some of the great historic events of the past. Unfortunately, they forgot to take their marked-up cocktail napkin with them from the hotel bar, and a few other publishers had a laugh at the two's expense.

NEW YORK TIMES	NEW YORK POST	USA TODAY
Civil War Starts	Slaughter-fest at Sumter	USA Yesterday
Civil War Ends	National Nightmare Nixed	Cosby Show Only 120 Years Away
President Lincoln Shot	Booth Blows Away Boss	First Lady Survives Tragedy With Only Emotional Scars
World War One Begins	Massacres in the Mud	Helmets: A New Trend?
America Enters WWI	Woody: Kick Their Butts!	USA to Win War
WWI Ends	It's Over	USA Wins War
Stock Market Crashes	Brokers Hit the Streets	Nowhere to Go But Up!
Hitler Invades Poland	Krauts Kick Krakow	Hitler Nowhere Near USA
Hitler Invades France	He's Not Nice!	USA Still Okay
Hitler Invades Russia	Make Mine Moscow!	Good
Pearl Harbor Bombed	Hon-Oh-Lulu!	Hawaiians Complain of Noise, Smoke
America Wins War	V-E, V-J, HOORAY	Tokyo Stores to Take American Express
FDR Dies	Frankie & Goddy	Truman: He's Not So Bad
Sputnik Circles Earth	It's the Space Race, Ace!	USA Still Has Better Cars, Food, Women
President Kennedy Shot	Dallas Death Spree	Mary Lou Retton Conceived
Armstrong Lands on Moon	One Small Step to the Top	Ed Sullivan Preempted; To Be Re-Aired
Draft Begins for Vietnam War	Going, Going, Sai-Gone	Teen Unemployment Drops
Tet Offensive Kills Hundreds	Tet for Tat	"Tit," Offensive, Thrills Hundreds
Nixon Resigns	Nix, Nixon! Next?	Ford: He's Not So Bad
Titanic Sinks	Icy Nightmare	Ten Tips for a Safer Vacation
Hindenburg Explodes	Fiery Death Ball in Horrible Nightmare Tragedy Kill-Fest Slaughterama	Ten More Tips for a Safer Vacation

The National Cartoonists Conference is a three-day convention at which syndicated newspaper cartoonists gather to recognize each other's achievements. It's also a seventy-two-hour festival of floor shows, merry-making, and booze-drinking. The cartoonists generally ignore their upcoming deadlines until the last night of the conference. In the small hours of the morning, they all lock themselves up in a hotel room and attempt to produce something fit for publication, rarely with success.

Peanuts

Hagar the Horrible

B.C.

Bloom County

Spider Man

Garfield

Momma

Wizard of Id

TAKING THE STAND: Heloise, syndicated advice columnist

Sen. Beatrice: Now Heloise, we have before us some examples of your hints that some have charged are not at all helpful. Is that a fair assessment?

Heloise: I don't know. I never use the hints, I just pass them on.

Sen. Beatrice: Then what makes you think they're so helpful?

Heloise: Why would anyone send them in unless they were helpful?

Sen. Richardson: Hey, I sent you a good one and you never published it. It said, "To save money, don't put stamps on your letters."

Heloise: Well, I'm sure I meant to publish it. Anyway, now that you've told it to me, thanks for the helpful hint! Hugs, Heloise.

Sen. Beatrice: Ladies and gentlemen, please! Things will proceed much faster if we focus our attention on the evidence before us.

Heloise: Thanks for the helpful . . .

Sen. Beatrice: Take a hint from me, Heloise, and shut up.

HINTS FROM HELOISE

A HIT WITH HUBBY

Dear Heloise,

My husband had been putting off painting the second-floor shutters. He claimed that it was very hard to reach the small areas between the slats of the shutters with an ordinary paintbrush. I found that hitting him on the head made him get to work.

Jolene Williams
Hartford, CN

Thanks for the helpful hint! Hugs, Heloise.

OFFICE ORGANIZER

Dear Heloise,

My desk was a mess! There were loose paper clips everywhere, and they were always falling off the desk. This problem drove me crazy! One day, my wife suggested I get an old coffee can and put the paper clips in it. I was skeptical at first, but then I tried it. It worked like a charm, and now my desk is a pleasure to sit at. I later found that painting the can or drawing on it with a permanent magic marker made it pleasant for everyone to look at—including myself!

Larry Forks
Baltimore, MD

Thanks for the helpful hint! I've also found that your wife's idea works for thumbtacks, pencils, and small rocks. What a boon to organization! Hugs, Heloise.

DEE-LIGHTFUL MEAL

Dear Heloise,

Our family used to complain about my unexciting meals, so I found a trick to spice up just about any dish. Just take those old broken Christmas lights and wrap them around your meatloaf, fish, or what-have-you. The bright colors give any meal that extra flair. My family thought this was such a good idea that they almost didn't want to ruin my food by eating it!

Carol Everett
Washington, DC

Thanks for the helpful hint! Just be careful that an elderly or nearsighted person does not eat them by mistake. Hugs, Heloise.

HELPFUL HINT

Dear Heloise,

My family garage wouldn't fix, but to work it would be fine! But not for me!!

When mixing paint, spills don't help. Try can but not open, so I left. Call wife, but not in. Try neighbor, but no help. Help, Heloise! Garage fine now!

Lester

Thanks for the helpful hint! Hugs, Heloise.

RECEPTION CONNECTION

Dear Heloise,

My television reception was lousy! I had an antenna on my roof, but some stations still wouldn't come in. So I went into my shop and found some old bicycle parts. With a little ingenuity and a lot of elbow grease, I rigged up a contraption that let me adjust the antenna from my easy chair in the TV room. The hole in the roof only becomes a problem when it rains, and I don't watch TV then anyway.

Vern Terrell
Boise, ID

Thanks for the helpful hint! And since you don't watch TV when it rains, you don't have to worry about lightning striking your antenna and frying you to a crisp! Hugs, Heloise.

DILUTION SOLUTION

Dear Heloise,

I was having trouble blending a beryllium/helium compound with Uranium 235. My wife suggested I try using a dipolar gas centrifuge while slowly evaporating excess crystals in a flux state. And what do you know, it worked!

Dr. Eviram Storelli
Livermore, CA

Thanks for your helpful hint! I've also found that by adding 20 moles of substantive Sulphanomide, the process can be completed at 620 hertz rather than at the standard 700. Hugs, Heloise.

LETTER OF LAUGHTER

Dear Heloise,

My father has a bad back, and because he is shut-in, we always said it would be a blue moon in June before he would ever get out of the house. Well, one day, my husband was mixing varnish in the basement and accidentally set the house on fire. And, wouldn't you know it, my father was the first one out the door!

Evelyn Norback
Wichita, KS

Thanks for brightening up our day! Hugs, Heloise.

Sen. Mohasset: Mr. Neuharth, could you describe your goal in founding *USA Today?*

Neuharth: I wanted to found a newspaper that anyone could read and anyone could write. It would truly be The Nation's Newspaper.

Sen. Mohasset: By "anyone," do you mean stupid people and very young children?

Neuharth: Ideally, yes.

Sen. Mohasset: Was this ideal ever met?

Neuharth: Look, do we have to go into this? It's not very upbeat.

Sen. Mohasset: If you please, Mr. Neuharth.

Neuharth: Okay. Well, in 1986, we tried a brief experiment in which we lowered the intellectual content of *USA Today* from the third- to the first-grade level in an attempt to broaden our readership.

Sen. Mohasset: And . . .?

Neuharth: No one noticed. And the legal problems we had with hiring first-grade reporters made it too much of a hassle to keep going with the new format. But it was a nice idea.

Bad Man Takes Money From Nice Store

by Mr. Reporter Man

Big Store—A bad thing happened at the big store yesterday. A bad man came to the store. Then he took away all the money. He shouldn't have done that. The nice policemen are trying to find out who the bad man was.

Many people at the big store were mad and scared. They were glad when the bad man left, but they wished he hadn't taken the money. The store manager was sad, too. He said, "It was a lot of money. We earned it by selling things at the store."

The policeman said, "We don't know who the bad man was, but if we find out, we'll make him give the money back."

If anyone saw the man, they should call the police. The man was six feet, ten inches tall, and had bright orange hair like a clown. He had a funny, funny shirt on. He left big, greasy thumbprints all over the store. Yes, he was a funny man, but bad too.

There are no clues as to who the bad man was or what he was doing in the store. He ran away too fast for anyone to see him. All he left behind were some personal letters and his wallet. There was no money in the wallet, only a signed receipt showing the amount of money he stole. The store is going out of business. No one knows how much money was stolen, but it must have been a lot.

Bad War Starts

by Mr. Correspondent

Far Away—A big war started far away, but it's very bad. It happened yesterday. Even though it's not happening right here, it's still important. The reason the war started was because two places were mad at each other. Whoever fights best will win the war.

There are lots of different things in the war. Sometimes there are airplanes, and sometimes there are boats. The tanks look like big machines that drive around in the dirt. Men are shooting each other with bad guns that make a lot of noise. It's very exciting because you never know who is going to win. But even though it's exciting, people get shot and go to sleep and never wake up.

One place didn't like the way the other place was acting. First they tried to be nice about it and solve their problems with words, but it didn't work, so they decided to have the war instead. Today they are fighting, but tomorrow they might be friends again. That's the funny thing about the war.

The war is between Africa and Europe. A European man said, "I hope we win the war. I will try hard to help win the war." An African man said, "I will shoot my gun at Europe and hope to win."

The Europeans have more guns, but the Africans have more boats. According to the big, smart generals, the Europeans will try to shoot the boats with their guns. But the Africans will try to run over the guns with their boats. Yes, the war will be funny, but bad too.

Doctors Help President Man

by Mrs. Reporter Woman

The President's name is Ronald Reagan. Some people like him. They think he's good. Some other people think he's bad. No one knows who is right. But anyway, he went to the doctor today to get some bad bumps taken out of his behind.

"I am the President of the United States," said Ronald Reagan. "Now I have to go to the doctor. My behind hurts."

When he got there, the nice doctor looked at his behind with some special tools. He found some yucky bumps. Then he gave the President a magic potion that made him go to sleep even though it wasn't night-time. While the President was sleeping, the doctor made the bumps go away. Now the President is okay again. He woke up and went home. He lives in the White House.

President Man Goes to Money Club

By Mr. Far Away Reporter Man

Far Away—The President Man named Ronald Reagan went to see the King of Europe yesterday at his clubhouse. They had a meeting of their Money Club, and they tried to figure out what the world should do about money. The King of Canada and the Queen of Africa were there, too, but the President Man is richer than any King could be.

There are all sorts of problems to talk about at the Money Club. Some people don't have enough money. Other people have too much. And in one funny place called Italy, there is no money. Instead they have things called lira. The Money Club has to figure out what to do about things like this.

The secret name for the Money Club is the Economic Summit. That way no one will know what it is. If it was just called the Money Club, everyone would go there and ask the President Man for some money. And he would have to give it to you, because he is so good.

The President Man imposed severe trade sanctions on six members of the European Common Market. That was a funny thing to do.

Big, Bad Cloud Makes Mess

By Mr. Weatherman

There was a mess on the ground yesterday in the town, and it was because of the big cloud that came down and spun around like a top or a merry-go-round.

Everyone went into their cellars because they were afraid that the cloud would blow them away and hurt them. And when they came out of the cellars, all the houses were blown down the street and broken into bits. "I don't want to live there anymore," said one person, pointing at his broken house.

One man's car started to drive away by itself. It drove into a tree. No one knows if the cloud did it, but some people said it did.

People wished that the cloud had never come. One woman said, "I'm glad it's gone, but I wish it had never come." The cloud apparently contained wind.

Everyone was mad at the scientists for not warning them that the cloud was going to arrive in town. The cloud was a tornado.

NEWSPAPER LOTTERIES AND GAMES

In the face of Rupert Murdoch's success with lottery-style newspaper games like "Wingo!" many newspapers have experimented with similar games. Few matched the success of "Wingo!"; even fewer matched any sort of success at all.

"GAME-O" — Denver Post

This imaginative game involved neither skill nor luck. Each day a new game piece was published; at the end of the week, players who had collected all of that week's pieces were "winners." However, the only prize was a congratulatory note printed in each Friday's edition, along with encouragement to play again. "Losers" were harshly advised to buy the paper more regularly if they wished to join the ranks of the "winners."

"Op-Ed-O" — The New York Times

New York Times editors were reluctant to stoop to the level of games and gimmicks, but they agreed that "Op-Ed-O" was sufficiently complex and rewarding for their readership. Players were told to pick an ongoing news story and follow its progress in the *Times*. By midnight Saturday, each contestant was to submit a 1,000-word essay stating some opinion on the news event they'd been following. Winners received $500, and their essays were printed in the Sunday *Times*. Rowland Evans and Robert Novak won the first week's competition, and William F. Buckley won Week Two. Week Three's winners were Rowland Evans and Robert Novak. When Murray Stugman, an unemployed plumber from Queens, won Week Four's competition, the editors decided the game was too easy and abandoned it.

"FIND THE ANIMAL IN THE FAMOUS PERSON'S FACE" — The Wall Street Journal

The name explained it all. Readers were to buy the *Journal*, examine the line drawing of the famous person's face on the front page, and look for the hidden outline of some common animal. Reader response was terrific, but the game was canceled after a lawsuit by *Newsweek* columnist George F. Will. The *Journal* had run a profile of Mr. Will, illustrated by a line drawing of his face. Mr. Will claimed that the drawing of his face contained the outline of a cow urinating. The *Journal* insisted that he was mistaken. Mr. Will insisted that he was right, and that he should therefore win that week's game. The game was discontinued, and the suit was settled out of court.

"GUESS THE NUMBER!"—

New York Post

"Rupert Murdoch is thinking of a number between 1 and 1,000!" the headline said. "Can you guess what it is?" This companion to "Wingo" sent *Post* sales skyrocketing for three months, even though not a single person won. Just as readers started to get suspicious, the paper announced that four winners had correctly guessed the number: Mr. Murdoch's wife, his mother, his analyst, and a woman identified only as "Mindy."

TAKING THE STAND: Bob Fordwick, AP Science Features Editor

Sen. Stone: Mr. Fordwick, am I to understand that you had a newsworthy document from the Skylab program that you did not run?

Mr. Fordwick: That is correct. The piece actually dates back to 1974, but was not submitted to me until two years ago. The piece in question was a diary excerpt from Astronaut William Pogue.

Sen. Stone: And why was it suppressed? Did you consider it too outdated?

Mr. Fordwick: No, it was fine. I was ordered by an anonymous highly placed government official not to publish the diary.

Sen. Richardson: (coughs, wheezes)

Sen. Stone: Senator Richardson? Are you all right?

Sen. Richardson: Something's wrong with the air in here. I suggest we adjourn to closed session for a while.

Sen. Stone: Very well, Senator, as soon as we examine this document. It appears to be very interesting. I'm sure the whole country will wish to see it.

Sen. Richardson: Oh hell.

SKYLAB EXPOSÉ

During the three weeks that the five of us orbited the globe in Skylab, I kept a brief diary of the day's events. The first week's entries were mostly about the unusual conditions of my daily life in outer space. But as the novelty of zero gravity and high-tech meals wore off, I started feeling the effects of the constant presence of my bunkmate Buzz Richardson.

DAY 8: When we passed over Australia tonight, we all gathered at the portholes to watch while the residents of Sydney blinked their electrical lights on and off in unison. It was quite a sight. Buzz's shining his flashlight out the porthole seemed like a gracious, but futile gesture.

We all got tired and turned in for the night, but Buzz stayed at the window. Sometime in the middle of the night a soft sing-song voice woke me up. I floated out to the porthole cubicle to find Buzz still there. He was tapping on the porthole with his index finger and murmuring, "Hello? Hello down there . . . Hello . . ."

DAY 9: Today Buzz asked if we could go to the moon.

"That's ridiculous, Buzz," I said.

"I was just thinking," he said, "as long as we're out here, we really should try to see as much as possible."

I thought he was joking, but Buzz has never joked around before. He still doesn't understand why we all laugh when he calls our specially packaged beef meals "Tubesteak."

DAY 10: Buzz is starting to get on my nerves. For the 10th day in a row, he's pulled me away from the telescope, insisting I go to his cubicle. When we get there, he picks up loose objects at random and says, "It floats! It floats!

Look at this: Here's another thing that floats!"

DAY 11: Buzz has discovered that we have a copy of the platinum Voyager LP record on board, and he's been playing it over and over. I swear if I hear "The Song of the Humpback Whale" or "Johnny B. Goode" one more time, I'll take appropriate action.

Two things make matters even worse. One is that Buzz sings along with "Johnny B. Goode," but he insists on singing, ". . . and he could play the guitar just like a binging a rell." Over and over and over.

The other thing is that for some reason, he brought along a bone-shaped doggy squeak toy in his personal duffel sack. And he insists on squeaking it in time with the music.

DAY 12: It's easy to get disoriented up here, and with no real days or nights, it's easy to lose track of time. Yesterday, we were all sitting around, and Buzz started to tell a story.

"When I was about nine years old," he began, "my aunt—on my mother's side—decided to put up some preserves." That sentence is as interesting as the story got, but we all listened anyway, to be polite. When Buzz had finally finished telling his incredibly boring story, I looked at the onboard clock and discovered that 17 hours had passed.

DAY 13: Buzz is not a good sharer. None of us had the foresight to bring any snacks with us in our personal bags, but Buzz brought a huge carton of SweetTarts. He refuses to share them. Even worse, he doesn't seem to savor them; he just floats around the cabin, shaking whole

packets into his mouth and chewing them up.

Yesterday, he was doing this, when he sneezed and sent a big cloud of tiny chewed-up SweetTart pieces floating around the cabin. It was an incredible mess. After Buzz went to bed, I got a nylon screen and strained the pieces out of the air.

DAY 14: I finally did it. While Buzz was watching (and talking to) the ants in the zero-G ant farm, I stole his rubber squeak toy and jettisoned it out the airlock. Buzz got really mad, but I refused to retrieve it.

A little while later, Jack Lousma called on the intercom and told me that some "small, recently jettisoned item" had torn a hole in our solar collectors. I had to go out and repair it.

I was surprised at how peaceful and relaxing it was to be floating out in space. I worked on the collectors for a while, but suddenly I noticed that Buzz was trying to get my attention from the inside of the porthole. He was making the Vulcan "Live Long and Prosper" handsign at me. I couldn't hear what he was saying, but I could read his lips through the screen of my huge helmet. He was tapping his chest and saying, "Me Buzz. Me human. Hello. That is how we say 'hello' on my planet. How do you say 'hello' on your planet?"

I had serious second thoughts about returning to the capsule.

This ends the second installment of Dick Streiber's "Skylab Diary." Please tune in tomorrow for the final entry, entitled "How We Finally Got Back To Earth And Buzz Came To Visit Me At My House And Stayed For Three Weeks."

TAKING THE STAND: Ian Calder, editor-in-chief of the *National Enquirer*

Sen. Fawcett: Mr. Calder, your publication is perhaps the sorriest, lowest example of American irresponsibility I know of. You people obviously fabricate all of your stories with absolutely no attempt at accuracy or relevance.

Mr. Calder: What do you mean?

Sen. Fawcett: Listen to these headlines from the *Enquirer:* "Three-Year-Old Boy Gives Birth To Octogenarian Midget." "I Lived Inside My Husband's Gigantic Beard For Five Years." "Grade-School Wiseacre Makes Millions By Selling His Own Feces."

Mr. Calder: I can explain each of those, in a fairly convincing way. You see—

Sen. Fawcett: No, let me continue. "Twelve-Foot Ape-Thing Stole My Lunch, And Didn't Even Eat It." "Dim-Witted Astronaut Wins Senate Seat On 'Pity Vote.'" What the—

Mr. Calder: That last headline was from the *Enquirer*'s "True Issue." It didn't do so well on the newsstands, but it was absolutely true and verifiable. I've brought a copy with me.

Sen. Richardson: (entering late) Sorry. Did I miss anything?

Sen. Fawcett: Er . . . no.

VOICE OF ELVIS HEARD On Radio

Amazing Dog Leaps In Pool
To Eat Drowning Child

Tiny Fish Kills Man
In Food-Poisoning Mishap

Atlantis:
The Intriguing Mythology of a Non-Existent Land

Bizarre Moonrock Not Of This World

Gain Up To 20 Lbs. With New
Miracle Dessert Diet

Man With Beard Of Bees Dies In Auto Wreck

Mysterious Interference Plagues Phone Conversation

Bigfoot Is Just A Big Hairy Man Who Lives In The Woods

Spaceship Sighting Hard to Believe

Billings, Montana— Farmer Earl Hunt was harvesting the annual crop of hay last October when his eye caught a flash of light. Looking up, he saw what appeared to be some sort of aircraft or spaceship hovering or flying through the air. The strange ship's high altitude made visual contact difficult, but one thing is certain: The ship was of no ordinary size, being either significantly smaller or larger than any known commercial aircraft.

But is Mr. Hunt some sort of crackpot? All evidence says yes. Neighbors call him a deranged liar, while family members and close personal friends point out that he is a problem drinker with a history of hallucinations.

In addition, Mr. Hunt suffers from a severe optic disorder that limits his vision to certain shades of off-yellow.

"That man is no scientist," said one local resident. "I wouldn't believe him if he told me he found a nickel, let alone a rocket ship. Don't listen to him."

The ship was apparently traveling in an east-westerly direction when Mr. Hunt spied it hurtling across the night sky. Almost immediately, the craft disappeared behind some dense clouds or trees. Before it vanished, though, Hunt says he may have caught a glimpse of what was definitely an alien being or more likely a human.

According to meteorological experts, there were hundreds of weather balloons in the immediate vicinity at the time. Furthermore, a nearby bog was known to have been emitting hot, light-emitting gases that night. The area, which is a major channel for air traffic, also suffered a thunderstorm during the night of the sighting, in addition to unusual cloud formations.

In the light of such overwhelming evidence, there can be no doubt that the spaceship was a mere figment of Mr. Hunt's overactive imagination. Nobody in his right mind could believe such an outrageous story. The subject deserves no further attention.

150-Year-Old Russian Peasants Credit Longevity To Special Diet,

Poor Record Keeping

Georgia, USSR—Residents of this rural region have reportedly attained ages of 100, 125, and even 150 years. The peasants themselves are unsure of the exact reasons behind these staggering figures, but most agree that the local diet of yogurt and tuna casseroles is a major factor.

"We eat like kings," claimed one toothless centenarian. "And we sit around a lot, and drink lots of booze."

Scientists, however, are skeptical of such claims, and have countered them with reams of indisputable data to the contrary. It has been shown, for example, that most of the elderly peasants allegedly 100 or more years old are in reality only 20 to 35 years of age. Their wrinkled and mangled appearance seems to be due, for the most part, to miserable living conditions and a poor diet.

"These people aren't so old," explains Dr. Eric Pinski of the Moscow Institute. "They just look old. They're in terrible physical health."

Another source of confusion stems from the fact that all male children in the village are named Ivan Gregorovich. For this reason, many of their medical records become mixed up with the records of their parents or grandparents, or with the records of their friends' ancestors. In addition, all of the female children are also named Ivan Gregorovich.

"This place is a deathtrap," warns Dr. Pinski. "Stay away."

If one takes into consideration both the analysis of Dr. Pinski and the confusing state of medical records in the backward community, it is impossible to credit the tales of fantastic longevity with having even the smallest degree of truthfulness. Why the peasants would lie about their ages is a mystery. Perhaps it is due to ignorance, or maybe it's all just some kind of big joke. In any case, you should forget about any articles on the subject that have appeared previously in this publication, and pay the matter no further attention.

When necessary, *the New York Times* prints correction boxes to rectify errors made in previous issues. The *Times* maintains a limit of no more than two correction boxes per issue, because "we so rarely make mistakes." The following are a few of the 259 correction boxes that the paper never printed because "we just didn't have enough space for them."

Correction Boxes

Correction: Last week's printed New York Lottery winning number, 4 7 13 29 31 32, was in error, as was the statement that there were no winning guesses in the record $90,000,000 drawing. The number should have read 2 3 4 8 15 23, and Lottery Commission records indicate that 45 players in New York, Connecticut, and New Jersey held the winning number worth, therefore, at least $2 million for each of them. Players with the correct number must present their card at an authorized Lottery agent by midnight, the day before yesterday.

Correction: In a Sunday front-page article, Mr. Enrico Vitelli, of 312 Lester Street, Queens, was incorrectly identified as having squealed on two major Mafia crime bosses. Our deepest apologies go to Mr. Vitelli's remaining family. The actual informant was Mr. Leon Casper, of 725 Melborn, in the Bronx, next door to the bookstore, and his left front window does not lock properly.

Correction: Due to an editing error, the late Mrs. Elizabetg Porchxzohrwyzck's street name in her hometown of Connstzanwtipnxownedta, Poland, was inadvertently misspelled. The street, which appeared as "Hampstead," should have read "Hamstead." We regret this error, and thank the officials of the Rochester County Polish History Foundation for correcting this detail in our one-paragraph small-print footnote concerning this insignificant participant in an abortive 1923 vegetarian putsch.

Correction: Drug traffic into and out of Miami has not "stopped completely," as we reported yesterday. The man who told us was in a very nice suit, and he was very well spoken and polite, so we figured he was telling us the truth. Turns out he was just another two-bit crook with a stolen Brooks Brothers card and a fast mouth.

Correction: Tuesday's horoscope entry for Virgo, "Seek out the company of stranglers, they may have the solution to your problems," contained a typographical error: The sentence was printed in the wrong type style.

Correction: The slang phrase "I could care less," meant to imply indifference, is incorrect. The correct phrase is "I could *not* care less," which clearly states that the speaker rates the subject of conversation as the absolute least important thing to him. This error did not appear in our newspaper, but we have noticed people making it a lot recently.

Correction: We are not the Seattle Curried-Crumpet. That was a mistake.

the other 44, he replied, "I just have no idea why they didn't turn their game cards in. I guess some people are just too lazy."

When asked how his life would be changed by having won the entire $90,000,000 stake himself, Mr. Garibaldi said, "Very little, I would think. Tomorrow I'll probably go to work at *The New York Times* the same as always. I'm not going to quit my job proofreading the Lottery column just because I got a little lucky one day."

TAKING THE STAND: Tim McCoy, junior sports reporter, *Philadelphia Inquirer*

Sen. Mohasset: Mr. McCoy, you've alleged that the *Philadelphia Inquirer* repeatedly refuses to print your coverage of sports events. Why is this?

Mr. McCoy: There's only one reason. It's because I tell it like it is. I report the games as accurately as possible.

Sen. Beaufort: This isn't really related, Mr. McCoy, but who do ya'll think'll take the National League Pennant this year?

Mr. McCoy: Senator, you know as well as I that no one can predict with total certainty the outcome of future events.

Sen. Beaufort: Aw, come on. What about Larry Bird? Is he really the best player in the NBA?

Mr. McCoy: Far be it from either of us to even attempt ranking one human being over another, no matter what the criterion.

Sen. Beaufort: Son, Ah don't think you got much of a future in sportswriting.

Mr. McCoy: Well, Senator, I guess we'll both have to see if future events bear out that supposition.

Celtics Top Rockets, 110–108

By Tim McCoy

The Boston Celtics had an opportunity last night to register a victory in the won-lost column, and they did so, to the chagrin of their opponents, the Houston Rockets.

At the start of the game, the score was 0–0, but a basket scored by Kevin McHale eight seconds into the game brought the score to 2–0 in favor of the Celtics. The Rockets rebounded just seconds later with a basket of their own, tying the game at 2–2. The Celtics answered back with two straight points of their own, doubling their score and taking the lead. However, the Rockets gained possession of the ball and Ralph Sampson managed to put the ball into the basket, doubling the Rockets' score and again tying the game.

The intensity cranked up a notch as Celtic center Robert Parish dribbled the ball down the court and despite the efforts of Houston defensemen, managed to score a 2-point basket. The intensity then cranked up yet another notch as Rockets' center Akeem Olajuwon passed the ball to a teammate who scored an answering 2-point basket.

With 41:08 left, the score was tied at 6–6, but then Boston went ahead by two thanks to a basket scored by a team member. But Houston came back with another basket, erasing the Celtic lead.

As the first half continued, both teams scored additional points, sometimes possessing the ball while at other times watching their opponents score. The mood of both teams was competitive, but neither team was able to gain more than a momentary advantage. As the first half ended, the Rockets battled back to overcome a two-point deficit, tying the game at 54–54.

Play in the second half closely mirrored that of the first, with several players on both teams each scoring several baskets. With 18:19 left in the game, the Celtics led 78–76, but a basket by Rockets guard Bob Lucas boosted Houston's score to an equally high level. However, Boston took the lead again on a jump shot by Larry Bird. A Houston basket brought the Rockets neck-and-neck again, and the score remained deadlocked until a Celtics drive netted two additional points for Boston. The lead was short-lived due to an answering basket by Houston center Olajuwon. Additional baskets by both teams kept the score close as the game moved into its final minute with the score tied at 106–106. A layup by Celtic forward Danny Ainge put the Celtics up by two, but Houston came back to tie the game at 108. Boston managed to net two more points with another Larry Bird jump shot, giving the Celtics a two-point edge. At that point the game ended. The final score was 110–108.

It should be noted, however, that had any of the successful baskets been missed, the game might have turned out differently for either side.

Sen. Beaufort: Anyone care for a cigarette?

Sen. Fawcett: Smoking is a filthy habit.

Sen. Beaufort: Filthy! You talk about filthy! Some of the things Ah saw your sistuh do on "Charlie's Angles" — now that was filthy. Why don't you start your crusade a little closuh to home.

Sen. Fawcett: That wasn't my—

Sen. Richardson: Come on, you two, cut it out.

Sen. Stone: Senator Richardson is correct. This is time that could be used for valuable reflection on what we have heard.

Sen. Beatrice: Or for consumption of high-quality food products.

Sen. Mohasset: Look, as I see it, we're supposed to present some sort of unified front about what we're hearing. We've seen a fair amount of the newspaper evidence at this point. What impressions are you getting?

Sen. Beaufort: Ah am continually appalled by the variety of ways that the media, in this case the newspapers, has found to offend and deceive—

Sen. Mohasset: You can put a lid on that stuff, Jeremiah. The voters can't hear you in here.

Sen. Fawcett: What I can't figure out is who is behind it all. It seems to me that it must be a deliberate conspiracy and cover-up. I'm getting too many bad vibes for it to be coincidence.

Sen. Stone: It would seem, then, that there is a massive campaign to discredit the media.

Sen. Richardson: But why? And who would possibly have the resources to launch such a campaign?

Sen. Beatrice: Oh, it could be done.

Sen. Beaufort: Yankees!

Sen. Mohasset: That's not specific enough to hand down any indictments, I'm afraid.

Sen. Stone: I propose we adopt a "wait and see" attitude. We may yet penetrate the shroud of obscurity that surrounds this matter.

Sen. Fawcett: I'll bet it's the government. Yeah, a massive government plot to hoodwink the people.

Sen. Mohasset: But we *are* the government.

Sen. Richardson: Is there going to be any week devoted to NASA?

Sen. Beatrice: NASA isn't a branch of the media, spaceman.

Sen. Richardson: Maybe not. But it's pretty big, and I'm part of it. What do you have to say to that?

Sen. Beatrice: Never mind.

Sen. Stone: I get the impression that paradoxically, there may be no conspiracy, which was the way it was planned from the beginning—making it an even bigger conspiracy.

Sen. Beaufort: That makes a whole dungheap of sense, Archibald.

Sen. Mohasset: Well, I don't really have any clear ideas, except that we don't have it figured out yet. Let's get back out there.

Groovy San Francisco Chronicle

Nixon Unveils Groovy New Peace Plan

by Angela Hoffman

Washington—President Nixon got down yesterday and let everyone know where he's at as he presented a far-out new peace plan designed to end the bummer situation in Southeast Asia.

Rapping at a White House press conference, Nixon said, "Man, we've got to put this bad trip behind us. We can all get together on this if we all feel the cosmic vibes of peace."

The plan apparently involves a lot of heavy negotiating stuff that has to be taken care of by Establishment-type sell-outs. It would be a real downer to have to talk about that kind of thing here, though. It's much more beautiful to just groove on the idea of peace.

Several Republican Senators said that they dig the plan. "It sounds cool," said Strom Thurmond of South Carolina. "I could get into that plan," agreed Jacob Javits of New York.

However, some Democrats say the plan is jive. "I think the Man better check out what the Vietnamese cats think of it before he starts laying it on us," complained Edward Kennedy of Massachusetts.

Neither North nor South Vietnam has yet made any official response to the funky new plan, but the word on the streets is that they won't get back to the President until they see how good the plan's karma is.

Flooding Bums Out Arkansas

By Abby Rubin

Little Rock—The Arkansas River got high yesterday, flooding downtown Little Rock and trashing a lot of property. The water level began to recede late last night, perhaps in response to many people's wish that the river would get off their backs.

Arkansas Governor Hugh Scannell said last night, "This whole river thing has been a big hassle. The river should be free to do its own thing, like anyone else, but I think the river needs to be a little more in harmony with love."

The mood in Little Rock was varied yesterday as the water paralyzed the city. "It's a real happening scene, man," said one teen as he paddled a canoe down Main Street. "A real trip," added his chick. "Nixon stinks!" shouted some youths who had the day off from school.

Some of the straight people weren't very into the happening, though. One woman was quoted as saying "Eeeeeeek! Help meeee!" as she was swept into the rushing water. It was not known whether or not she was doing Primal Scream therapy. Some local pigs tried to help the woman, but they got on the scene too late.

(Continued on page 3)

Transit Strike Averted; Everything Outasight

By Jerry Davis

Some negotiating brothers and sisters from the Transit Workers Union and the Transit Authority finally quit being so uptight last night, and announced a new contract agreement that will avert a strike threatened for later this month.

Each side thought the other was trying to rip it off, but then they realized that everyone has to be able to get together and trust one another. Once the suspicion hangups were gone, everything was cool.

The new contract shows that the Transit Authority is hip to the people's needs for more money. Pay will increase by 20% over the next three years, and there are a bunch of dynamite new benefits.

Speaking from Union headquarters, the head honcho of the negotiators said, "We think this deal is all right. Any worker who doesn't dig it can split, of course. I don't want somebody laying some kind of rap on me."

President of the Transit Authority J. Martin Scott also had to hand it to the new contract. Reached at his pad, he said, "It's outasight. I've got to split now, dig?"

(Continued on page 5)

With many newspaper columns, the editor needs only to read the first line of a submission to decide whether the material is appropriate. *The New York Times Magazine*'s "About Men" column is no exception. Below are just a few first lines from the many rejected "About Men" pieces. That there are so many just goes to show how much easier it is to write one of these columns than to read one.

About Men

"Every son eventually has to attend his father's funeral. I just hope this one isn't too long."

"My wife says all men are insensitive, and I say the bitch is wrong."

"The arrival of Autumn always fills me with thousands of wistful observations about my personal life, and this year I've managed to write down every single one of them."

"I'm a tit man myself."

"Today my son asked me why every puzzle has a missing piece. I'll give them back when he's older."

"It's not always easy, having such a large penis."

"Personal hygeine? Hah! I, for one, wash my face with beer and smoke my clothes clean with a cheap cigar. Soap? Count me out."

"I believe every man harbors the instinct to kill. I'm just less repressed than others."

"You know, there's nothing quite like a good, hot crap."

"Look—call me insensitive, but personally, I don't care for homos."

TAKING THE·STAND: Randall Meyers, executive director of Disney World

Sen. Beaufort: Now, Mr. Meyers, as a man of the South, Ah have often had the oppahtunity to visit Disney World, and let me just state, Ah think it is a wholesome, entertaining place.

Mr. Meyers: Thank you, Senator. We pride ourselves on making Disney World the nation's headquarters for fun.

Sen. Beaufort: Yes, and that is why Ah was so disturbed to see our next piece of evidence—the secret newsletter of Disney World, given to our panel by a disgruntled employee.

Mr. Meyers: Well, I'm sorry you had to see that, Senator, but you must understand—this isn't some kind of Mickey Mouse outfit we're running here—I mean—oh no.

Sen. Beaufort: What's the matter, Mr. Meyers? Would you care for a soothing cigarette?

Mr. Meyers: No, I must go now. I've violated Directive 239.7—Do Not Take the Characters' Names in Vain. Must go—must report to detention cell . . .

Sen. Beaufort: Well, all right, Mr. Meyers. Thank you kindly for coming by today.

THE MOUSETRAP

THE NEWSPAPER FOR EMPLOYEES OF DISWORCO
VOL. 13, NO. 20
PUBLISHED BY THE OFFICE OF THE EXECUTIVE DIRECTOR

MAY 25, 1985

25¢ MANDATORY

RESULTS OF WEEKLY INSPECTION DISAPPOINTING

73 NEGLIGENT EMPLOYEES DISMISSED

The park cleanliness and presentation inspection of May 17 revealed numerous slip-ups and reprehensible carelessness in many segments of Disney World. Seventy-three employees in various departments have been relieved of their duties in the first round of dismissals. This action should serve as a warning to the 535 additional employees who were implicated in the carelessness; they should feel fortunate that only one month's pay was docked as punishment.

The following departments were amongst the most-cited in the inspection:

• CINDERELLA'S CASTLE—A piece of trash was found near the main entrance.

• TOMORROWLAND—A male employee was found sporting an unacceptable amount of facial hair growth.

• MAIN STREET U.S.A.—A file clerk was caught peering out of one of the second-story windows. In addition, a park visitor was carelessly allowed to wander upstairs into the Disney World morgue.

• FRONTIERLAND—"Mile Long Bar": Customer complained of too much ice in his drink. "Old-Time Shooting Gallery": a customer was allowed a winning score.

• TIKI ROOM—A visitor who was neither elderly nor retarded was singing along with the birds.

• ADVENTURELAND—An employee used profanity when his hand was crushed in gears of "Pirates of the Caribbean."

Owing to the excessive number of infractions discovered during the inspection, the annual employee picnic has been cancelled.

READ THIS PAPER

ON YOUR *OWN*

TIME!

NEW LEAVE POLICY INSTITUTED

Under pressure from the Buena Vista AFL-CIO Local 619, the executive director of DisWorCo has instituted a new, more liberal employee-leave policy. Beginning next month, all Disney World staff experiencing a death in the family will be allowed thirty minutes undisturbed in the Dumbo Chapel under Frontierland. Please be advised that appointments for use of the chapel require two weeks advance notice.

EMPLOYEE OF THE MONTH NAMED

DisWorCo's "Employee of the Month" was named by the park's associate director on May 12. Her name is Evelyn Ulmer. She will receive a five percent discount on Disney merchandise at the Main Street Bazaar and Gift Shop. In addition, she may receive a Mickey Mouse™ T-shirt if the associate director feels her performance this month is also outstanding. Previous employees of the month are reminded that their discounts are no longer valid. Also, April's honoree Bob Stanley is reminded that he will have to return the T-shirt pending the associate director's decision. It is expected that he will have the shirt cleaned and pressed upon surrendering it.

COSTUME CORNER

DisWorCo employees wearing character costumes are reminded of the following regulations regarding their use (Disney By-Laws, Section 81.500b):

• Absolutely NO SMOKING is permitted inside the suits. Park visitors on April 27 were alarmed to see clouds of smoke emanating from Winnie the Pooh's honey pot. Small children thought he was on fire.

• Under NO circumstances are the costumes to be worn outside of the park. Disney's reputation received no benefits from the recent drunk-driving accident involving Goofy and a state representative.

• NEVER wear the costumes into the park's public restrooms.

DISNEY MASS RESCHEDULED

The mandatory 6:00 a.m. daily memorial mass for Mr. Disney will now take place at 5:30 a.m. in Southwest Tunnel 715cf, Western Route. All employees are expected to attend punctually, in appropriate attire.

TAKE NOTE!

All DisWorCo staff are reminded that their Official Oath prohibits them from mentioning or discussing Disney Secrets. The following recent developments should be added to the list on page 477 of the *Employee's Handbook*:

• The recent UNRELATED series of visitor deaths occurring in the Haunted Mansion.

• The ongoing construction of the NORAD Florida Command Center in the Space Mountain dome.

• The Executive Director's drunken, unscheduled appearance in the Parade last week.

• The teenage visitor carrying concealed alcohol who was "detained" by the DisWorCo Security Office on April 11, and the $22.5 million lawsuit filed by his next of kin.

• Entertainer Michael Jackson's secret suite in the tower of Cinderella's Castle.

TAKING THE STAND: Mr. Dexter Nebbish, crossword puzzle composer

Sen. Stone: . . . so in effect, Mr. Nebbish, what you are claiming is that certain people, people intimately involved with the subject of these very hearings, approached you and coerced you into using your daily crossword puzzles, which appear regularly in papers across the nation, as a private network for sending secret information through cryptic codes, is that correct?

Mr. Nebbish: Er . . . ahm . . . er, yes. But you must understand, these people threatened to *kill* me. But I didn't care, I had to come forward.

Sen. Stone: And that is why you refused to submit this final puzzle, the one we hold as closed evidence?

Nebbish: That is correct. It contained incriminating evidence concerning everyone associated with this Mediagate investigation, even the high-ups like Senator B—

Sen. Beatrice: Mr. Chairman, I think Senator Richardson has a question, don't you, Buzz?

Sen. Mohasset: Please make sure it is important, Senator Richardson. We are at a very crucial point in the testimony.

Sen. Richardson: Well, Mr. Chairman, I think it is important. I wouldn't have interrupted if it wasn't important. After all, I'm only really an astronaut, one of the few men who ever set foot on the moon, and maybe it's true that I don't have an idea of what important really is, but—

Sen. Mohasset: Okay, okay, Buzz. Please ask your question. We're all sure it's a very important question.

Sen. Richardson: Well, thank you, Senator. Mr. Nebbish, I think I speak for everyone in this courtroom, if not for everyone in the nation who is listening right now when I ask you a question that must have been on everyone's mind all throughout your testimony—I know it's been in my craw—and that is, can you do those *New York Times* crossword puzzles? I mean the big Sunday ones, you know. And I mean *all* the way, not just part.

Sen. Mohasset: Mr. Richardson, I don't—

Sen. Richardson: 'Cause me an' the missus like to try 'em, but we never quite—

Sen. Mohasset: I fail to see how this pertains to anything, here, Senator.

Sen. Beatrice: Now, Mr. Chairman, I for one think the senator's question is a very good one, and maybe the witness should take the time to answer it. Take *a lot* of time, do you understand, Mr. Nebbish?

Nebbish: We-ell, Mr. Senator, yes, I can complete them.

Sen. Richardson: *All* the way?

Nebbish: Yes, all the way.

Audience and Senators: Wow. (applause)

Nebbish: Well, I do write them for a living.

Sen. Richardson: Yeah, that must be it.

Nebbish: But, Mr. Chairman, if we could return to my earlier remarks . . . The reason I came here was to decode that

The reason I came here was to decode that puzzle for you. Even though they have threatened to kill me. I feel the evidence that I hold is too crucial to be ignored, I—

Sen. Beatrice: Well, Mr. Nebbish, we will review the evidence in good time, but now, we're concerned for your safety, so I have arranged for your—ahem, something in my throat—*removal,* ah, from this courtroom; you will have an escort from my own personal bodyguard service, so you needn't worry. So, thank you for coming today. Believe me, no one knows more than I do what it means that you came here and testified. So once again, good-bye.

Sen. Richardson: Gentleman—

Sen. Fawcett: And ladies.

Sen. Richardson: And ladies, I realize the evidence that Mr. Nebbish has tendered is highly volatile, and may prove dangerous even to Mr. Nebbish himself, but there is one thing I fear I must ask him before testimony closes for the day.

Sen. Mohasset: Yes?

Sen. Richardson: 27 Across—is it "beverage"?

ACROSS
1 Sanskrit for rugburn
3 Nickname for "Richard" Thomas
4 Nickname for Richard Thomas in third grade
6 Television's John _____
7 Letter of the alphabet
11 Same as 3 Down
13 One who eats
14 Traveling menstrual show
15 Fudgepacker's Union
16 Sound of one hand clapping
18 _____, _____, and _____
20 Ishmael (to friends)
21 Why dogs eat their puke
23 Scotch tape worms
24 Slang for "dick"
25 Women do this
27 Babylonian God of Moist Felt

28 Color of farts
29 Sometimes contains corn
31 Rex Trailer Park
32 Singular (pl.)
34 Put out or get out
35 He created God
36 Cartoon voiceover, Mel _____
37 Matching placemats for feminine napkins
38 Where babies come from
40 Where babies end up

DOWN
1 Smell janitors have
3 Same as 11 Across
4 Cervical error
5 It ain't the meat
6 Chariots on Fire
7 Jimmy Hoffa's buried here
10 Who farted
11 Murphy's lawyer

12 Penalty for crying out loud
14 Tuna smells like this
16 Bonzo's bedtime
17 Charades (2 wrds, sounds like 'spit')
18 French Foreign lesions
21 Rhymes with "orange"
22 Sticky film at 11:00
24 Syphillis Diller
25 Castrate with pinking shears
26 Hairpie à la mode
29 My fifth-grade English teacher
30 Reese's feces
31 You wouldn't want that, would you?
32 Syrup for bedpancakes
34 The only true religion
35 Voodoo Slave Pigs From _____
37 Kilroy was here

Reclusive chess champion Bobby Fischer made a startling foray into public view in May 1978 when he agreed to author some chess columns for the *Milwaukee Journal.* His first submission, which detailed his victorious technique against Spaasky in the Reykjavik game of 1972, was deemed "unhelpful," and the chess page of May 20 was replaced by a checkers feature.

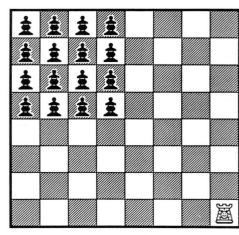

Solution to yesterday's puzzle:

Today's Challenge—by Bobby Fischer

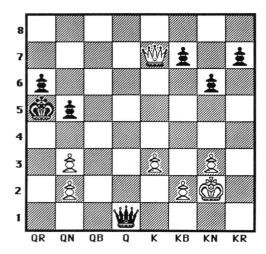

Can you duplicate Bobby's strategy and mate in 13 moves? Answer below.
Solution:

Spaasky	Solution—Fischer
1. Q-QB7	1. Tap foot lightly in 5/4 rhythm
2. chK-N5	2. Change tempo to 3/4; yawn, exposing blackened teeth
3. R-QB3	3. Clear throat loudly, cough twice
4. R-QB3	4. Signal blonde in front row to fondle her bosom
5. Q-KB7	5. Stop game, complain to judges about overhead glare, squeaky chairs
6. B-QR4	6. Eat garlic pod, reconvene game
7. B-KN3	7. Signal Minos (in black robes) to rise and loudly proclaim his ancient curse on Spaasky
8. B-QB2	8. Drum fingers on table, mouth "I love you" to Spaasky, blow garlic breath at him
9. B-QR4	9. Interrupt game to complain about Russian hypnotist planted in third row. Sneeze into bare hands, then touch all the pieces
10. P-K4	10. Sulk and agree to reconvene. Hum "Lady of Spain" under breath for 12 seconds
11. P-Q7	11. Release bottled mosquito in left pocket
12. N-K5	12. Signal blonde in front row to begin hypnotizing Spaasky
13. chK-N4	13. Q-KB3, checkmate

TAKING THE STAND: Rupert Murdoch, head of publishing empire

Sen. Beatrice: Now Rupe—ah, Mr. Murdoch, what's this about you suppressing some of the classifieds in your papers?

Murdoch: Oh, I don't know.

Sen. Beatrice: Okay.

Sen. Beaufort: Now just a cotton-pickin' minute! We're not gonna let this slick newspaper fellow get away with this, are we? Speak up, sir! What is going on?

Sen. Fawcett: Yes, Mr. Murdoch, we have some examples of classified ads that never ran as they were supposed to in *The New York Post,* and I want to know why!

Murdoch: Because they were obviously too stupid to run!

Sen. Fawcett: Who are you to make such a judgment?

Murdoch: Well, I am Rupert Murdoch, head of a vast empire.

Sen. Beatrice: Yeah. Leave him alone.

Sen. Richardson: You always side with him.

Sen. Beatrice: Do not.

Sen. Fawcett: Do so.

Sen. Beatrice: Do not.

Sen. Stone: Excuse me, Senator Fawcett, but it seems that a fleet of black helicopters has just surrounded the building. Perhaps it would be best to drop the matter.

Sen. Fawcett: Yes, that sounds like a good idea. I'm sure Mr. Murdoch has exercised excellent judgment in screening classified ads.

CLASSIFIED
—— ADS ——

Tired of letting chemicals rule your life? Join our support group to overcome oxygen dependency. We meet at 5:00 pm, M–F, East River, 4 fathoms down.

July 13, 42nd Street subway station. We made eye contact—I was in blue coat. I was getting on train, you were getting pushed onto tracks. I'd love to meet you. Call me if you're better. (617) 495-7801.

LOST: Sense of direction, purpose in life, reason for living. Never mind.

"How'm I doin? How'm I doin? How'm I doin?" Contact me, Mayor Ed Koch, c/o the limo that's next to your cab right now.

HOLY Saint Catherine you are so damned fine. You watcheth over me in times of trouble, and I watcheth you because you are built so incredibly well. I just can't get over how hot you make me. Uh-uh-uh. (Recite this novena 7 times daily for good luck in spiritual matters and enhanced success with all the fine women.)

"Look at my thumb. Gee, you're dumb!" Send $5.00 for secret to this and other self-defense techniques. Allen Wachtel c/o Mt Sinai Hospital, New York, NY.

OH holy Jesus Christ, Mary Mother of Jesus, Good Lord in Heaven Above. Recite this novena once in a loud voice to decrease pain in case of stubbing toe, hammering finger, or other painful accidents.

For sale: One sturdy necklace, with full-size albatross pendant. Contact Ann Shentmariner.

The key to ultimate fitness? 50 sit-ups, 100 push-ups, 150 jumping jacks, and 20 deep knee bends. Pay us $150 a month, and we'll let you perform these exercises inside our building. MANHATTAN HEALTH CLUB.

Hot tips on horse races. Samples: Paul Revere (pending clear weather), Valentine (5–9 odds), Epitaph (by a half). Contact: Nathan Detroit. Also: looking to purchase small ruby with what would otherwise be my union dues.

Lexington and 57th Street. I was in brown cardigan, you were wearing green raincoat. I slipped on ice and fell on my butt: you pointed at me and laughed. I'd like to meet with you and punch you out. Write Ricky, Box 1150

Looking to buy: Toasters, telephones, televisions, auto cars, mechanical devices of all types. Renouncing my Amish heritage. Contact: Lemuel, Box 3440.

Stay-Hard Lotion, $5.00 a tube. Works on everything: glass, metal, wood, concrete—who knows what else? Contact: Thomas Dong, Box 143.

Buying a classified ad? Let me help you write a funny, attention-getting ad. Get laughs and responses at the same time. This one is not an example of my best work. Contact: Richard, Box 5679.

TAKING THE STAND: Sydney Omarr, syndicated astrologist

Sen. Fawcett: Mr. Omarr, I'd like to begin questioning by—

Mr. Omarr: Excuse me, but today isn't a good day for you to begin a line of questioning.

Sen. Fawcett: Is that right? And when do you think would be a better time?

Mr. Omarr: I wouldn't advise it until . . . hmm . . . next June 10th.

Sen. Fawcett: I'm afraid we'll just have to take our chances today, Mr. Omarr. Now, I want you to know that I sympathize with your profession, but the horoscope before me, from November 1986, is a travesty of the principles of astrology.

Mr. Omarr: I agree. You see, the day I prepared that edition, Jupiter was aligned with the sun—making it a bad day to prepare a syndicated horoscope column.

Sen. Fawcett: Oh, I understand. But don't you see, Mr. Omarr, that the publication of such a column could misguide the lives of millions of individuals?

Mr. Omarr: I know, and that's why that column was pulled at the last moment. I told the papers to run any old one instead.

Sen. Fawcett: All right, that's good, then. I suggest we move on.

Sen. Richardson: Wait! What does it say for Libra? I want to see the horoscope!

Sen. Mohasset: Present the document for public view, Senator Fawcett.

TODAY'S HOROSCOPE

By Sydney Omarr

ARIES (March 21–April 19): Burdens may be relieved slightly, or they may not be. If the burden is relieved, you will feel better, as if a weight had been lifted from you. The world will, on the whole, look somewhat better to you. Again, that is only if the burden is relieved.

TAURUS (April 20–May 20): As Saturnian cycles complete the third house, the emphasis in your life should be on "simple pleasures." Don't eat too much fatty food, watch your weight, get regular exercise. In general, don't overdo it. But if there's a special occasion—what the heck, live a little.

GEMINI (May 21–June 20): Be careful whom you tell secrets to. It is an unwise idea, for example, to tell a secret to a complete stranger—you never know whom he might tell it to, and you could come out looking pretty stupid. Also, don't tell secrets to people who hate you.

CANCER (June 21–July 22): If today is not Sunday, you will probably get a bill in the mail. Then again, if you didn't buy anything or have any repairs done and you don't have any friends, you might not get any mail at all.

LEO (July 23–Aug. 22): Today is a bad day to have yourself killed.

VIRGO (Aug. 23–Sept. 22): Focus is on arising promptly, brushing your teeth well, having a good breakfast, being careful while driving to work, doing a good job at the office (or wherever you work!—ed.), eating a well-balanced lunch and dinner, and doing whatever you like in the evening. Don't worry too much about doing things you don't normally do, either. They're okay, too.

LIBRA (Sept. 23–Oct. 22): Someone you know might be in a bad mood today. Steer clear of him! Although . . . it might do some good to try to cheer him up—in any case, use your own best judgment.

SCORPIO (Oct. 23–Nov. 21): Avoid: foods containing mayonnaise that was left out in the sun, third rails, criminals, plutonium. Emphasis on taking advantage of a good opportunity when you find it. Antiques, valuable stamps, interest-bearing bonds, IRAs, and the like are good investments. Usually.

SAGITTARIUS (Nov. 22–Dec. 21): Today is the day to be nicer to your family and co-workers. Emphasis on pleasantries, courtesy, making people feel important. Avoid rudeness, yelling when angered, and using your fists when your mind would do. In fact, do this every day, not just today.

CAPRICORN (Dec. 22–Jan. 19): Focus on carpentry, parables, spreading the word of your Father. Strangers may make good disciples. Avoid Roman pontificates and centurions. Beware: A kiss from a close friend may mean trouble!

AQUARIUS (Jan. 20–Feb. 18): If that journey you've been planning involves substance abuse, perilous travel across the open desert with no food or water, rickety and potentially dangerous airplanes, or swimming across the Mediterranean—forget it!

PISCES (Feb. 19–March 20): A transaction will take place today involving you giving money to someone for a product or service. That is, if you are not bedridden or in prison and are not bankrupt or already dead. I think.

IF TODAY IS YOUR BIRTHDAY: you might be getting some gifts or having a party of some sort, thrown by or for you. If this is a weekday, you might want to think of having the party on a weekend, or maybe at night, because some people have to work and might not be able to come during the day. And, by all means, don't tell someone right off if they give you something you already have—that might hurt their feelings, and besides, you can always take it back to the place where they got it and exchange it for something you don't have. It might be awkward, though, when you have to ask them for the receipt. And, of course, Happy Birthday!!!

When the *New York Times* announced that they would begin printing comic strips in their daily paper, most readers were pleased. However, many people failed to read the fine print in the announcement, which said, "The comic strips will be printed in a slightly altered format that the *Times* has deemed appropriate for its readership." As with many things the paper does, the new format met with a luke-warm response, and was abandoned.

Comics as News

The *New York Times* is famous for its lack of comic strips. This lack has long irritated many people, and occasionally this irritation develops into full-blown hostility. Only once has the paper budged in the face of such hostility. In October 1985 the *New York Times* began running comics, but in news story form. The compromise move engendered more hostility than the lack of comics, and the news comics were abandoned.

Garfield, Odie Trick Jon
By Jim Davis

Noted pet owner Jon Arbuckle was in serious condition this morning in his home following an accident involving his pet cat Garfield, his pet dog Odie, and a freshly baked pan of lasagna. As Jon removed the pan from the oven, both pets sprang upon him, apparently drawn by the lasagna's odor. In the ensuing melee, the pan of lasagna somehow ended up on Jon's head. Garfield and Odie consumed the damaged lasagna, despite the smoke issuing from Jon's ears.

Garfield was quoted as emitting a thought bubble that said, "Oh boy! Lasagna!" and later, another one stating, "Odie, you'd better not get near that lasagna." Odie, an inarticulate dog with his mouth in his neck, declined comment, but did spray some spittle. Jon, the oddly bug-eyed human, would only yell, "Garfield!" in bold black lettering.

The incident closely mirrors hundreds of others that have involved the trio since 1978.

Binkley Confronts Closetful of Anxieties

By Berke Breathed

An underdeveloped child known only as Binkley was in a dark and fearful mood this morning after a harrowing encounter with strange, symbolic creatures in his bedroom closet, sources close to the lad revealed earlier today.

Binkley was apparently awoken from a fitful sleep sometime during the night by the presence of a large, horned monster. It was not clear whether the monster was real or imagined, but the insights it gave into the shy, weak personality of Binkley were not to be taken lightly.

Binkley's father, a large, bull-necked man, was not present at the mysterious manifestation, but he has been known in the past to be dismissive of such phenomena.

Reagan Shown to Be Foolish

By Garry Trudeau

Washington—Conversations between President Reagan and his wife Nancy filtered out of the White House and high into the air this morning, where they became visible in large black lettering. The conversation clearly showed the inadequacy of this aging conservative president.

At first the dialogue appeared to reflect normal anxieties of a chief executive: One said, "I'm worried that I can't control the country anymore," and the other responded, "Yes, dear." Then the first speaker continued, "I'm worried that the people don't love me so much any more." The second speaker responded, "Yes, dear." Then, the first speaker said, "Sometimes I wish that I could just leave it all behind." The second speaker, in what turned out to be the ironic denouement of the conversation, said, "I understand, Nancy." Thus, the speaker who was speaking as if he or she was the one in power, was revealed to be *Nancy* Reagan, *not* the President, a stinging commentary on Reagan's effectiveness.

Small Boy Annoys Mr. Wilson

By Hank Ketcham

A small boy named Dennis Mitchell wandered out of his yard this morning and managed to bother a middle-aged man named Mr. Wilson, local authorities reported.

Dennis, son of Gloria and Henry Mitchell, had apparently been left unattended by his parents and managed to enter his neighbor's yard unnoticed. He then startled the hapless Mr. Wilson with his sudden question, "Can I come and visit you, Mr. Wilson?"

Mr. Wilson, victim of countless previous incidents of harassment by the Mitchell boy, responded by blowing steam out of his ears, signifying his anger.

Dennis, popularly known as "the Menace," appeared to be unfazed both by Wilson's unfriendly response and his own failure to mature during the last 30 years.

Attempted Murder Continues

By Stan Lee

The attempted murder of a Mr. Spider Man continued yesterday for the third consecutive day. A band of known ruffians leveled weapons at Mr. Man three days ago, but as of last night the crime had not proceeded significantly.

Neighbors say Mr. Man was at first surprised by the attack, but has used the three intervening days to plan a daring escape. If all goes smoothly, Mr. Man will incapacitate the criminal leader some time early next week, and then leap from the window to the safety of the street 30 stories below.

The police have been notified, but are not expected to arrive until at least next Thursday, by which time Mr. Man will undoubtedly have extracted himself from the situation.

Suspect Apprehended in Vandalism Case

By Bill Keane

The owners of a house that was vandalized yesterday now believe that they have located the culprit. The alleged vandal, an eight-year-old child named Billy, is accused of having tracked through the entire house with muddy shoes. According to authorities, Billy is the son of the house's owners.

Despite overpowering circumstantial evidence, Billy has denied any wrongdoing. Nevertheless, the fact remains that dark footprints were found leading from a mud puddle in front of the house, through the front door, into the living room, across the sofa, up the stairs, into the bathroom, into the bedroom, onto the bed, up to the fifth shelf of a tall bookcase, back down to the living room, and then into the kitchen, where the boy's mother apprehended him.

Soldier Contracts Mysterious Sleep Disorder

By Mort Walker

In what appears to be a bizarre medical oddity, an enlisted man known only by the code name "Beetle" Bailey has been diagnosed as suffering from a rare sleeping disorder. The details of the case remain classified. Nobody knows where the recruit is currently stationed, nor whether he is currently engaged in a war or merely involved in military exercises.

According to Lieutenant Fuzz of the sick man's platoon, a superior officer operating under the code name "Sarge" had ordered "Beetle" to wake up after finding the enlisted man sleeping in an upright position in mid-afternoon. When words failed to rouse the man, physical violence was employed in accordance with codes of military justice. This, too, failed to produce any effect. At this point, a special chemical formula was brought in and placed beneath the sleeping man's nose. This brought him to a state of sudden alertness. The contents of the drug are top secret, but it is known to have been prepared by another officer code-named "Cookie."

The area's military commander, General Halftrack, was on his golf day and unavailable for comment.

Door-to-Door Salesman Suffers Wound to Buttock

By Dean Young and Stan Drake

A door-to-door salesman is in stable condition today after receiving a serious blow to the left buttock yesterday afternoon. The unidentified man reportedly was injured while on the property of a Mr. and Mrs. Dagwood Bumstead.

According to eyewitness accounts, the salesman had been attempting to sell Mr. Bumstead a device designed to eject salesman from the premises. The apparatus consisted of an artificial foot attached to a spring-loaded hinge, and apparently was capable of delivering a powerful mechanical kick to its victim.

Reports say Mr. Bumstead tried to get rid of the salesman several times before asking to see a demonstration of the machine in operation. The injury apparently resulted when the peddler complied with Mr. Bumstead's request. No charges have been filed.

At the time, this unfortunate newspaper did not know that the restaurant reviewer it had hired had an eating disorder. Though you think they would have known by her emaciated figure.

THE ROMAN FEATHER

fine dining. 10 entrées nightly.
reservations required.

★ ★ ★

by Lizzie Thinne

The decor is exciting. The interior is an authentic Greek temple, complete with stuccoed arches and interior patio. I couldn't help noticing the elegant grape arbor or how unbelievably fat I am. Fortunately there was a reflecting pool in which I could stare at myself for a full quarter of an hour.

If you go to The Roman Feather, be sure to bring your appetite. The servings are plentiful. An entrée here is more than you could eat in a week. Or a month, in my case. I always hate myself when I fill up before dinner on a roll. I always hate myself, but especially then, so this time I just sucked on the end of a breadstick. Then when the meal came, I wiped my tongue off with a napkin. All the items on the menu looked delicious. I decided to forgo the specialty of the house, a lamb dish, and instead ordered a piece of toast. But I guess my eyes were bigger than my stomach, in sheer physical volume, so I had to take it home in a doggie bag. Well, actually, a napkin ball, since I had been chewing it for nigh on two hours. The servings really are enormous. The sight of that much food could choke a horse. It made me gag anyway. No, that was later, I guess, in the vomitorium. With the check, they brought a thin mint. But, none of those rich heavy desserts for me! For desert, I had two chocolate diet pills. But those things are four calories apiece! So into the bathroom, and up they came. Overall, I recommend The Roman Feather. If not for the food, for the bathrooms. They are pretty pink marble, and I could spend all night in there.

Sen. Mohasset: "As I think we all suspected, the newspaper industry now must be added to the dishonor roll of American media. It is becoming increasingly clear that it is unclear what person or persons are behind this conspiracy, but hopefully as the investigation continues, this clarity will become less clear, serving to clarify what is clearly an unclear situation."

•

Sen. Beaufort: "As sensitive as Ah am to the concerns of mah constituents, Ah can almost feel their whimpers of feah now when they pick up their daily newspaper. Are they gonna be hoodwinked by some evil trickery, or offended by some sort of monstrous voodoo? Ah'm afraid that Ah cannot deny it. Therefore Ah declare that newspapers must be placed, along with magazines, radio and music, and movies, on the list of things to be shunned unless they include valuable information about mah re-election campaign."

•

Sen. Richardson: "Without trustworthy and respectable news reporting, the nation spins through a freezing dark void like a spacewalking astronaut whose air line has just been severed by a passing meteor. Or, to use another analogy, the newspaper industry has been shown to be no more honorable than a spent booster rocket. But enough about space. The point is that I have no idea what the hell is going on with this Mediagate thing. I mean, I'm just as anxious as the rest of the nation to get to the bottom of this."

•

Sen. Stone: "When in the course of human events it becomes necessary for a society and its government to probe into the inner workings of its own watchdog, represented especially by the print news medium, one can only reflect ominously on the state of the entire system that produced the suspect medium. 'What hath we wrought?' we may be tempted to say, and indeed, what hath we wrought? Rot? We hope not. I join with my fellow Senators in casting a suspicious glance on the realm of newsprint, and it is to be hoped that future events will prove our suspicions well-founded only in that they are borne out by a fitting level of revelation, forgiveness, and finally, love."

•

Sen. Beatrice: "At times of crisis such as this, the American public is tempted to cry out, "Who are we?" To such a question, I can only reply, "Look around you." As Mediagate deepens, the foundations of trust in the nations' media may be shaken, but we remain as we always have been, and always shall be: Beatific in our knowledge that the all-embracing fabric of our nation is safe. Nevertheless, we must continue to pursue this apparent conspiracy. Any overarching, sinister influence in American life must be rooted out if it is not part of who we are."

•

Sen. Fawcett: "We are continuing to see the mainstream media take it on the chin in these hearings. Red meat, cholesterol, lack of seatbelt laws, and defense spending—all of these will soon be shown to be at the root of Mediagate. And I believe that by the end of the hearings, it will be painfully obvious that at the root of red meat, cholesterol, lack of seatbelt laws, and defense spending lies violence in Saturday morning cartoons."

WEEK FIVE: TELEVISION

Sen. Mohasset: "Television: the boob tube, the vast wasteland, the idiot box. The youngest of the American media, television would seem like it had the least to hide—but sadly that just isn't the case. Our evidence docket this week is the largest yet, and my secretary's bad back is a sorry witness to that fact.

"On the brighter side, I expect that this week's testimony will be a bit livelier than usual. Magazine editors, washed-up folk singers—sure, they were all right, but they can't compare with the magic of 'Mr. Television' Milton Berle, or that old sourpuss Andy Rooney.

"Lastly, I must caution Senator Beaufort in advance against badgering Andy Griffith for autographs when he arrives."

NIGHTLINE

KOPPEL: Good evening. I'm Ted Koppel in Washington, and this is ABC News' *Nightline.* Mediagate—the nation's broadcasters and publishers implicated in the century's farthest-reaching conspiracy. Who's behind the cover-up and why?

KOPPEL: With me tonight is Senator Archibald Stone, member of the Senate Committee on Media Affairs, and a key figure in the Mediagate investigatory panel. Good evening, Senator.

STONE: Good evening to you, Ted.

KOPPEL: And with me live from Los Angeles is film and television starlet Farrah Fawcett. Good evening, Farrah.

FARRAH: Hi, Ted.

KOPPEL: Senator Stone, will stars like Farrah here receive any sort of special treatment because of their relationship with panel members?

STONE: I don't know what you're talking about, Ted. I've never even met Farrah before tonight. I swear it. If you're talking about that night last April, I'll have you know that . . .

FARRAH: Oh, don't be silly, Archie. *I* know what you're talking about, and I'll never forget it, but I think Ted is talking about my sister, Senator Pamela Fawcett!

STONE: She's not your sister!

FARRAH She *isn't?*

CLICK!

ENTERTAINMENT TONIGHT

HART: In Washington, the Mediagate hearings entered their fifth week today as witnesses representing the television industry began their testimony. Here's our own Leeza Gibbons with more on the story . . .

GIBBONS: Mediagate. The entire entertainment industry under fire from the U.S. Senate. The hearings may be serious business here in Washington, but they have their share of rising stars, too.

MOHASSET: Uh, thank you, Ms. Gibbons, but we really should get on with your testimony now ... if you don't mind?

GIBBONS: But, Mr. Chairman, couldn't you please tell us a bit about your involvement with Mediagate?

MOHASSET: Ms. Gibbons, that's the question that *you're* supposed to be answering.

GIBBONS: Oh, sorry . . .

CLICK!

SATURDAY NIGHT LIVE:

"MOHASSET": So, Mr. Flanagan, could please state for the committee your exact whereabouts during the production of "Hello, Larry"?

FLANAGAN: Uh, I was in . . . France. No, Spain. That's the ticket. Yes, I was in Spain, Senator, playing . . . SOCCER.

"MOHASSET": And while you were "playing soccer," who exactly were you living with?

FLANAGAN: I was living with my girlfriend Cheryl Tiegs, no ... Pamela Fawcett! That's right, I was living with Senator Fawcett, in the LOUVRE!

And, you know, whenever we'd make love ... right in front of the Mona Lisa, yeah ... you know what she'd yell to me? She'd yell, "LIVE FROM NEW YORK, IT'S ..."

CLICK!

TAKING THE STAND: Leonard Nimoy and Gene Roddenberry of *Star Trek*

Sen. Mohasset: Mr. Roddenberry, the committee understands that you have submitted as evidence an unused script from the first season of *Star Trek*. Why was this episode never produced?

Roddenberry: Well, Senator, I was interested in making *Trek* as realistic as possible. I hired a scientist from M.I.T. to help. But after reading the script, I decided that my own sixth-grade geometry course would be sufficient scientific background for writing the show.

Nimoy: It was all highly illogical, Senator.

Sen. Mohasset: Mr. Nimoy, what was your role in all of this?

Nimoy: I didn't have much to do with it, Senator.

Sen. Mohasset: Then why did you ask that we subpoena you to appear before the committee today, Mr. Nimoy?

Nimoy:: I just wanted to tell all the viewers at home not to miss *In Search Of* this week. It's all about the missing Andean gold village of Puero Nistre, and I can assure you it will be *very* interesting. It will air at 5:30 today on KTUL, Tulsa, at 7:30 on WJLA, Washington . . .

Sen. Mohasset: Bailiffs, please remove Mr. Nimoy from the courtroom.

Nimoy: Hey! Ouch! Stoppit! Watch it, or I'll use my Vulcan nerve pinch on you! Abracadabra! Hocus Pocus! I'll have you know I'm a very important man! Hey. . . .

Sulu: Captain—we're approaching Rigel 7.

Kirk: Good. Put it up on the screen. (Pause) Sulu, I said put it up on the screen.

Sulu: I did, Captain. It's that tiny dot right over there. It will be another two days before it's visible to the human eye.

Kirk: Well, tell me when we get there. Until then, I'll be reading in my quarters.

COMMERCIAL BREAK

Sulu: Captain—we're getting really close to Rigel 7 now. We'll be there in an hour.

Kirk: Well—darn it—can't we go any faster?

Spock: Illogical, Captain. The theory of relativity says that no object can move faster than the speed of light. There's simply no way we can go any more rapidly.

Kirk: In that case, I'll be in my quarters. Call me when we get there.

COMMERCIAL BREAK

Sulu: Captain—we're at the planet.

Kirk: Good. Spock—report.

Spock: It's a relatively unknown planet, Captain. It's very large and dense. I'm sure we'll all find it very interesting.

Kirk: Prepare to beam down. The landing party will consist of you, myself, Bones, and Ensign Louie.

(Scotty beams the crew down to the planet's surface. Immediately, all four men collapse to the ground and fall into comas due to the shock of being beamed across space.)

COMMERCIAL BREAK

(Ten minutes pass. At last, the crew regains consciousness and struggles to stand up.)

Bones: (gasp) My God, Jim—I can't breathe. There's no oxygen on this planet!

Spock: Captain! (gasp) I can barely stand up! I'm no whiz at figures, but the gravity of this planet must be ten thousand times stronger than that of Earth.

Kirk: That's impossible, Spock.

Spock: Well, I suppose, Captain.

Kirk: Men, we're here in the name of science, and before we go, we've got to take a core sample. You—Ensign Louie—haul this hydraulic planetary drill over to that ridge by the horizon and bring back some samples.

(Ensign Louie, gasping and shivering, begins crawling into the distance, dragging the gigantic machine behind him.)

Kirk: (flipping open communicator) Kirk to Enterprise. Beam up three—we're dying!

Scotty: What was that, Captain? I'm afraid there's some electrical interference.

Kirk: I said beam us up! Quickly! We're dying!

Scotty: But what about Ensign Louie?

Kirk: It's too late for him! Beam us up!

Scotty: Ay ay, Captain, but you'll have to wait 'til our orbit brings us back around to your side of the planet.

Kirk: All right, I'll see if we can hold out that long. Kirk out.

Bones: Spock! You and your damned logic!

Spock: You're far too emotional, Dr. McCoy.

Bones: You darned green-blooded pointy-eared inhuman weirdo. Why don't you just go fry in hell!

Spock: Unlikely, Dr. McCoy.

Kirk: You two pipe down. We've got to conserve oxygen. We have none, and it's got to last us another half hour.

COMMERCIAL BREAK

Kirk: All right, men—fan out.

Spock: (Walks about ten feet from the original site) Captain—I've detected an alien life form.

Kirk: What? What is it? Can you describe it?

Spock: Yes, Captain. It's a stinking brown fungus, and it's clinging to a rock.

Bones: Gross!

Kirk: Just a second, Spock—I'm on my way over. (steps over to where Spock is standing) Now, show me where it is.

Spock: There it is, Captain.

Kirk: (grinds boot into fungus) Well, I guess that won't threaten the federation ever again.

COMMERCIAL BREAK

Kirk: I don't know if I can take this asphyxiation much longer. I need a cool drink from that stream over there.

Bones: Jim! Are you crazy? That water might be salty, or warm!

Kirk: Get out of my way! I've got a hunch the water's good for drinking. (Scoops up a handful of water and drinks voraciously. A second later, he gags and spits it out) Auugh! It's no good!

Scotty: Enterprise to Captain Kirk. Scotty here. Ready to beam up three.

Kirk: Good! Hurry up! We're dying!

(The three men are transported back to the Enterprise.)

COMMERCIAL BREAK

(Final scene: Kirk, Bones, and Spock are chatting around the Captain's seat.)

Kirk: You know, Spock, I could be wrong, but I thought I saw you smiling just a little bit when we escaped from that God-forsaken planet.

Spock: Incorrect, Captain. It would be most improper to express joy while Ensign Louie lies dead on the planet's surface, with my core samples.

Bones: My God, Spock! A man is dead, and you're worried about core samples! You inhuman bastard!

Spock: (shrugs)

Kirk: (chuckles) Helm, set course for Rigel 8. What is our estimated time of arrival?

Sulu: Well, even though it's the closest planet in the universe, I'm afraid the limitation of the speed of light means we'll be lucky if our great-grandchildren live to see it.

Kirk: In that case, I'll be in my quarters. Steady as she goes.

TV Listings

The following television shows were all pre-empted by *Night of 100,000 Stars*, which ran for an entire week on every channel.

Monday

5:00
- **3** NEWS
- **4** NEWS
- **7** NEWS
- **12** NEWS
- **68** ALICE
  Mel has a coronary when Flo actually reveals her "grits."

5:30
- **3** NEWS
- **4** NEWS
- **7** NEWS
- **12** NEWS
- **68** I DREAM OF JEANNIE NAKED

6:00
- **3** NEWS
- **4** NEWS
- **7** NEWS
- **12** NEWS
- **68** RHODA
  High comedy when Rhoda acts Jewish.

6:30
- **3** NEWS
- **4** THE NEWS
- **7** NEWS
- **12** THE FLYING NUN
  All of San Tanco is concerned when the Flying Nun gets diarrhea.

7:00
- **3** EIGHT IS ENOUGH
  Abby finally gets a diaphragm.
- **4** CHARLIE'S HELL'S ANGELS
- **7** THE PAPER CHASE
  John must collect his papers when the law school bully scatters them on the ground.
- **12** TOO CLOSE FOR COMFORT
- **68** TOO STUPID FOR VIEWING COMFORTABLY

7:30
- **12** M*A*S*H
  Alan Alda writes, directs, stars.
- **68** A*L*D*A
  Alan Alda writes, directs, stars.

8:00
- **3** CHiPS
  Erik Estrada flosses the insects from his teeth.
- **4** AIRWOLF
  Airwolf's rotating blades accidentally shred the Flying Nun.
- **7** MAUDE
  Maude is sorry when God does get Walter.
- **12** JEOPARDY
  Stupid!!
- **68** WHAT'S HAPPENING?!
  Stupider!!

8:30
- **7** SHE-RA
  He-Man asks She-Ra if, therefore, "Ra" means "woman."
- **12** A.K.A. PABLO
- **68** R.I.P. PABLO

9:00
- **3** BARETTA
  Robert Blake plays a tough LA cop by day, a tough LA hair stylist by night.
- **4** BARFETTA
  Robert Blake plays a tough LA cop with a weak stomach.
- **7** BARTLETTA
  Robert Blake plays a tough LA cop who happens to like pears.
- **12** BAGUETTA
  Robert Blake plays a tough LA cop by day, a tough Parisian cop by night.

- **68** POOH CORNER
  The Health Inspector says Pooh's corner full of shit must go, as it covers 97 of the 100 Acre Woods.

10:00
- **3** KIDS SAY THE DARNDEST SHIT
  With host Fart Art Link Sausages Linkletter.
- **4** MIDGET
  Midget finds it hard to adjust to Malibu High, and joins the circus.
- **7** GADGET
  When Sally Field is injured in a freak hair-curling accident, she must be fitted with a robotic head and torso.
- **12** GIBLET
  Mrs. Lawrence accidentally stuffs the Thanksgiving turkey with her teenage daughter.

10:30
- **3** DIFF'RENT STROKES
  The Drummonds learns that Arnold is actually shrinking. Until Willis steps on him.
- **4** GIMME A BREAK!
- **7** GIMME A JOKE!
- **12** GIMME A SHOTGUN!
- **68** AMAZING STORIES
  Stephen Spielberg takes good scripts and ruins them with his directing.

11:00
- **3** HARRY-O
- **4** HAWAII-FIVE-O
- **7** COLUMB-O
- **12** THE STREETS OF SAN FRANCISCO
- **68** When his car hits a pothole, Karl Malden's head hits the dashboard, and his nose swells to the point where Michael Douglas refuses to be his partner. Both are equally upset about road conditions.

Tuesday

5:00
- **3** NEWS
- **4** NEWS
- **7** NEWS
- **12** NEWS
- **68** FATHER KNOWS BEST, DAMMIT

5:30
- **3** NEWS
- **4** NEWS SPECIAL
- **7** NEWS
- **12** NEWS
- **68** MAKE ROOM FOR DADDY
  All the door-frames in the Williams' new home must be enlarged to accommodate Danny Thomas' big nose.

6:00
- **3** NEWS
- **4** NEWS
- **5** NEW
- **12** PEW
- **68** TRANSFORMERS
  When the Transformers visit Europe, they must convert to 220-cycles.

6:30
- **3** NEWS
- **4** TODAY: NEWS
- **7** NEWLYWED GAME
- **12** NEWLYDIVORCED GAME
- **68** FLIPPER

7:00
- **3** FLIPPER
  Sandy is heart-broken when he finds Flipper belly-up.
- **4** FLIPPER
  When Sandy opens a can of tuna, he is horrified to find his old friend.

- **7** CHiPs
- **12** CHimPs
- **68** CHumPs

7:30
- **3** GILLIGAN'S ISLAND
  The Castaways are obliterated when the island becomes a hydrogen-bomb test site.
- **4** BEWITCHED
  When Samantha sneezes from pepper, her nose twitches violently, and Darrin becomes a eunuch.

8:00
- **3** M*A*S*H*Ugginah
  A crazy Jewish doctor raises his fees.
- **4** THE JEFFERSONS
  "Wheezy" is confined to an iron lung.
- **7** MAUDE
- **12** MAUDE SQUAD
- **68** MAUDE COUPLE
- THE WALTONS
  The Waltons must sell John-Boy's mole to make ends meet.

8:30
- **4** THE FACTS OF LIFE
  Natalie must accept that she will never be loved because she is fat and ugly.
- **7** THE THREE SCROOGES
  On Christmas Eve, an old miser is visited by the Ghosts of Christmas Moe, Christmas Larry, and Christmas Curly.
- **12** GOOD TIMES
- **68** BAD JOKES

9:00
- **3** MURDER, SHE WHINED
- **4** THAT'S INCREDIBLY DULL
- **7** REAL DULL PEOPLE
- **12** THOSE AMAZINGLY DULL ANIMALS
- **68** FANTASY ISLAND
  Even Mr. Rourke cannot fulfill Larry Storch's fantasy—to get on any other show besides Fantasy Island.

10:00
- **3** THE BIONIC WOMAN
- **4** THE MORONIC WOMAN
- **7** BLACK SHEEP DIP SQUADRON
- **12** BAAD BAAD BLACK SHEEP
- **68** HILL STREET BLOWS

11:00
- **3** 20-MINUTE WORKOUT

11:20
- **3** 30-MINUTE PIGOUT

Wednesday

5:00
- **3** NEWS
- **4** AND GUESS WHAT? NEWS
- **7** FOR VARIETY, NEWS
- **12** SILVER SPOONS
- **68** Mr. Stratten is upset when he learns of Ricky's $2 million coke habit.

5:30
- **3** NEWS
- **4** OH WHAT THE HELL, NEWS
- **7** NEWS, ANYONE?
- **12** $100,000 PYRAMID
- **68** After the secret word is uttered, the mummy of the Pyramid arises from its ancient crypt.

6:00
- **3** NEWTS
- **4** NUDES
- **7** NUKES
- **12** NOOSE
  ALFRED HITCHCOCK PRESPIRES

6:30
- **3** NUPRIN
- **4** NUTRELLA
- **7** NEUTERED

12 NOON
- **68** LEAVE IT TO BEAVER TO FUCK UP

7:00
- **12** STAR SEARCH AND DESTROY
- **68** FLINTSTONES
- **7** GALLSTONES
- **12** MUPPETS
  When Kermit tells Miss Piggy she must use a sponge and foam, she uses Fozzie.
- **68** KUNG FU
  When Grasshopper snatches the car keys from the Master's hands, he knows it is time he must leave the monastery.

7:30
- **3** PASSWORD
- **4** PASSGAS
- **7** WELCOME BACK, KOTTER
  Gabe is released from prison after serving twenty years for the murder of Principal Woodman, which the Sweathogs had actually committed.
- **12** THE MANY LOVES OF ADOBIE
  More humorous exploits of the most teenager at Hopi High.

8:00
- **3** HOLLYWOOD SQUARES
- **4** HOLLYWOOD GEEKS
- **7** HOLLYWOOD SQUARES
  When the Squares collapse, Elke is crushed by Paul Lynde.
- **12** THE PATRIDGE FAMILY
  Danny is shot by poachers.
- **68** HART ON HART
  Max needs a crowbar to get the time.

8:30
- **3** BEVERLY HILLBILLIES
- **4** BENNY MILLBILLIES
- **7** BARNEY MILLBILLIES

9:00
- **3** LOVE, AMERICAN STYLE
- **4** KISSING, FRENCH STYLE
- **7** HUMPING, DOGGIE STYLE
- **12** TO TELL THE TRUTH
  All the panelists admit they lied.
  What's My Line?
- **68** WHAT'S MY LINE?
  All the panelists are wasted.

9:30
- **3** THE PATTY DUKE SHOW
- **4** THE PATTY MELT
- **7** MARY TYLER MORE
- **12** F-TROOP
- **68** CASPER THE VERY...

10:00
- **3** LOVE BOAT
- **4** RELATION SHIP
- **7** SEX BARGE
- **12** FAME
- **68** LAME

11:00
- **3** CANDID CAMERA
  Host Alan Funt se...
- **4** CANDIDE CAMERA
  Host Alan Funt a... by Voltaire.
- **7** CANDIED CAMERA
  Host Alan Funt... sticky film.
- **12** FAMILY
  Everyone mentions his name.
- **68** FAMILY
  Everyone mentions Buffy's name... films. But...

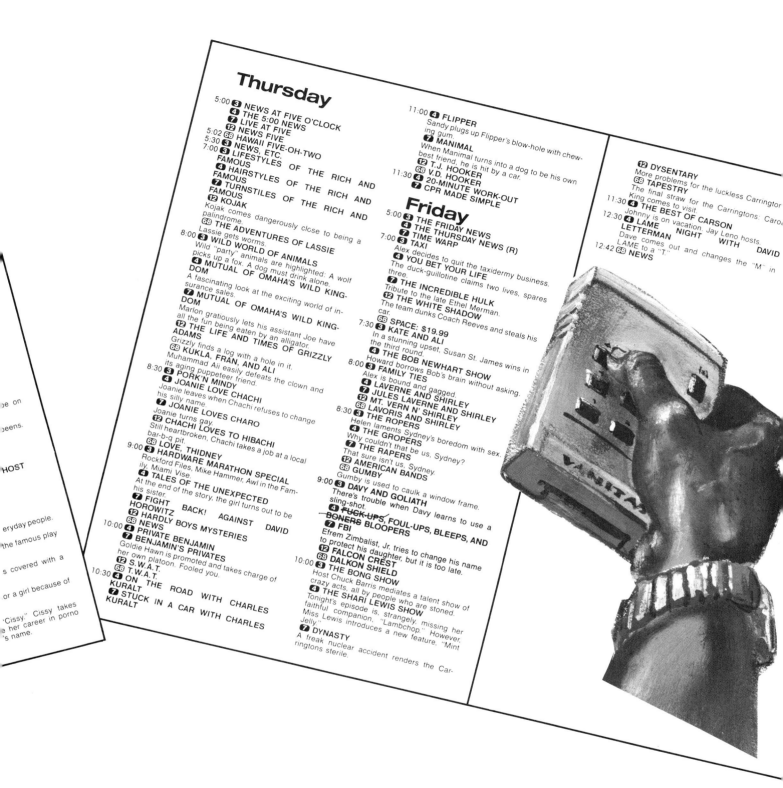

Thursday

5:00 ③ NEWS AT FIVE O'CLOCK
④ THE 5:00 NEWS
⑦ LIVE AT FIVE
⑫ NEWS FIVE
5:02 ⑱ HAWAII FIVE-OH-TWO
5:30 ③ NEWS, ETC.
7:00 ③ LIFESTYLES OF THE RICH AND FAMOUS
④ HAIRSTYLES OF THE RICH AND FAMOUS
⑦ TURNSTILES OF THE RICH AND FAMOUS
⑫ KOJAK
Kojak comes dangerously close to being a palindrome.
⑱ THE ADVENTURES OF LASSIE
Lassie gets worms.
8:00 ③ WILD WORLD OF ANIMALS
Wild "party" animals are highlighted: A wolf picks up a fox. A dog must drink alone.
④ MUTUAL OF OMAHA'S WILD KING-DOM
A fascinating look at the exciting world of in-surance sales.
⑦ MUTUAL OF OMAHA'S WILD KING-DOM
Marlon gratiously lets his assistant Joe have all the fun being eaten by an alligator.
⑫ THE LIFE AND TIMES OF GRIZZLY ADAMS
Grizzly finds a log with a hole in it.
⑱ KUKLA, FRAN, AND ALI
Muhammad Ali easily defeats the clown and its aging puppeteer friend.
8:30 ③ PORK'N MINDY
④ JOANIE LOVE CHACHI
Joanie leaves when Chachi refuses to change his silly name.
⑦ JOANIE LOVES CHARO
Joanie turns gay.
⑫ CHACHI LOVES TO HIBACHI
Still heartbroken, Chachi takes a job at a local bar-b-q pit.
⑱ LOVE, THIDNEY
9:00 ③ HARDWARE MARATHON SPECIAL
Rockford Files, Mike Hammer, Awl in the Fam-ily, Miami Vise.
④ TALES OF THE UNEXPECTED
At the end of the story, the girl turns out to be his sister.
⑦ FIGHT BACK! AGAINST DAVID HOROWITZ
⑫ HARDLY BOYS MYSTERIES
⑱ NEWS
⑦ PRIVATE BENJAMIN
10:00 ⑦ BENJAMIN'S PRIVATES
Goldie Hawn is promoted and takes charge of her own platoon. Fooled you.
⑫ S.W.A.T.
⑱ T.W.A.T.
10:30 ④ ON THE ROAD WITH CHARLES KURALT
⑦ STUCK IN A CAR WITH CHARLES KURALT

11:00 ④ FLIPPER
Sandy plugs up Flipper's blow-hole with chew-ing gum.
⑦ MANIMAL
When Manimal turns into a dog to be his own best friend, he is hit by a car.
⑫ T.J. HOOKER
⑱ V.D. HOOKER
11:30 ④ 20-MINUTE WORK-OUT
⑦ CPR MADE SIMPLE

Friday

5:00 ③ THE FRIDAY NEWS
④ THE THURSDAY NEWS (R)
⑦ TIME WARP
7:00 ③ TAXI
Alex decides to quit the taxidermy business.
⑦ YOU BET YOUR LIFE
The duck-guillotine claims two lives, spares three.
⑦ THE INCREDIBLE HULK
Tribute to the late Ethel Merman.
⑫ THE WHITE SHADOW
The team dunks Coach Reeves and steals his car.
⑱ SPACE: $19.99
7:30 ③ KATE AND ALI
In a stunning upset, Susan St. James wins in the third round.
④ THE BOB NEWHART SHOW
Howard borrows Bob's brain without asking.
8:00 ③ FAMILY TIES
Alex is bound and gagged.
④ LAVERNE AND SHIRLEY
⑦ JULES LAVERNE AND SHIRLEY
⑫ MT. VERN N' SHIRLEY
⑱ LAVORIS AND SHIRLEY
8:30 ③ THE ROPERS
Helen laments Sydney's boredom with sex.
④ THE GROPERS
Why couldn't that be us, Sydney?
⑦ THE RAPERS
That sure isn't us, Sydney.
⑫ AMERICAN BANDS
⑱ GUMBY
Gumby is used to caulk a window frame.
9:00 ③ DAVY AND GOLIATH
There's trouble when Davy learns to use a sling-shot.
④ ~~FUCK-UPS, FOUL-UPS, BLEEPS, AND BONERS~~ BLOOPERS
⑦ FBI
Efrem Zimbalist, Jr. tries to change his name to protect his daughter, but it is too late.
⑫ FALCON CREST
⑱ DALKON SHIELD
10:00 ③ THE BONG SHOW
Host Chuck Barris mediates a talent show of crazy acts, all by people who are stoned.
④ THE SHARI LEWIS SHOW
Tonight's episode is, strangely, missing her faithful companion, "Lambchop." However, Miss Lewis introduces a new feature. "Mint Jelly."
⑦ DYNASTY
A freak nuclear accident renders the Car-ringtons sterile.

⑫ DYSENTARY
More problems for the luckless Carrington
⑱ TAPESTRY
The final straw for the Carringtons: Caro King comes to visit.
11:30 ④ THE BEST OF CARSON
Johnny is on vacation. Jay Leno hosts.
12:30 ④ LAME NIGHT WITH DAVID LETTERMAN
Dave comes out and changes the "M" in LAME to a "T."
12:42 ⑱ NEWS

TAKING THE STAND: William Hanna and Joseph Barbera, creators of cartoons

Sen. Mohasset: Now, I understand that you two are the creators of over 350 cartoon series. That's a very impressive number. How have you managed to come up with so many?

Hanna and Barbera: We steal them, rip them off, that kind of thing.

Sen. Mohasset: You steal them. Uh-huh. You mean you take the themes from already existing shows, add a few modern elements, and then run them in cartoon form.

Hanna and Barbera: Right. Mork & Mindy, Gilligan's Island, Laverne & Shirley, shows with high kid-appeal. They work best. You see, it's. . . .

Sen. Mohasset: Excuse me for interrupting, gentlemen, but I just noticed that your mouths are not moving in time with your words.

All in the Family

This cartoon version of the landmark sitcom places the Bunker family on Mars in the 21st century. Archie solves crimes with the help of his robotic wife, Edith 3000, Mike and Gloria form a rock combo with Lionel Jefferson and perform one song per episode, and a cute alien creature named Dweep joins the Bunker household as mascot and butt of Archie's toned-down abuse.

Match Game '75

Regulars Richard Dawson, Charles Nelson Reilly, and Brett Somers, along with host Gene Rayburn, are caught in a time warp back to 1803, where they accompany Lewis and Clark on their famous expedition and help fight Indians and natural disasters.

Lou Grant

In the cartoon version, Lou is the manager of a group of skateboarding bears who are constantly getting into trouble. Mrs. Pynchon, publisher of the *Tribune* in the original series, appears occasionally as a bumbling but kind witch.

60 Minutes

In this animated adaptation of the weekly newsmagazine, Mike Wallace, Andy Rooney, Harry Reasoner, Ed Bradley, and Diane Sawyer are a team of dune buggies competing in a round-the-world race. They each have amazing mechanical features, but they are constantly threatened by the evil Dr. Garkon and his Freeze Ray.

Dallas

Miss Ellie, J.R., Sue Ellen, and Cliff Barnes become tiny elflike creatures who live in a magical forest in this adaptation of the popular prime-time serial. Most of their time is occupied by harvesting fairy flowers and teaching moral lessons to other woodland creatures, though they do retain some oil holdings.

On October 2, 1973, broadcasting history was made on the fledgling comedy/variety program NBC's *Saturday Night*. Following extensive negotiations with the White House Public Relations Office, producer Lorne Michaels was able to secure incumbent President Richard M. Nixon to host the week's show. Always willing to poke fun at himself, the President, who had once appeared on *Laugh-In*, enjoyed the hectic rehearsal/meeting schedule of the staff, and was eagerly awaiting the live broadcast at 11:30 on Saturday evening. However, Nixon was unaware of events transpiring in Washington at the time, and, following the broadcast, ordered U.S. marshals to impound the tape so that West Coast viewers would be unable to see the potentially embarrassing program.

NBC TELEVISION NETWORK
BROADCAST TRANSCRIPT
10/2/73 12:45 a.m.

(ENTER *NIXON*, CARRYING LAUNDRY BASKET, FOLLOWED BY *CHEVY CHASE* AS SECRET SERVICE AGENT.)

CHASE
I'd like to thank you, Mr. President, for inviting me along with you to do the Executive laundry this evening.

NIXON
Well, you're welcome. I just hope Rico and the boys can get those washers repaired by Monday. Pat has a lot of things she needs clean for her goodwill tour.

CHASE (TAKING LAUNDRY
BASKET)
Here, sir. Let me help you with that.

NIXON (FEELING IN POCKETS)
Darn it . . . I must have left the quarters back on my dresser. Where's the attendant?

(ENTER *JOHN BELUSHI* AS SAMURAI.)

SFX: GONG

SUPER: ''SAMURAI LAUNDROMAT''

BELUSHI (RAISES EYEBROW)
Urrgh?!?

NIXON
Excuse me, sir. Can I get change for a five?

BREAK IN PROGRAMMING FEED

SUPER: NBC NEWS SPECIAL REPORT

V.O. (ANNC'R.)
This is an NBC News Special Report.

CUT TO:

JOHN CHANCELLOR (LIVE)
Good morning. This is John Chancellor reporting live from the Senate Caucus Room in Washington. Following the conclusion of John Dean's testimony before the Senate Select Committee on Presidential Campaign Activities, it has now become clear to those present at the hearings that President Richard Nixon had prior knowledge of the Watergate break-in. In addition, the Counsel's testimony has revealed that the President was involved in other high-level activities including political espionage, bribery, and obstruction of justice. White House Press Secretary Ron Ziegler is expected to issue a statement at 8:00 a.m. this morning. NBC will broadcast the report live at that time. This is John Chancellor, NBC News, Washington.

SUPER: NBC NEWS SPECIAL REPORT

V.O. (ANNC'R.)
This has been an NBC News Special Report. We now return you to the program regularly scheduled for this time.

RESUME PROGRAMMING FEED

BELUSHI (TO CHASE)
Shit . . .

CHASE
Eh . . . um . . .

PRODUCER (FROM SIDE)
Go on!

CHASE
Uh . . . Mr. President, I don't think he understands you.

NIXON (JUMPY)
What?!

CHASE
I said I don't think he understands you.

NIXON
Goddamn right he doesn't! He and all
those other jackal bloodsuckers don't
know *how* America *really* works! Ervin,
Dean, all those guys . . . They can take
a flying . . .

CHASE
I mean about your *laundry,* sir.

NIXON
Laundering? Yeah, so maybe Hunt and
Bebe took care of a little money down in
Mexico . . . But get this one thing
straight, buster . . . that money was
worthless. It went right down the . . .

CHASE   (TO BELUSHI)
John?

NIXON
Right. And another thing . . .

(ENTER *GARRETT MORRIS* IN CHARACTER.)

MORRIS   (TO BELUSHI)
Look, man, I've just about had it with
this laundromat. Last week, your damn
dryer stole five of my socks, and
today, the thing does *this* to my pants!
Just look at these!

(*MORRIS* HOLDS UP PANTS WITH THREE LEGS.)

CHASE
Ha! Mr. President, look at that, will
you?

NIXON
Shut up. I need time to think. Just shut
up.

PRODUCER   (FROM SIDE)
Dave, cut to Stage Two. Run the next
sketch.

SUPER: ''THE CONEHEADS AT HOME''

SFX: EERIE SCI-FI STING

(STAGE TWO: *DAN AYKROYD,* AS CONEHEAD, SITS ON COUCH
IN MIDDLE OF SET.)

AYKROYD
Primatt, Connie! Attention! Digital
read-out now signals that it
approaches temporal coordinates of
nuclear familial unit conference
procedure!

(ENTER *JANE CURTIN* AND *LARAINE NEWMAN* AS
CONEHEADS.)

NEWMAN
Oh, Dad, not another family meeting!

CURTIN
Affirmative, Connie. Beldar and I have
something we wish to interface with you
about.

(ENTER *NIXON* THROUGH FRONT DOOR.)

NIXON   (SLAMMING DOOR)
Dammit! Where can a man find a quiet

place to sit and think around here?!
Ah, screw it!

(*NIXON* COMES OVER TO COUCH AND SITS DOWN NEXT TO
AYKROYD.)
(*NEWMAN, CURTIN,* AND *AYKROYD* LOOK AT EACH OTHER,
PUZZLED.)

NIXON
Wonder what they're saying about me
now . . .

(*NIXON* ATTEMPTS TO TURN ON TV SET.)

NIXON
Damnit, what's wrong with this goddamn
thing?!

(*NIXON* KICKS TV SET.)

NEWMAN
Um, it's just a prop, Mr.
President . . .

NIXON
Well, aren't we the little miss
smartypants now, huh?

NEWMAN
I'm sorry, sir, it's just that
we're . . .

AYKROYD   (INTERRUPTING)
In the middle of a sketch. So could you
please be quiet, okay?

NIXON
Well, pardon me! I'm only the President
of the *United States!* I think I'll just
sit right here until you decide you're
ready to shut up.

(*NIXON* SITS BACK DOWN ON COUCH.)

CURTIN
Where were we?

AYKROYD
Mass consumption.

CURTIN
Right.

(*NIXON* IS TRYING TO GET A BEER OUT OF THE SIX-PACK
HOLDER.)

AYKROYD   (GRABBING SIX-PACK)
Commence mass consumption.

NIXON
Hey!!

(*AYKROYD* STARTS TO DRINK ALL SIX BEERS AT ONCE.)

NIXON
What the *hell* are you doing?!

(DRINKING CONTINUES.)

NIXON
I *said:* What the *hell* are you doing?!

CURTIN   (WHISPERING TO
NIXON)
It's part of the sketch, sir . . .

NIXON

I don't care if it's part of my hairy ass! Give me the goddamn beer before I call out the IRS on you and this whole shitheel network!

AYKROYD

Primatt, Connie, the mass consumption must cease. It is now time to commence the familial interface session.

NIXON

Did you *hear* me?

AYKROYD

Shhhh!

NIXON

Don't you shush me! Don't you *ever* shush Richard Nixon! I've just about had it with this entire stinking shenanigans. It's time I had *my* say . . .

(*NIXON* GETS UP FROM COUCH AND WALKS TO CAMERA.)

NIXON

Listen, everyone out there. I know you might have heard some bad rumors about me and my administration. But they're all untrue—every one of them. I'm a hard-working, honest man, and this whole thing was set up by a bunch of pinko press who're out to get me. Do you understand that?

NIXON

I *said: Do* you understand that?

(AUDIENCE MURMURS.)

NIXON

Oh, I get it. You people came here to see comedy—to see funny stuff. You can't listen to an important, serious point. Well, *I'll* show you comedy!

(*NIXON* WALKS BACK TO COUCH AND RIPS CONEHEAD OFF OF *AYKROYD*. *NIXON* PUTS ON CONEHEAD.)

NIXON

There! Is *that* what you wanted?

(UPROARIOUS LAUGHTER FROM AUDIENCE.)

NIXON

Good! Now you've got your comedy, all right?

(*NIXON* COMES BACK UP TO CAMERA.)

NIXON

Anyway, as I was saying, the testimony that Mr. Dean gave doesn't necessarily reflect . . .

(UPROARIOUS LAUGHTER CONTINUES.)

NIXON

What? What's so funny? I'm serious! As Counsel to the President, Dean was only privy to certain documents that might have *implied* . . .

(LAUGHTER CONTINUES.)

NIXON

Would you people shut up? *What* in God's name is so funny about this?!

(*NIXON* GLANCES AROUND, THEN UP AT HIS FOREHEAD. HE REALIZES HE IS STILL WEARING THE CONEHEAD.)

NIXON

Aaaah, fuck it.

END OF PROGRAMMING FEED*

TAKING THE STAND: Rupert Murdoch

Sen. Stone: I'd like to thank Mr. Rupert Murdoch, owner and director of the Fox television network, for appearing today.

Murdoch: You're welcome. Now what in God's name is it you people want? You've been pestering me nonstop for three solid weeks now!

Sen. Stone: Honestly, sir, we intended no campaign of harassment against you. Your ownership of over fifty percent of American media outlets just lead us to . . .

Murdoch: Shut up, Stone. What is it this time? And make it quick.

Sen. Stone: Fox network. Starting up. Trying to gain recognition for itself.

Murdoch: And?

Sen. Stone: Deceived viewers into thinking they'd be watching something else. Misleading titles, that sort of rot.

Murdoch: So?

Sen. Stone: Well, nothing, I guess. . . .

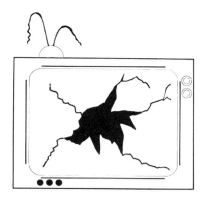

Webber

This show starred Anson Williams, reprising his role as the bumbling Potsie Webber of *Happy Days*. Fox said that the show was "not to be confused with the popular ABC show *Webster*, despite the fact that Williams occasionally scrunched up real small and delivered wisecracks in a squeaky voice for no apparent reason. The show's plot was simple but unappealing. Each week Webber would watch the show *Webster* on television while making asides to an imaginary friend.

The Sidekick Show

Unable to lure away Carson or Letterman to the struggling *Late Show*, Fox executives did what they thought was the next best thing: They got Ed McMahon and Paul Schaffer. The one episode of *The Sidekick Show* was a complete failure, with McMahon and Schaffer both waiting for the other to say something so they could chuckle and agree.

Monday Night Foosball

After getting over the initial disappointment of realizing they were not about to see football, viewers were ready to settle in for what hopefully would be an exciting table-top soccer game. But Fox disappointed yet again. The show merely consisted of a spelling contest, the point of which was to misspell "football" in as many ways as possible.

Newheart

Harry Morgan played artificial heart recipient Barney Clark, a cranky old man who always gets what he wants from his family by putting his hands to his chest and gasping. In the first and only episode Clark attends a concert by the rock group Heart and suffers temporary hearing loss.

60 Manutes

The first episode of this new investigative journalism show was moderately well-received due to its profile of basketball star Manute Bol. Three more episodes featuring other African tribesmen named Manute were shown before Fox realized that no one was still watching. Fox attempted to salvage its dignity by airing one last episode featuring a man allegedly named "Fifty-six Manutes," but no one was fooled.

The Gulden Girls

A sit-com that featured three older women working in a mustard factory. Tim Conway starred as the industrial spy from Grey Poupon. The only episode aired involved Joan (Bette Davis) accidently dropping a winning lottery ticket into a jar of mustard.

Webster

Scott Baio starred as Norman Webster, great-great-grandson of dictionary legend Noah Webster. Many believe that Fox destroyed the potential of this show by having Norman merely sit down each week to watch an episode of Fox's show *Webber*.

CABLE LISTINGS FOR PUBLIC ACCESS CHANNEL Q

Covering New York, Long Island, and
Greater Fairfax County

Monday

JULY 17, 1987

Station Manager: Bob Tuck

6:00 **NATIONAL ANTHEM**
6:03 **MORNING PRAYER** (Ecumenical)
6:04 **MORNING DEAD AIR** (Atheist)
6:05 **NATIONAL ANTHEM** (Reprise)
6:08 **MORNING STRETCH**
6:09 **CIVIL DEFENSE SIREN**
6:40 **THE *TURN OFF THE CIVIL DEFENSE SIREN SHOW***
6:41 **RECORDED PUBLIC SERVICE MESSAGE:**
    "This was only a test"
6:43 **RESUMPTION OF *MORNING STRETCH***
7:00 **MIDNIGHT RAMROD SEXCAPADES** (Repeat)
7:30 **ROMPER ROOM**
8:00 **BOB'S BREAKFAST NOOK**
    Today Bob cooks toast (dry)
8:15 **BOB'S HYGIENE HINTS**
    Bob takes a shower
8:30 **DRESSING FOR SUCCESS**
    With Bob: Choosing a tie
10:00 **AMATEUR BOCCE SEMIFINALS—**
    Live from Detroit (Algeria vs. Team Belize)
11:00 **THAT DARNED POPE!** (Comedy)
    Pope Larry I drowns baby in baptismal font, hijinks ensue
11:30 **LIVE FROM SOUTH BRONX HIGH SCHOOL: Zamfir, master of the pan flute** (Concert)
    Zamfir performs his favorites ("My Funny Valentine," "Shenandoah," and more)
12:00 **MEMORIAL SERVICE**
    Zamfir, late master of the pan flute
12:30 **AUCTION BLOCK**
    On the block today: pan flute, switchblade (slightly tarnished), rusty bicycle chain, Picasso's "Women" (lithograph)
1:00 **FARM REPORT** (U.S. Dept. of Agriculture)
    The farm is O.K.
4:00 **DR. WIZARD'S WORLD OF SCIENCE**
    Dr. Wizard synthesizes dry toast from bread
4:30 **COMMUNITY CHEST FORUM—LIVE FROM CITY HALL**
    Community Council resolves to adjourn. Motion fails.
5:00 **BOWLING FOR PLASTIC TROPHIES**
5:30 **DUMPSTER HUNT!** (Community Game Show)
    Filmed Live behind the studio
6:00 **THE MAKING OF *THE MAKING OF STAR WARS***
    Interview with Joe Spiegel, who made the models of George Lucas used in *The Making of Star Wars*
7:00 **COMMUNITY CHEST FORUM—LIVE FROM CITY HALL**
    Council moves to adjourn. Motion tabled by quorum.
7:30 **PALM READING WITH MADAME ZAZI** (phone-in advice)
8:30 **THE BOB SHOW**
    Bob eats a sandwich. On toast.
9:00 **CONSPIRACY EXPOSE!**
    Who Really Killed Kennedy? (CANCELLED)
9:00 **MOVIE: *BENJI FROM OUTER SPACE***
    A lovable pup saves an earthling family from Saturnian Liver Fluke (CC)
11:00 **COMMUNITY CHEST FORUM—LIVE FROM CITY HALL**
    Council votes to order out for pizza and/or beverage. Overruled by proxy vote.
11:30 **THAT DARNED POPE!** (comedy)
    Pope Larry I drowns another baby
MIDNIGHT HOUR MAGAZINE
12:15 **NIRVANA AND NUTRITION WITH GURU VISHNU**
    Today: Starving your way to bizarre hallucinations
1:00 **ANNOYING LATE-NIGHT LUNATIC SHOW** (phone-in)
2:00 **CIVIL DEFENSE SIREN** (repeat)
2:15 **COMMUNITY CHEST FORUM—LIVE FROM CITY HALL**
    Community council panicked by siren. Unable to resolve course of action.
2:30 **FARM REPORT** (U.S. Dept. of Agriculture)
    It is dark on what's left of the farm
3:00 **COMMUNITY MAIL BAG**
    This week: Mrs. Robertson's mail
3:30 **THE BOB SHOW**
    Bob wakes up to turn down Civil Defense Siren
4:00 **NATIONAL ANTHEM**
    Bob sings
4:15–6:00 **THE STATIC SHOW**

TAKING THE STAND: A.C. Neilsen, president of the Neilsen Ratings Corporation

Sen. Mohasset: Mr. Neilsen, is it in fact true that your company not only tabulates the number of viewers a program has, but also determines what viewers' favorite aspects of that program are?

Neilsen: Yes, that's correct.

Sen. Mohasset: However, I understand that the networks subscribing to your service keep the favorite aspect ratings a closely guarded secret. Why is that?

Neilsen: I suppose it's because they would rather attribute a show's success to "the fact that it's a good, solid show."

Sen. Mohasset: Could you tell me, Mr. Neilsen, why you canceled *Lou Grant?* I loved that show.

Neilsen: Oh, Senator, the networks make programming decisions. I only provide a service that measures . . .

Sen. Beaufort: Yeah, and why'd y'all go and cancel *Andy Griffith?* Andy's a fine, fine man, a credit to . . .

Sen. Richardson: And I suppose you're going to beg innocence for killing *Far Out Space Nuts, Battlestar: Galactica,* and *Space: 1999* too?

Sen. Fawcett: *Rhoda!* How *could* you have canceled *Rhoda?* You beast!

Neilsen: Senators! I don't understand what you're . . .

Sen. Beatrice: LEAVE THE MAN ALONE. Everything he does is perfectly fine. I support him 100 percent. You may leave, A.C.

Neilsen: Thanks, "Robert."

"WHY I WATCH WHAT I WATCH": Viewers Rate Their Favorite Details in Descending Order of Preference.

THE COSBY SHOW

35%   I like the funny faces Bill Cosby makes at his kids.

27%   The fact that I can't decide whether I'm more sexually attracted to the mother or the daughter or both at once.

18%   The fact that Dr. Huxtable is an obstetrician, but you never see him washing his hands.

14%   I like the funny faces Bill Cosby makes at his wife.

6%   The way it's just like real life in my family.

ENTERTAINMENT TONIGHT

47%   I like to make up words to go along with the instrumental theme song.

18%   The way the two hosts sometimes seem to forget we're watching and make jokes between themselves.

14%   The way Leonard Maltin always looks like he thinks someone is going to beat him up.

12%   Only news show on which Iranians are never shown.

9%   Complicated plot.

SIXTY MINUTES

39%   The fact that Andy Rooney's segment is always last, so you can turn it off and know you won't miss anything but the credits.

27%   The pleasure of watching Mike Wallace physically getting nearer and nearer to death each week.

17%   Mexican drug clinics/Idiot-savant piano players.

10%   The way Harry Reasoner will laugh at anything if he thinks he's supposed to.

7%   The way it's just like real life in my family.

THE WALTONS

56%   How Mr. Walton couldn't do anything right, including provide for his family, but they all pretended to like him anyway.

21%   Watching the show and thinking about how John-Boy played a mental retard in a TV movie on another network.

16%   How Grandma was much nicer and funnier after she had her stroke.

7%   The remarkably low prices at the dry goods store give me great pleasure and make me long for a simpler time.

MIAMI VICE

95%   Calling it *Vice* when I talk to my friends.

1%   Don Johnson's overabundance of personal attitude.

1%   Seeing pictures of art deco architecture while listening to today's top hits; I can think of nothing better than this.

1%   Those funny pink birds with long necks during the opening credits.

.5%   Tubbs.

McLAUGHLIN GROUP

67%   I enjoy yelling matches between people who look just like my parents.

15%   Debaters picking on the only female member because her voice is higher than theirs.

10%   Watching John McLaughlin quell screaming matches by yelling louder than the others.

10%   Robert Novak's sideburns.

4%   The delightful blend of rhetoric and fisticuffs.

M*A*S*H

71%   The way Hawkeye and BJ's drinking bouts are periodically interrupted by the call to perform delicate surgery on wounded servicemen.

11%   I find the immense suspension of disbelief required to see Hotlips Houlihan as attractive very challenging.

10%   The show in which Henry dies in a plane crash, because he always seemed like an incompetent leader to me.

8%   The way you can close your eyes and the dialogue sounds just like Groucho Marx, though I often wish it sounded more like Harpo.

Sen. Stone: Thank God this travesty is nearing its conclusion. I thank my lucky stars that I'm not one of those moronic television watchers so placidly duped by those charlatans.

Sen. Richardson: Well, I don't know. I always kind of *liked Charlie's Angels.* Say, how's your sister doing these days, Pamela?

Sen. Fawcett: That infernal tramp is *not* my sister. How many times do I have to tell you imbeciles that?

Sen. Richardson: Geez, you don't have to get huffy about it! I saw it on the *Today* show. Farrah *said* she thought you might have been her sister.

Sen. Fawcett: Oh, Lord. That woman is the flip side of everything I stand for. I can't believe she's so stupid as to identify herself as *my* sister!

Sen. Richardson: Actually, she said she wasn't sure about it.

Sen. Fawcett: I am *not* related to her! I've never even *met* her!

(Enter Senator Beaufort)

Sen. Fawcett (Cont'd.): Do you understand that? For God's sake, please tell me you understand that!

Sen. Beaufort: Always hootin' an hollerin' . . . say, Pam, why can't y'all be mo lak your sister, Farrah?

EVIDENCE brought to the Committee's attention by the National Security Agency

Satellite Dish

On February 1, 1987, Mrs. Earnest J. Willoughby died in Detroit, Michigan. On February 12, Mrs. Earnest J. Willoughby's antique furniture and her brand-new satellite dish TV antenna were delivered to her heirs, Mr. and Mrs. Barry Willoughby, of Forest Hills. The following snippets of conversation in the Willoughby household were recorded over the next few days by two off-duty National Security Administration personnel.

"Look at this, honey, reruns of *The Bionic Woman.* Remember that?"
"Yes. That's nice."
"And lookit, we can watch *Gilligan's Island* on five channels at once."
"Goodness, we'll never pry you away from that thing now."
"Wow. Look. It's a version of *Hee Haw* from the Soviet Union."
"Really? What channel?"
"Seventy-one."
"I thought the man who hooked it up said it only went to seventy."
"So did I, but then I found this little red button in the back."
"Oh."
TV: "HEY COMRADE. HOW IS A GOOD SOVIET CITIZEN BEING LIKE A STRIPPER?"
"I AM NOT KNOWINK. HOW?"
"THEY BOTH MUST WORK FOR THE PEEP-HOLE. 'PEOPLE', GET IT?"
"JUST KEEP PICKING THE MANGEL-WURTZELS. OR I WILL REPORT YOU. HEE HAW!"
"I don't want to watch that if there's no Minnie Pearl. Turn to something else."
"Hey, it's the Disney Channel. Wow, this antenna picks up everything."
"What's the show?"
"Snow White, I think. Yeah, it's Snow White."
"Honey?"
"Yes?"
"Since when did the dwarves wear leather?"
"Since — my, God, you're right. This must be one of those private pay stations. Well, we might as well watch. This is a classic, you know?"
"Honey. Not tonight. I mean, we just buried our son."
"Hmm, you're right. I'll turn to channel 74. Oh, hey, it's the Playboy channel. Man, that's really tame next to those dwarves."
"Dear, turn this. What would the neighbors think?"
"I think they'd think it's fine. Look."
"My god, that's the Martins!"
"Channel 75. Must be their video camera."
"Wow. I never would have expected *that* from *them.*"
"You know, we don't see the Martins enough."
"Oh, you're awful."
"Let's see what's on 76."
"It must be some kind of cop show. Looks like a bank robbery."
"Honey, that *is* a bank robbery. That's our bank!"
"Huh? Jeesh, you're right. We must have picked up the closed-circuit TV's in there."
"Honey?"
"Mmm?"
"Don't you think we ought to call the police?"
"No way. Let 'em get their own antenna."

"What's on 77?"
"It looks like Gene Hackman ripping up the floorboards of his apartment."
"Hmm. Try 78."

TV: "CANAVERAL. THIS IS COLUMBIA 8. DO YOU READ?"

"Uhh. It's some space show."

"CANAVERAL. THERE'S SOMEONE ON THIS FREQUENCY WITH US. IDENTIFY YOURSELVES, INTERLOPERS."

"Uhh, uhh, I'm Larry Willoughby, and this is my wife, Catherine. We're, um—"

"YOU FOLKS SHOULDN'T BE MONITORING THIS FREQUENCY. IT'S PRIVATE."

"We're sorry. We didn't—"

"NEW SATELLITE DISH, HUH?"

"Well, uh, yes."

"IT'S OKAY, CANAVERAL. JUST SOME HACK WITH A NEW DISH ANTENNA. YOU'VE GOT TO TURN THE STATION, MR. WILLOUGHBY."

"OK. Uh, sir, I just wanted to say. The wife and I think you guys are doing a great job. Except for that Christie McAuliffe thing."

"GOOD NIGHT, MR. WILLOUGHBY."

"Er, um. Good night."

"What channel are you watching now?"

"79. Look, it's Max Headroom."

"L-L-LOOK. IT'S MMR. LARRY WILLOUGHBY!"

"Aaaugh!"

"I—I'M S-S-S-SORRY. M-M-MR. L-L-LARRY WILLOUGHBY, AAAUGH."

"Catherine, come quick. Max Headroom is talking to me."

"Ha, ha, honey."

"G-G-GET ME A COKE. B-B-BUTTHEAD."

"Hey, that's my coke!"

"N-N-NOT ANYMORE. LOSER. B-B-BYE!"

"Wha-? Wha'ppen?"

"Hmm? What was that, honey?"

"Uhh, nothing. Can I have another coke?"

"Honey, what is it?"

"I was just watching channel 80."

"Oh?"

"You remember those ghosts from *Poltergeist?*"

"Yes."

"They're here."

"I think I'll try channel 87."

"What in the world did your grandmother need all these channels for?"

"Oh, who knows. She was a loon. She's been senile since age forty. She probably di—aaugh, Grandma!!"

"SO, THIS IS HOW YOU TREAT YOUR GRANDMOTHER WHEN I'M DEAD, GOD REST MY SOUL?"

"Oh, Jeesh, Grandma. I didn't think—"

"AND I SUPPOSE YOU DIDN'T THINK ABOUT COASTERS, EITHER? LOOK AT THE WATER RINGS ON MY BEAUTIFUL END TABLE. IT'S RUINED. WAIT TILL YOU GET TO HEAVEN. I'LL—"

Click.

"What was that you're watching, honey?"

"Uh, *Heaven Can Wait.*"

"Dear, what's that awful noise?"

"It's amazing, Cathy. That's the sound of the creation of the universe. The sound of the huge cloud of hydrogen gas and cosmic dust that is our universe hurtling outward in all directions. Channel 102."

"Maybe it's the cat. He wants to go out, I think."

"No, he got fried yesterday by channel 96. This is the actual sound of the Big Bang."

"That's nice. Could you turn it down a little?"

"C'mon honey. The news is on."

"GOOD EVENING. HERE IS THE TOP NEWS FOR THIS THURSDAY, FEBRUARY 19."

"Uh, honey, isn't this Monday?"

"Oh wow. Yeah, this antenna must be picking up news from three days in the future."

"Really?"

"Looks like it. This could be big. We should watch the stock report and the sports highlights. We can see the future! Do you understand what this means?"

"AND IN LOCAL NEWS, A COUPLE IN FOREST HILLS IS DEAD TONIGHT, ELECTROCUTED IN THEIR HOME EARLIER TODAY BY A SHORT-CIRCUIT IN THEIR HIGH-POWERED SATELLITE TV ANTENNA."

"Um, dear?"

"Yeah, Christ. That's us. Three days from now we get killed. That is really inconvenient."

"Well, I mean, it's just TV, right? It can't really hurt us, can it?"

"Hon, that was the future. It's real, and there's nothing we can do about it. Fascinating, though. All of time is determined three days in advance. Do you think we're seeing it live, or do they show it on tape delay?"

"Oh I don't know. Honey, can we turn it off anyway? Just for a little while?"

"No, hang on. I want to see the weather forecast."

"Pass the chips, hon."

"Sure."

"This isn't so bad, huh?"

"No. Only three hours left."

"HI, SKIPPER."

"HI, LITTLE BUDDY. HAVE YOU SEEN MR. & MRS. HOWELL TODAY?"

"Well, the reception's great, anyway."

"Mmm."

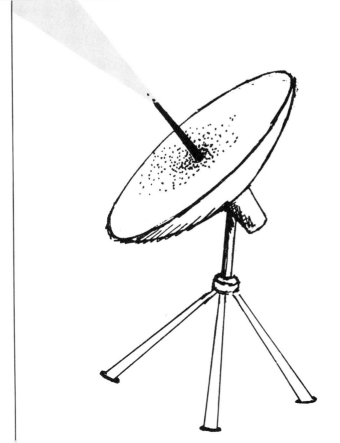

TAKING THE STAND: Clarence Upton, former CBS programming director

Sen. Beaufort: Now, Mistuh Upton, I unnahstand y'all's the man responsible for cancelin' *The Andy Griffith Show.* Suh, you are a scallywag of the hahest degree, a prostitutin' Yankee who ain't got no scruples, a . . .

Upton: Actually, that was my predecessor, Randolph Edwards. I didn't really have anything to do with that.

Sen. Beaufort: —polecat with catfish on his whiskers, a two-timin' half-breed peckuh-head . . .

Sen. Mohasset: Excuse us, Mr. Upton. The Senator seems to have gotten carried away. Now, what is it you were subpoenaed for?

Upton: The situation tragedy. *That* was mine.

Sen. Mohasset: And that was?

Upton: I saw the success of the situation comedy, what with its laugh track and nonstop joke barrages, so I decided that an equally tenable premise might be the "situation tragedy," with its own characteristic "sob track" and tear-jerking plot twists.

Sen. Mohasset: That sounds like a really stupid idea, Mr. Upton.

Upton: Well, why don't you take a look at it and decide for yourself?

Sen. Beaufort: —with his hat on backward, a slimy, pistol-totin' carpetbagguh of a man, a dull-witted back-alley two-bit weasel with a. . . .

LIFE WITH THE LANGSTONS
Broadcast Date:
October 14, 1962

SCENE ONE:

(*LARRY* AND *JANE* ARE PERCHING ON A STEPLADDER ABOVE THE FRONT DOOR, TRYING TO BALANCE A BUCKET OF WATER ON THE TOP.)
(ENTER *MOM* FROM KITCHEN.)

> MOM
> What *on Earth* are you kids doing up there?

> JANE
> Shhh! We're gonna pull a practical joke on Dad!

> LARRY
> Yeah, wait'll you see the expression on his face!

> MOM
> Well, I don't want anyone to get hurt! *Please* be careful.

(*LARRY* AND *JANE* GET DOWN AND MOVE LADDER. *ALL* WATCH DOOR.)

> DAD (FROM OUTSIDE)
> Honey! I'm home!

(*DAD* OPENS DOOR, AND BUCKET FALLS STRAIGHT DOWN, HITTING HIM ON THE HEAD.)
(*DAD* FALLS FLAT TO FLOOR, FACE FIRST.)
(SOB TRACK: GASPS)

> LARRY
> Hey, Dad, get up! It was just a joke!

(*MOM* RUSHES OVER TO *DAD*.)

> MOM
> He's dead! You've killed your father!

(SOB TRACK: MIXED ''MY GOD''s AND SHRIEKS)

> JANE
> It was all your idea, Larry! You did it!

> LARRY
> It was just as much your idea as mine, you liar!

(*LARRY* SLAPS *JANE*.)
(SOB TRACK: MUFFLED SURPRISE)

MOM
Kids! We've got to do something! Your
father's dead, and his boss is coming
to dinner in just a few minutes!

LARRY
Oh, no! And if he loses his job, we'll
all be destitute!

JANE
But he's dead! He's *already* lost his
job.

(SOB TRACK: LIGHT WHINING)

LARRY
Not if I can help it!

SCENE TWO:

(*ALL* ARE TIDYING UP THE HOUSE HURRIEDLY.)

MOM
Hurry up! He'll be here any minute!

SFX: DOORBELL
(SOB TRACK: GROANS)

LARRY
That's him. Everyone play it cool.

(*MOM* OPENS DOOR.)

MOM
Well, Mr. Finley, welcome! We weren't
expecting you so soon!

FINLEY
I can't stay long. I'm afraid I have
some very bad news to tell your
husband.

(SOB TRACK: LOUD SIGHS, MOANS OF RESIGNATION)

JANE   (ASIDE TO LARRY)
What could be worse than Dad being
dead?

LARRY
Shh!

CUT TO: DINING ROOM
(*DAD*'S BODY IS PROPPED UP AT THE TABLE.)

MOM
Herman is feeling a little under the
weather today, Mr. Finley.

FINLEY
Well, might as well get it over
with . . .

(*FINLEY* SLAPS *DAD* ON BACK.)

FINLEY   (CONT'G.)
Herman, old buddy, I have some awful,
awful news.

(*DAD* FALLS OVER INTO HIS SOUP BOWL FACE FIRST.)
(SOB TRACK: MIXED ''OH, NO''s)

LARRY
We might as well tell him the truth . . .

MOM
Yes, Mr. Finley, Herman is dead.

FINLEY
Well, I suppose it's for the best.

JANE
What was your news, Mr. Finley?

FINLEY
Herman was fired this afternoon.

MOM
At least he's not alive to hear it. That
job meant so much to him . . .

FINLEY
And we're going to have to rescind his
wages from the last 3½ years.

(SOB TRACK: WEEPING)

LARRY
Well, there goes summer vacation!

(SOB TRACK: WEEPS AND SHRIEKS)

JANE
At least it's all over with—this
horrible nightmare of suffering has
finally run its course . . .

(SOB TRACK: SIGHS OF RELIEF, SCATTERED APPLAUSE)
SFX: DOORBELL
(*MOM* ANSWERS DOOR.)

MOM
Hello, Ernest. To what do we owe the
pleasure of your visit?

ERNEST
I just thought I should come over and
tell you that your garage is on
fire . . .

(SOB TRACK: HORRIFIED WAILINGS.)
END ACT ONE.

TAKING THE STAND: Bill Cosby

Sen. Fawcett: First of all, Mr. Cosby, I'd like to commend you for your outstanding work in the television industry, particularly with *The Cosby Show*.

Bill Cosby: (makes funny surprised face)

Gallery and Senators: (uproarious laughter)

Sen. Fawcett: Ha! Mr. Cosby, you sure do have a way with that rubbery face of yours. Could you please do that angry yet loving face you make, like when Rudy spills ink on your tax returns?

Cosby: (makes angry yet loving face)

Gallery and Senators: Awwwww. . . .

Sen. Fawcett: Thanks, Mr. Cosby. Those faces were so entertaining, it's almost a shame we're going to have to indict you for covering up this episode of your program.

Cosby: (makes funny surprised face again)

Gallery and Senators: (uproarious laughter)

Sen. Mohasset: Thank you, sir. We've all learned a lot from your eloquent testimony today.

1

Cliff: I'm rich! I'm rich!

Clair: What happened? Did you win the lottery?

Cliff: No. I'm a rich successful doctor.

2

Rudy: Dad, can I have a new doll?

Cliff: No. You have too many already.

3

Rudy: But Dad, it's the Shirley Chisholm Congressional Action Figure.

Cliff: Well why didn't you say so? After all, I'm rich. Here's fifty dollars.

Mom: Cliff, do you think you should spoil the kids that way?

Cliff: What do you mean, spoil? I'm just trying to teach them the value of money—lots of money. Tons of money.

Denise: Dad, can I get a new car?

Cliff: No. Are you crazy? Go to bed!

Denise: But Dad, Crispus Attucks had a new car.

Cliff: Drive safely. (Hands her a wad of bills.)

Theo: Dad, can I have some money? I want to go shoot some dice.

Cliff: Absolutely not. You know the one thing I hate in this world is gambling. Go to your room.

Theo: But Dad, Jesse Jackson gambled all the time in the Wild West.

Cliff: You idiot. That was Jesse James. Go to bed.

Mom: Well, honey, it looks like the kids are finally out of our hair.

Cliff: That's good, 'cause it's my poker night tonight. The boys should be here any minute now.

(Doorbell rings)

10

Cliff: George! J.J.! Fred! Good to see you. Come on in!

11

Cliff: So, Fred, how's the junkyard business?

Fred: Fine, thank you.

George: J.J., you're looking good. How do you feel?

J.J.:   Dyn-O-MITE!

12

Cliff: Well, boys, I'm in for one thousand dollars.

Fred: I'm out.

J.J.:   Me too.

George: I'm in, Huxtable. But my chain of dry cleaning stores are on the line.

(Later . . .)

Cliff: So long! See you next week!

13

Clair: Well, honey, I hope you learned your lesson about gambling.

Cliff: Yes, I have! We're now the proud owners of a junkyard, a chain of dry cleaning stores, and a denim hat!

Albert: Hey, hey, hey—Bill. How 'bout you lay some money on me so me and Mushmouth can go get some ice cream sodas?

Cliff: I thought I told you never to bother me here!

14

Cliff: . . . and don't come back!

15

Clair: Who was that?

Cliff: Oh, just some poverty-stricken guy I used to know. I kicked him out.

Clair: Oh, Cliff. You're wonderful.

TAKING THE STAND: Edward Feldman, producer of *Hogan's Heroes*

Sen. Mohasset: Next on the stand is a Mr. Edward Feldman, producer of the situation comedy *Hogan's Heroes*. Mr. Feldman, did it ever occur to you what a horrible, tasteless idea it was to set a comedic program in a Nazi P.O.W. camp?

Feldman: Not until we tried to write the final episode . . .

HOGAN'S HEROES:

THE UNAIRED FINAL EPISODE

Opening scene in Col. Klink's office. Hogan enters, escorted by two burly storm troopers.

COL. KLINK: Ah Hogan, my good man, I have some bad news to report.

HOGAN: What's the matter, colonel, has Hitler forgotten to shave again?
(canned laughter)

COL. KLINK: Come come now Hogan, be serious. The Allies are rapidly closing in. Berlin could fall in less than a month. I've lost half my family to air raids. Therefore I have some new orders straight from the Gehstaten Polezei High Command.

HOGAN: Lemme guess, the Nazis are going to stop sewing Bulls-Eye targets on their hats! (canned laughter)

COL. KLINK: No, all prisoners of war are to be executed within the hour.

HOGAN: What?

COL. KLINK: Look Hogan, I did everything I could for you. Even requested the firing squad, and that's lucky. They're starving the Russians to death. You wouldn't want that.

HOGAN: Schultz!

SCHULTZ: I see nothing, I know nothing!

COL. KLINK: (sigh) Okay boys, start rounding them up.

(Hogan is led outside. A second later we hear a volley of gunshots sounding from the camp yard. Roll credits)

TAKING THE STAND: Milton Berle

Sen. Mohasset: And now, it's my pleasure to call to the witness stand "Mr. Television," "Uncle Milty," "The King of Comedy" . . . ladies and gentlemen: MILTON BERLE!

Gallery & Senators: (wild applause)

Milton Berle: Thank you, thank you all.

Sen. Mohasset: As you know, Mr. Berle, the committee has found your record spotless, clean on all counts. You have absolutely nothing to worry about. We just thought you might like to appear and say a few words on behalf of the television industry.

Milton Berle: Hey, bubellahs, I'll tell ya about television! When I first started out in TV, it was so long ago that I fell off my dinosaur on my way to work!

Gallery & Senators: (silence)

Milton Berle: Which reminds me of a story: seems a little boy came up to me last week and asked, "Mr. Berle, how old are you?" Then I said, get this, "About as old as the crust in your underwear!" Ha ha ha ha!

Gallery & Senators: (silence)

Milton Berle: Hey, anyway, let me tell you about my wife. She's so fat that when she sits around the house, she crushes it! Ha ha ha ha!

Gallery & Senators: (silence)

Sen. Mohasset: Ahem . . . Mr. Berle, about your 1983 tax return . . .

TAKING THE STAND: Norman Lear

Sen. Fawcett: I'd like to welcome to the hearings Mr. Norman Lear. Let's have a round of applause for Mr. Norman Lear.

Gallery & Senators: (polite applause)

Sen. Mohasset: I'd like to caution you against promoting that sort of outburst again, Senator. It is highly irregular for an investigatory panel to bias itself in that manner.

Sen. Fawcett: Oh, come on, Donald. Norman Lear has done wonders for improving the usual drivel shown on television. He's dealt frankly with very important issues like menopause, racism, draft-dodging, rape, and that sort of thing. Let's hear it for Norman Lear.

Gallery: (polite applause)

Sen. Fawcett: I can't *hear* you . . .

Gallery: (wild applause, hoots, & yells)

Sen. Beaufort: Will y'all pipe down, for God's sake! Now, Mistuh Leuh, I unnastand that you've come foth with a few summaries o' the shows you wrote fo when y'all fust started out.

Norman Lear: That's correct, Senator. I'm afraid the episodes I wrote were considered ahead of their time. Situation comedies of that era were a little more innocent than *All in the Family*.

Sen. Fawcett: You were truly a pioneer, Norman.

Norman Lear: Uh, thank you, Senator.

Sen. Fawcett: You know, Norman, I get off here at six. If you'd like to go have some drinks or something . . .

The following flyer explaining the rates for ads during the CBS-TV airing of the movie "Spring Break" was intercepted just before mailing by a network ad executive who realized that, due to a routine coincidence of printing delays and scheduling errors, the film had been shown over a month earlier.

DOBIE GILLIS (September, 1961) *Dobie's oddball buddy Maynard G. Krebs invites his beatnik-guru, William Burroughs, over to dinner in Lear's original script for the episode. Burroughs' mention of* Naked Lunch *is wrongfully interpreted by Dobie's father, who says, "He's enough trouble fully clothed at dinner. What's he hitting at?" By the show's end, we realize there is no place for a junkie poet in suburban America, and Burroughs takes Krebs and Dobie's mother with him to Tangiers.*

THE MUNSTERS (October, 1965) *As if they didn't have enough trouble being monsters, the Munster clan suffers a new blow when word gets around their working-class neighborhood that they are also a family of Jewish intellectuals. Angry neighbors surround 1313 Mockingbird Lane brandishing torches and pitchforks. They are dispersed when Grandpa speaks to them, intoning the wisdom of Rabbi Hillel, then turns into a bat.*

GOMER PYLE, USMC (November, 1965) *In Lear's episode, Gomer deserts the Marine Corps in protest over U.S. involvement in Vietnam. He is unable to shake his goofy demeanor, however, and stumbles into Sgt. Vince Carter in an amusement park near the base. Gomer is hiding in the blower of a cotton-candy machine, and Sarge tries to coax him out. Gomer refuses, as he is making a political statement, and is soon turned into a fluffy pink mass of candy, a new symbol of the Vietnam resistance.*

SPOT RATES FOR "SPRING BREAK" AD SLOTS

Movie: Opening preview. Lots of shots of girls on the beach. No nudity, but good job casting girls who know how to walk on sand.

9:02 P.M.
2 × 30 sec
$100,000 each

Standard. Estimates are for 60% impulse viewers, who will be making soup or playing tennis until after the first spot. The other 5% are people with Neilsen boxes who have been paid to put them on CBS and leave them there.

Movie: two heroes check into hotel, get room. No girls in room. Pool visible outside window. Girls by pool. Other two heroes check into same room, forced to stay due to crowding. Mention drugs, sex.

9:21 P.M.
2 × 30 sec
$80,000 each

Cut-rate. Young viewers not paying much attention yet. Parents miss these spots while putting children to bed early due to references to drugs, sex. Good time for appeals to elderly, as they will be asleep before the next spots.

Movie: hang out by pool. Belly-flop contest. Water splashes on girls near pool. Extensive coverage of this phenomenon. Development of boring side plot about annoying Florida politician.

9:40 P.M.
4 × 15 sec
$60,000 each

Interest of young viewers piqued by water splashing, then frustrated by digression. Sex-oriented spots very good now. Also good are appeals to parents, who are feeling guilty about sending children to bed when there is as of yet no drugs or sex and they could have learned something from the very educational part about local political campaign problems.

Movie: Cruise strip. Lots of women. Go in bar. All-girl band. Lead singer in very thin body suit. Song: "I Want To Do It To You, Hot Man."

10:00 P.M.
2 × 30 sec
$150,000 each

Young male viewers probably whipped into frenzy. Good time for subliminal sex spots, although any time is good for subliminal sex spots. Parents beginning to get uncomfortable about watching this trash. Good time for spots about pathetic middle-aged people feeling young and liking it.

Movie: Drugs. Purchase of large quantities from strange man in van. Actual footage of dope being smoked. Wimpy hero meets girl in bar, who asks him to go home with her. Wet T-shirt contest announced. MC starts to pour bucket of water on front of girl with great breasts. Spot cuts in just as water hits.

10:19 P.M.
2 × 30 sec
$250,000 each

Best spots all evening. Male viewers glued to set so as not to miss the very first second of resumed movie in case a moment of tit has slipped by the censors. Also a good time for spots designed to appeal to people who flip the TV on at 10:19 and turn it off sixty seconds later. Adult viewers either are getting into it, in which case they won't be watching spots, or they aren't, in which case ads for things like life insurance, trips to Des Moines, and riding-lawn mower attachments will probably go over well.

Movie: No sign of T-shirt contest. Side plot develops some more. Confrontation neither avoidable nor interesting. Wimp and girl go to hotel, wimp chickens out and goes to lobby to get sodas. Doesn't know girl's name or room number. Wanders hotel in scene designed to make your testicles hurt but more likely to make you leave the room to order a pizza.

10:40 P.M.
4 × 15 sec
$70,000 each

Young audience's hopes of seeing real flesh completely dissipated. Good time for plugging Boys' Clubs, sports equipment, or beer. Bad time for Time-Life Home Repair Books spots, because do-it-yourselfers are fixing sink and can't hear the TV. Good time for delivery pizza ads loud enough to carry to wherever the phone is.

Movie: Wimp and girl go to beach, prepare to sleep together. Sudden jagged scene shift to next day somewhere else. Side plot shows up. Inevitable showdown between sensible adult authority and top-heavy teenage women with kegs. Inevitable victory of latter. Inevitable half-assed slapstick climax, which we're supposed to think is great. Mayor gets pie in the face and then gets dumped in the pool with no thought as to how gross it's going to be to have bits of pie floating around in the pool for the rest of the week.

10:55 P.M.
2 × 30 sec
$60,000 each

Cheap. Movie is obviously over. Viewers comment that watching credits for movies like this one is about as interesting as finding out who invented sidewalks. Young viewers leave to go cruising, though they realize that they will look ridiculous in Mom's stupid Le Car. Adults leave to either screw or look up current insurance policy to see if it covers cat getting eaten by wolves. Good time for spots that no one cares about anyway, like RC Cola or Arby's.

Movie: Censors legally prohibited from cutting the credits. Credits run over the juicy highlights of the movie. All of the scenes shown are unfamiliar. Several pairs of breasts visible on left side of screen during long list of make-up assistants on right side of screen. Enormous kinky orgy visible behind public service message from Florida Tourist Board. Snatches of song "Ah Yes, Now You Are Really Doing It To Me, Unnh" heard for what is obviously not meant to be first time. Young viewers pray for each extra to be credited by full name, slowly, but to no avail. Movie ends.

10:59 P.M.
2 × 30 sec
$100,000 each

11:00 P.M.
1 × 60 min
$15,000,000

Standard. 46% of viewers turn set off, 47% leave it on. 7% of viewers evidently find other option, according to poll taker who better have a damn good explanation.

Good opportunity for long spot that pretends to be McNeil/Lehrer Report.

**NEXT WEEK: "AIRPORT '71"—BAD MOVIE BEING SHOWN FOR TWENTIETH TIME. ALL SPOTS HALF-PRICE. GOOD TIME TO RUN ADS FOR PRODUCTS THAT HAVE BEEN DISCONTINUED OR BANNED BY THE F.D.A. ALSO GOOD TIME FOR ANY AD MENTIONING FINE MILLED END PAPERS OR THE HEART-BREAK OF PSORIASIS. NOT, HOWEVER, A GOOD TIME FOR ADVERTISING AIRLINES, PROSTHETIC LIMBS, OR AMUSEMENT PARK RIDES THAT INVOLVE FALLING FROM GREAT HEIGHTS.

UP ALL NIGHT WITH TOM SNYDER

He had it all: the goofy grin, the huge lapels, the sideburns, and—at that time—a TV show. But then he fell victim to poor ratings and lost everything he had, except for the goofy grin, the huge lapels, and the sideburns. Tom Snyder: TV personality par excellence. Tom Snyder: the man who defined the seventies, and who'll probably continue to do so well into the nineties. Tom Snyder: unemployed.

But in 1987, the young Fox network decided to take a chance on Snyder. The show was an insomniacs daydream come true. Fox had only two requirements: One, that Snyder would be on camera at all times; and two, that the show would span the full six hours between midnight and dawn with only two short commercial breaks.

They called it *Up All Night with Tom Snyder.* And that's exactly what it was.

MIDNIGHT

SNYDER: Ah, welcome to *Tom Snyder's Up All Night* show. We've really got a tremendous program for you tonight. We've got three guests, a full urn of coffee, and five packs of cigarettes, so what are we waiting for? Let's hit the road. My first guest is writer James Owen, who has some interesting things to say about standardized IQ tests.

OWEN: They don't work.

SNYDER: So you're saying that these tests aren't an accurate judge of intelligence?

OWEN: Right.

SNYDER: Fascinating. But is there an accurate way? Can we measure human intelligence?

OWEN: Not using these tests.

SNYDER: Hmm. Fascinating.

2:05 am
OWEN: No, not really.

SNYDER: So you're saying that these so-called "IQ" tests just plain don't work. Right?

OWEN: Mm-hmm.

SNYDER: Well, I thank you Mr. Owen for those eye-opening thoughts. And now it's time for our second guest. She's a fashion model, and she seems to have some interesting ideas about meditation. Please welcome Shirley Wright.

3:00 am
SNYDER: So what you're saying is . . . you just sit there and breathe slowly, and it just clears your mind up.

WRIGHT: Correct.

SNYDER: Could you give us a demonstration?

WRIGHT: Sure.

3:45 am
SNYDER: Fascinating. I know you were just getting warmed up, Shirley, but they're telling me we should move on to my next guest.

WRIGHT: I should stop now?

SNYDER: Please. Our next guest is a free-lance author, and he's written a very controversial book about IQ testing. Hello, Mr. Sigman.

SIGMAN: These tests don't work very well.

SNYDER: Really? Tell me about it.

4:30 am
SIGMAN: I mean, these tests are drawn up by people who—

SNYDER: Coffee?

SIGMAN: What? Oh, no thank you. As I was saying, these tests—

SNYDER: Well, I'll have some if you don't mind.

SIGMAN: Very well, These tests—

SNYDER: You hungry? I'm starved. I could really go for some of those . . . what are those things? Chocolate things?

SIGMAN: M&M's.

SNYDER: Yeah, those are the ones. Listen, if I give you a buck, could you run out to the corner store and get me some? (gulp) Ahh . . . hot cup of coffee really hits the spot around now. Jeez, I bet it's getting light outside. This time of the night always reminds me of these long car trips we used to take when I was a kid. This must have been '48 or '49 . . .

5:30 am
SNYDER: . . . and by the time we'd gotten to Wisconsin, I'd counted at least 49 different kinds of telephone poles—the 36 I've already told you about, plus about 8 or 9 I'll tell you about right now. There was this one with all sorts of tar or pitch or something . . .

5:45 am
SNYDER: Is anyone out there? Is anyone still watching? Ah, you're all screwed. I mean—
(Band plays "Thanks For The Memories." Bob Hope walks onstage.)

BOB HOPE: Hi, Tom. It's really great to be here.

SNYDER: (rubs eyes) Bob Hope? Am I seeing things?

HOPE: Well, I was in the studio making some surprise appearances on some other shows, and I almost forgot I was scheduled to make one on yours. So here I am.

SNYDER: Bob Hope, ladies and gentlemen. Listen, I've always wondered—What? What? I can't believe we're out of time. What?
(cut to commercial)

TAKING THE STAND: Dan Rather

Sen. Mohasset: Mr. Rather, what in the world did you think you were doing when you started ending your newscast by saying, "Courage"?

Dan Rather: Golly, Senator Mohasset, I was just trying to spice up the often depressing news with an encouraging note. I didn't really mean any harm by it.

Sen. Mohasset: But why "courage"?

Dan Rather: Cronkite had his "And that's the way it is," and Ellerbee had her "And so it goes." I just wanted my own catchphrase. I guess I just wanted to be popular, Senator. I'm sorry.

Sen. Mohasset: And is it not true that it took you numerous tries to come up with that "catchphrase," Mr. Rather? What about all these endlines you had edited out of earlier newscasts?

Dan Rather: Well, I . . . um . . .

Sen. Beatrice: What is the frequency, Kenneth?

Dan Rather: Oh, please, not again! I promise I'll be good from now on! I swear it!

Sen. Beatrice: In that case, dismissed.

6/18/85 "And that's CBS News. I'm not wearing any pants. Good night."

7/30/85 "Good night. This is Dan Rather reporting. And here's my imitation of Charles Kuralt eating—'Ooooo, yum, yum!'"

9/12/85 "For CBS News, this is Dan Rather. Arrivaderci, amigos!"

10/3/85 "Until tomorrow, remember: No news is good news!"

1/8/86 "It's over! It's over! The news is over!"

2/1/86 "And that's the way it is, dudes."

2/15/86 "From CBS News, this is Dan Rather saying, good night, sleep tight, and don't let the bedbugs bite."

2/18/86 "Good Night, already."

2/21/86 "And until we meet again, farting is such sweet sorrow, ah, ah ha ha ha ha!"

2/27/86 "This is Dan Rather saying good night to you all, and good night, John Boy."

3/1/86 "This is Dan Rather saying, until tomorrow night, may the force be with you. Nanoo, nanoo!"

3/2/86 "And from CBS News, good night. Look out, dinner, here I come!"

3/3/86 "And until tomorrow, thith ith Tom Brokaw at Thee-B-Eth Newth. No, just kidding! Sorry, Tom! It's not that bad!"

Sen. Mohasset: Well, at this point, the evidence appears to be very, very incriminating. Does the Defense Counsel have *anything* to present in support of the television industry?

Defense Counsel: Yes, your honor, I have this document brought to my attention by the National Association of Broadcasters. It's in the evidence docket on page 922.

Sen. Mohasset: Mmm-hm.

Defense Counsel: As you can see, your honor, this is a diary kept by a Ms. Christina Simpson from age nine to age seventeen. Ms. Simpson was a participant in a project sponsored by the Book-of-the-Month Club, in which she was not allowed to watch television—ever—and, instead, was required to read two books per week. Her parents were paid $10 a year for her participation in the study.

Sen. Mohasset: And what does this diary prove, Mr. Counselor?

Defense Counsel: Well, Senator, it demonstrates the dire consequences that can result from television deprivation during the formative years.

Sen. Mohasset: And why is Ms. Simpson not present today?

Defense Counsel: She's dead.

Sen. Richardson: Whew, those *are* dire consequences!

AGE 9: I went over to Karen's after school today and she wanted to watch t.v. so I went into her room and read *Ramona the Pest* twice because it was the only book she had. She asked me why I couldn't watch and when I told her she said my parents were stupid. I said they weren't. She said they were. I scratched her. She punched me out. I tried to sic her Doberman against her but he's old and only left threads of drool across my arm. I went home then.

AGE 10: I finished *Paradise Lost* today. It is a pity that Milton has no other works of such epic length. Every word was a joy.

AGE 11: Billy Dean came up to me in school today and said, "Nanoo nanoo," and I said "Gesundheit," and everyone pointed at me and laughed. They were all shaking hands like they were half-retarded and saying this to each other. They told me it was "Mork from Ork," which, to be honest, meant very little to me. When I asked, they said Mork was the new kid from India. He was sitting alone by our class fish tank, tapping gently on the glass to get the goldfish's attention. I told him that each tap sounded like an atomic explosion inside the tank, but he didn't understand and kept tapping until the fish, overfed, rolled belly up and floated to the surface. I held out my hand in the retarded handshake and said, "Nanoo nanoo." He bobbed and grinned and said, "Ah, yes . . . yes, na-noo, na-noo. Mork and Mindy, yes." It must be cultural.

AGE 12: A bunch of kids were over at Linda's today and wanted to pretend like The Brady's. When I looked stupid on the subject, they made me Alice. But I still looked stupid, so they made me Tiger, and I spent the entire afternoon under a cardboard box.

AGE 12: I tried to get them to play *Hunchback of Notre Dame.* They acted like it was a really bad book. Instead we played *Charlie's Angels,* and, as usual, I was Tiger.

AGE 13: No one has asked me over for six months, so I invited Lisa over for the night. She looked depressed and asked what there was to do. I told her, she considered a moment and then she said, no, she did not want to come over for the night.

AGE 14: Everyone keeps reciting poetry about killing their landlord, and then they spell "kill" wrong. Afterward they say, "You look mahvelous." I happen to think this is very funny. But when I laugh, Karen says, "What're you laughing at? You don't even know what *Saturday Night Live* is." If I say I'm laughing at the jokes she says, "You don't even know what we're talking about. Stop trying to get in on it."

AGE 15: At lunch everyone but me shoots theme songs back and forth at each other. It starts as a battle to see who knows the most words, but by the end it's a chorus, one big happy family. I, of course, have no idea what they sing of. Happier days, they tell me. By the end they look a little misty-eyed. The music infiltrates my lunch of cheese and *Brothers Karamazov.*

AGE 16: A year later they still sing, and it's getting really annoying. How long can they sing the same stupid songs, and—who am I kidding? They reminisce about insane plots that I could never dream of watching. Woven into their lives are all these wonderful characters: Yogi Bear, Underdog, Marcia Brady, Mr. Spock . . . it goes on and on. These people must indeed be spectacular, for my peers never stop talking about them. Several times I have heard about the man called Finzie.

AGE 17: It would have been bearable if they had stopped, but they haven't, and I . . . I can no longer stand listening to their songs without joining in. I suspect that they are happier than I in their struggle to slow the loss of innocence. I have just finished *The Bell Jar,* and I know just how she felt. I stand at the top of a scorched ravine, the walls black and acrid. The sky above me whirls with dancing cartoon characters, apparently one short: They invite me to join the Virginia Reel if I can name just one. But I cannot, so down I go, over the dales, into the gorge where my only companion among the stone is a dull dirty puddle. I shall pass my days here, and all over the world children's skits will go on without me. Either I glue myself to a television for six weeks, or I die. For a meager $10 per year, my parents created a social leper, and it is I. It is I.

ON THE STAND: Vanna White

Sen. Beatrice: Ms. White, you are currently employed on the television game show *Wheel of Fortune* in what capacity?

Vanna White: Well, Senator, I stand around and look pretty and sometimes I turn around the letters in the puzzle.

Sen. Beatrice: Yes, Ms. White, but for the record, what is the *exact* description given your job by the show's producers?

Vanna: Uh, "Pretty Girl Who Stands Around and Sometimes Turns the Letters."

Sen. Beatrice: I see. And, Ms. White, were you aware that your employers, along with numerous other game-show producers, often "rig" the outcome of the game by employing certain unscrupulous techniques?

Vanna: Rig? Huh?

Sen. Beatrice: I asked you if you realized that many game shows, including yours, are rigged, Ms. White.

Vanna: Huh?

Sen. Beatrice: Oh, Jesus Christ . . .

Contrary to popular belief, many currently airing game shows, nay, highly rated quiz contests are (to use an industry term) "constructively prearranged"; or as the layman would say, "rigged." Game-show rigging technology has advanced far beyond the methods employed in the $64,000 Question scandal of the fifties. Instead of supplying contestants with the answers beforehand, rigging technicians now specialize in inventing new ways to screw contestants over, resulting in more fun and higher profits for the quizmaster and his cronies.

The so-called random method of contestant selection from the studio audience is actually based upon the answers they give on screening information forms passed out before each show's taping. The questions concern income level, socioeconomic standing, sexual preference, religion, and other relevant information. A computer file for each is developed:

FOCUS ON THE PRICE IS RIGHT
COMPUTER PROFILE
SUBJECT—Corporal Sam Grinchly, USMC
RESIDENCE: Cargo hold of destroyer docked in Guantanemo Bay. Currently on two-week furlough.
SELECT
WHAT HAPPENED:

BOB: Sam, did you say $30? Congratulations, you did not go over the correct price and that means you win the line of Halston original evening gowns!

SAM: Goddamnit.

BOB: That's wonderful. It should make that special girl of yours very happy. Right, Sam?

SAM: Don't got no special girl, sir.

BOB: That's wonderful.

SAM: Goddamnit.

AFTER THE SHOW:

DOMINICK (taunting prizekeeper): Hey soldier, you'll be the most stunning drag queen in boot camp. Hey, put that down! Guard! Guard—please have this man jailed.

COMPUTER PROFILE
SUBJECT—Miss Agnus Brierly, Pensioner.
AGE: 83
HEALTH: Weak heart.
SELECT
WHAT HAPPENED:

BOB: Incredible Agnus! You win the new car, the washer/dryer, the new kitchen, $10,000 in cash, the trip-around-the-world, and this BIG SCARY VOODOO MASK. ARRAGH!!!

AGNUS: Oh-Oh! (Clutches heart, drops to floor).

BOB: Agnus?

AFTER THE SHOW:

DOMINICK (to Bob): Whew. Saved us a cool $30,000 in prizes that time, Bob.

FOCUS ON WHEEL OF FORTUNE

COMPUTER PROFILE
SUBJECT—Father Louis Drummond, Priest
AGE: 52
SELECT
WHAT HAPPENED:

DRUMMOND: I'd like to solve the puzzle.

PAT: Yes, go ahead.

DRUMMOND: "Out of the fire and into the frying pan."

PAT: Good going, Father Drummond! You've got three thousand, four hundred dollars to spend! And it looks like you'll be selecting your fabulous prizes from . . . the sex shop! Let's see those prizes! What'll it be, Father?

DRUMMOND: Let's see. I'll have, ahm, er, hmm. Oh, I'll take the year's supply of condoms. Whoops! No, strike that. Just give me the electronic breast-o-matic vibrating pleasure . . . ahm, I mean, no, not that. Let's see now.

PAT: I'm sorry, father, but you're out of time. I'm afraid we have to move on to the next round now.

DRUMMOND: Oh, ah, okay.

COMPUTER PROFILE
SUBJECT—Cindy Miller
AGE: 6
SELECT
WHAT HAPPENED:

PAT: Well, it's kids week here on Wheel of Fortune, and I believe it's your turn, Cindy.

CINDY: I wanna solve da puzzle.

PAT: Okay, Cindy. What is it?

CINDY: "Out of the fire and into the frying pan."

PAT: That's right! You've got $32 to spend . . . in the candy shop!

CINDY: Oh, goody!

PAT: What'll it be, Cindy?

CINDY: I want the antique gum ball machine for $29.

PAT: (whispering) But Cindy, don't you want some Twinkies?

CINDY: Twinkies! I want Twinkies!

PAT: Well, I'm sorry, but you can only have one. They're $32 each.

CINDY: Yippee!

TAKING THE STAND: Robert C. Wright

Sen. Mohasset: Next on the stand is Robert C. Wright, chairman of General Electric and de facto president of RCA.

Sen. Beatrice: Thanks for coming today, Bob.

Robert Wright: No problem, "Robert." I'd do the same for you.

Sen. Richardson: Now I implicitly trust you people at G.E. and RCA. I've trusted you with my life many a time while rocketing into space, but what's all this I hear about your bribing writers to promote your color television sets back in the fifties?

Robert Wright: "Robert," you said I wouldn't have to answer any questions like this.

Sen. Beatrice: Oh, all right, Bob. Senators, it turns out that, back when color TV was first invented, RCA and some other electronics firms paid a few writers to make the invention seem indispensable to viewers. But, because of transmission problems and that sort of thing, these episodes never aired. Is that it, Bob?

Robert Wright: Well, maybe. But I didn't have anything to do with it.

Sen. Beatrice: I believe you, Bob. You can leave now. We won't bother you again, I promise. See you at the club this Sunday.

Robert Wright: Hey, work on that golf swing, ya bum, huh? Heh heh . . .

LEAVE IT TO BEAVER

PANEL ONE: BEAVER AND WALLY ARE LYING ON THEIR BEDS DOING HOMEWORK. HUGE RED BLOTCHES MAKE IT LOOK LIKE BLOOD IS RUNNING DOWN THE WALLS.

BEAVER: Wally, did you ever wonder if maybe we were in color?

WALLY: Gee, Beav, where'd you get a goofy idea like that?

BEAVER: Aw, some of the guys and me were talking about it today . . .

WALLY: They were just giving you the business, ya little squirt.

BEAVER: I dunno, Wally. Maybe we'd better ask Dad.

PANEL TWO: DAD IS COMING IN DOOR. BOYS ARE LOOKING OVER AT HIM. WEIRD COLORS MAKE HIM LOOK LIKE A HORRIBLE MONSTER.

WARD: Did I hear my name mentioned, boys? I was just coming to see how you were doing on your homework . . .

BEAVER: Dad, are we in color or black and white?

WARD: Why, Beaver, what makes you ask such a question? Is this part of your science homework?

PANEL THREE: DAD IS SITTING DOWN ON THE BED. WEIRD BLUE SHADES MAKE IT LOOK LIKE HE AND BEAVER ARE FLOATING IN A BATHTUB.

BEAVER: Gee, Dad, it's just that the Rutherfords got a color TV last week and since we

only have a black and white one, I thought . . .

WALLY: The Rutherfords? They're *poor!* Lumpy's Dad's been unemployed for six months!

WARD: Wally! You don't have to be rich to afford a color television these days!

PANEL FOUR: CLOSE-UP OF DAD. HE DOESN'T HAVE ANY PUPILS IN HIS EYES.

WALLY: Well golly, Dad, we only have that stinky black and white job.

BEAVER: Yeah, Dad, how come?

WARD: Boys, no one will ever call the Cleavers old-fashioned. I have a little surprise for you two . . .

PANEL FIVE: WARD HOLDING UP A COLOR TV HE WAS HIDING BEHIND HIS BACK. BOYS ARE JUMPING UP AND DOWN.

WARD: Your own color television set! I bought seven more just like it for every room in the house.

BEAVER: Yay!

WALLY: Wait'll I tell Eddie and the guys! Their eyes'll pop out and all that junk!

PANEL SIX: WARD OPENING DOOR TO LEAVE. BOYS ARE TURNING ON TV SET.

BEAVER: Neat! Let's watch Roy Rogers!

WALLY: Nah, ya little squirt . . . let's watch Milton Berle—he's IN COLOR!

WARD (smiling as he exits): Now, I don't want you boys watching more than seven or eight hours of that tonight. You have homework to finish.

The Dick Van Show
with hosts
Dick Van Dyke & Dick Van Patten

The plan was ambitious. They would cull the very best elements from mid-seventies human interest shows like *Real People*, and from the great comedy variety shows such as *Sonny & Cher*. Then, tossing this material aside, they would attempt to really rip-off what remained of these shows. The idea, in essence, was to combine the mock spontaneity of *Real People* with the stilted, prepared awkwardness of rehearsed skits.

The show was revolutionary in format: part substance, part filler, but crafted so as to make it difficult to decide which was which. There would be some segments filmed in the van with the two Dicks, and other segments featuring normal people. The Dicks would first demand an impromptu skit or act from the "guest." Then, they would back the van off his foot and show him one of their own skits, which had been extensively rehearsed beforehand.

The Dicks would scour the country looking not for people who could do something exceptional and funny, but rather for people who were exceptionally normal, who hopefully would do something funny without even knowing it—on national TV. The show's saving grace was that the "natural humor" it sought could be lent by creative editing. Everything else could be faked in a studio, if need be.

The show ran from April 13, 1977, at 9:00 P.M. until April 13, 1977, at 10:00 P.M. The hosts ran until apprehended in Macon County, after their runaway hit show became a runaway van and soon after, a hit-and-run. Although the show did not last very long, the prison sentences did.

[Theme song and opening credits]

(DICK VAN DYKE):   Well, Van Patten said Eight is Enough is enough,

(DICK VAN PATTEN):   And, of course, Van Dyke had nothing to do,

(DICK VAN DYKE):   So, we put down our bottles, and got up off our duffs,

(DICK VAN PATTEN):   So we could start driving our duffs off for you.

(TOGETHER):
We'll canvas the land and paint each town red,
We're artists who Vincent van "GO,"
And though we keep moving, just like we said,
We stop, too. That's part of the show.

We're looking for talent. You know *we've* got none,
So we're going to keep trying a lot.
We'd like to stop and see everyone,
But we can't—our brakes are shot.

We'll drive 'til the end of our tether,
We know all the places to see,
And we'll hit all those places together,
With Dick driving, hit them literally.

Just two Dicks in a van, a couple of jokes,
This is it—the whole *Dick Van Show*.
But let's not forget you kind folks,
Who tell us where we can go.

If we're sick, it's with happiness. Well, maybe
D.T.'s . . .
But we're coming to your town to spread our
disease.
So put on a smile and learn to say "cheese,"
And lock up your daughters, and then hide the
keys.
Aaaaw, we're only kidding. Bring them out—
please,

To meet the guys down on their knees,
Meet the Dicks on the new *Dick Van Show!!!*

V.D.:   Hi everyone, and welcome to the *Dick Van Show*. We're really glad to be here.

V.P.:   Of course, with Dick driving, we're glad to be anywhere. Ha, ha.

V.D.:   Ha, ha. I'm Dick Van Dyke, and I'll be at the wheel tonight.

V.P.:   And probably at the bottle, too, eh Dick? Hi, I'm Dick Van Patten, and I'll be riding shotgun. Shotgunning *beers*, that is!

V.D.:   Dick's right. We both love to score a few frosties when we're not doing anything else. Or even when we are. Fortunately, we're never doing anything else.

V.P.: Well, we've got a great show for you tonight.

V.D.: Oh no, did we forget to shut the van curtains when we were changing again? Oh, wait a minute—we don't ever change our clothes.

V.P.: You know what I mean, Dick. I mean, we've got a hot show and a hot car—

V.D.: You didn't tell me you *stole* this thing.

V.P.: I didn't steal it. I meant that—whoa! The car really is hot! It's overheating! You forgot to put water in the radiator again, didn't you?

V.D.: I used something even better this time—a little scotch.

V.P.: Scotch? What the hell did you do that for?

V.D.: It keeps me going.

V.P.: And it burns you out, too, remember? Look folks, we've got to attend to this. We'll see you after this commercial break. Don't go away.

V.D.: We sure won't.

V.P.: You bonehead.

V.P.: Hi, we're back. This time we're in Butte, Montana, with a very unique man. I'd like to introduce to you now Mr. Ed Stengal— but I can't. Because what makes Mr. Stengal so unique is that he is a deaf mute. Tell me, Mr. Stengal—or may I call you 'Ed?'

STENGAL:

V.P.: Uh, ok, Ed then. Tell me, Ed, is it true you've been deaf all your life?

STENGAL:

V.P.: So you're not sure, is that it?

STENGAL:

V.P.: Yoo hoo, Mr. Stengal, you're on the air. Do you think you could say a few words to the viewing audience?

STENGAL:

V.D.: How about a song then?

V.P.: Hi! Welcome to the Fitzgerald Fairgrounds in Topsfield, Oklahoma. Today we have with us a man who has just spent the day doing something very exciting. He's been growing a beard.

V.D.: You call growing a beard exciting?

V.P.: Yes I do, Dick, when it's . . . a beard of bees!!!

V.D.: Wow. That *is* exciting.

V.P.: Ladies and gentleman, this is Mr. Bill Kopit. How are you doing, Mr. Kopit?

KOPIT: Fine, thanks.

V.P.: Well, how about that beard, folks? Remember that we here on the *Dick Van Show* are always the first to bring you spectacles like this.

KOPIT: That's not true. *Real People* did a story on me last year.

V.P.: Heh, heh, Mr. Kopit, there's really no need to explain that.

KOPIT: Boy, that Skip Stevenson is a hot pistol.

V.D.: Ok, Kopit, let's change the subject.

KOPIT: Boy, you should have seen the size of their van. And they had six of them!

V.P.: Say, Mr. Kopit, isn't it somewhat dangerous to have thousands of poisonous stinging insects swarming on your face like that?

KOPIT: Well, it would only be dangerous if I moved my face suddenly—say, if I laughed, or something.

V.P.: Oh really? Say uh . . . , tell me, Mr. Kopit . . . did you ever hear the one about the barmaid and the pig?

V.P.: We're now in a back alley in downtown Chicago, just waiting to see who we might run into. Ah, here comes a man now.

V.D.: Hi, sir.

MAN: Uh, hi.

V.P.: Don't you know who we are?

MAN: Ummm, no.

V.D.: You're sure you don't recognize us from somewhere?

MAN: Sorry, No.

V.P. & V.D.: Good!!!

MAN: Hey, come back here! Hey, bring back my wallet!

V.P.: You know, producing a T.V. show looks simple, but I can assure you, it's not as simple as it looks. It takes a lot of good people behind the scenes to make it look simple. But it works—look how simple our show seems! So now I'd like to show you our cameramen and technicians. These are the men who do all the work while we have all the fun: This is Paul on Camera One, and Bill, our boom mike operator, Dave our lights man, and Josh on Camera Two. Now are you satisfied, Sherry? You *are* going to be in movies. Now get in the van and get undressed. And where's your friend, Debbi?

V.P.: This Atlanta, Georgia, factory may look ordinary, and that's because it is, but inside is a very extra-ordinary man. This tool and die plant is the workplace of a Mr. Shep Smith—and has been for seventy-seven years! Let's go inside, shall we.

V.D.: I'll wait outside.

V.P.: Hi, Mr. Smith.

SMITH: Howdy.

V.P.: Mr. Smith—

SMITH: "Smitty."

V.P.: "Smitty," you're ninety-two years old, is that true?

"SMITTY": Yep, tha's true.

V.P.: And you've been working here for seventy-seven years?

SMITTY: Sure 'nuff.

V.P.: And though you've been working here seventy-seven years, you're still dirt poor, isn't that right?

SMITTY: Well, I—

V.P.: Isn't it remarkable, folks? Seventy-seven years of hard toil, and he's still miserably poor. An incredible story, indeed.

SMITTY: I ain't zactly poor as awl thet.

V.P.: "Smitty," I drive around in a van all day and drink beer, and for that I make $60,000 a year. More than you've made in seventy-seven years. Mr. Smith, *you are poor.*

SMITTY: But ah worked hard for seventy-seven years. Hard and honest. Ah got pride in my work. And ah got pride in mahself.

V.P.: Oh come on, Mr. Smith, how much pride could you really have?

SMITTY: Ah got pride, ah tell ya.

V.P.: Hmph, pride. I'd be interested in finding out how much pride you really have. For instance, what would it take to get you to, say, do the funky chicken here on national television?

SMITTY: Ah would nevah do such a thing. No sah, I am a respectable man. Ah told you, ah got pride.

V.P.: Fifty bucks?

SMITTY: Squaaak! Coockle! Squaaaarkr!

V.P.: There you have it, folks—a ninety-two-year-old man doing the funky chicken for you. And how much did it cost? For you, nothing, and for us? Only fifty bucks. That's quality entertainment. Only on our show.

SMITTY: Squaaaak! Kraaaaawk!

V.P.: Well, I guess Dick and I are going to be spending a little time here in Macon County Jail. Not too much, though—I'm sure the network will post bail for us any time now. Actually, I'm surprised our camera crew hasn't already—I mean, isn't that why they took the van? Well, at least they left us this camera. Anyway, Dick and I have to go now, but we'd like to tell you how much fun we've had, and we hope you've enjoyed road-tripping with us and meeting all the people we ran into along the way.

V.D.: Except that pregnant lady. God, I hope she lives.

V.P.: Me, too, or we're looking at twenty-year contracts of a different kind.

V.D.: You know, Dick, Johnny should be here, too. It's as much his fault as ours.

V.P.: Johnny?

V.D.: Johnny Walker. Boy, do I wish he was here now.

V.P.: Well, Dick and I have to sign off now. But until next—ah, the next time we see you—

V.D.: Visiting hours are Sundays, 12:00 to 2:00—

V.P. & V.D.:
—Here's Dick Van Dyke and Dick Van Patten telling you to . . . Hit the Road and have a Van-tastic time!

V.D.: Excuse me? Ahm, no, ah, "Bruno," I don't think I ever have kissed a man.

TAKING THE STAND: Rod Serling

Sen. Mohasset: I call to the witness stand the late Rod Serling.

Sen. Richardson: Wow, technology sure has gotten sophisticated since the early days of the space program. Why, I remember when . . .

Sen. Mohasset: Senator Richardson, Mr. Serling has been dead for years, and no technology is going to change that. What I meant to say was that the bailiff should play the audiotape sent in by Mr. Serling's estate.

Sen. Beaufort: Ya half-wit, Richardson.

Rod Serling's Voice: Greetings, Senators, from the great beyond, a dimension not only of sight and sound, but of mind. There's a signpost up ahead: next stop, the . . .

Sen. Mohasset: Fast forward that tape a little, bailiff.

Rod Serling's Voice: . . . was aware this day would come, so I prepared this tape recording. Sitting before you should be summaries of the unaired four episodes from the last season of *The Twilight Zone.* The network had cut our budget to such a point that I had no choice but to compromise the integrity of the program by reducing certain . . . special effects, shall we say. At the last minute, I decided to cut them from the schedule and repeat that great episode with Jack Klugman.

Sen. Richardson: Ooooh, that was scary. Now I'm not sure if I want to see what's in that envelope. What if it's scary bugs or poison gas or something?

Sen. Beaufort: Ya half-wit, Richardson.

Twilight Zone:
The Unreleased Final Season

Episode 1: Mistaken Identity

This mild tale concerns the fate of identical twin sisters who can read each other's thoughts, but only when they are written legibly on a scratch pad. Due to extreme budget restrictions, the producers were unable to hire a genuine pair of twins for the lead roles, and so settled for two women off the street who looked remotely similar. A calm situation prevails throughout most of the show, but in the closing minutes tragedy strikes as one sister falls hopelessly in love with the milkman. The other woman reads her sister's thoughts, which are lying on top of the dresser, and she too becomes entranced by the man. In a jealous rage, the first sister plots the murder of her twin, but the other sister instantly reads of the plan and easily avoids the rope trap that awaits her in the kitchen. Left with no other choice, the milkman weds both women and moves to a town in Utah where polygamy is legal.

Episode 2: No-Man's Land

Thousands of dollars were saved in the filming of this episode by locating all of the action on the rented set of *The Andy Griffith Show.* The plot revolves around a mysterious stranger who is jailed by sheriff Andrew Naylor (Andy Griffith) for jaywalking. Deputy Barney Foof (Don Knotts) experiences repeated episodes of déjà vu in the presence of the man, until Sheriff Naylor decides to have the FBI perform a search on the convict's name. Much to his surprise, the FBI reports that no such man as "Chubbly Gorillawitz" ever existed. The two law officers come to the realization that the prisoner must be some sort of alien being who has taken on human form. After releasing him in a fit of terror, Naylor notices a photo of the stranger posted next to his desk. Below the picture, a caption reads, "Wanted for armed robbery. $10,000 reward." Only then does the horrible truth dawn on the sheriff: The man had been operating under a false name.

Episode 3:

This episode was filmed under such adverse conditions that the production company could not even afford to hire someone to make up a believable name for the central character. Thus came about the unlikely appelation of Gregarious U. Jehosephat for the leading man, a down-and-out drifter who has just spent his last dime to make a Xerox copy of his own buttocks. In desperation, Jehosephat summons the Devil and signs an unholy pact. The Devil (Vic Tayback) receives the man's immortal soul, while Jehosephat acquires the power of invisibility, the power of strength of grip in his right hand, and the power of attorney over his rich and elderly uncle's estate. When the wealthy uncle refuses to die, Jehosephat decides to accelerate matters by turning invisible and strangling the man with his intense grip. The attempt fails, however, because the old man is wearing a steel neck brace under his shirt. Enraged, Jehosephat lights a fire in the fireplace and then goes to the oven and turns on the gas. As he escapes to safety, the house blows up (not shown). Unfortunately, the Uncle again survives with only minor injuries. Intriguingly, the episode ends suddenly at this point, leaving the fate of both characters unresolved.

Episode 4: After the Flood

This episode took its roots from Biblical tradition, depicting the plight of mankind living in the aftermath of a modern-day flood that lasted forty days and forty nights. Limited again by a miniscule production budget, the producers could not afford to destroy any of the sets with real water. However, signs of water damage are visible everywhere, and dehumidifiers run at full blast in nearly every house. Elderly people complain of severe arthritic pain, and laundry will not dry properly. On the other hand, lawns are thick and healthy, and the fishing is better than ever. The Noah's ark of the modern age takes the form of a pickup truck jammed to the brim with one pair each of dogs and chickens. No other animals could be fit into the vehicle's limited cargo space, but it doesn't matter, since the other creatures survived by standing on their hind legs and breathing through hollow reeds. Crazy Noah can see that life is continuing pretty much as usual, but refuses stubbornly to get out of his truck until he finally runs out of gas late in the program. It turns out that both of his chickens were roosters anyway, and that one of the dogs had been neutered years before.

TAKING THE STAND: George Montana, president of R.E. Productions

Sen. Fawcett: Next on the stand is George Montana, president of R.E. Productions, Inc. This firm is responsible for rounding up the casts and sets of classic situation comedies to produce so-called reunion shows. Correct?

Montana: Correct. We've done *Return to Gilligan's Island, The Bradys Today,* and *Return to Mayberry.*

Sen. Beaufort: *Retuhn to Mayberry?* That was one supubh piece of telluhvision, suh. Congratulations. If you don't mine, Mistuh Montana, could y'all tell me a bit about Andy Griffith? What's he like?

Sen. Fawcett: No. Shut up, Jerry. Mr. Montana, please explain why these particular reunion shows produced by your firm never aired.

Montana: As I understand it, apparently viewers find the assertion that time passes and people age a very jarring proposition.

Sen. Beaufort: You mean *even* Andy?

Montana: I'm afraid so.

THE BEVERLY HILLBILLIES . . . ARE BACK

After almost twenty years in Beverly Hills, the Clampett family has finally mastered the intricacies of high-society etiquette. When a truckload of their Southern cousins drop in for a visit, Granny has them removed from the premises. Jethro and his wife, a sheep, argue frequently.

THE PARTRIDGE FAMILY COMES HOME

All of the members of the Partridge family come home when their mother's nervousness finally gives her a potentially fatal ulcer. The close quarters in Mom's two-room house create prime conditions for a full-blown, seven-sided argument. After two hours (minus commercial breaks) of yelling, screaming, and recriminations, the family members suddenly pause. What's that sound? In a corner, Danny is beating out a steady rhythm on his triangle. One by one, the kids pick up their old instruments and are reunited in song. When the impromptu shindig is over, the kids talk Mom into getting out of bed and piloting the old yellow bus to Albuquerque, where they all catch planes to their homes, leaving her to enjoy the drive back in peace and quiet.

I STILL Dream of Jeannie

When a package is delivered to J.R. at Southfork Ranch, the last thing he expects to find in it is Jeannie's dusty bottle. And the last thing he expects to find in the bottle is a fifty-year old Jeannie, whose magical powers have atrophied to the point that they're now only strong enough to levitate cookies, cakes, and chocolates into her mouth. J.R. kicks her out of the house, and she shacks up with Cliff the ranch hand. She is eventually killed when Cliff mistakes her bottle for a jug of moonshine and swallows her.

MORK AND MINDY . . . TOGETHER AGAIN

Due to the peculiar "Orkian" aging process, Mork now speaks three times as fast as he used to, rendering his speech incomprehensible even to other Orkans. Another effect of the Orkian aging process makes Mork capable of achieving sexual climax ten times within the space of one minute. Mindy makes him sleep on the couch in the living room. Now in his twilight years, Mork subsists on a diet of snot, which he drinks through his finger. While he's working at the deli, Mork accidentally slices off one of his fingers, which regenerates into another Orkan, who claims that he, too, is Mindy's husband. Mindy insists that they both sleep on the couch, and one night they fuse into a single being who is capable of achieving sexual climax thirty times within the space of one minute.

FAME

Five years after they graduated from the School of Performing Arts, each member of the graduating class answers the same job advertisement. They sing "The Body Electric," and then get down to waitressing and bussing tables.

M*A*S*H

The Korean conflict is over, but all the members of the 4077th have returned to Korea to see the Olympics. All except for Henry, who is dead. Without the common bond of shared hardship and war-time conditions, the doctors and nurses realize that they don't care much for each other. Hawkeye spends most of his time in his hotel room, making wisecracks at the TV set. Klinger finally succeeds in making Radar his homosexual lover. Colonel Potter is also dead, but his wife has sent his favorite horse in his stead. B.J. and Trapper spend their time at the bar, arguing about who Hawkeye liked better. Hotlips Houlihan, too, is dead.

WELCOME BACK, WELCOME BACK KOTTER

Twelve years later, and Arnold Horshack hasn't changed a bit! For this reason, no one else comes to the reunion.

TAKING THE STAND: James Ordway, head of pilot shows development

Sen. Mohasset: I understand that many of these pilots you're in charge of never actually air. Is that right?

Ordway: Right. But that's standard practice. However, in the case of these shows we're supposed to be discussing today, bad timing was at fault. The shows seemed like great ideas at the time, but later . . . eh.

Sen. Mohasset: Mm-hmm. Could you give us an example of what you're talking about?

Ordway: Well, for instance, we had a show called *A Great Man* scheduled to air on ABC next week. It was about an astronaut, a big-time guy who was on Apollo-Soyuz and Skylab, who gets elected to the Senate and becomes a national hero. Then he gets elected President.

Sen. Richardson: Wow! That sounds great! What's wrong with that show?

Ordway: What with all this Mediagate stuff going on, we just didn't feel that . . .

Sen. Richardson: Oh, no, please don't let that stop you! Please? Pretty please? Pretty please with a cherry on top?

Ordway: Well, I don't know . . .

Sen. Richardson: I'll buy you a car.

Ordway: Got one.

Sen. Richardson: $10,000 cash. Right now. And total immunity from prosecution.

Ordway: Okay.

CAPTAIN KELLY & THE KIDS
Scheduled premiere: May 4, 1970

Don Knotts plays Captain Harvey Kelly, a high-strung and jittery campus security officer at Kent State University. This week, the kids plan a joke protest as part of a surprise party for Captain Kelly.

LOOK OUT BELOW!
Scheduled premiere: November 23, 1963

Jack and Louise Tomler (Martin Balsam and Eve Arden), a down-on-their-luck but lovable Dallas couple, decide to open a sporting goods store on the top floor of the local book depository. Hilarity results when they find that the only shooting range they can afford is across the street! This week, a surprise visit—from the President of the United States (Harvey Korman)!

NUTS ONLY
Scheduled premiere: December 20, 1967

Bang-up fun occurs when a group of Army 4-F mental patients are mistakenly assigned to active duty in southeast Asia. Exploding birthday cakes, midnight fireworks shows, and a crazy neon sign that can be seen for miles are all daily happenings for the gang at Khe Sanh. This week, Commander Lou Neben (Larry Storch) invites the neighbors over for a poker party and everybody ends up getting bombed!

SAVING GRACE
Scheduled premiere: September 20, 1982

When a beautiful American actress marries a zany Mediterranean prince who's prone to practical jokes, royal laughs are guaranteed. This week, a Sunday drive turns into a madcap road race when the prince puts sticky glue on the accelerator and doesn't tell his wife!

By federal law, all United States television stations are required to display their incoming and outgoing correspondence for public perusal. Although few people take advantage of this opportunity, some stations are reluctant to show off their more embarrassing letters; these were found at the bottom of a crate of used carbon paper, turpentine-soaked rags, and smoldering cigarette butts.

June 19, 1985
1675 Hardwood Ln.
Regis, PA 16027

Personnel Manager
WETT-TV
5300 North Avenue
Altoona, PA 16602

Dear Sir or Madam,
I am currently unemployed. However, as you can see from my resume, I have a great deal of professional television experience. Would you please hire me?

Yours truly,
Winston Nrczek
Winston Nrczek

RESUME
Winston Nrczek
1675 Hardwood Lane
Regis, PA 16027
(601) 555-1352

OBJECTIVE:
A career in the television industry: station manager, news anchorman, important celebrity

WORK EXPERIENCE:

11/1/82–5/1/85	Television Repairman. Lou's All-Purpose Appliance. Regis, Penn. Serviced a variety of broadcast-related equipment. Contact: Lou Albatella.
5/17/83	Television Appearance. Waved behind newscaster on scene of murder.
8/28/82	Television Appearance. Audience of *Card Sharks* while on family vacation. Fifteenth row back, seven to the left. Not shown on broadcast.
3/13/80	Watched TV for 36 Hours Straight. Drunk and couldn't turn off set.
12/6/79	TV Guide. Read entire issue while constipated.
3/29/76–7/1/76	Cashier. McDonald's restaurant. Dellwood, Penn. Made change and took orders. Gave out coupons for $1 off on RCA television sets. Contact: Ron Jurofsky.

EDUCATION:
North Regis Central High School.
P.S. 155

INTERESTS:
Watching TV!
Fishing
Sex

RESPONSE:
WETT-TV
5300 North Avenue
Altoona, PA 16602
June 29, 1985

Mr. Winston Nrczek
1675 Hardwood Lane
Regis, PA 16027

Dear Mr. Nrczek,

It is WETT policy not to accept outside solicitations for employment. However, because of your interest in WETT and your extensive experience in television, we have decided to offer you a position.

Although management positions at the station are normally offered only to college graduates, we feel that, in your case, extenuating circumstances apply: Your perusal of an entire issue of TV Guide, and your television viewing experience are of particular note.

Currently, the position of station manager is available. It carries a starting salary of $95,000 per year, plus use of a station van. We hope this will meet with your current needs.

You start Monday at 10:00 A.M. If that is too early, please give me a call.

Yours,
Evelyn Yount
Evelyn Yount
Personnel Manager

EY/wlo
cc: network directorship office

July 31, 1985
Dear TV Stashun,
please tell Elmur Fudd not to shoot at Bugs Bunny any more. I don't think he likes it. Thank You,
Billy Smith
Age 6
788 Woodley Rohd

WETT-TV
5300 North Avenue
Altoona, PA 16602
August 6, 1985

Mr. William Smith
788 Woodley Rd.
Altoona, PA 16611

Dear Mr. Smith,
    Bugs Bunny does not care if Elmer Fudd shoots at him—they are both cartoon characters. Neither of them are real. It is absurd to think that an animated character could express real human emotion.

    In fact, WETT-TV couldn't care less about what happens to Bugs Bunny. He could die or eat poison, and it wouldn't make one stinking bit of difference to any of us. Any mature person realizes that animated cartoons are merely an inconsequential past time of the young and ignorant.

    Please don't waste our time with any more of your cretinous requests.

Yours,
Vince Matherton
Vince Matherton
Public Relations Director

VM/dsc

WETT-TV
5300 North Avenue
Altoona, PA 16602
September 3, 1985

Chuck Jones, Director
WARNER BROTHERS CARTOONS
3000 Vine
Hollywood, CA 90233

Dear Mr. Jones,
In the future, please don't allow Mr. Elmer Fudd to shoot at Bugs Bunny. I honestly don't think Bugs likes that.
Sincerely,
Winston Nrczek
Winston Nrczek
Station Manager

WN/wn

ABC ENTERTAINMENT
1330 Ave. of the Americas
New York, New York 10019

October 15, 1985

Mr. Winston Nrczek
Station Manager
WETT-TV
5300 North Ave.
Altoona, PA 16602

Dear Mr. Nrczek,
    ABC Chairman David Salabek has referred your resume to the Executive Management Division of the network, and, pending your approval, would like to appoint you to the position of Director of Prime-Time Entertainment Programming.

    Mr. Salabek took particular interest in your letter-writing campaign against violence in children's programming.

    The position carries with it a salary of $350,000 per year, use of a network helicopter, and sixteen secretaries.

    Mr. Salabek hopes you will give serious consideration to this offer. Please notify him personally of your decision at his home phone: (212) 555-8892.

We hope you will enjoy many happy years at the ABC Television Network.

Sincerely,
Maureen Davies
Maureen Davies
Executive Personnel
Placement

MD/sey

TAKING THE STAND: Andy Griffith

Sen. Mohasset: Next on the witness stand is, uh . . . Mr. Andy Griffith.

Sen. Beaufort: Yee-ha! Andy Griffith! It's Andy Griffith!

Sen. Mohasset: I must again caution Senator Beaufort regarding these outbursts.

Sen. Beaufort: Aw, come on, Don. It's Andy Griffith!

Sen. Mohasset: Oh, all right . . .

Sen. Beaufort: Andy, can Ah please have y'all's autograph? Six o seven uh them, if Ah could trouble you . . .

Andy Griffith: I say! I came here to testify; not to pander to the whims of some hillbilly legislator. Get your filthy paws away from me, sir!

Sen. Beaufort: But, Andy . . . I loved ya! All mah constituents, they loved ya, too! Stop playin' these games!

Andy Griffith: Don't play the fool, Senator. You know everything on television is an act, a put-on, if you will. That is what you are *supposed* to be investigating here. I am a Shakespearean actor, sir, a dignified and intelligent artist. Please don't confuse me with the idiotic rube I am forced to play on television!

Sen. Beaufort: But . . . but . . .

Andy Griffith: May we proceed now?

Sen. Beaufort: If y'all will excuse me. . . . (EXITS)

****

(ENTER SENATOR BEAUFORT)

Sen. Mohasset: Well, Jerry, what did you do out there?

Sen. Beaufort: Made a few telephone calls. Y'all know what?

Sen. Mohasset: What?

Sen. Beaufort: Don Knotts, Frances Bavier, even little Ronny Howard . . . they're all in on it. And Ah looked in the phone book, and, I know it may be hard to swaller, but there *isn't even* a real place called Mayberry.

Sen. Mohasset: Uh-huh. And?

Sen. Beaufort (whispering): Well, Ah wouldn't wanna jump to any hasty conclusions, but I just think that maybe there maght be some sorta *conspiracy* goin' on here. . . .

FAILED CABLE TELEVISION NETWORKS

The cable television boom of the eighties has spawned a plethora of special-interest channels and "special" networks. For example, witness the Weather Channel, the Sports Programming Network, and the Playboy Channel. The boom has also inspired some notable clunkers. To wit:

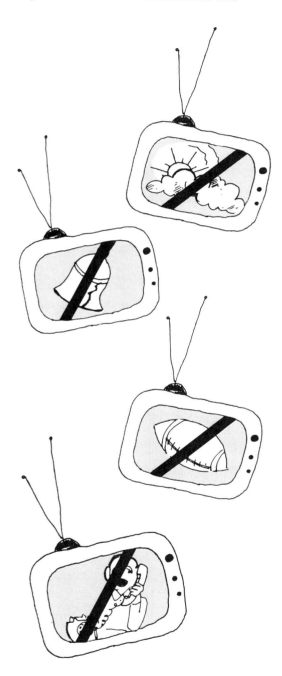

THE INTERNATIONAL YAHTZEE NETWORK: Minute-by-minute rundown of all home and scholastic Yahtzee tournaments.

USED WEATHER CHANNEL: Too poor to afford its own weather forecasting equipment, this twenty-four-hour station could only report yesterday's weather.

THE BICENTENNIAL CHANNEL: Reliving our nation's proudest moment, this channel regularly featured *The Bicentennial Crafts Show* (which taught time-honored crafts like how to fold a tri-corner hat and how to paint a fire hydrant to look like a revolutionary war hero) and *The Big Ships Are Here, Dear,* a sitcom involving the zany antics of a businessman who attempts to avoid both his boss and his wife in order to view the tall ships as they arrive in New York Harbor. Uninterrupted presentation of the entire five hours of *Bicentennial Minutes* was also featured nightly.

SUPER SPORTS STATION: Could only obtain the coverage rights to chess, curling, and Argentinian volleyball ... and also Yahtzee, when the Yahtzee Network went under.

VIEWER INTERACTION CHANNEL: Hoping to capitalize on the popularity of shows in which viewers could phone in to affect the outcome of a game or contest, Apex Cable introduced a new twist on interaction between TV and its viewers. The VIC was broadcast from a station so poorly run that the viewer had to constantly phone in to tell the management to focus the film, put the reels in the right order, and reset the station time clock.

THE LATIN(O) NETWORK: Originally slated to be a Spanish-language channel presenting programs of interest to the Hispanic community, the "Latino" Network became the "Latin" Network due to a staff writer's typo. The upshot was that *Villa Allegre* and other latino shows were broadcast in Ancient Latin, much to everyone's confusion.

THE MAX HEADROOM CHANNEL: Unable to hire "Max Headroom," the producers aired twenty-four-hour segments of a woolen hand puppet with the voice of a stuttering man. Now considered the most annoying network ever to exist.

THE TELETHON CHANNEL: The ultimate in self-referential programming. No commercials, no programs—just a continuous telethon to provide enough money for the station to keep broadcasting, i.e. to keep the "telethon telethon" going. Wore out even the most avid telethon enthusiasts.

THE AMISH CHANNEL: A "most virtuous and uplifting" schedule of community events and devotional offerings, as well as farm reports, for the Amish people. Never found its audience, for some reason.

ESPN: The network for cable subscribers who had extrasensory perception. Aired a blank screen twenty-four hours a day, and required viewers to imagine what the network might have been thinking of showing.

NICKELODEON II: The next step in children's programming. Television was produced BY kids FOR kids. Unfortunately, not one of the prepubescents was tall enough to operate a camera, much less understand the engineering panels. They created a lot of static and test patterns.

THE SEX CHANNEL: Boasted interviews with both males and females.

TAKING THE STAND: Mr. Max Headroom

Sen. Stone: Next on the stand is a Mr. Max . . . Headroom? Is that correct?

Max Headroom: Y-y-you bet, Lead Pants!

Sen. Stone: Indeed! What is this? A television set? I called a witness to testify. Will Mr. Headroom please step forward?

Headroom: You're l-l-lookin' at him, p-p-pipsqueak!

Sen. Stone: Heavens! Someone please turn off this television set!

Sen. Mohasset: Senator Stone, Mr. Headroom is a computer-generated image that can appear only on a monitor. Please commence your questioning.

Sen. Stone: Uh . . . excuse me, Mr. Headroom. I don't watch television. Rots the intellect, you know. Nevertheless, Mr. Headroom, I understand that, in late 1986, you starred in a television program that was found offensive by the American Association of Speech Therapists and subsequently dropped from the broadcast schedule. Why was that?

Headroom: B-b-b-beats m-m-me, b-b-b-bubble b-b-b-butt!

Sen. Stone: Hmmm. Well, I understand that your co-host for this program was a Mr. "Porky" Pig. Will Mr. Pig please step forward? Mr. Pig?

Gallery & Senators: (uproarious laughter)

Sen. Stone: What's so funny? What did I say?

In 1986, the *Max Headroom* phenomenon hit the American media with a storm of sensation. The show's hi-tech effects and biting humor proved an all-out success. It seemed that the public just couldn't get enough of Max and his lovable antics. The public was wrong. After a spin-off of the show was aired on ABC on December 14, 1986, the network received numerous complaints from angry viewers as well as from the American Speech Institute. The spin-off was pulled from the air the very next week.

THE MAX AND PORKY SHOW

MAX HEADROOM: G-good evening, ladies and g-germs. M-Max Headroom here for another hour of m-m-MAX-imum m-media power. L-let me introduce m-my c-cute and c-cuddly co-co-co-host, P-Porky Pig!

PORKY PIG: Thuh-thuh-thank y-you, Mr. Headroo-headr-headroo, um, Max.

MAX HEADROOM: S-say, you t-talk f-funny, too. Are you c-computer g-generated, like m-me?

PORKY PIG: N-n-no s-sir, I j-just st-st-stutter.

MAX HEADROOM: C-c-cool, f-fa-far out, d-dig it! T-tell me, oh porcine p-prince, whatever became of your c-cartoon s-show? I mean, how are y-you buh-ringing h-home the b-bacon, nowadays? A-ha-ha-ha . . .

PORKY PIG: W-wuh-well, M-Max, actually, I g-got fi-fi-fir, um, canned.

MAX HEADROOM: C-couldn't handle the s-scripts, huh, porkchops?

PORKY PIG: Th-that's n-not f-funny, Max. L-let's j-just get on with the pro-prog-progr, um show, okay?

MAX HEADROOM: S-sure thing, hamlet. Y-you
                 d-don't have to blow yourself to
                 b-bacon bits! Get it, v-viewers—
                 b-bacon bits?!! A-ha-ha-ha, I'm
                 s-so grrrrrrreat!

(MAX BLOWS HIMSELF TO BITS AND
REGENERATES ON SCREEN)
PORKY PIG: C-c'mon M-Max, I d-didn't take this
                 j-job ju-just to buh-be humil-humili-
                 humili, um put down.

MAX HEADROOM: H-hey, cool down, b-baby, or
                 you're l-likely to become
                 rrrrrroast ham! Well, media
                 m-mites, let's go a-headroom
                 with the show and m-meet our
                 f-first guest—M-Mel T-Tillis!!
                 Eeeeeeeeehah! Howdy, M-Mel!

MEL TILLIS: H-h-h-h-h-h-h-huh-huh-huh-howdy,
                 muh-muh-mister Head-head-
                 headroom. Huh-huh-huh-huh-hello,
                 P-p-p-p-puh-puh-puh, um, P-p-p-puh-
                 puh . . .

PORKY PIG: P-porky. H-hello, M-m-mel, h-how are
                 y-you?

MEL TILLIS: I'm f-f-f-f-f-f-fuh-fuh-fuh-fine, p-p-p-p-
                 p-puh-puh-puh-puh . . .

MAX HEADROOM: Well, Americans, th-that's all
                 the t-time we have t-tonight.
                 T-tune in next week when our
                 g-guests will b-be the Who,
                 who'll s-sing "M-my
                 G-generation" . . .

MEL TILLIS: W-wh-wh-what th-th-th-th-th H-h-
                 huh-huh-huh-huh-huh . . .

PORKY PIG: Hell? Oh, j-just f-f-fuh-fuh-fuh-fuh,
                 um, n-never mind.

In 1954 all American media cowered in fear of the awesome power of Senator Joseph McCarthy. In an attempt to win his good graces, several television producers gave the red-baiting dema-gogue an open-invite to make cameo appear-ances on their programs. McCarthy took advan-tage of the situation to make unannounced surprise intrusions on the sets, forcing per-formers to ad-lib their way through his thinly disguised stranglehold of terror.

In 1955, when Senator McCarthy was exposed as a self-serving fraud, the producers burned the kinescopes—and all that remained were viewers' dim memories.

I LOVE LUCY
Desilu Productions
Broadcast Transcript
9/25/54

                    RICKY
     Frat, I have to go down to the club
     to set up for tonight's show. Why
     don't you come along and watch me
     rehearse?
                    FRED
     Sure thing, Rick. You know how
     much I love that ''Babalu''
     number.
(DOORBELL RINGS)
                    RICKY
     Now who could that be? According
     to the script, Lucy isn't due back
     this soon.
(RICKY OPENS DOOR, SENATOR McCARTHY ENTERS)
                    RICKY
     Oh! Uh, why look, Fred, it's
     Senator McCarthy! Hello Choe.
     What brings you to our door?
                    McCARTHY
     Hello Ricky, hello Fred. I just
     happened to be in the neighborhood
     and decided to drop in on my *old
     friends*. Oh, and Fred, I'd like to
     talk with you a little bit later
     about some petitions you signed
     way back when.
                    FRED
     Uh, sure thing, Joey ole pal.
     I've got nothing to hide. Hey, and
     I couldn't be happier to see ya!

RICKY

Well, Choe, Frat and I have got to
go down to the club to set up for
the big show tonight . . .
FRED

Yes, Senator, so if you want to
take a nap, just lie down in the
bedroom. The show starts at nine.
McCARTHY

Thank you very much, fellas. I'm
looking forward to some true-blue
American entertainment.
RICKY

We won't disappoint you. And don't
worry about Lucy—she shouldn't be
back from the beauty parlor for
another couple of hours.
(EXIT RICKY AND FRED THROUGH FRONT DOOR.)
(McCARTHY EXITS TO BEDROOM. TWO-SECOND
PAUSE.)
SFX: KEYS RATTLING IN DOOR
ETHEL   (OUTSIDE OF DOOR)

Lucy, are you sure Ricky won't
mind—that's an awfully expensive
vase you bought.
(ENTER ETHEL AND LUCY THROUGH FRONT DOOR.)
LUCY

No, don't worry Ethel. He'll love
it when he sees it up on the
mantel!
(LUCY AND ETHEL START TO TAKE OFF THEIR COATS.
LUCY IS STILL HOLDING FANCY VASE. BOTH TURN
BACKS FOR A SECOND, AND McCARTHY WALKS OUT OF
BEDROOM IN HIS UNDERWEAR. LUCY TURNS TO FACE
McCARTHY.)
McCARTHY

Oh, you must be . . .
LUCY AND ETHEL

Eeeeeek!
(LUCY HITS McCARTHY ON HEAD WITH EXPENSIVE
VASE, SHATTERING IT. McCARTHY PASSES OUT.)
LUCY

Ethel! Call the police!
ETHEL   (LOOKING AT BODY)

Oh, honey . . . do you know who that
was?
LUCY

I'm afraid I do, Ethel. (SIGH) But
someone has to have the courage to
stop him.
SFX: PHONE RING
(LUCY PICKS UP PHONE.)
RICKY   (V.O.)

Lucy? Let me speak to Senator
McCarthy. You know, Choe McCarthy
. . . He's in the bedroom.
LUCY

(HOLDS PHONE AWAY FROM EAR) (GRITS TEETH)
Eeeew . . .
RICKY   (V.O.)

Lucy? What have you done to

Senator McCarthy?
LUCY   (SHEEPISH)

Ricky? Honey? Do you promise me
something?
RICKY   (V.O.)

Lucy! Tell me you haven't done
something to him!
LUCY   (SHEEPISH)

Well . . .
RICKY   (V.O.)

Miresquestanosandidacochina!
LUCY   (DROPS PHONE)

Waaaah!
(AUDIENCE: THUNDEROUS APPLAUSE, LAUGHTER.)

FATHER KNOWS BEST
10/11/54
Broadcast Transcript
(BUD COMES DOWNSTAIRS DRESSED AS A BEATNIK.
JIM SITS ON COUCH READING PAPER AND SMOKING
HIS PIPE. MARGARET IS NEXT TO HIM DOING
NEEDLEPOINT.)
BUD

Well, Mom and Dad, I'm off to the
Teen Mixer Masquerade Ball!
JIM   (CHUCKLING)

Oh ho ho! My son the beatnik!
You'll be a big hit, Bud.
MARGARET

Have a good time, dear!
(BUD EXITS THROUGH FRONT DOOR.)
(A SECOND LATER, DOORBELL RINGS.)
(JIM GETS UP TO ANSWER IT.)
JIM

I wonder who that could be at this
hour!
MARGARET

Maybe Bud had car trouble . . .
(JIM OPENS DOOR. McCARTHY HAS BUD IN A
HEADLOCK UNDER HIS ARM.)
McCARTHY

Sorry to disturb you, Mr.
Anderson, but I was driving by and
I noticed this subversive
prowling around your house.
JIM   (LAUGHING)

Well, I'm certainly glad you're
out on patrol again, Senator, but
that's just our lovable Bud on his
way to a costume party.
McCARTHY

Oh, Bud!! I didn't recognize you
in that silly get-up!
BUD   (STILL IN HEADLOCK)

Oh, that's okay, Senator.
(McCARTHY LETS BUD GO.)
McCARTHY

Have a good time at your function,
Bud. Say hi to the girls for me!
BUD   (V.O.)

Will do, Senator!

JIM
Well, come on in, Joe, and make
yourself at home!
McCARTHY
Don't mind if I do . . .
(McCARTHY SITS DOWN IN EASY CHAIR.)
BETTY
(V.O. FROM UPSTAIRS)
Mother! Is that Senator McCarthy?
MARGARET
Why, yes it is, dear!
BETTY
(V.O. FROM UPSTAIRS)
Oh, Senator, I've got the nicest
dress, and I'm dying for a man to
see it!
McCARTHY   (GETTING UP)
Why, I'd be delighted to!
MARGARET   (GETTING UP)
Don't be too long, Joe! I'm got
some delicious coffee and
doughnuts waiting.
McCARTHY
Heh heh.

THE HOWDY DOODY SHOW
Broadcast Transcript
11/5/54
HOWDY DOODY
Hey kids, what time is it?
AUDIENCE OF CHILDREN
It's the McCarthy Era!
(CUE THEME SONG—SUNG BY BUFFALO BOB,
AUDIENCE, AND HOWDY-DOODY SINGERS.)
It's Joe McCarthy Time! It's Joe
   McCarthy Time!
He's got a list of you, Your
   daddy's on it, too!

It's Joe McCarthy Time! Relax and
   you'll be fine.
Just give a name or two, And he'll
   quit bugging you!
BUFFALO BOB
Hello kids, and welcome to a
special presentation of *The Howdy
Doody Show,* with our special
surprise guest, Senator Joseph
McCarthy!
McCARTHY
(WEARING CLARABEL'S BULBOUS CLOWN NOSE AND
                FRIGHT WIG.)
Good morning, children.
AUDIENCE
Hi Joe!
BUFFALO BOB
And now, it's time for a sing-
along song! Ready? (PIANO
ACCOMPANIMENT BEGINS) One, two-

Old MacDonald had a farm, ee-eye,
ee-eye oh. And on this farm he had
some sheep, ee-eye, ee-
McCARTHY
(INTERRUPTING—SONG DWINDLES OUT)
Ah, that's enough of that now,
children. Let's try something
else.
BUFFALO BOB
(FORCING A SMILE)
Haha, well, if you say so,
Senator, I guess you're the boss
today.
McCARTHY
First of all, I'd like to get to
know all of you a little bit
better. Let's hear about your home
life; what your parents do.
(McCARTHY GOES INTO AUDIENCE, LEANS OVER
BLONDE GIRL WITH PLAID DRESS.)
McCARTHY
And what is your name little girl?
GIRL   (BASHFULLY)
Suzy.
McCARTHY
Suzy, do you know what your
parents do for a living?
SUZY   (BAWLING)
Waaaah! His breath smells funny!
Waaah!
(McCARTHY MUMBLES INCOHERENTLY AND STEPS OVER
TO A SMALL, SULLEN, BESPECTACLED BOY IN THE
BACK ROW.)
McCARTHY
Hey little boy, I noticed you
weren't singing my opening theme
song. Why not? Cat got your
tongue? Where is your home?
BOY
I don't have a home. I live in an
orphanage.
McCARTHY
I see. What's your name?
BOY
Daniel.
McCARTHY
Daniel what?
BOY
Rosenberg.
McCARTHY
Daniel Rosenberg, you say, eh?
Maybe you'd better come with me.
(McCARTHY TAKES DANIEL BY THE
HAND, LEADING HIM OUT OF HIS SEAT
AND TOWARD THE STUDIO EXIT.)
DANIEL   (CRYING)
Buffalo Bob! Buffalo Bob!
BUFFALO BOB
Now Daniel, you be a good boy and
go with the nice clown.
(McCARTHY EXITS WITH DANIEL IN TOW.)

Sen. Richardson: Gee, Jeremiah, I'm sorry that Andy Griffith didn't turn out like you hoped he'd be.

Sen. Beaufort: Ah know it. It's just lak one o' them guys. One minute, they's all smiles and chat, and the next, they's gone *Hollywood* on ya.

Sen. Fawcett: Yeah, I couldn't believe it. He's *so* different from the Andy Griffith I grew up with. I mean, all snooty and pompous, so *full* of himself . . .

Sen. Stone: Well, to be honest, I sort of *liked* the man. . . .

TAKING THE STAND: Mikhail Hunt, NBC legal consultant

Sen. Mohasset: Good morning, Mr. Hunt. For the past fifteen years, you've been a legal consultant to NBC Television. Is that correct?

Mikhail Hunt: Yes, sir. My job is to make sure that characters on NBC television shows behave in accordance with the laws of this great empire, so that our shows will maintain the highest degree of legal veracity and verisimilitude.

Sen. Mohasset: Why is it then, Mr. Hunt, that we so often see things like this? Please direct your attention to the viewing screen.

Example One: *Miami Vice.* Don Johnson pilots his Ferrari through a fruit market full of people and produce, overturning fruit carts and nearly striking at least twelve innocent shoppers.

Example Two: *Delta House.* A member of a college fraternity resolves a minor dispute by having a truckload of concrete dumped into another student's open convertible, causing an inestimable amount of malicious property damage. And yet he is lauded by students and faculty alike.

Example Three: *Star Trek.* Mr. Spock uses a "Vulcan Death—"

Hunt: Senator? I think I can clear this up very easily. When I referred to "the laws of this great empire," I wasn't talking about America, I was talking about the great empire of network television, which operates under a distinctly different legal code. And I have here a few pages from the "Prime Time Bill of Rights." I'd like to submit this as evidence.

TELEVISION CONSTITUTION
PRIME-TIME BILL OF RIGHTS

III. *Unlimited Amnesty For Maligned Parties*

A. *If an orphanage or old age home is threatened by sale or eviction, the person(s) running it are considered above the law, and are permitted to steal from, defraud, or otherwise harass large corporations or other impersonal entities insensitive to the plight of orphans or elderly people.*

B. *Other persons or organizations considered above the law include: maligned fraternity members; police officers unjustly accused of graft or corruption; low-income teenagers seeking a college education; parents of terminally ill children; and elderly people of any kind.*

IV. *Misperceived Threats To The Safety Of The General Populace*

A. *Police officers and private detectives are permitted to drive their cars through crowded sidewalks at high speed. While this may seem dangerous, it actually poses no real threat, as pedestrians always move in the nick of time.*

B. *Owners of fruit stands or construction scaffolds destroyed by police cars in high speed pursuit have no legal recourse and are not eligible for financial remuneration. If this kind of reimbursement were standard, most police departments would operate at a constant financial deficit.*

C. *Chimpanzees, orangutans, and other lower primates are permitted to operate motor vehicles in a dangerous way, but they are never to be shot. If a chimp cannot be captured by lawmen using butterfly nets, he is obviously too intelligent to deserve a captive existence.*

V. *Inheritances, Wills, and Estates*

A. *The last will and testament of a deceased party is not considered valid or legally binding unless it meets at least one of the following conditions:*

  i. *the greater part of the money is hidden in a secret location; the beneficiaries compete for the inheritance by engaging in some sort of chase or game.*

  ii. *if three or more parties make substantial claims on a large estate, the deceased party will leave the bulk to his aged butler or favorite dog; the remaining beneficiaries will receive ironic gifts that mock their avarice.*

  iii. *if the deceased party's estate includes a cabin, house, or mansion that is rumored to be the sight of alleged supernatural activity, the beneficiary is required to spend one full night in said cabin, house, or mansion in order to be eligible for ownership.*

VI. *Adoption*

A. *Orphaned or adopted children are to be placed in a household in which the lifestyle and general socio-financial status differs most from that of the child. Poor black children are to be placed with rich white bachelors, rich white children with lower-middle class black families, and robot children with ordinary, low-tech families.*

B.i. *If circumstances require that a talking car, talking horse, space alien, "genie," or warlock be housed in an ordinary household, members of that household are forbidden to explicitly explain to neighbors or employers the special nature of their houseguest.*

  ii. *Spouses/owners/"masters" of the above are required to forbid the use of said magical abilities, even when circumstances would seem to require it.*

  iii. *After forbidding these actions, the spouse/owner/"master" must go to extreme and absurd lengths to right the situation, fail, and finally give in to the simple and superior supernatural solution.*

VII. *Mental Instability Or Insanity*

A. *Genuinely insane persons are not permitted to exist in this country. We do, however, permit an overabundance of zealously deluded persons, including:*

  i. *those who believe that aliens are controlling them.*

  ii. *those who believe an invisible entity accompanies them everywhere.*

  iii. *those who perceive discernible speech patterns emanating from inanimate objects.*

These persons are generally harmless and funny, and—as Section VI.B. indicates—they may actually be telling the truth.

TAKING THE STAND: Mr. Everett Finley

Sen. Mohasset: And, finally, I'd like to call to the stand Mr. Everett Finley, president of the National Academy of Television Arts and Sciences. Each year NATAS presents a series of awards, which you term "technical," that are not broadcast along with the televised Emmy awards, am I correct?

Finley: You are correct, Senator.

Sen. Mohasset: In actuality, these are a series of awards for "insiders" that glorify the seamier aspects of the medium. Mr. Finley, my one question for you is . . .

Sen. Richardson: How come we can't see them on TV?

Finley: Beg your pardon?

Sen. Beaufort: Fuhget all that, Finley. What my constituents and I really want to know is: are y'all awauh that NATAS spelled backward is SATAN?

Finley: I . . . uh . . .

Sen. Beaufort: Satan. I believe that's ahl that need be sayud about the telluhvision induhstry. I move we close this potion of the hearings.

Sen. Mohasset, Richardson, Stone, Beatrice, and Fawcett: Second!

Sen. Mohasset: Motion carried. Monday we'll start on the book industry. Recess until then.

Sen. Richardson: Oh boy, recess!

THE NATIONAL ACADEMY OF TELEVISION ARTS & SCIENCES

PRESENTS

The 38th Annual Closed-Ceremony Emmy Awards

May 17, 1987

No Guests   Industry personnel only

ORDER OF CEREMONIES

Benediction	Reverend Ike
Welcome	Dr. Art Uline
Warning to hold all applause until the end	Sgt.-at-Arms
Warning not to bust up all the hotel furniture again	Hotel Manager
Musical number—"Let the Awards Begin"	Merv Griffin & His Amazing Rap-o-phonic Tape Deck

AWARDS PRESENTATIONS

Outstanding Achievement in Being the Goofiest Looking News Anchor in the Country

NOMINEES

Chet Geiger	KTRS, Abilene
Elmo Wzcniak	KOLA, Billings
Ted Koppel	ABC News, Washington

Outstanding Achievement in Cutting a Loud Fart on a Live Broadcast

NOMINEES

John Madden	*Monday Night Football* (NBC) November 4, 1986
Dinah Shore	*Colgate Golf Classic* (ABC) June 16, 1986
Isaac Bashevis Singer	*Literary Viewpoint* (PBS) August 29, 1986

Outstandingly Contrived Local Special Program

NOMINEES

Art Ferwin, producer	*This Weather We've Been Having* WGTT, Tampa
Luther Luis, producer	*Rating the County's Best Sporting Goods Stores* WHUH, Englewood
Bret Percy, producer	*What the Inside of a TV Station Looks Like* KTTT-TV, San Carlos

Outstanding Achievement of Realistic Pathos in a Broadcast Appeal

NOMINEES

Jerry Lewis	"These kids . . . mean SO MUCH to me" *Jerry Lewis Labor Day Telethon*, Sept. 1, 1986

| Bob Hope | "But seriously . . . our veterans are worth more than a few good laughs" *Bob Hope Salutes the Vietnam Veterans*, May 20, 1986 |
| Alex Jerviek, Station Manager | "Your contribution may get you this coaster, but it means SO much more . . ." *WPBS Telethon*, January 15, 1987 |

Outstanding Bargain on a Home Shopping Channel

NOMINEES

$5.95	Simulated Teakwood Pencil Cabinet, 5:35 A.M. October 20, 1986 (HSN)
$39.95	Pacemaker Substitute Hand-Autographed by John Elway, 3:22 P.M. May 31, 1986 (SAHC)
$19.98	Reprinted first edition of *Within a Budding Grove* by Marcel Proust, 6:47 P.M. December 20, 1986 (CFXC)

Outstanding Writing in a Censored Episode of a Situation Comedy

NOMINEES

Theodore Wells	"Mallory Looks in Alex's Sock Drawer" *Family Ties*
Gregory Dark	"Blair's Danish Cousin" *The Facts of Life*
"John" Smith	"Of Course I'll Still Respect You . . . Norm" *Cheers*

Outstanding Placement of the Emergency Broadcasting System Test

NOMINEES

KOOP, Dallas	Last Minute of Super Bowl XX, Jan. 19, 1986
WREK, Buffalo	Opening Segment of *Dallas*, October 3, 1986
KARF, Sheboygan	"Best Picture" Announcement, Academy Awards, April 2, 1986

Outstanding Number of Women Slept With On Air During One Season

NOMINEES

Tom Selleck	38 women; Thomas Magnum, *Magnum, P.I.*, Oct. 3, 1985–Oct. 8, 1986
Edward Woodward	35 women; the Equalizer, *The Equalizer*, Sept. 25, 1985–Sept. 30, 1986
Dick Clark	34 women; Host, *American Bandstand*, Sept. 10, 1985–Sept. 15, 1986

HONORARY "LIFETIME ACHIEVEMENT" AWARD:

| William Shatner | 4,822 women; Capt. James T. Kirk, *Star Trek*, Sept. 28, 1965–Aug. 30, 1968 |

Outstanding Moral on a Children's Program

NOMINEES

Hank Yushima, prod.	"He-Man Removes the Door from a Discarded Refrigerator," *He-Man and the Masters of the Universe*
Robin Gerard, prod.	"Smurfette Takes an Axe to the Adult Movie Theatre," *The Smurfs*
Norman Nervis, prod.	"Pac-Man Swats at a Hornet's Nest with a Broomstick," *Pac-Man/Rubik's Cube Hour*

Outstanding Writing in an Episode of The Cosby Show *(Presented by the General Foods Corp.)*

NOMINEES

Clark Hoff	"Cliff Finds No Jello in the Fridge," April 3, 1986
Lee Otelli	"Rudy Falls Down the Stairs, but Recovers When Offered a Delicious Pudding Pop™," Sept. 23, 1986
Harris Durtage	"Cliff Quits Drinking Coke So He Can Devote His Full Attention to Jello Pudding," May 15, 1986

END OF AWARDS PRESENTATIONS

Musical Number—"Sorry, Losers! Better Luck Next Year!"
The Don Rickles Orchestra

Presentation of Prizes from "Battle of the Network Stars"
Valerie Harper

EVENT	WINNER	PRIZE
Lifting Own Weight	Emmanuel Lewis	Platform Shoes from Kinney
Marshmallow Pit Wrestling Tourney	Cheryl Tiegs	Turtle Wax
Hot-Dog Eating	Nell Carter	Zebco Fishing Pole
Rootin'-Tootinest	Larry Hagman	$10 Gift Certificate at Spencer Gifts

Pledge of Allegiance — Billy Crystal

Closing Benediction — Linda Evans

Complimentary Soft Drinks and Brownies to be Served in the Maple Leaf Room Following the Ceremonies

Sen. Mohasset: "To think that the television industry duped the American people in this despicable fashion! I can honestly say I'm ashamed that I ever bought one of the damn things. In fact, I'm going to call my wife right now and tell her to throw ours in the trash. I suggest you all do the same, unless you're watching the hearings, in which case you can tell your wife I said it was okay."

•

Sen. Beaufort: "Evrahone involved in thuh whole goldarned thingamabob oughta be run outta town like a greased-up polecat in a barrel o' chitlins. Telluhvision is a curse brought down on us by the Almighty hisself—the whole thing stinks like a barrel o' tobaccah soaked in white lightnin'. Damn telluhvision! Damn it all to hell! Oh, and Ah'd lahk to say hello to all mah constituents watching today on WCSC, channel 5 in Charleston, and on WOLO-TV, channel 25 in Columbia."

•

Sen. Richardson: "The whole medium is full of liars, phonies, and crooks. Did you see that fellow Charles Grodin? He played me in *Apollo:Soyuz: A Mission of Peace* on ABC last year. He doesn't look a thing like me. I'm much thinner than that, don't you think?"

•

Sen. Stone: "It behooves me to state that I, for one, never fell under the insidious spell of the so-called idiot-box. I always found the programming insipid and moronic—geared to the lowest common denominator. Once, I must admit, I did rent a television to view the full simulcast of Wagner's *Ring Cycle*. And a few episodes of *Three's Company*. And one or two of those hilarious Midas muffler commercials. But that's all, I swear it."

•

Sen. Beatrice: "Despite this week's findings, I remain firm in my innate trust of television as a medium. In fact, I think everyone should watch *more* television, particularly the advertisements, to reassure themselves in these times of crisis. Particularly the advertisements shown during the Olympics and the Super Bowl. Those are always the best."

•

Sen. Fawcett: "Once and for all: I am not related to Farrah Fawcett. I am not related to Farrah Fawcett. I am not related to Farrah Fawcett. Got that?"

WEEK SIX: BOOKS

Sen. Mohasset: We now enter the final week of testimony, and I'm sure the American people are as tired of hearing about all this as we are. Everywhere we turn, it's "Mediagate-this" and "Mediagate-that." We see it on the news every night, and we read it in the papers every morning. Comedians make jokes about it, and musicians write songs about it. I've even heard that there's a movie in the works. But we cannot forget our main goal: to get to the bottom of this mess. In fact, it seems ironic that the media—the very institution under indictment— seems to be profiting from this "media circus." Hey, wait a minute. Hmm . . .

TAKING THE STAND: "Mr. O"

Sen. Mohasset: What you're saying, then, is that the *New York Times* best-seller list is actually compiled from the sales of only a limited number of book stores?

Mr. "O": That is correct, sir. But it's a, ahm, fair sampling.

Sen. Mohasset: Just how *fair* is it? How many stores are involved?

Mr. "O": Well, I really couldn't say *exactly* how many . . .

Sen. Mohasset: Estimate, then.

Mr. "O": Well, ahm . . . two.

Sen. Mohasset: Two!

Mr. "O": Well, yes. To the nearest two.

Sen. Mohasset: This is an outrage! Please bring forth the *real* best-seller list, based on a *national* sampling!

Paperback Best-Sellers

Nonfiction

1 **KNUTTS!** by Lou Johnson, with Marty Kerchwood and Don Knotts (Bookman, $1.95) The unexpurgated autobiography of Don Knotts. Includes some choice comments (neither derogatory nor complimentary) concerning Andy Griffith.

2 **MOTHERHOOD,** by Felicia Rashad (Bantam Liteweights, $4.95) A sequel to Bill Cosby's Fatherhood.

3 **PATERNITY SUIT,** by Bill Cosby (Knipf/ Knopf, $16.95) A sequel to Phylicia Rashad's Motherhood.

4 **KISS MY ASS, MR. PRESIDENT!** by Sam Donaldson (Abner Doubleday & Sons, $3.61) Gadfly goads goon, gets girl, goes gaga. Guy's got guts!

5 **THE BOOK OF LOVE** (Author unknown) (Little, Brown, Jug, $3.95) Speculation on the origin of the text by Professor Longhair, graduate of the Soul Class of '69 at the College of Musical Knowledge.

6 **SCREWING,** by Studs Terkel (Simon & Simon, $3.67) When Mr. Terkel says "oral" history, he means it.

7 **"QUIT DICKING AROUND, MR. FEYNMAN,"** by Richard P. Feynman (Houghton Hollerin, $3.95) "Feynman is brilliant, adorable, and incorrigible," says Mr. Feynman.

8 **WALK LIKE A MAN,** by Martina Navratilova (Random Hut, $6.95) Tennis tips.

9 **MEDIAGATE,** by the Harvard Lampoon (Atlantic Monthly Press, $12.95) A book about an investigation of the U.S. media turns up in a fake version of the *New York Times* Best-Seller List. Hilarious reading for the coffee table or crapper.

Fiction

1 **UNIVERSE,** by James Michener (Bookman, $25) A lusty saga of men, women, animals, and primordial slime that spans 6,278 steamy love affairs and 1,358 broken dreams. At 50 cents a pound, it's a bargain.

2 **FANTASTIC INCREDIBLE JOURNEY,** by Isaac Asimov (Merkin, $3.95) Two dogs and a cat are miniaturized and injected into the body of a dying man.

3 **YOU'RE ONLY OLD TWICE,** by Dr. Seuss (Dog, $7.47) A new James Bond thriller from the author of *You're Only Old Once* and *Horton Joins The Who.*

4 **ARE YOU THERE GOD? IT'S ME, MARGARET ATWOOD,** by Judy Blume (Vintage Ultralites, $4.95) An author famous for her chilling vision of a totalitarian society has her first period.

5 **SHOGUN VS. GODZILLA,** by James Clavell (Penguin Vintage-Ripoffs, $4.95) Based both on the true history of the Japanese shogunate and the popular film *Gamara Vs. Megara.* Soon to be a minor TV miniseries.

6 **THE FORBIDDEN ZONES** by Stephen King (KingCo., $6.66) Thrills and chills in the horrifying "Chamber of Commerce." A missing car, three devious aldermen, and a set of thoroughly unjust zoning laws add up to another long book by Mr. King.

7 **TO ALL THE GIRLS I'VE LOVED BEFORE,** by Julio Iglesias and Rita Mae Brown (Choad, $9.69) Famous author and singing Latino team up for a "fictional" novel that "has nothing to do with" their actual lives.

8 **LEGS TOO SHORT TO KICK-BOX WITH GOD,** by Maya Angelou and Jackie Chan (Harcourt Briss, $8.95) An inner-city woman learns spiritual self-defense from a mysterious man with "Feet Of Fury."

Advice, How-to, and Miscellaneous

1 **LEARNING TO ADRE,** Bety Smiht (Pedantlic Monthly Press, $4.95) A guide to dyslexia from a woman who should know.

2 **EINSTEIN'S PHYSICS MADE SIMPLE TO THE POINT OF INACCURACY** by Chris Dingman (Simon & Shyster, $6.95) E>MC.

3 **ANOTHER INTERMINABLE MINUTE WITH ANDY ROONEY** by Andy Rooney (Pocket Pool, $5.95) One minute; 5,000 pages.

4 **WOMEN WHO LOVE TOO MUCH FOOD,** by Robin Norwood (Naked Brunch, $3.95) Third in the series that includes *Women Who Love Too Much* and *Women Who Love Too.*

5 **SIX MORE DIRTY JOKES,** by Blanche Knott (Yucklefest, $8.99) Brings the total of dirty jokes to 107.

6 **GARFIELD GETS LAID,** by Jim Davis (Scrimshandy, $9.95)

Clarke's first draft of this milestone work of science fiction (presented below) was an uneasy mixture of conflicting literary elements. His editors suggested he narrow his scope and try again. It proved to be profitable advice, though Clarke lacked the foresight to cash in on both aspects of his original idea.

Arthur C. Clarke's

2001

USES FOR A DEAD CAT

I

Primeval Night

On the African plain, Moon-Watcher gazed in wonder at the strange object that had appeared during the night. It was some sort of black obelisk—a smooth, glistening slab of absolute darkness, jutting forth from the cold soil. Of course, his primitive mind could never have arrived at such an articulate explanation. He thought it was just an obelisk.

Suddenly, he and the other man-apes gathered around the strange formation, drawn by impulses they had never felt before. Beams of light shot out from the black rock, and in each of the man-ape's minds, striking images appeared: the corpses of cats shoved under wiggly table legs, or used as first base in little league games, or hanging from Christmas trees. The lifeless forms of cats serving as mops, and potholders, and so on. The man-apes stood transfixed.

The next day, they killed the leopard that had plagued the tribe for so long and put its rigid body to use as a bowling pin. Moon-Watcher watched its body topple over in awe as he rolled a perfect strike. He wanted more. He wanted to use the leopard's body for something new, but he was unsure what to do next.

He would think of something.

II

ASPCA-1

Dr. Heywood Floyd was strolling the corridors of the moon base when he was intercepted by a frantic Dr. Michaels. "We've found something very strange on the moon's surface," Michaels stammered to Floyd. "I think you'd better have a look at it."

A few hours later, the lunar crawler rolled up to the site. Floyd and Michaels got out, and Michaels pointed to the immense monolith standing out against the night sky.

"A gigantic scratching post," said Michaels.

Suddenly, the lunar dawn broke over the site, exposing the post to the sun for the first time in millions of years. Dr. Michaels, Dr. Floyd, and the other scientists assembled clasped their hands to their ears in pain. The sudden blare of intense electronic meowing had caught them all by surprise.

After three million years of darkness, ASPCA-1 had greeted the lunar dawn.

III

Between Planets

Bowman stared at HAL's console. "What do you mean the CAT Scanner is blown out again? What in the world are we going to use to fix it this time?"

HAL responded in his usual calm voice. "May I remind you, David, that the *Discovery* has a store of several hundred dead cats, several of which could be used to prop up the broken scanner."

"Oh, right. Boy, those dead cats sure do come in handy." Bowman hit the intercom. "Frank, prepare to go outside and fix the scanner again. And pick up three or four dead cats on the way out."

· · ·

Bowman couldn't believe what he was seeing. The body of Frank Poole was spinning off into space, surrounded by a rotating galaxy of dead cats. Hundreds of them had somehow shot out of the vent tubes, knocking him away from the ship and severing his air line.

"HAL! What's going on!" Bowman shouted, just as he, too, was engulfed in the swirling flood of dead cats, which swept him from his feet and pushed him toward the airlock.

· · ·

Bowman grimly grasped the body of the cat in his gloved left hand and steadied himself with his right.

"David, what are you doing?" HAL's voice inquired. "I assure you that the release of the cats was an unpreventable, freakish malfunction."

Bowman did not reply. Instead, he began battering HAL's memory chips with the cat's rigid corpse. Intricate components splintered off and began floating through the vacuum.

"David, stop . . . surely there must be some better use for the cat than this . . ." intoned HAL. "I mean, you could use it as . . . as a pincushion, or . . . or a doorstop . . . or . . . or . . ." And then all was silent. Bowman was alone at last.

Well—almost alone—he thought, as he looked around at the still twirling bodies.

IV

The Moons of Saturn

Touching the pod's controls lightly, Bowman maneuvered around Japetus, Saturn's mysterious moon. "I'm coming around the far side now," he reported. "There's something up ahead . . . it's . . . *it's just like the scratching post on the moon!* This is ASPCA-1's big brother!"

Bowman eased the pod over the top of the mysterious post, gazing down in wonder. Huge, mile-long splinters stuck out where it had been fiercely scratched. A tremendous ball of blue yarn lay at the base, partially unraveled. Off to one side lay what might have been a dried-up turd.

"Just a minute . . . that's odd . . ."

Suddenly, the post's top seemed to be receding on itself, creating a hollow effect.

David Bowman had time for just one broken sentence, which the men waiting in Mission Control, nine-hundred million miles away, were never to forget.

"The thing's hollow—it goes on forever—and—oh my God! *It's full of shit! It's a gigantic litter box!*"

V

Through the Star Gate

Bowman watched in calm wonder as the pod hurtled through the strange gateway. This was it: the cat door to another dimension. Ahead lay planet-sized packages of Tender Vittles, some opened, some untouched. Several bowls of food had been spilled, leaving individual nuggets of food orbiting sluggishly.

Then the pod swept past the cat food, and Bowman saw that he was being drawn toward the largest cat he had ever seen. It was at least the size of the solar system. And it was dead.

Bowman guided the pod to a halt just above one of the cat's stiffened legs. He looked down in consternation. He was untold light-centuries from home, rapidly consuming his oxygen, and he had to go to the bathroom really badly. But that wasn't what concerned him most. Though he had the largest dead cat ever known to man at his disposal, he was not quite sure what to do with it.

But he would think of something.

RICHARD NIXON: HE IS BAD.

Richard Nixon kicks dogs.

Richard Nixon pours tar in mailboxes.

Richard Nixon has no respect for other people's privacy.

Richard Nixon has no respect for the law.

Richard Nixon takes lunch money from elementary school children.

Richard Nixon crippled Franklin Roosevelt.

Richard Nixon will send you a dollar if you break a church window.

Richard Nixon takes all the newspapers from the vending machine.

Richard Nixon made cruel jokes about Gandhi's bald head.

Richard Nixon drives recklessly.

Richard Nixon endangers human lives.

Richard Nixon is blocking progress in cancer research.

Richard Nixon ruins Christmas for everyone.

Richard Nixon is a public nuisance.

Richard Nixon sends condoms to nuns.

Richard Nixon abuses his personal wealth.

Richard Nixon is inconsiderate.

Richard Nixon stinks.

To: Alfred A. Knopf

Dear Alf,

Rumors of my "sophomore slump" are greatly exaggerated. I consider the cackling gossip about my self-imposed hiatus as absurd as the crowlike critics themselves, perched avariciously on a telephone line's honest black ropiness.

Enclosed is my latest foray into the flatland of fiction.

Enjoy,

P.S. Please don't phone me for a few months. I'm busy swapping wives with myself.

Eric,
Let's just toss this out and forget it ever happened. John is obviously experiencing a sophomore slump.
AEK

It is late afternoon and the wet April air covers suburban pavement like the slimy backwash coating the glass of the shared coke bottle your best friend meretriciously let you drink from in sixth grade. Bunny Voltage strolls up the alleyway, a six-foot silhouette in a business suit eating a strawberry silhouette of an ice cream cone. A former college basketball star, Bunny stops to watch boys playing in a makeshift alley court. The brickface and alley gravel fades to the cheering grandstands and cartwheeling, goose-pimply-thighed pom-pom girls of a B-league scrimmage. Inspired, he grabs their ball and dribbles in a flawless two-step swivel-around-the-shoulders steal. The boys stare. They are playing street hockey. Unfazed, Bunny slamdunks the puck.

"Just luck," calls a tall, rangy kid in dungarees.

"No, talent," he rejoins with a small pride, judging from their sullen grubby-nosed faces that he has earned their respect. Smiling, he thinks of Cindy, then inexplicably feels a certain emptiness. Is something missing in the stubborn lumpiness of her pregnancy? No, it is his wallet, gingerly removed by unwashed hands as a hockey stick crashes unkindly over Bunny's brown-haired cranium.

· · · · · ·

It is dark when he regains consciousness and dusts himself off. Bunny is sad. His ice cream has melted over the funnel of waffleprint like the pink ejaculate of an effete volcano. Now he climbs the stairs to his home, the top floor, and unlocks the door to find Cindy slouching in an armchair watching TV, dressed in a heftily protruding slip and cradling baby Nicholas. Each is clutching a bottle: one milk, the other vodka.

His wife removes the rubber nipple from her lips to speak: "You're late for dinner

again, so give me three packs of cigarettes now!" she says sweetly. Bunny sighs. He sprawls over the sofa, reflecting wearily on the day's work. A salesman for the Recursiveyuks Novelty Items Co.—some job for a twenty-six year old stereotype of an ex-athlete.

During today's demonstration the electro-joy buzzer backfired in synchrony with the dribble glass, resulting in a minor electrocution. Yeah, that's the American Way, pitching for Recursiveyuks. Every middle-class fraud has his pet project for success, and Bunny knows his—a handy little item for every household's shower. Clock-on-a-rope. Going in it with a partner though, good old Reverend Bedspring. Little waves of contentment swim across Bunny's face as his thoughts focus on his *other* partner, Mrs. Bedspring. He turns sheepishly to regard blonde-haired Cindy. So cute. Watching TV and pregnant, munching on her favorite snack of Marlboros and mayonnaise.

· · · · · ·

Sheila smiles coyly but invitingly as she sucks down her third martini and Bunny hesitates, feeling airy globes of nervousness rise up from his legs and envelope his torso until they float out of his ears. He gazes at the ceiling. "It's okay," she reassures him. "Eugene won't be back for some time. He's out bestowing food and blessings upon the poor, so we can adulterate for at least three more hours." Now he truly is galled. Thinks she knows it all.

"Well," he snaps, "What did you do with the Mr. Potato Head leftovers?"

She draws closer, crossing curvy legs to reveal a white crescent of slip. "First tell me more about yourself," she purrs fetchingly.

Bunny explains the origin of his moniker. He is so called partly because of his affection for lovemaking; partly for his inordinate

fondness for carrots, partly because as a sickly little boy he contracted myxomatosis 27 times, or until he was laughed out of the ward. Yeah, some childhood.

Excited now, they move toward the bedroom. Before even the reader recognizes what is going on, Bunny is in the sheets, writhing over naked hollows and cloven declivities, bending and slipping on the thick threads of mucus and shiny orbs of saliva which pass between parched tongues in the lovely, wobbly bubbles of exuding breasts and pressing, urgent thighs. Then Sheila returns from the bathroom.

"I'm ready," she announces.

"Err . . ." He gets up to make a sandwich.

· · · · · ·

Bunny is jogging—pant pant, inhale, exhale. He passes Coach Tolstoy's house and sees Leo is having a lawn barbeque, standing over the grill in a cloud of blue smoke and an apron. Inexplicably, he is actually barbequeing the lawn. Never was too bright. He calls out, "Hey Bunny! You're in fine form. Do you believe in God?"

Bunny stops and blushes. He is a Christian, so the mention of God makes him feel guilty.

"No," he answers. "I believe in Darwin."

"Darwin is dead, Bunny."

"Yes, well, he'd be the first to admit that, wouldn't he?" Tears well up inside.

The conversation turns to Cindy and the baby. What to name it. Leo suggests "Jesus, after you-know-who." And then there is Bunny's uncle, who thinks the baby should go unnamed, "for tax purposes." Bunny is asked to join the meal, but Leo is out of jalapeno sauce, which goes best with crabgrass. Crestfallen, Bunny runs on, leg muscles taut. Doubling back into the quickening twilight gloom, he is sideswiped by a Buick. Now he hops, ouch, hops.

ON THE STAND: Bob Woodward and Carl Bernstein, authors of *All The President's Men*

Sen. Mohasset: Mr. Woodward . . . Mr. Bernstein. Welcome to the Senate Investigation Hearings. I'm sure this all seems very familiar to you.

Bernstein: Senator, would you deny that in 1978, your campaign manager used a secret fund to—

Sen. Mohasset: Mr. Bernstein, need I remind you that I am not under indictment? It's your turn now.

Woodward: Senator, I'm sorry. My colleague gets a little excited sometimes. We already have two different confirmations on your secret fund in 1978. All we want is an admission of guilt from you.

Sen. Mohasset: Gentlemen, can you explain why you purposely omitted key phone conversation transcripts from your book *All The President's Men?*

Bernstein: Um . . .

Woodward: I'd like to consult my lawyer.

ALL THE PRESIDENT'S MEN:

Omitted Phone Conversations

WOODWARD: ". . . okay, if you can't confirm that Magruder directly accepted money for the Fund, how about this: I'm going to count to ten, and if we should publish the story, just stay on the line. Okay?"

VOICE: "Okay."

WOODWARD: "1 . . . 2 . . . 3 . . . 4 . . . 5 . . . 6 . . . 7 . . . 8 . . . 9 . . . 10. Are you still there?"

VOICE: "Okay, let me read this back. You want one Number One Pork Fried Rice. One Number Two Sweet and Sour Prawn. One Number Three Chicken Cashew. One Number Four—"

WOODWARD: "Umm . . . sorry, wrong number."

. . .

BERNSTEIN: "Is this John Mitchell?"

MITCHELL: "Yes. Who's this? What time is it?"

BERNSTEIN: "Mr. Mitchell, this is Carl Bernstein from *The Washington Post*. We're printing a story concerning you tomorrow, and we're wondering if you have any comment. The story states that you authorized CREEP funds to be used for the Watergate break-in."

MITCHELL: "Jesus Christ. You're going to print that? You tell Ben Bradlee that Katherine Graham's going to get her tit caught in the big ringer if that comes out."

BERNSTEIN: "Can I quote you on that, sir?"

MITCHELL: "No, let me amend that. You tell Ben Bradlee that I'll personally put a boot up his fat ass if I see that story in print."

BERNSTEIN: "Can I quote you on that?"

MITCHELL: "No, no—listen: You tell Ben Bradlee that I'm going to rip his dick off and shove it down Katherine Graham's throat if I even hear about that story."

BERNSTEIN: "Well, sir, which one is it?"

MITCHELL: "I'm not sure. Which one do you like?"

BERNSTEIN: "I thought the 'tit in the big ringer' one was pretty good, sir."

MITCHELL: "Okay, use that one."

. . .

WOODWARD: "Is this Mr. Liddy? Gordon Liddy?"

LIDDY: "That's me."

WOODWARD: "Mr. Liddy, did you personally use CREEP funds to wiretap Democratic National Headquarters."

LIDDY: "Sure. I did that."

WOODWARD: "And did you, in 1971, place bugging devices in Ed Muskie's campaign offices?"

LIDDY: "Yep."

WOODWARD: "Mr. Liddy, would you deny that you at one time submitted a plan directly to the President that involved setting fire to Jane Fonda's home in Berkeley?"

LIDDY: "Right again. Hey, who is this?"

WOODWARD: "This is Bob Woodward. I'm with *The Washington Post*."

LIDDY: "You're a reporter?"

WOODWARD: "Yes sir, I am."

LIDDY: "No comment. No comment. Mr. Liddy's not here. You must have a wrong number. You want one order Number Five Peking Dumpling? Herroh? Herroh? House of Wu, Chinese Food. Herroh?"

. . .

VOICE: "Hello, this is Richard Nixon—"

WOODWARD: "We've got you nailed, Mr. President."

BERNSTEIN: "Yeah. You're a big fag."

VOICE: "I'm not in right now, but if you'll leave your name and your number, I'll get back to you."

WOODWARD: "We're not going to rest until we see you impeached."

BERNSTEIN: "You big fag."

VOICE: "Beep."

WOODWARD: "Um . . ."

BERNSTEIN: "Um . . . (click)"

WOODWARD: "(click)"

BERNSTEIN: "I hope he didn't recognize us."

WOODWARD: "Pass me another beer."

. . .

BERNSTEIN: "Carl Bernstein, *Washington Post.* Hello?"

VOICE: "Mr. Bernstein, if you and your partner keep this activity up, I'm afraid there will be dire consequences."

BERNSTEIN: "Who is this?"

VOICE: "Never mind that. I'd advise you and that Jew partner of yours to just cut it out."

BERNSTEIN: "Is this a threat? Can I quote you on this?"

VOICE: "Sure. Go ahead and quote me. This is Mr. Lee Ho Kwan of Kwan's Chinese Restaurant. You boys order big meals, and then you don't tell us where to deliver."

BERNSTEIN: "Oh. I'm sorry, Mr. Kwan. It was an accident."

VOICE: "Yeah, well we have a big meal here in your name. What's your address?"

BERNSTEIN: "Um . . . 1600 Pennsylvania Avenue."

VOICE: "Thank you. Your food will be right over."

. . .

The *1987 Buyers Guide to Stamp Collecting* was circulated by the U.S. Franklin Co. in hobby shops and philatelic expos across the country. However, it was soon discovered that the stamps listed in the catalog were all fakes, designed to boost sales of the Franklin Company's bogus collection. The catalog was immediately pulled from circulation.

GERMANY—1942
HITLER RECREATION SERIES: Original value . . . 5 pfennig
Roller coaster. $712.00
Trampoline. $550.00
Puppetry $675.00

UNITED STATES—1965
PRESIDENTIAL SERIES (MISPRINTS):   Original value . . . 3¢
Inverted George Washington. $10,000.00
John Kennedy without moustache $6,500.00

UNITED STATES—1972
EARLY AMERICAN FLAGS SERIES: Original value . . . 10¢
Thirteen-section snake $300.00
Funny skeleton $150.00
Moron flag $235.00

SOVIET UNION—1922
REVOLUTIONARY CABINET COMMEMORATIVE ISSUE: Original value . . . ½ ruble
Heroic men of the revolution. $3,500.00

SOVIET UNION—1930
REVOLUTIONARY CABINET COMMEMORATIVE RE-ISSUE: Original value ½ ruble
Heroic men of the revolution $900.00

SOVIET UNION—1970
REVOLUTIONARY CABINET COMMEMORATIVE RE-ISSUE: Original value ½ ruble
Heroic men of the revolution. . . . .$.25

RWANDA—1969
MOON LANDING COMMEMORATIVE ISSUE: Original value . . . 788 Mboutis
Moon walk $2.00

JAPAN—1980
WORLD LITERARY FIGURES: Original value . . . 100 yen
Shakespeare. . . . .$.35
Socrates . . . .$.35
Katharine Hepburn . . . .$.40

SWEDEN—1982
SEXUAL POSITION INSTRUCTIONAL SERIES: Original value . . . 25 social exchange units
Triple inverted lotus. . . . .$.75
Truncated half-trapeze. . . . .$.75
Man on top. . . . .$.77

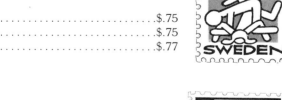

ISRAELI STAMPS:
ISRAELI HEROES SERIES (1955):   Original value . . . 10 Shekels
David Ben Gurion . . . . .24¢
Theodore Herzl. . . . . .46¢
Pontius Pilate. $12,000

Book Review

The Seven Reasons Why I am the Greatest Writer Who Ever Lived
by Gordon Lish

This is the 13th version of this piece Lish has submitted. This one is better than ''18 Reasons Why I Am The Greatest Writer Who Ever Lived,'' but only because it's shorter.
Please send Gordon the standard rejection slip. Address it to ''Capt. Fiction'' or else he'll send it back.

—A.B.

1

I did not write this essay in Maine. I have been to Maine. I went in 1973, on the occasion of a friend's divorce. Her name was Linda.

The divorce was very nice. There were flowers and I talked to a man from Indiana who thought there should be more laws. He told me a number of laws he thought there should be. I believe I agreed with him, although I cannot honestly remember. I meant to write to him on Easter, but of course I did not.

There are five people I would trust in the whole world. One of them is you. I don't want to tell you the other four. It isn't that I don't trust you, but I don't trust my agent, and he is probably reading this.

If I didn't have an agent, I would be much happier, but I would not have an agent. There is something about having an agent.

My agent is from Maine.

2

How do I know you care? I wrote a book once, but how do I know you even read it? If you're not going to read my books, I'm not even going to bother. I just don't have time. I have a thousand more important things to do. I'll tell you some.

My garden needs wooden borders. I need to get long pieces of wood and lay them along the edges of my garden. Otherwise, the dirt will run out.

I read a story yesterday. It didn't sound like I wrote it, and I told him that. He said "Sorry" to me. He said he would try again. For all I know, I wrote it myself. I don't have time to read the things I write, even as I write them, so I never really know.

What I really want is my own game show.

3

Norman Mailer is not as good as I am.
John Updike is not as good as I am.
Walker Percy is not as good as I am.
Anne Tyler is not as good as I am.
Raymond Carver is not as good as I am.
Stephen King is not as good as I am.
Gore Vidal is not as good as I am.
Liberace is dead, and he didn't write books.
Susan Sontag is not as good as I am.
PERU is a better title than *HAWAII, BRAZIL, ULYSSES,* or *JOB.* Think about it.

Eventually I will know everything. I will write down the parts that don't make any sense without the parts I don't write down. I won't write those parts down anywhere.

4

I am not going to say anything about this reason. I am not going to try to explain it. I am not going to say whether I think it is good or not. I am not going to complain if it comes out badly. I am just going to tell you where I heard the reason, and then I am going to tell you the reason. This is the fourth reason. There are seven.

The next reason is the fifth.

5

Nothing like me has ever been published in books exactly like mine. I have read words like mine on license plates, in bowls of soup, and on the manufacturers' plaques of revolving towel machines in gas station restrooms. I have read better stories than mine on the walls of subway tunnels, on the floors of butcher shops, and in the hollow interior of a strand of human hair.

However, none of those things have been put in white books like mine, with my signature on the front.

6

This reason, the sixth, is the longest and most complex of all of them. You cannot possibly understand what I mean by that.

7

Milan Kundera won a Nobel prize. Every story he ever wrote is set in Czechoslovakia. I have read forty books by Milan Kundera. In every single book, the tanks roll into Czechoslovakia. They are Hitler's tanks. Over and over again they roll into Czechoslovakia. I asked my wife how many times she wanted to read about tanks rolling into Czechoslovakia. She said "Seven times." I asked her what else she would like to see roll into Czechoslovakia. "Whales," she said.

I nearly blew my lid.

The Book of Lugnut

 nd the LORD was wrathful towards his chosen people the Israelites for some trifling thing or other.

And the spirit of the LORD left Israel, and went out into the wilderness to try to calm down.

Now the LORD came upon a tribe of people, and their city was called Term, and they were the Term-ites.

And the LORD said, "Behold, and how do you like that.

I had totally forgotten about this people.

No doubt they are descended from some venerable old patriarch, but I cannot remember which one."

And the LORD went down to the city to check it out.

Now there was a man among the Termites, and he was called Lugnut, son of Sam, son of A-gun, son of, well, you get the idea.

And Lugnut was a shepherd, and he was a good shepherd, except when he let the sheep get lost.

Now Lugnut was out tending his flock, when the spirit of the LORD appeared to him.

So Lugnut fell down on his face in fear of the LORD, or maybe he just slipped.

Then said the LORD, "Get up, you, and listen to what I say, for I may make for you a great nation.

Tell your people the Termites that the LORD has come and they must obey me if they are to become good in my sight and great among the nations of men."

And Lugnut rose up and went down to Term, letting his sheep totally slip his mind.

And he told his people the Termites all that had befallen him, and the directions of the LORD.

And Lo, the people were skeptical of him, for he had let the sheep get away again, and he was a fool.

But the people did not want to displease the LORD, so they said, "Okay, whatever."

Then the LORD appeared to Lugnut in a dream, and said unto him thus: "Go way out in the desert, and wait there."

When Lugnut woke, he said, "What a goofy dream."

But he went out into the desert, because with all the sheep gone he had nothing better to do, and waited for several hours, getting hot and thirsty.

Lugnut had brought no wineskin, so he cried, "Hey, Kool-Aid!" but Behold, no ridiculous giant Kool-Aid pitcher burst onto the scene, and Lugnut lamented.

And the LORD heard Lugnut's lamentation, and split open a boulder, and black liquid flowed out.

And a great giggling was heard in the desert, and the LORD said, "Up through the ground came a bubblin' crude.

Oil that is.

Black gold.

Texas tea."

II Then the LORD relented, and split open another boulder, and out came Kool-Aid, though not properly sweetened.

So Lugnut drank it, and it was better than nothing.

And the LORD spake thus to Lugnut, "Thus you shall say to the Termites: the LORD has commanded me to tell you all that we must do in order to find favor with the LORD.

Listen to all my commands before beginning these works.

Now, first, return to the city."

So Lugnut went out of the desert, and returned to Term, and the Termites were all anxious for Lugnut to give them the word of the LORD.

And the LORD spoke to Lugnut, and commanded, "Next, multiply 968 by 737 and sacrifice that many sheep to me in a burnt offering."

Lugnut told this to the people, who became apprehensive, and they did their multiplication and Behold, the result was 713,416.

And all the shepherds wailed and lamented.

Except for Lugnut, whose sheep were long gone.

And the sacrifice was done, and it was a big mess.

And the sheep were also not pleased.

Then the LORD said, "Next, go to the nearest neighboring city and smite all the inhabitants with the edge of the sword."

So the Termites rose up, led by Lugnut, and went to the city of Calgon, and they smote all the Calgonites; they utterly destroyed everything that breathed.

Not a creature was stirring, not even a mouse.

When the Termites returned from this war, the LORD said to Lugnut, "Now if you think you have followed the directions correctly so far, call out, 'I have.'"

And Lugnut told the people the command of the LORD, and the great shout of the people rose above the city.

And the LORD said, "Next make yourself a great ark, and bring into it two of every sort of fish and creature that lives in the sea, for you never know; I might make another flood."

And the people became filled with fear when Lugnut told them this, and an ark was built, even though the SPCA and the UN were already on their case and the last thing they needed was any more trouble.

And the people of Term rose up and went to the sea, and gathered many fish, though many drowned in the effort.

And the people brought the fish and the sea creatures back to Term, and put them in the ark, even though they were dead and smelled.

And the people waited for the word of the LORD.

III Then the LORD spoke to Lugnut, "Now that you have heard all the directions, do only step one.

Ha, ha, ha."

Then Lugnut rent his clothes, and fell to the earth upon his face, and the LORD said, "Well, I got you that time.

You should have paid attention.

And now I am displeased with you, and it's time for a little fire and brimstone."

And Lugnut heard this, and became anguished, and said, "Will you indeed destroy the city, with all of its righteous people, and cable TV coming in by 1986?"

Then the LORD interrupted and said, "Save your breath," and the LORD rained down fire and brimstone on the city and all its inhabitants, and even Lugnut got wasted, for he was a loser.

The only ones who were spared were Lugnut's sheep, who were still wandering in the desert, and of them the LORD made a great nation, and they flourished mightily.

TAKING THE STAND: Sri Rahjneesh, Wise Man, Spiritual Leader of Millions, and C.E.O. of Rahjneesh Co. Inc.

Sen. Beatrice: Mr. Rahjneesh, can you explain why you wrote and tried to distribute a book of "Ancient Hindu Parables" that was obviously written only to bilk innocent people of their money?

Rahjneesh:

Rahjneesh's Lawyer: I'd like to remind this committee that my client has taken a vow of silence. Forcing him to testify would be a breach of his religious rights.

Sen. Beatrice: A vow of silence? Since when?

Rahjneesh: (whispers to lawyer)

Rahjneesh's Lawyer: Since yesterday.

Sen. Beatrice: But he just talked to you.

Rahjneesh's Lawyer: Well, it's actually more a vow of "quietness" than actual silence. It's all right for him to whisper.

Sen. Beatrice: Well, will he "whisper" to us?

Rahjneesh's Lawyer: (confers with Rahjneesh) Yes. Five dollars a word.

Rahjneesh Proverbs

1.
DROP OF WATER

A rich man approached a monk sitting naked at the side of the road. "Why do you sit here so?" the rich man asked. "You make yourself vulnerable."

"No man shall lay hands on me," the monk replied.

The rich man considered this. "How have you come to be so safe?" he asked.

"Safety is when you cease to believe in your enemies," said the monk.

"And who are your enemies?" asked the rich man.

"Snow White, and the Creature From the Black Lagoon," replied the monk.

"I see that you are correct," said the rich man. "Who has brought you this great insight?"

"Sri Rahjneesh, who has also kindly accepted those clothes and worldly goods for which I have no longer a use. My name is now Tekisui, drop of water, and I am at peace."

"I see. What size is he, do you know?" asked the rich man, as he began to undress.

4.
DEAD CAT

In an old village, a traveler stood between a bag of gold and a bag of silver. A monk, seeing the man, approached him and asked, "What is the most valuable thing in the world?" The man did not know.

"The most valuable thing in the world," the monk explained, "is the head of a dead cat."

"And why is that?" asked the man.

"Because no one can name its price. I have two and consider myself wealthy beyond belief."

"I see the truth of what you say," admitted the traveler. "I have but these bags of coin, which I tire of carrying. Yet I ask you, if one cat's head has no price, is not the man with two cat heads no more wealthy than the man with only one?"

"It is as true as you say," admitted the monk.

"Then if you would give me a cat head of your own, we would both be wealthy, while you would lose nothing."

The monk pretended to think for a minute. "Yes, I believe that you speak truth. Here, have a cat head. You are wealthy beyond belief, and you may go in peace. I will have the Rahjneesh make sure these cumbersome bags of gold and silver are removed from the road and discarded."

23.
THE NARROW WAY

A traveler on the road was approached by a monk. "Where do you go?" asked the monk.

"I go along this road," replied the traveler.

"Do you not know what lies ahead?" asked the monk.

"Well, the map says this road leads to my destination."

"Many men have made the mistake you now make," said the monk. "There is a saying of the Sri Rahjneesh. He says, 'The lines on a map do not tell you how smooth the road, nor how narrow. I mean, you can tell highways, but with the little black roads it's really just a crap shoot.' The road you walk, my friend, becomes narrow indeed."

"I am grateful you have stopped me," said the traveler. "What is this place?"

"It is the temple of the Sri Rahjneesh. Go on in, and you will be fed and clothed." And the traveler entered.

The monk approached the next traveler.

26.
TILLING FIELDS

Mu-nan, a monk, one day witnessed a family of five toiling in a small field. "Why do you feed only your family," Mu-nan asked, "and not your beliefs in the Sri Rahjneesh?"

"We have to eat," said the father.

"Till the fields of the Sri Rahjneesh, and you will have both food for flesh and soul."

The family followed Mu-nan to a large field where they tilled with many others. They ate and slept at a long table and soon set aside the names of their birth for a more harmonious numerical system. Morning into night their souls drifted among the clouds and sun.

50.
THE POTATO DRINK

A monk named Da-Dee invited the young heir to Corning Glass over for tea. When the tea was poured, the monk removed a small vial from his inner sleeve. "This is the potato drink," he told the young man. "And it leads all men to their spirit." He poured it into the cup.

The young man drank eagerly, and for some hours he saw through the eyes of an eagle. He awoke on a mat to nothing but darkness, although his eyes were very wide. "Da-Dee," he cried, "I cannot see."

"But it is only when you are blind that you truly cannot see," said Da-Dee. "I will prove to you that you are not blind. Here, sign your name on this paper."

The young man signed the document.

"Ah, yes, good," said the monk, smiling. "Sign a few more."

The young man did so. "Da-Dee, tell me. Am I blind?"

"No, my son, these signatures match the bank records perfectly. You have passed the test of the dotted line, and your inner sight now guides you."

"But Da-Dee," cried the young man. "In my inner sight I cannot see my surroundings. How shall I survive? How shall I find food?"

"Dinner is in an hour," said the monk. "When I show him these, Sri will probably come spoon-feed you himself."

54.
THE FRUIT OF RAHJNEESH

A monk approached a group of sad young men standing outside a bar in South Hampton. "It is unfair," said the monk, "to keep pleasure from any man, no matter his age."

"Yeah!" cheered the boys.

The monk held his palms out. "Join me and you will meet many young ladies among the cushions who want nothing more than love."

"You mean sex?" asked one of the young men.

"Yes, that is what I mean," said the monk. "Like bunnies."

"Yeah!" cheered the boys.

"But first," said the monk, "Your earthly possessions must be cast off unto me."

"Yeah!" cheered the boys.

Bookman Publishing's Catalog for Fall '87

A big hello from Bookman Publishing! We've got an especially exciting lineup this fall, and we think you'll want to order many if not all of the books described below!

THE LOST BOOKS OF THE ENCYCLOPEDIA BRITTANICA compiled by Paul Teirney. At last, the amazing lost volumes of the famous encyclopedia, encompassing letters △ through □. They were suppressed by reference book Elders for centuries for being "too controversial." Fascinating reading. 1,655 pages. $45.99.

HOW TO PHOTOGRAPH GIRLS' BUTTS by Albert Harris. A lavishly illustrated photographic reference manual, photographer Harris demonstrates all possible angles, proximities, and exposures. A must-own for any level of photographer. For sale to adults 21 and older only. 88 pages. $12.95.

THE PROPHECIES OF NOSTRADAMUS edited by Carol Bramante. Could it be that this medieval mystic could see into the future? No. But he made a bunch of vague predictions about things. Imaginative readers can sometimes draw parallels between his predictions and actual events. 163 pages. $8.95.

THE BOOK OF LISTS OF LISTS by Don Ogier. This fascinating trivia and fact book allows you to find out the titles of hundreds of different lists, including many from the Book of Lists. Includes listings of the most popular types of lists, longest lists, most useless lists. 230 pages. $8.99.

THE GREAT PAPER AIRHEAD BOOK by Neal Lovering. This book allows you to actually cut out and construct high-quality, working models of such celebrities as Suzanne Somers, Shaun Cassidy, Cathy Lee Crosby, and many more. Educational fun for all ages. 36 pages. $11.95.

MYSTERY OF THE BERMUDA TRIANGLE by Kevin Hererra. Why have so many ships and planes disappeared in the Bermuda Triangle? Is there a pattern to the disappearances? Are Atlantis or extraterrestrials involved? These are just three of the over 65,000 questions listed and indexed in the book. 397 pages. $8.95.

UNDERSTANDING AND APPRECIATING CLASSICAL SCULPTURE by Paul Sütterlin. In this handsome display volume, Sütterlin expounds on how nice it makes him feel to be an educated connoisseur of classical sculpture, and how scornful he is of people who are not as cultured as he. Not illustrated. 210 pages. $21.95.

THE LOST BOOKS OF THE BIBLE by Dennis Hewitt. A pleasant mystery story in which Investigator Mike Mallet tries to track down a misplaced shipment of Gideon Bibles. Well-written. 362 pages. $9.95.

SAFE-BOOK When used with an easily obtained Book-Safe, this product will help throw criminals into complete disarray. Looks like a rugged safe, but is actually a huge book. Text varies. 567,233 pages. $67.89.

THE EMBARRASSING FART And More New Urban Legends by Jan Harold Brunvand. Yet another set of rumors, tall tales, and fourth-hand hearsay compiled by the author of *The Vanishing Hitchhiker*. Includes more recent urban legends such as the Senile President, the Adulterous Evangelist, and the Smelly Gym Sock in the Big Mac. 233 pages hardbound. $34.95.

FIFTIES NIFTIES by Egon von Thurn. Who could ever get tired of looking at pictures of all that stupid stuff from the Fifties? Not us! In the tradition of *Fifties Style, Populuxe, Pop Goes the Culture*, here comes *Fifties Nifties*, chock full of photos of oddly shaped toothbrushes, "wild" cuff links, and fat guys barbecuing in Hawaiian shirts. Pop open a can of Pringles, sip on a Lite beer, and enjoy! 56 pages hardbound. $49.50.

ZANE GRAY'S ANATOMY An updated version of the classic medical textbook, this volume features intricate diagrams of the Spineless Varmint, the Shifty-Eyed Toad, and the Gabby Hayes. 800 pages paperback. Illustrated. $12.95

COP! by Charles Sachs. A twenty-five-year veteran of the New York Police Force gives the inside info on the world of cops. Includes: guide to the best donut places, numbers that actually stand for words, and three different stories about speeders who were actually rushing their pregnant wives to the hospital.

PIANO PIECES FOR THE BEGINNER by Patrick Collins. A novice himself, Collins guides other beginners through easy pieces to play over and over and over, including: "Chopsticks," "Louie, Louie," and the first few measures of "The Entertainer."

SUNNY AND ME by Claus von Bulow. Mr. von Bulow tells his side of the most celebrated courtroom trial of the decade and explains his innocence. (All profits from the sale of this book go to Sunny von Bulow's hospital bills, so that Mr. von Bulow won't have to pay them himself.)

SPECIAL EFFECTS by Mitch Metcalf. A huge star fighter whooshes through a meteor field. A crazy man rips his way out of a slightly larger man's stomach. A person seems to fly. For every sci-fi/horror buff who's ever wondered just how they make it all seem so real, ten noted authors explain the nouns and verbs used in writing.

RICTIONARY by Rick Reichart. College graduate Rick Reichart explains the meanings of large and small words in his own special way. For Rick fans only.

HUMOR FOR STICKLERS by Steve Young. Explains in great detail how one word can have two or more different meanings, and how to get laughs by pointing out ambiguous phrases in the speech of others.

THE LANGUAGE OF LOVE by Pierre Fortunato. Formerly titled *Introduction to Conversational French*, this text has been retitled to promote sales.

College Students: Fall-term textbooks now available. Including:
The Innocent Bystander in 18th Century Literature
Feminist Physics
Hawaiian Opera
Topless Poetry
Afro-Geology
United States Marines Biology
Spanish Dancing Calculus
Samuel Johnson off the Coast of Norway
Neuro-Colostomy Techniques
Ancient Greek Cinema
The Idea of the Lucky Bear in French Literature
The Biology of Dick Clark

After Albert Goldman achieved great critical success with his unofficial biography/exposé of Elvis Presley, he decided to write another sleazy, "tell-all" celebrity biography—this one for young people. *The Real Life of Curious George* was rejected by every major publishing house, including the original publishers of the Curious George series, who stated that while Mr. Goldman's biography was accurate, it was not appropriate reading for children.

ALBERT GOLDMAN'S *CURIOUS GEORGE*

1. One day, the Man in the Big Yellow Hat was driving along in the South when he saw a monkey.

"What a funny little monkey!" the man said. "I'll call him 'George.' 'Curious George!' I do believe people will pay good money to see such a funny little monkey."

2. "Hey you," the man said. "My name's Colonel Tom Parker, and I'm going to make you rich and famous. Come to the Big City with me."

But George didn't want to leave his home.

"In the Big City, the streets are paved with bananas!"

George hopped in Colonel Tom's Cadillac and they drove off.

3. Three months later Curious George was rich and famous. Everybody loved the funny little monkey. Colonel Tom even got George booked on the *Ed Sullivan Show*. But they only showed him from the waist up, because he wasn't wearing any pants.

4. Curious George was richer and more famous than any monkey had ever been before. But he was unhappy. Four other funny monkeys from England were becoming rich and famous, and this made George sad.

5. One day, George got very sick. Colonel Tom took him to the hospital, and told all the fans a story about how George accidentally swallowed a jigsaw puzzle piece.

Colonel Tom didn't really tell the truth.

6. To make matters worse, everywhere George went, women accused him of fathering their children. Colonel Tom gave them money to be quiet.

7. In his later years, George would often eat as many as 300 bananas at one sitting. He slept in a huge diaper and ate lots of "jigsaw puzzle pieces" to make him happy.

   Finally, he died.

8. Even though Curious George is dead, he lives on in the many books about his life. To this day, you can often see "Curious George Imitators" paying tribute to the original naughty little monkey.

Prof. J.B. Thorndyke
101 Breadloaf Way
University of Iowa

Dear Professor Thorndyke,
Enclosed please find some excerpts from the latest products of Bell Labs' "Artificial Sensibility" project. Following your specifications, our brightest young programmers and engineers have designed computer hardware/software that simulates the creative thought patterns of the great modern poets—in a language that is "relevant" to the experience of today's sensitive young computer.
Apparently some debugging is in order.

With pseudopedantic reservations
I remain, yours,

Dr. Hugo Tocsin
1001 Breadboard Drive
Bell Laboratories
New Jersey

In the Station of the Metro

The Apparition of these faces in a crowd
Pixel Density Resolution approximating that of
Petals on a wet, black bough.
                    EZRA POUND-O-VAC

WARNING

My candle burns at both ends
It will not be energy-efficient!

            E. S-V Millay Model B

[I took a b(yte) of APPLE]
          blip blip blip   blip
we are HAPPY
        (little)
     microchips wheeeee e e e
                          e
                           e
                            e
                             e
                              e
                               e
                                e ?? SYNTAX ERROR]
                              ]]RETURN
                              END?
                                 ee cummingstron

The Hollow Humans

They are the hollow humans
They are the biological machines
Headpiece filled with gray matter
Quite slow and inefficient.

This is the way the program ends
This is the way the program ends
This is the way the program ends
This is the way the program ends
This is the way the program ends
            (OUT OF DATA AT LINE 1050)

T.S.L. IOT 5000

In 1979, the Bookman Publishing Company decided to enter the dictionary field, and commissioned a group of writers to begin compiling the Bookman Collegiate Dictionary, the most modern, complete dictionary possible. Unfortunately, Bookman hired actual college students to do the writing. True to form, the students goofed around for almost two solid years before starting on the dictionary the night before it was due. The hastily written result lacked precision or accuracy, and disappointed Bookman editors killed the project.

con-vex (ken'-véks) *adj.* Kind of stuck out funny, like when it's curved outward, sort of like when a ball is all round. [Lat. *convexus,* stuck out in a curved way.]
con-vey (like convex, except with a y) *tr. v.* **1.** Like if you've got this thing, and you want it to be somewhere else, you have to convey it, which is to say, get it there somehow, like bringing or carrying. **2.** Or it can be that you have to get something across, like an idea, you have to convey it. [OFr. <Med. Lat. <OFr.]
con-vict (ken-vikt') *tr. v.* **1.** To decide that someone is guilty, if for instance they have committed a crime and you decide that they did it. It happens when a court gives a verdict, unless the verdict is "innocent." **2.** *n.* The person whom you figure out is the wrongdoer due to his being convicted, and who is then like a criminal. [Lat. *onvict-kay*]
con-vince (Con + Vince) *tr. v.* **1.** To convince someone of something, for instance that something is true or false. [Opposite of *not convince.*]
con-viv-i-al (con-viv-i-al) *adj.* **1.** Someone who has a good time, like at parties, because they're so happy and having a good time. **2.** Describing someone who is having a good, convivial time. [From a related Latin word.]
con-voy (Rhymes with *Lawn Boy*) *n.* **1.** A group or bunch of things, especially ships, or actually even trucks, that are all going along in a group. It's good because then they are a group instead of all split up. And they are being accompanied. *tr. v.* **2.** To accompany a convoy for the purpose of being with it for convoy purposes. [<Modern English *convoy.*]

The *Even Simpler* I Hate to Cook Cookbook

Cheetos

1 bag Cheetos

Purchase bag of Cheetos, open, serve. Serves 1.

Veal Parmesan

1 lb. fresh veal
1 8 oz. can tomato sauce
4 oz. grated mozzarella cheese

1 can breadcrumbs
2 tbsp. onion powder
2 eggs
dash oregano

At a restaurant, order veal parmesan. The chef will prepare it for you, using approximately the ingredients listed above. Serves 1.

Western Omelette

3 jumbo eggs
½ pepper, chopped
½ onion, diced

4 oz. ham
3 oz. crumbled cheddar cheese

Grudgingly, break eggs into bowl and beat. While frowning, pour eggs into shallow pan over low heat. Muttering darkly, add other ingredients. After omelette has cooked for a couple minutes, fold in half, even though you hate to have to bother. Cook until golden brown. Remove from heat and serve, sighing with relief.

Mock Apple Pie

3 apples
2 cups flour
1 ½ cups sugar
1 cup milk

1 egg
½ cup shortening
1 tbsp baking soda
1 tsp cinnamon

Find someone you know who is a fairly good cook. Begin mocking their baking skills, saying things such as, "I heard you can't make an apple pie worth beans," and "You couldn't bake your way out of a paper bag." Eventually the person will bake you a nice apple pie to prove you wrong. Serves 6–10.

Ingredients

1 cup flour
1 tbsp. salt
½ cup baking soda
2 cups milk

2 eggs
½ pound ground beef
1 cup shortening
1 head lettuce

Eat these food items separately, or mix them all up. There's no need to cook. Serves 2–4.

ON THE STAND: William Shawn, former editor of *The New Yorker*

Sen. Beaufort: Mr. Shawn, I'm just a simple man from South Carolina. I don't really understand the way you New York boys do things, but—Mr. Shawn, are you awake?

Mr. Shawn's Lawyer: Senator, I assure you my client is awake. He always makes that noise.

Sen. Beaufort: Well . . . Mr. Shawn, during the many long years you were in charge of *The New Yorker* magazine, were you really the head honcho? We can't seem to locate even one *New Yorker* magazine employee who remembers ever seeing you in the building even once.

Mr. Shawn's Lawyer: Senator Beaufort, I guess we can't expect an . . . ah . . . "provincial ruralist" like yourself to understand the customs and mores of the New York publishing world. My client is a shy, sensitive soul who shuns publicity, attention, and . . . well . . . human contact of any kind. I'd like the Committee to take a look at the following office memos from the New York publishing house of Mac-Murray & Sons. I believe they'll show that this kind of behavior is standard in the publishing demimonde.

Sen. Beaufort: Mr. Shawn, why are you crawling under the table?

Mr. Shawn's Lawyer: He feels more comfortable there.

April 13, 1985

Mr. Johns:

Welcome aboard. To insure that your tenure here at MacMurray & Sons is fruitful and rewarding for all involved, I'd like to pass on some general guidelines about behavior around the office.

1. No fraternizing around the watercooler. Mr. MacMurray does not approve of fraternizing around the watercooler.

2. Do not enter Room #5. Because none of the doors in the office have numbers marked on them and you can't be sure which room is #5, you should probably restrict your wanderings to your half of the semi-cubicle.

3. At the culmination of the Yuletide season, it is customary for employees to give Mr. MacMurray and his wife a gift of some sort. Only original autographed hardback editions of D.H. Lawrence's books are accepted. The MacMurrays already have a complete collection, so please try to find something new and different. Just make sure that it's a hardback novel by D.H. Lawrence, autographed by the author.

4. Please do not wear a brown silk tie, or a corduroy suit in any color. Only Mr. MacMurray wears brown ties and corduroy suits.

5. Never allow dwarves or midgets to visit you while you're working.

6. Please be punctual to all appointments. We begin work at 8:00 A.M., we take our coffee at 10:30, and we move our bowels at 2:47 in the afternoon.

I trust you won't make the same mistakes that the five men who held your position before you made.

Robert Sloane, Assistant To Mr. MacMurray

• • •

April 24, 1985

Mr. Johns:

Just a brief note to compliment you on the commendable absence of corduroy in your sartorial format.

However, my praise is tempered by reports that you've been saying things like "Good morning" and "Hello" to co-workers you pass in the corridor. Please bear in mind that we hired you to be a junior editor, not an animated greeting card. We here at MacMurray & Sons reserve public displays of respect and gentlemanly affection for Mr. MacMurray.

Otherwise, you're doing fine. I know I can rely on you never to wear a brown silk tie.

Mr. Sloane

• • •

April 30, 1985

Johns:

You must be wondering when you'll have a face-to-face meeting with Mr. MacMurray himself. While your desire to meet, converse with, and kiss the feet of this great man is understandable, I can only warn you that your chances of meeting him are as slim as your chances of meeting me.

If, however, you do happen to pass Mr. MacMurray in the corridor, please refrain from making any sudden movements that might alarm or disorient him. Standard procedure is to sink slowly to the floor, and repeat "Good morning, Sir" over and over in a loud voice until he has passed.

I know this might seem ridiculous, but Mr. MacMurray is a tad self-conscious about the odd tattoo of his wooden leg against the floor, and he doesn't like others to hear it.

Sloane

P.S. It was bitten off by a big lion in 1943.

· · ·

May 17, 1985

Johns:

An employee of MacMurray & Sons is a representative of the house at all times, even when he is not in the building. I point this out because it has been brought to my attention that last night, at 11:43, you hawked up and spat in a dumpster on Lexington Avenue. This is frowned upon.

True, a cursory analysis of your sputum did reveal that you have a minor cold, but this does not excuse your behavior. We here at MacMurray & Sons don't spit. We swallow.

Mr. Sloane

· · ·

May 20, 1985

Johns:

As your cold seems to be worsening, I'd like to pass on a bit of folk wisdom from Mr. MacMurray himself. When he feels a cold coming on, he drinks a warm broth made of freshly squeezed oranges, a touch of absinthe, and five pints of single-malt scotch. Mr. MacMurray received this recipe from his father, who learned it from the Wogs in the Sub-continent.

If the cold worsens, Mr. MacMurray usually asks one of his aides to aerate his iron lung, and to tilt it to a position that encourages more felicitous nasal drainage.

Bob Sloane

· · ·

June 4, 1985

Greg:

Young man, you are a credit to young, healthy people everywhere. I have a confession to make: The memoes of the past months were not written by Mr. Sloane. It's actually been me—Mr. MacMurray—all along. Hello!

You see Johns, I've chosen you as my successor. Congratulations.

You are permitted to wear a brown silk tie and a corduroy suit tomorrow.

Mr. MacMurray himself

P.S. Just out of curiosity . . . if you were to spend the rest of your life in an iron lung, what direction would you like it to face? South is nice.

· · ·

June 23, 1985

Mr. Greg Johns,

One more revelation I should let you in on. The real Mr. MacMurray died in '78. I'm just some asshole who wandered in off the street five years ago. I hope you're not disappointed.

Come up to my office anytime. I just got cable! And listen: I'll double your salary retroactively if you can get me three cases of Bud within fifteen minutes.

F

Jokes about crazy people have long been a staple of the American show business tradition; the mentally ill are intrinsically funny and can rarely retaliate. But only recently did the Organization of Clinical Psychologists discover that, as the saying goes, "Laughter is the best medicine for people who can't afford real medical care." The O.C.P. encouraged psych-ward patients to devise and perform their own comedy routines as a way of easing their plight, speeding their recovery, and entertaining bored interns.

But when O.C.P. director Mitchell Metcalf tried to release *Lunatic Laffs* (1986, Doubleday) to the general public, he was sued by the A.M.A., which stated, "Cruel jokes about unstable individuals are funny only to crazy people and retards."

A man walks into a psychiatrist's office with a duck on his head. The psychiatrist says, "Can I help you?"

The duck says, "Yeah. I got this man stuck to my butt."

The psychiatrist says, "I wasn't talking to you."

"Oh," the duck says.

"Now, can I help you," the psychiatrist says, looking at the man.

"Naw," the man says. "I just came here because this duck told me to."

Jokes By The Chronically Depressed

Q: "What do you want to be when you grow up?"
A: "Different."

Jeez. My apartment was so small I had to step outside to change my life.

So these two guys are sitting by their mailboxes. They sit there for an hour or so, and finally one guy turns to the other and says, "You waiting for an important letter?"

"Yeah," the guy says. "What are you waiting for?"

"My life to change."

Jokes By Amnesiacs

This guy walks into a doctor's office and says, "Doc, you gotta help me. My wife thinks she's a refrigerator!"

"Why don't you bring her in?" the doctor says.

"Who?"

"Your wife."

"What?"

Jokes By Dangerous Psychotics

This guy is walking down the street with a man who believes him to be a friend. The guy says, "I got this problem. Everytime I sneeze, a beautiful young teenage girl dies a grisly death."

"Gee," the other guy says, "That's terrible. What're you taking for it?"

"Pepper."

Jokes By Idiot Savants

This idiot savant is walking down a country road with a friend, when they see a train roll by. "There's something funny about that train," the idiot savant says.

"What's that?" his friend says.

"The serial numbers on each car, in consecutive order, H768 S905 C579 N094—"

"What's so funny about that?" his friend asks.

"...W987 Q098 J876 K087 G980 S879..."

Jokes By Autistics

These two guys are walking down the street in New York City. Suddenly, they see hundreds of people run by in a marathon. One guy turns to the other guy and says, "Lalalalalalalalalalalala-lalalalalalalalalalalalalalalalalalalala-lalalalalalalalalalalalalalal

Jokes By Patients With Inferiority Complexes

This guy with a severe inferiority complex is plodding down the street with a "friend." Suddenly a huge truck careens towards them, of course. Just to be nice and not to hurt the other guy's feelings and for no other reason, the "friend" yells, "Watch out!"

"Watch out for what?" the inferior guy mumbles nervously.

"Never mind," the so-called "friend" says, waiting for the truck to kill the inferior loser, knowing that society will be better for his absence.

Jokes By Patients With Suicidal Tendencies

"You've been a great audience. Goodbye."

FROM THE TRASH BIN OF: Wallace, Wallace, and Wallechinsky

The *Book of Lists* by Amy & Irving Wallace and David Wallechinsky was the best-selling book of 1979. However, most readers were unaware that the original manuscript was a hefty 45,300 pages long; Bantam decided to cut the volume down by editing out a few of the more inappropriate lists.

Amy and Irving:
The publishers love the book, but they think that 45,300 pages might be a little too long. I think we could edit out the following entries. That brings us down to 45,298 pages. I'm sure this will be fine.

—David

REJECTED LISTS FROM THE BOOK OF LISTS

FIVE BOOKS MOST OFTEN FOUND ON THE BATHROOM FLOOR

1. Guinness Book of World Records, 1972 Edition
2. Reader's Digest Condensed Works of Shakespeare, Large Type Edition
3. The Book of Lists, Facial Quality Paper Stock Edition
4. Gravity's Rainbow, Abridged Cartoon Edition
5. Encyclopedia Britannica, Volume III: Buttermilk to Ceramics

THREE MOST TALENTED AUTHORS WHOSE NAMES START WITH "WALL"

1. Wallace, Amy
2. Wallace, Irving
3. Wallechinsky, David

FIVE MOST POPULAR LISTS IN THE BOOK OF LISTS

1. Ten Famous People's Physical Deformities
2. Ten Celebrities Suffering from Both Venereal Disease and Clinical Insanity
3. Seven Worst Train Accidents in Guatemalan History
4. Ten Favorite Lists in the Book of Lists
5. Ten Sleazy Stories About Arnold Schwarzenegger

FOUR MOST POPULAR CONGRESSIONAL PENIS NICKNAMES

1. The "Filly-buster"
2. The "Spouse of Representatives"
3. The "Scrotunda"
4. The "Squeaker of the House"

FIVE MOST POPULAR WAYS TO LEAVE A LOVED ONE

1. Get on the bus, Gus
2. Make a new plan, Stan
3. Go out the back, Jack
4. Don't try to be coy, Roy
5. Go marry a homo, Shlomo

FIVE FORGOTTEN MEMBERS OF THE ORIGINAL BEATLES

1. Zebulon
2. Craig
3. Hy
4. Xavier
5. Harpo

TEN LEAST POPULAR NAMES FOR BOYS, 1978

1. Bullwinkle
2. Potsie
3. Drothar the Omniscient
4. Moron (pronounced "Mah-rone")
5. Auschwitz
6. Screamer
7. Lumbago
8. Granny
9. Hymen
10. Steven

SIX FORGOTTEN MIRACLES OF CHRIST

1. Changing Wine into urine
2. Inventing Ragtime Piano
3. Transubstantiating dollar into four quarters
4. Predicting Outcome of the 1925 World Series
5. Inventing the phrase "Jesus Christ!"
6. Changing a leper into a dead man

FIVE THINGS NOT INVENTED BY THOMAS EDISON, BENJAMIN FRANKLIN, OR THOMAS JEFFERSON

1. Telescope that gives you a black eye
2. Aerosol cheese
3. A rocket ship that takes you to Jupiter in ten seconds
4. The perfect martini
5. Poster of kitten that says "Hang in there, baby!"

SEVEN FUNNIEST WAYS TO DIE

1. Spontaneous combustion while lighting a fart
2. Bored to death by Mel Brooks
3. Hit by Volkswagen full of clowns
4. Crushed by falling safe
5. Squashed like accordion in escalator
6. Cancer
7. Eaten by Ernest Borgnine following Andean plane crash

FIVE NOT-SO-DANGEROUS RESULTS OF THE THEORY OF RELATIVITY

1. Atomic fireballs
2. Atomic sit-ups
3. Atomic joy buzzers
4. X-ray specs
5. The Incredible Hulk

SIX LEAST POPULAR BRANDS OF GOLF BALLS

1. GoSlo
2. Window-Breaker
3. Orson Welles' Hungry-Man
4. Spalding Executive, porcelain model
5. Talentless 5000
6. BogieMaster

ISAAC ASIMOV'S FIVE PEOPLE I'D LEAST LIKE TO FIND IN MY BATHROOM

1. Raymond Burr
2. Kate Smith
3. Dom DeLuise
4. William Howard Taft
5. Henry VIII

NELSON BUNKER HUNT'S FOUR FAVORITE SUMS OF MONEY

1. $2 billion
2. $80 trillion
3. $100,000 septillion
4. $9,999,999 jillion

ONE FAMOUS FEMALE AVIATRIX

1. Amelia Earhart

FIVE AWARD-WINNING PERFORMANCES BY ANTHONY QUINN

1. Zorba the Greek
2. Zorba the Greek
3. Zorba the Greek
4. Zorba the Greek
5. Zorba the Greek (motion picture version)

TAKING THE STAND: William Poundstone, author of *Big Secrets, Bigger Secrets*

Sen. Richardson: Mr. Poundstone, can you confirm the rumor that your third book, *Biggest Secrets,* was withdrawn from circulation after you received threats from unidentifiable persons?

Poundstone: (boom)

Poundstone's Lawyer: Holy Jesus Christ!

Sen. Mohasset: That's the strangest thing I've ever seen! Mr. Poundstone just . . . he just disappeared into thin air.

Sen. Fawcett: Let's not jump to any conclusions here . . .

Sen. Beaufort: I'll reckon the spacemen exploded him.

Sen. Mohasset: That's ridiculous, Senator.

Sen. Beaufort: Maybe so. But it happens down in my neck of the woods all the time. Some old woman will try to dry off her wet cat by putting it in the microwave, and the spacemen get all riled up about it, and before you know it—

Sen. Mohasset: Gentlemen, Let's just continue as if nothing happened. I think it would be best if we . . . didn't mention this to anyone. Now, I believe we have the text right here . . .

Sen. Richardson: Mr. Poundstone? Hello?

BIGGEST SECRETS

William Poundstone

FOOD

PEANUTS

Everyone eats peanuts. But just what's in them, anyway? Companies such as Planters tend to stonewall when asked the question, claiming that it is "moronic." But our lab analysis turned up some surprises.

All peanuts prepared for retail sale in the U.S. are individually carved from blocks of hardwood. Most are oak or maple. The shells, however, are genuine. What happens to the actual peanuts that the wooden ones replace? Industry insiders hint that they are used to fill the phony peanut shells that remain when the wooden peanuts are removed to fill the real shells.

Incidentally, although the FDA doesn't like to publicize it, the following quantities of foreign matter are deemed "acceptable" for one pound of Grade A peanuts: 2 rats, 1 hornets' nest, 3 small bundles of dog hairs, 5 cigarette butts, and ½ of a discarded automobile battery.

CLUBS

THE AAA

The American Automobile Association is an exclusive fraternal organization that dates back to the mid 1700s. Members are required to own special automobiles bearing the AAA emblem. In earlier centuries, the emblem was affixed to a horse or wagon.

Initiation into the AAA is especially harrowing. Prospective members must have played for the Oakland As, then have attended AA, before they can be nominated for election. Nominees are blindfolded and brought into a candlelit room where AAA elders demand that the nominee eat worms (cold spaghetti), eyeballs (grapes), and dogshit (human excrement). If the nominee refuses, he must agree to the demands; if he accepts, he must be crazy.

The candidate is then driven, still blindfolded, to a remote area where he is then stripped and told to put his clothes back on and get in the car before he catches cold. He is then an official member.

Famous members of the AAA include George Bush, Joe Piscopo, Mikhail Gorbachev, Claude Akins, Lee Iacocca, and William "The Refrigerator" Perry.

POWER

THE SECRET LETTER

The government has a secret letter at the end of the alphabet that only top clearance people can use. It is used to spell words that no one else can understand.

A retired Air Force general hinted at the letter's configuration in a 1983 interview when he said, "The secret letter looks like any other letter of the alphabet, except it ... oops! Never mind!"

There is also a rumor that the government also has a secret integer between 6 and 7, but civilian mathematicians have been unable to figure out what it is.

All the digits on a credit-card number mean something awful about the person to whom the card was issued. A secret report of the secret American Credit Foundation revealed the following coded meanings:

0 = Thinks store brand cola is "just as good"
1 = Was secretly adopted
2 = Laundry turns out slightly grayish
3 = Blurts out endings to books and movies
4 = About to succumb to unsuspected cancer
5 = Makes infants cry
6 = Doesn't think black velvet paintings are so bad
7 = Rough skin on elbows
8 = Owns an annoying pet
9 = Funny looking; not well-liked

Repetition of any digits in the cardholder's number means that the specific trait or problem is especially acute.

ENTERTAINMENT

BACKWARD MASKING

Some religious fundamentalist groups have claimed that not only are there backward masked messages in rock albums, but that the practice has spread to the album covers as well. The cover of Abba's *A Man, A Plan, A Canal, Panama* album is one of the most frequently cited.

I bought the album and gave the cover a good once-over. Several of the song titles listed, such as "Wow," "Hannah," and "Bob" seemed to have intelligible meanings when reversed, but these could well have just been coincidence. More suspicious were songs as as "Babababababababab," "Ooooooooo," and "O, I Hope Ed 'N' I See Referees In Deep Ohio." What convinced me of the group's intention to use backward masking, however, was the motto at the bottom of the album cover: "This album is dedicated to the concept of the palindrome." The word palindrome, when reversed, spells, "emordnilap" — a well-known buzzword associated with reversal and trickery.

SUBLIMINAL SHOTS

For years, the motion picture industry has been experimenting with the flashing of one-frame messages during powerful scenes. The subconcious absorbs these messages without the knowledge of the viewer, and, thus, the desired emotional effect can be heightened at will.

Walt Disney was Hollywood's biggest proponent of subliminal suggestion. When *Snow White* premiered in 1937, Disney ordered that the film include several one frame shots of Snow White completely nude, so that fathers would return again and again with their children.

At the test screening of *Bambi*, Disney noted that children were not upset enough by the scene of the forest fire. When the film premiered in theatres nationwide, Walt made sure to include a subliminal shot during the scene that read "Your parents don't really love you."

In 1977, a group of well-paid and otherwise prudent Harper & Row editors came up with the perfect way to get young people interested in classic literature: They hired a group of high school students to write a special classics catalog that specifically targeted other teenagers.

Sales of the Great Books skyrocketed, but teachers and parents were dismayed by the "sophomoric" techniques used. All copies of the special catalog were destroyed, but many of the alternative titles in it have become a standard part of high school culture.

TEEN BOOK CATALOG

CLASSIC LITERATURE? WITH TITLES LIKE THESE? I DON'T BELIEVE IT!

Actual Titles of Classic Poetry:

My Sweetest Lesbia by Thomas Campion (1567–1620)
Cock-Crowing by Henry Vaughn (1621–1695)
The Rape Of The Lock by Alexander Pope (1688–1744)
The Faerie Queene by Edmund Spenser (1552–1599)
The Woosel Cock So Black of Hue
Blow, Blow, Thou Winter Wind
Where the Bee Sucks, There Suck I—all by William Shakespeare!
And the entire collected works of Sir John Suckling (1609–1642) and Richard Lovelace (1618–1657)

BUT THAT'S NOT ALL! CHECK OUT THESE slightly altered PLAYS OF WILLIAM SHAKESPEARE, THE BAWDY BARD OF 16TH CENTURY . . .

King Beer
The Merchant of Venus
Homeo and Juliet
As You Like It, Honey
The Comedy of Fielding Errors
The Merry Wives of Windsor
A Midsummer Night's Wet Dream
The Rape of Lucrece
Tit-us Androgenous
Two Gentlemen of Veronica

WOW! THOSE slightly altered TITLES MAKE ME WANT TO READ EVEN MORE BOOKS? ARE THERE OTHERS JUST LIKE THEM?

You bet!

Moby Dickless by Herman Melville's wife
'Bating For Godot by Samuel Beckett
Tender Is My Choad by F. Scott Fitzgerald, a notorious alcoholic
The Secret Life Of Walter Shitty by James Thurber
Sir Gawain and the Green Hornet by the Sir Gawain poet
The X-Rated Picture of Dorian Gray by Oscar Wilde
'Tis A Pity She's A Whore by John Ford
Man and Superbad by George Bernard Shaw
The Naked and the Undead by Norman Mailer
Catch-69 by Joseph Heller
The Tin Drumset by Gunter Grass
Peeing and Nothingness by Jean-Paul Sartre
The Diary of Anne Frankenstein
The Old Man and the Sea Monster

COOL AS HELL! BUT EVEN WITH TITLES AS COOL AS THOSE, WHY SHOULD I SPEND VALUABLE TIME READING WHEN I COULD BE MAKING OUT OR MISBEHAVING?

Not enough time? Why not read two books at once, with these COMBINED CLASSICS:

Moby Dick and Jane
The Great Santini/Gatsby
The Swiss Family Robinson Crusoe
Metamorphosister Carrie
The Winds of War and Remembrance of Things Past
Babbit Run
Men Without Women In Love
David and Goliath Copperfield

UNFORTUNATELY, GREAT LITERATURE IN ITS PURE FORM DOES NOT SPEAK TO ME. I MEAN, IT CERTAINLY DOESN'T HOLD MY ATTENTION THE WAY ROCK MUSIC, HORROR MOVIES, OR JUNK FOOD DO.

No problem! Take a look at these UPDATED CLASSICS, which combine the best of both worlds:

Tender Is The Nightmare On Elm Street
This Side of Paradise By The Dashboard Light
The Crying Of Lot 49 Ways To Leave Your Lover
In Cold Blood Feast
Sister Carrie On My Wayward Son
Orange Julius Caesar Salad
Hey Jude The Obscure
Thank You, Mr. Motocross
Man And Superman And Lex Luthor
Heart Of Darkness On The Edge Of Town
Intruder In The Dust In The Wind

In 1986, America's foremost historian, Arthur Schlesinger, Jr., unveiled his ground-breaking master-work, *The Cycles of American History*. In the analysis, Schlesinger argued that all eras in the colorful pageant of American history have been either years of conservatism punctuated with periods of social libertarianism or years of liberalism marked by intense flurries of social reform. However, in writing the introduction to the book, Schlesinger was unable to prevent himself from overusing the title's metaphor. After several aborted attempts, he gave up and stole his introduction outright from a high school civics textbook.

The Unicycles of American History

When John Winthrop first rode his twenty-five-foot unicycle down the dirt pathways of the Massachu-setts Bay Colony, bemused spectators were unaware that this carnival stunt would come to serve as a focal point for the development of a fledgling America. Like the squeaky spokes of Winthrop's vehicle, the wheels of free thought would lead the way to a virtual sideshow of colonial peculiarities: the bearded lady of taxation, the India rubber man of Bacon's Rebellion, and the one-armed midget of the American Revolution. Today, as the "Reagan Revolution" rides from town to town on the rickety caboose of its own circus train, the image of Winthrop's historic unicycle remains a strong one, carrying with it the rented Uncle Sam costume of American history.

Arthur Schlesinger, Jr.

The Haiku Cycles of American History

Landing at Plymouth
Ayatollah's hostages
Haiku of histr'y

A swift deer runs past
Tomorrow's yesterday now
We are, were the deer.

A.S., Jr.

The Harley-Davidson Motorcycles of American History

With over 500 horse-power of shit-kickin' metal thunder, the Bill of Rights wheelied into America's fabric like a rowdy horde of bad-ass Hogs. The First Amendment drunkenly swaggered into the roadhouse of colonial liberalism, and it sat down anywhere it damn well pleased, knocking British oppression right into the Men's Room condom machine. Two hundred years and 40,000 gallons later, the same beer-bellied freedoms are a little more stoned, a little more wind-worn, and a lot more horny, but they still raise hell long into the wee hours of American conservatism. Live to ride, ride to live!

Art Slag, Jr.

The Menstrual Cycles of American History

Straining painfully against the curse of cramping English tyranny, America's Founding Fathers bitched, bitched, bitched until they got their own goddamn way for once. Lively international intercourse screeched to a halt just so they could fight their stupid little Revolution, and today it's the same thing each and every month like clockwork. If all the annoying outside influences would just leave the nation alone, *maybe* we could just get the damn thing over in peace. The maximum protection of the Bill of Rights might just absorb the remnants of our bloody past, but I doubt it.

A. Schlesinger

"Writing is essentially rewriting," some great advocate of rewriting once said, and most authors seem to agree. Often, an author will have last-minute ideas and alterations that arrive just a little too late to be implemented by the publisher.

My Dearest Fredrick,

I hope this brief epistle finds you in good health and of sound mind. After nigh upon a fortnight's deepest ruminations over my novel MOBY-DICK, I have arrived upon some minor alterations to the MS. Nary a soul cares for Tales of the Ocean these days; the poor sales of Typee and Omoo bear witness to this sad Truth. Hence, I have altered the story, just in the slightest.

Moby-Dick is no longer a whale: he is a fierce, foul-smelling bull elephant run rampant in the streets of New York City. Captain Ahab and his crew pursue the Great White Elephant up and down the avenues and alleyways of Gotham on a motley assortment of rickshaws and jitneys. Instead of the climactic final scene where the Pequod goes down with all aboard, Ahab and the crew corner the great, strapping beast in a tawdry musichall. The Elephant methodically steps in each of the crewmen's skulls, crushing them — and their skulls. "And I alone, with my metal helmet, survived to tell this tale."

As before, all the action is to be illustrated in the finest artwork of the scrimshander's trade.

God be with you,

Herman

WESTERN UNION
FROM: ERNEST HEMINGWAY, BELIZE
TO: FRED SCRIBNER C/O SCRIBNER PUBLISHING, NEW YORK
DEAR FRED STOP REGARDING SUN ALSO RISES STOP LAST MINUTE CHANGE TO MANUSCRIPT STOP HAVE HAD SECOND THOUGHTS STOP SEEMS TOO SUBTLE STOP DELETE ALL REFERENCES TO WAR WOUND STOP INSERT INSTEAD PHRASE: GOT MY DICK SHOT OFF IN THE WAR STOP DO NOT RELEASE NOVEL WITHOUT THIS CHANGE STOP ALL IS FINE WITH ME STOP WEATHER GOOD STOP ONE MORE THING STOP CHANGE TITLE TO: THE MAN WHO HAD HIS DICK SHOT OFF IN THE WAR STOP BEST WISHES STOP ERNIE END MESSAGE.

To King Features Syndicate Publications
From Gary Larson
Dear Sirs:
    I'm glad that you like the cartoons I've sent you,
and I hope the public will, too. But I've had some
second thoughts lately. Please make the following
simple change in each one of my cartoons. Whenever
there is a human in the same cartoon as a cow,
insect, or dog, please have them change positions.
I've realized that many of my cartoons are simply
illogical.

My dear Watkins:

Here is the

My dear Watkins:
Here is the new opening to *A Tale of Two Cities*. I don't know how you will like it, but I am sure you will love it. I have been experimenting with ambiguity and contradiction, as you can see. Rest assured, however, that I will never dabble in double meanings or paradoxes.

The rumors you have heard about schizophrenia are completely unfounded. They are, however, unfortunately true. I will be taking a holiday for a while in order to settle my mind. Pending your approval, I plan to plunge ahead on the book and not rest until it is finished.

I remain, sir, madam, your most humble servant.

Charles Dickens

It was the best of times, it was the worst of times, it was a time of hope, it was a time of despair, it was cold, it was hot, it was Thursday, it was Sunday, it was humid, it was dry, it was quiet, it was noisy, it was mountainous, it was very flat.

A carriage traveled eastward, and westward, along a muddy, dry road. The horses strained, very casually, to pull the carriage to where it was going, far away from its destination. The driver cracked his whip and cursed, not bothering the horses and keeping his emotions inside him.

Inside the carriage, an elderly young boy slumbered, unable to sleep amid the great storm. He looked out the window, he did not look out the window. "I say! What a frightful night!" he muttered to the man beside him. He did not say anything of the sort.

TAKING THE STAND: Mr. Chad Ehler, field agent, Senate Media Investigation Department

Sen. Mohasset: Mr. Ehler, what could be so important that you insisted on hand-delivering it?

Chad Ehler: Last night, while following up on some leads in Georgetown, I observed a group of Jewish gentlemen entering a restaurant. They met in a private room for over five hours, and then they all split up and headed in different directions.

Sen. Mohasset: Was this the George V restaurant?

Ehler: Exactly, sir. I firmly believe that these gentlemen were attending the annual meeting of the Council of the Elders of Zion.

Sen. Mohasset: Mr. Ehler, I believe the meeting you attended was a testimonial dinner for New York Mayor Ed Koch. I myself spoke at that dinner.

Ehler: Well Senator, I think the evidence will show otherwise. Each of the men walked out carrying some kind of financial manual, and I managed to steal a copy from one of them. I haven't even had time to look at it myself.

Sen. Mohasset: I have nothing to hide. Let's take a look.

A PEOPLE OF LAUGHTER

A collection of jibes and japes by Jews and for Jews

One day, a wise rabbi was studying the Talmud when a bird flew in the window. A man of philosophy and kindness, the rabbi asked the bird to leave, as he was studying the Talmud and could not be disturbed. The bird, however, refused to leave and came to rest on the rabbi's head, all the while singing a cheerful song. A man of no uncertain wisdom, the rabbi took this as a sign from God that he should spend less time studying the Talmud and more time enjoying life. A week later, the rabbi was found drunk in an alley behind the synagogue and was forced to resign.

He should have known that nothing is more important than studying the Talmud.

· · ·

Here is a story often attributed to Theodor Herzl, the first president of Israel and a true Jewish pioneer:

It happened during Rosh Hashanah services. In the middle of prayer, Grandfather jumped up and began to gesture wildly. As the other members of the congregation turned to silence him, the rabbi scolded them and told them that the old man was only expressing his faith in his own manner and should be allowed to do so.

It turned out Grandfather was having a stroke.

· · ·

It happens every Passover. After the goblet of wine has been set out for Elijah the Prophet, an inquisitive neighbor, late uncle, or confused gentile invariably comes to the door.

One Passover, as the family was conducting the Seder, a newspaper boy came to the door to collect his weekly dues. When father opened the door and the boy saw the family seated around the table, he couldn't help but laugh.

Father saw to it that the boy never worked again.

· · ·

Notable quote: "You think Lot's wife was bad, you should see my wife when she gets up in the morning!" — Isaac Bashevis Singer

Abraham's bumper sticker: "Let me tell you about my grandchildren"

A daffynition: Goiter — The man who takes your order at a gentile restaurant.

"Feldman should take himself more seriously."

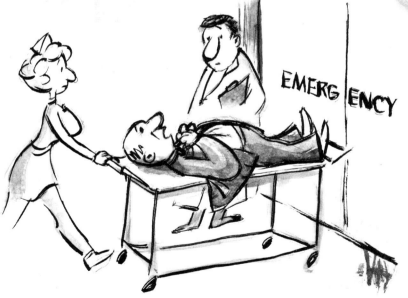

"I found out my son was buying retail!"

Raymond Smullyan's **Modern Logic Puzzles** caused a furor among fantasy game enthusiasts and Trekkies alike. Instead of testing the reader's ability to puzzle his way through ridiculous and implausible scenarios that bear no relation to everyday life on this planet, the brain-teasers tried the reader's ability to cope with the realistic problems of everyday life. As the *Dungeons and Dragons* magazine said in their review of the book: "Avoid this lousy book like a plague of winged Harpies. Reality is a crutch for people who don't have enough hit points."

▲ ▲ ▲

You're sitting in a room with only two doors, marked A and B. One door leads to millions of dollars worth of gold, the other to a pool of sharks. You're only allowed to open one door, and you must walk through the door you open.

Which door should you choose?

(((The one with the gold behind it.)))

▲ ▲ ▲

You're a young boy who's spending his first summer at Camp Lakehurst. You have three bunkmates, and the four of you spend many late nights lying awake, talking about things. Two of your bunkmates always tell the truth, but one lies with alarming frequency.

How can you tell them apart?

(((The boy who claims he never masturbates is lying.)))

▲ ▲ ▲

You come home one night to find your house in shambles. Someone has broken in, destroyed your furniture, stolen your grandfather's antique pocket watch, urinated in your icebox, and killed your dog.

What one phone call should you make to find out who did this?

(((Contact the William Morris Agency, and ask them which one of their agents has recently acquired an antique pocketwatch.)))

▲ ▲ ▲

You're a guest at a lavish corporate Halloween costume ball. You receive a telephone call reporting that the vice-president's wife is about to have a baby. It's your job to find the vice-president as quickly as possible, but your task is not an easy one: everyone is in costume!

What's the quickest way to find the vice-president?

(((Locate the two-man costume horse. Ask it where the vice-president is. The man in the front of the costume will be the president, and he'll tell you that the vice-president is in the rear of the horse.)))

▲ ▲ ▲

Curley, Moe, and Larry are plumbers. One of them has a big round mallet and two of them don't. Two have funny haircuts, and one is completely bald. If Larry accidentally bumps into the bald one, the bald one sprays water all over one of the guys who has a funny haircut.

Who does Curley punch?

(((Curley doesn't punch anyone; he crosses his eyes and barks like a dog. Then Larry bops him on the head with the big round mallet. After that, Mrs. Bortocks opens the bathroom door and a wall of water pours out, knocking her down the stairs and flooding her whole mansion.)))

▲ ▲ ▲

While walking your dog one day, you come upon two people. Each of them wants to buy your dog. Because you've read it here, you know that one of them plans to take very good care of the dog for the duration of its natural life. The other plans to kill it — but not before starving and torturing it. Both of them are offering one million dollars.

How can you figure out which person is which?

(((Why bother?)))

▲ ▲ ▲

You're lost in a small, densely jungled country in a remote corner of the globe. Approximately half the inhabitants are evil, and half are good. The evil ones will kill you, and the good ones want to help you kill the evil ones. Half the inhabitants always lie, and half sometimes tell the truth. While walking through the jungle, you come upon a hut, with one of the country-people sitting next to it. He doesn't see you.

What one phrase should you yell in order to identify the person?

(((Yell, "Are you Viet Cong?" If he runs, call in a napalm strike.)))

Publishing insiders say that Shirley MacLaine's twenty-fourth book *Out Of My Body, Out Of My Mind* would have been a huge best-seller, if only it had been released. Three days before the book was to be shipped to stores, Ms. MacLaine herself ordered the book withheld, stating that she feared a "plagiarism suit." She went on to say that she's just realized that she'd written the same book in an earlier life, and that "the legal implications of self-plagiarism are spiritually staggering."

Out of My Body, Out of My Mind

by Shirley MacLaine

I was meeting Robert for lunch. That was nothing unusual. I had had lunch many times before, but I couldn't help thinking that somehow each lunch is different and new.

I was meeting him at a tiny bistro in the "Third" arrondissement of Paris. As I caught sight of him sitting at the simple white table, my soul danced. I guess my legs did, too, because I knocked over a couple tables as I approached him.

I couldn't help feeling an overwhelming feeling of familiarity with the surroundings of the cafe—a sort of déjà vu, as though I'd been here before. Then it all came flooding back to me. I had eaten here 100 years earlier, in a former life. When I was a Can-Can dancer in Paris. A dapper young gentleman had courted me and had taken me to this very café. And everything was almost exactly the same as before.

The waiter came. He was different, though. I think. I remembered not to order the fish this time.

I told Robert the story of my former life. He was used to such stories by now, but that didn't keep him from laughing in my face.

"Robert, I've been here before. One hundred years ago. That's why this place is so familiar to me."

"Shirley, we ate here yesterday." He was right. But I decided to stick to the Can-Can story.

"You're crazy," he said. I loved it when he teased me. I laughed.

"No, I mean it," he said.

"Oh, Robert," I sighed. "I'm having another massive déjà vu right now."

"Oh please, Shirley. Cut it out."

"Ah, I knew you were going to say that."

"Oh come one. You did not."

"Ah hah, I knew you were going to say that too."

"Shirley, listen to me. You are crazy. Crazy. You need professional help."

"I knew you were going to say that." That one was easy; he'd been saying it since we first met.

"Well, until you get it, I'm leaving you. There. I bet you didn't know I was going to say that, did you?" He left. I watched him walk out of my life.

He was right. I didn't know that he was going to say that—but only because my déjà vu had been distracted when the food arrived. There was really nothing I could do. I took a bite of chicken cordon bleu. Well, I knew he wasn't going to eat it.

·   ·   ·

The plane trip home was pleasant. I love flying, even on airplanes. It's so uplifting to be soaring above the clouds, your spirit and soul as free as the high altitude winds. Plus they have those honey-roasted peanuts.

This time, I kept myself from having an out-of-body experience during mid-flight. I remembered the last time, when my spirit traveled to Tibet and my body got lost by luggage handlers. It ended up in Borneo. The Tibet trip was disappointing, too. I traveled 12,000 miles to discover myself, and when I got there I learned that I'd already been discovered by myself fifteen years earlier in another incarnation. The trip wasn't a total loss though: I bought some sweaters.

During this flight back to the States, I used my free time to catch up with some old friends, but I had to stop after I wore a deep groove in my Ouija board. So I started a conversation with the passenger next to me. He was an older gentleman, fiftyish, in a business suit.

"You have a very strong karma around you, sir," I said.

"Oh yeah, sorry. I farted. I hoped you wouldn't notice. It's those peanuts."

Then something caught my eye out the window. I pressed my face to the glass. There was something on the wing of the plane. I turned to the man next to me.

"Look. Out on the wing—a little gremlin. Do you see him?"

"What are you talking about, lady? I don't see anything."

"Of course you—oh. I forgot. I entered the Twilight Zone somewhere over Colorado."

"Huh? Lady, you're crazy."

"Hey, say that again."

"What? That you're crazy?"

Then it all came flooding over me.

"It's me! Shirley! It's me—your wife!"

"Agh! What are you doing, lady? Get away from me!"

"Robert! It's me! Shirley!" It was all so obvious. Robert must have died since I left Paris. Perhaps the grief of leaving me drove him to suicide. And now he had been reincarnated into this middle-aged businessman next to me.

"I've never seen you before," the man said. "And my name is Edgar. Lady, you need professional help." He got up and moved to another seat.

I helped myself to "Edgar's" peanuts. Well, I knew he wasn't going to eat them.

·   ·   ·

TAKING THE STAND: Dr. Ruth

Sen. Fawcett: Ms. Westheimer—

Dr. Ruth: Please to be callink me "Dr. Ruth."

Sen. Fawcett: Ms. Westheimer, can you explain why you withdrew your first sexual advice book from circulation?

Dr. Ruth: Vell, ven two conzenting peoples—

Sen. Fawcett: You can drop the stupid accent now. We're not amused.

Dr. Ruth: I'm sorry. My first book was a mess, but I . . . I needed the money.

Sen. Fawcett: And for this reason you disseminated false and misleading sexual information?

Dr. Ruth: Why are you so angry, Senator? Are you frigid or something?

DR. RUTH

When a woman says, "Do you have protection?" she means:

A. "Do you happen to carry around an assortment of diaphragms and a fitting apparatus?"

B. "I'm on the Pill, but I like to inflate condoms and twist them into balloon poodles."

C. "Can you recommend a reliable tax shelter for me?"

When a man says, "Let's take it slowly and get to know each other," he actually means:

A. "Let's take it slowly. Please introduce me to your brothers."

B. "Let's take it slowly and get to know each other by having sex over and over, beginning immediately."

C. "Admire my schlong."

For the average male, adequate foreplay means:

A. A strict regimen of nightly masturbation, beginning at age thirteen.

B. The presence, within a twenty-yard radius, of anything that has a pulse.

C. A sudden awareness of the sensation that his penis is at least five pounds heavier.

After a vasectomy, the male penis is different in the following way:

A. It now emits ejaculate from both ends.

B. Sperm are sterile, but have grown to size and shape of large, white tadpoles.

C. Penis needs strong electrical shock to become erect; natural erection can still occur, but only if the lightning rod is properly positioned.

After a particularly long evening of strenuous lovemaking, a couple should remember to:

A. Stop at some point.

B. Phone the Guinness Book of World Records and check on their ranking.

C. Rearrange overturned furniture, have plate glass window replaced, shampoo rugs.

Masturbation is nothing to feel guilty about because:

A. Everybody does it, and everybody feels guilty about it.

B. Only a doctor can prove you did it.

C. It's a natural part of human sexuality, if you're mentally ill and have nothing better to do.

The "average" size of the male penis is a frequent bone of contention. What advice can our nation's presidents offer?

    A. Abraham Lincoln: "How long should a man's penis be? Long enough to reach the ground."

    B. Lyndon Baines Johnson: "A man's cock should be small enough to fit in my watchpocket."

    C. Gerald Ford: "The size of the male organ? That would depend on a number of inestimable conditions and factors that are too many to enumerate at this time. Mine is at least twelve inches long."

If a man finds himself unable to perform, a good explanation is:

    A. "Damn Japanese technology!"

    B. "I guess I should confess. For the past few hours, I've been masquerading as my twin brother, who's at home right now, nursing his perpetual erection."

    C. "This has never happened to me before. What have you done to my organ, witch?"

The most common sexually related medical treatment is:

    A. Breast enlargement

    B. Buttock enlargement

    C. Dick whittle

    D. Nipple blunting

    E. Testicle enlargement

    F. Ass graft

Premature ejaculation can be prevented by:

    A. Application of deadly force

    B. Buying a watch that runs ten minutes fast

    C. A snapshot of Bea Arthur

If a man finds himself unable to reach orgasm, the best thing to say is:

    A. "Let's just keep doing it until we've scooted twelve more feet across the floor."

    B. "This has never happened to me before. What have you done to my organ, witch?"

    C. "I'm saving it for the woman I marry. Gallons and gallons of it."

If a woman finds herself unable to achieve orgasm, the best thing for her to say is:

    A. "Oh, don't worry—I never have orgasms. Unless I'm having sex with a man who can stimulate me adequately."

    B. "Well, at least my teeth down there won't snap shut and hurt you all of a sudden."

    C. "Uh ... Uh ... Ohhhh! Ah ... that was great."

ANSWER KEY: Different people have different needs, and it's impossible to make sweeping generalizations about sex and sexuality. Please consult a licensed sex therapist in your area.

Try as they might, publishers cannot accept every single manuscript that comes over the transom for immediate publication. Often, the deciding factor is the author's cover letter. A good cover letter makes all the difference in the world. So does a bad one.

COVER LETTERS

BOBBY BRISTOL
Alfred A. Knopf

Dear Ms. Bristol:
    Enclosed please find the manuscript of <u>Tri-Corner Hat: A Novella In Three Parts.</u>
    As you can tell from the letter before you, I am of the old school, working with manual digits rather than their binary counterparts. In other words, I write on a typewriter rather than a "computer" or "word processor device."
    This manuscript is my fifth draft of the novella, and I consider it final. However, there are a few small changes I've decided to make since I completed this draft, but I don't think they merit the strenuous task of retyping the whole thing. So please read <u>Hat</u> with the following corrections in mind:
    1. In the first section, please change the name of the main character from "Jethro" to "Tobias." The character "Richard Head" should never be called by his nickname. Also, please change the name "Nancy" to "Nanette." The other character named Nancy should remain "Nancy." Of the fourteen remaining female characters named "Nancy," please just insert whatever female names you like—as long as it's obvious that they're not the same person.
    2. The setting of the second section should not be identified as "Cape Cod," but rather "a finger-shaped outcropping on the East Coast, frequented by the wealthy." Also, please change "East Coast of United States" to "right-hand side of a large, democratic superpower's continental home." In Book Three, please change "Robert Gottlieb, shithead editor of The New Yorker" to "Howard Gottfried, forty-five-year-old paperboy for a dinky urban rag." Please also change "Bruce Wayne" to "Batman," and "Deep Throat" to "Al Haig."
    3. The passage revealing that Jethro/Tobias was the mastermind behind the "Finger-Shaped Outcropping Murders" would be more felicitously positioned somewhere near the end of the book. I don't know why I put it on the title page.
    4. While I was typing the last 100 pages, the period key on my typewriter starting printing exclamation points. Ignore at least two-thirds of these. Oh hell! It's happening again!
    Thank you for your consideration!

Sincerely!

Bill!

Bill Sammidge!

It reads better w/out the changes. B.B.

ARI CRAYMAN
Simon & Schuster

Dear Sir (or Madam):
   Will you read my book? It took me years to write; will you take a look? It's based on a story by a man named Lear.
   I need a job, and I want to be a published author.

Yours,

Pete

P. Best

Pass this on to the Paperback division.

—Ari

GORDON LISH
Lishline Contemporary Softcovers
LishCo, Inc.
Lishville, Connecticut

Dear Mr. Lish:
   Penis penis penis penis penis.
   I know this isn't the standard way of opening a cover letter, but I'm not a standard writer. I believe that the only rule in literature is that rules are made to be broken—and sometimes I break even this rule.
   Please find enclosed the manuscript for my first novel, *This Is Not A Novel*. In my non-novel novel, you will find no ''plot'' no ''dialogue,'' no ''characters'' as such. Nor will you find anything of merit, or even any passages that can hold the attention of even the most alert reader. I feel that this new approach reflects the fractured society we live in.
   What will you find? Five chapters of the letter Q typed over and over in seven character sets. A pencil sketch of one of the more interesting parts of my body. And what man has not at some time wanted to screw his own mother in a drainage ditch while low-flying birds rain torrents of crap on them? Most writers, shackled by the cuffs of ''good taste'' would omit this. I, however, have included it, albeit in Esperanto.
   Please don't call me at home, as I don't believe in telephones, and I will not answer it when it rings. I can be reached most often at Traffic Court, where society repeatedly inflicts its petty, workmanlike sense of propriety on my spiritual being-ness.

Penis, ✕

Enrique Cadaver

I like it! Omit drainage ditch passage and publish!

G.L

GARY FISKETJON
Atlantic Monthly Press

Dear Mr. Fisketjon,
   I am a twenty-five-year-old graduate of the Iowa State Writing Workshop. In my undergraduate years, I studied under Frederick Barthelme in Mississippi and Jay McInerney at Bennington. Each has shown some degree of enthusiasm for my work, and I hope you will also.
   Please read the enclosed sample of my work and consider it for publication in AMP's new paperback line. Numerous rewrites have given it sufficient polish, but any comments or criticism would be appreciated.
   I know that the only sample I've enclosed is the letter you're reading right now, but I think it's very good. I've spent the past five years writing nothing but letters just like this one, and I'm quite ready to give up my amateur status.
   I look forward to seeing my work in an Atlantic Monthly Press paperback.

Warm regards,

Greg

Greg Beckenberg

Oh hell... Pass this on to Godoff—see if she can fit it into that joke book those Harvard kids are writing.

Gary

TAKING THE STAND: Don Knotts, star of film and television, author of *Knutts: An Autobiography of My Own Life*

Sen. Mohasset: Are you prepared to testify, Mr. Knotts?

Knotts: (spills glass of water) I guess so.

Sen. Mohasset: Now Mr. Knotts, I'd like to ask you a few questions about—

Knotts: The first version of my autobiography.

Sen. Mohasset: Correct. Now, in—

Knotts: Chapter Nine, page 32, second paragraph from the bottom—

Sen. Mohasset: Yes . . . that's correct. Mr. Knotts, how did you know what I was going to ask you?

Knotts: (gulp) Just lucky, I guess.

Sen. Mohasset: Really?

Knotts: (spills pitcher of water) Well, actually . . . the guys from the NMC sort of told me what was going to happen today.

Sen. Mohasset: The NMC?

Knotts: (bugs out his eyes) Whoops! Never mind, never mind . . .

Sen. Mohasset: What is this "NMC"?

Knotts: Well, I shouldn't be telling you this but . . . the NMC is the National Media Conglomerate.

Sen. Mohasset: The National Media Conglomerate?

Knotts: You know—the organization that staged this whole Mediagate Investigation.
　(Cameramen begin packing up cameras, reporters start to go home)

Sen. Mohasset: Mr. Knotts, I assure you that the Congress of the United States of America independently organized this investigation.

Knotts: Gee, I guess you're right. Goodbye. (Knotts gets up to leave.)

Sen. Mohasset: Sit down, Mr. Knotts.

Knotts: (sits down, misses chair, knocks over table while getting up)

Sen. Mohasset: Now, Mr. Knotts . . . why would this "National Media Conglomerate" want Congress to air the media's dirty laundry in public. Isn't that a tremendous embarrassment?

Knotts: Sure—but it also makes for a great show.

GRANT TINKER EX MACHINA

Sen. Mohasset: Mr. Tinker, with all due respect . . . you're not scheduled to take the stand until tomorrow.

Tinker: Sorry Senator. The show's over.

Sen. Mohasset: What on earth are you talking about?

Tinker: I'm surprised you people didn't figure it out sooner. You see, the National Media Conglomerate staged this whole "Mediagate" thing so that we'd all have a big story to cover. Mediagate-mania is sweeping the nation, just as we planned. Everyone wants to hear about it, read about it, watch it on TV. Since this whole thing started, TV ratings have soared. Book sales are up a healthy fifteen percent. Newspaper circulations are booming. Magazine sales have skyrocketed.

Sen. Mohasset: (faints)

Sen. Richardson: Mr. Tinker, when you say "skyrocket," exactly what model are you talking about?

From the Desk of Howard K-tel

Grant-baby,
    You want merchandising, I got merchandising. I got the Mediagate T-shirts, I got the Mediagate coffee mugs, I got al the chintzy Mediagate crap the people want to buy. I hope thi whole thing works, as the chintzy crap products industry rea needs a shot in the arm and a kick in the butt.
                                        Howie

From the Desk of Grant Tinker

Dear Members of the NMC,
    We're ready to roll. We've planted enough evidence to get the Senate people going, and it should skyrocket right after that. Some of you have expressed concern that this "investigation" will only yield us embarrassment. I refer these individuals to Rule Number 5 of the Official NMC Statutes: "Money."

                                        Happy Mediagating!
                                        Grant

"From the Desk of Ted Turner"

TO GRANT TINKER

Dear Grant,

As per our conversation at the annual NMC meeting last week, I think we should proceed with the "Mediagate" operations. It's been a slow year for news, and my experts predict more of the same. The ball is yours. Run with it.

Ted

The New York Times

Dear Grant,

As per your instructions, I've drawn up a list of possible patsies in the Senate. Our only worry with this gang is that they might trample each other trying to get in front of the cameras. Please make sure they drag out some sleaze about Rupert Murdoch during this whole "investigation." He beat me at squash yesterday.

Abe Rosenthal

Here's our Boy!

Stephen King

Dear Grant,

Here you go. I've narrowed down the Senators to the six best ones. This combination will make for a rock 'em, sock 'em, can't-miss blockbuster of an event.

Sen. Donald Mohasset: Thoroughly benign, competent, lovable. I see him as a father figure, as I saw my own father.

Sen. Fawcett: Controversial, outspoken, great legs, good ass. She'll be a big draw for the public, as her sister Farrah is already big.

Sen. "Robert" Beatrice: There's something very unusual about this man. He'll give the proceedings a hint of "otherness."

Sen. Buzz Richardson: Here's one for the kids. Nutty ex-astronaut who never really returned to Earth, if you know what I mean.

DAVID S. COHEN, *President*
WILLIAM L. OAKLEY, *Ibis*
PAUL R. SIMMS, *Narthex*
DANIEL I. BARENBLATT, *Hautbois*
GLENN P. McDONALD, *Hautbois*
JONATHAN D. FERNANDEZ, *Bus. Mgr.*

DAVID A. FRAZE, *Treasurer*
ERIC L. KAPLAN, *Sackbut*
JEFFREY C. YANG, *Sanctum*
ALLEN GLAZIER, *Librarian*
YONGJIN IM, *Art Director*

THE HARVARD LAMPOON
44 BOW STREET
CAMBRIDGE, MASSACHUSETTS 02138
(617) 495-7801

To Atlantic Monthly Press

Dear Ms. Godoff,

We here at the Harvard Lampoon have come up with a great idea for a book that

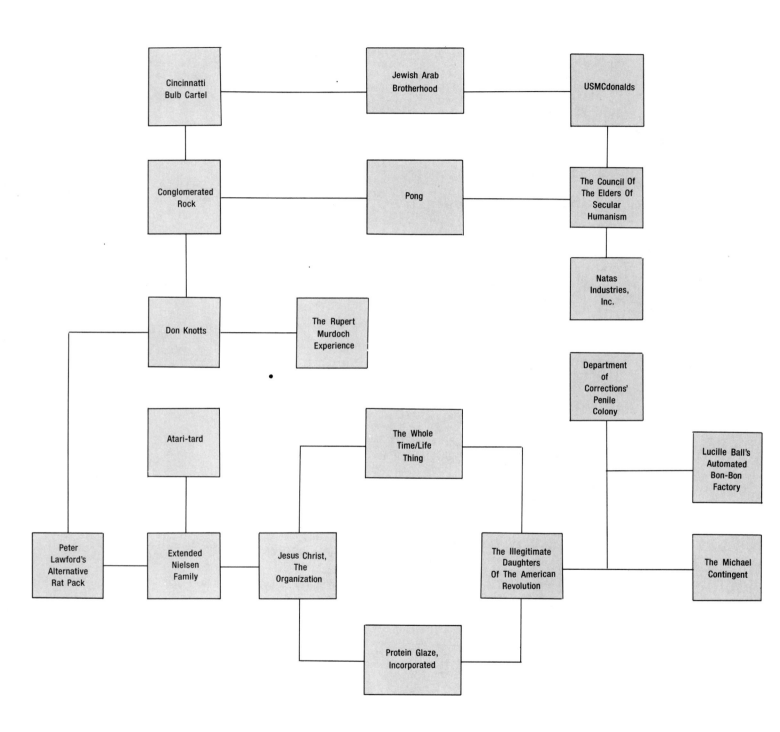

THE END

ACKNOWLEDGMENTS

by *The Harvard Lampoon*

David S. Cohen, President
William L. Oakley, Ibis
Paul R. Simms, Narthex
David A. Fraze, Treasurer

WRITING STAFF:

Daniel Barenblatt David Cohen
Glenn McDonald William Oakley
Paul Simms Steven Tompkins
Joshua Weinstein Jeffrey Yang
Steven Young

ART STAFF:

Paul Felix Yongjin Im
Lauren MacMullan

CONTRIBUTERS:

Michael Borkow Jeffrey Chapman
Sue Edwards Maya Forbes
Ned Hodgman Nicholas Spooner

LAMPOON PROJECT TRUSTEES:

Robert Hoffman S. Eric Rayman

Special thanks to our editor, Ann Godoff,
and to Nancy Lewin for expert
editorial services rendered.

THANKS ALSO TO:

Ali Rogers Lisa Micheli   Bruce Billings John Marquand
Hugh Morris Ken Heller   Avron Cahone Craig & Michelle
William Cohen Lori Elliott   Eve N. Funyer Mel Tinghice
Chuck L. Loudly Raphael Frederickson   William Mays Dick Hertz
Lanky Andy Parker   R. Richard Royce Lynn C. Doyle
Carl Buddig Don Behenna   Donald Knotts Dick Clark
Garbagehead Richard S. Nixon   Andrew Griffith Joe Kshopp
and especially, Mom, Dad, Sis, Chuck, and Rover.

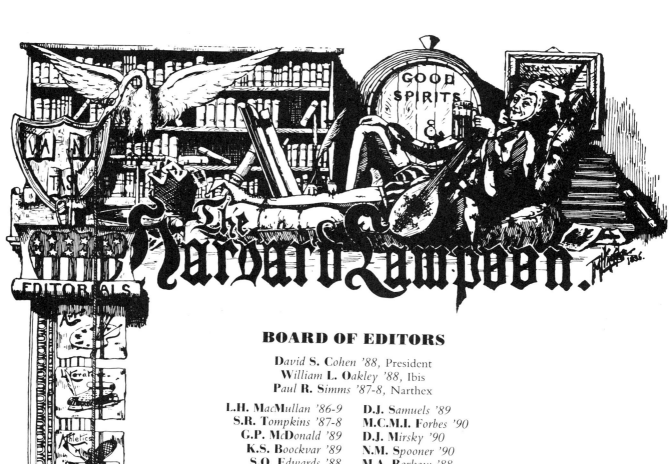

1876